PORTRAIT OF QUEEN ANNE. *Courtesy of Pennsylvania-German Society.*

Early Eighteenth Century Palatine Emigration

A British Government Redemptioner
Project to Manufacture
Naval Stores

By

Walter Allen Knittle, Ph.D.

Department of History
College of the City of New York

With a Foreword by
Dixon Ryan Fox

Baltimore
GENEALOGICAL PUBLISHING CO., INC.

Originally published: Philadelphia, 1937
Reprinted, with an Added Preface,
Genealogical Publishing Co., Inc.
1001 N. Calvert St., Baltimore, Md. 21202
1965, 1970, 1976, 1979, 1982, 1989, 1997, 2004
Copyright © 1965
Genealogical Publishing Co., Inc.
Baltimore, Md.
All Rights Reserved
Library of Congress Catalogue Card Number 65-21924
International Standard Book Number 0-8063-0205-4
Made in the United States of America

PUBLISHER'S PREFACE

It remained for Mr. Knittle in Early *Eighteenth Century Palatine Emigration* to present the only exhaustive study of so remarkable an episode in the history of the American Colonies as the Palatine migration from the Rhine Valley through England to America. The nearly three thousand emigrants who landed in New York in 1710 made up the largest group of people to arrive at any one time in the early colonial period. About the same time a company of seven hundred had gone to North Carolina, and another group to Virginia. In succeeding years they were followed by many thousands, the vast majority of whom settled in Pennsylvania. There have previously been scattered mention of these migrations, but of the movement of the people as a whole no complete or connected narrative appeared until Mr. Knittle's book.

The appendices listing about 12,000 names of the Palatines who came to America are of especial interest to genealogists, since the most difficult problem confronting the genealogist is to establish the exact date when the colonial ancestor arrived on these shores. Published here together for the first time are the several lists, compiled from the Public Record Office and elsewhere, of the names of those emigrants who settled in the American Colonies in the early part of the seventeenth century. Five of these lists were chosen for inclusion in the revised edition of Lancour's *Bibliography of Ship Passenger Lists* (1963), because their authenticity establishes proof of overseas origin. Similar books containing lists of immigrants have been reprinted by us and others are planned for future production.

INTRODUCTION

SOME FORTY years ago a country clergyman serving parishes in Schoharie and Saugerties developed an interest in their German backgrounds. There in upstate New York he found German names, German customs and remnants of German speech. The Reverend Sanford H. Cobb had a deep concern for backgrounds—witness his *Rise of Religious Liberty in America*—and he set about to write *The Story of the Palatines*, which he published in 1897. He made no great pretense to scholarship, as such would be esteemed today, and confined his reading, apparently, to accounts in the English language and, among these, to very little source material. As anyone might infer, his work was sketchy and superficial, however well intentioned, and yet, surprising as it may seem, it has remained from that day to this our only extended general narrative on the Palatine migration from the Rhine Valle through England to America.

In Mr. Cobb's day our colonial history, so far as it proceeded from the universities, concerned itself largely with the slow manufacture of states. The techniques of the historical seminar had not been applied to population and except for some attention to the Dutch, there was comparatively little apprehension of the various stocks outside the English making up about a third of the nation which declared its independence in 1776. Had the Germans come earlier, had their records all been written in a language which most American historians readily understood, had they settled in New England near those centers where for a long time most history was written or, particularly, had they founded a whole and separate colony, the story would have been different. Forty years ago, it is true, there were several accounts of one phase or another of the Palatine migration, but they were by

Germans and in German, as though the Palatines and their descendants were merely Germans abroad, exiles from the Fatherland. But a century before that it should have been realized that they were as much Americans as those whose ancestors had come from Devonshire or Norfolk. Even their names were becoming naturalized: Werner had become Warner, Benker had become Banker, Schneider Snyder, Leyer Lawyer, etc., to say nothing of straight translations. Today only in Pennsylvania is there any considerable group of the German colonial stock which remains primarily German in speech and culture; most of the old German blood has been intermingled and most of the old culture has been thoroughly merged in what we call American culture. Where could one find more typical American careers than those suggested by the names of Wanamaker and Rockefeller?

Instead of this being a reason for neglecting the peculiarly German elements in our colonial life, it is a reason for studying them with increasing thoroughness. If the culture which they represented has lost its clear identity, if it is hidden in the general mass, its contribution has been more essential. If the Germans have become somewhat English in social habit, then the English have become somewhat German. All this is a factor in making the American temper what it is.

Dr. Knittle's book is significant not only as the first thorough study of the first large German immigration. It may possibly be contended that it is the first thorough study of colonial immigration of any kind. This is not to say that the general subject has been neglected; it has had almost constant attention. But much of it has had to be developed by ingenious inference, for in scarcely any case except that of the Palatines has there been at hand a full record of the motives, the process and the experience of the migration. The phrase "at hand" must not be understood, however, as meaning that the record had been accumulated and arranged. The accounts in the invaluable *Documents relative to the Colonial History of the State of New York*, of course, have been accessible everywhere, and more recently Todd and Goebel's edition of *Christoph von Graffenried's Account of the Founding of New Bern* and the British *Calendar of State Papers Colonial;* Pennsylvania Germans have dug out Rhineland background; and there have been fragments published here and there in historical magazines. These which had satisfied others were merely introductory exercises for Dr. Knittle's driving zeal. As will appear in his notes, he went over the German materials again, combed the manuscripts in the Public Record Office, the British Museum and the private collections in the great houses of England, made his way through a maze of eighteenth-century periodicals and pamphlets, and visited Ireland to discover the remaining influence of Palatine settlement. No such thorough and intensive study had previously been made.

As this book is published American political sentiment is divided on the question of planned economy. Can the government determine what kind of production is desirable? If so, can it wisely organize and direct that production? Should the government produce its own materials? Is government enterprise likely to face betrayal by the private interests of coöperating contractors? Can the government fuse its ancient function of relief with such planned production? The Resettlement Administration, which is now attempting this fusion, may or may not be a success, may or may not be temporary. With all the variable factors involved, historical analogies are treacherous and there is no desire to force them. But our situation makes especially interesting a study of planned production and charitable resettlement seen in long perspective.

Any writer is tempted to magnify the influence of his subject and in no field has this been more prevalent than in that of the history of social groups. With a scholar's honesty Dr. Knittle has conquered this temptation; however much he may have increased our knowledge of the Palatine immigrants, he has steadfastly avoided extravagant claims for their influence. He has even challenged and reduced claims previously thought to be established. For example, it has usually been stated that the Palatines' disgust for the treatment they had received in New York was an important factor in diverting subsequent German settlement from that province into Pennsylvania. By cool analysis the present author reveals how untenable is this thesis. He has been ready to throw out the dramatic and the picturesque when clouded with doubt or founded on error. He cites the "interesting legend" set forth by his predecessors which had it that the five Mohawk Indians taken by Peter Schuyler to London were so grieved at the plight of the Palatines, then encamped on Blackheath, that they gave the Schoharie Valley to the Queen on consideration that she would bestow it upon the emigrants; then he points out that the Palatines sailed from London before the Indians sailed from Boston, that four of the five Indians were not sachems and had no authority to grant Mohawk lands and that these lands were subsequently ceded at Albany to the province with no reference to the Palatines. Though eschewing partisanship he is quick to repel unwarranted aspersions on the group, and disposes of Archdeacon Cunningham's contention that the Palatines' success in Ireland was explained by the unnecessary favor of their subsidy by showing that the subsidy was necessary to establish them but that their individual prosperity came chiefly from their frugality and competence. Three examples out of innumerable such cases may assure the reader that he is in the hands of an alert and thoughtful scholar.

The appendices listing about 12,000 names of Palatines who embarked from the homeland might strike some as of slight historical worth. But these lists, carefully compiled for the first time in the Public Record Office and elsewhere, are an event for genealogists. The baffling difficulty at the head of every family history in this country is to establish the exact date when the American progenitors reached these shores.

Here is filled for the first time the gap in German immigration lists between that of the Pastorius settlement in 1683 and those covering the years 1717–1818 published recently by Strassburger and Hinke for the Pennsylvania-German Society.

History is never written finally. New materials are exhumed; new interpretations spring from new experience and new curiosities. But Dr. Knittle's *Early Eighteenth Century Palatine Emigration* is not likely to be superseded for many long years. It covers a stirring group adventure, a well-defined and significant experiment in political economy and a contribution to the making of a nation; it covers this complex enterprise with thoroughness and sympathy and presents its record with insight, force and clarity.

Dixon Ryan Fox

PREFACE

THIS MONOGRAPH is written from the view-point of the British government. This attitude is not only proper because the so-called "American" colonies were then British in name as well as in fact, but also because the Palatine emigration was carried out under the auspices of the British government. Indeed, the British government itself engaged in the manufacture of naval stores, putting the Palatines to work at its own expense, consonant with the mercantilist aims of the times. The subject therefore may be described as remarkable because in dealing with the Palatines the British government exhibited in practice the mercantilist theories on immigration, naval stores and colonies.

This study would have been impossible without the aid and encouragement of many scholars. Acknowledgment in this brief space can be made only to a few of the many. Important suggestions and advice were given generously by President Dixon Ryan Fox of Union College, Professor Charles M. Andrews of Yale University, Professor Robert G. Albion of Princeton University, Mr. Victor H. Paltsits of the New York Public Library, Mr. Albert Cook Myers of the Historical Society of Pennsylvania and Mr. Henry S. Borneman, Secretary of the Pennsylvania-German Society.

I am particularly indebted to Professor William Thomas Morgan of Indiana University, who gave me my first graduate training and who introduced me to my present subject. He has been my most active and interested contributor. To Professor W. T. Root of Iowa University I must express my thanks for an amicable division of this subject with which one of his graduate students was engaged. To Professor Edward P. Cheyney I am grateful for sponsoring this study before the faculty of the Graduate School of the University of Pennsylvania. Professor Henry R. Mueller of Muhlenberg College, whom I am so fortunate to count among my teachers, has given the manuscript the benefit of careful reading. Dr. Dixon Ryan Fox has not only extended to me the advantage of his editorial wisdom, but he has also written the introduction to this book. To him I am deeply grateful.

I must also express my appreciation of the great patience and many courtesies extended to me by the librarians of these institutions: the University of Pennsylvania Library; the Columbia University Library; Library of the College of the City of New York; the Historical Society of Pennsylvania; the Holland Society of New York; the Huntington Library of San Marino, California; the Widener Library of Harvard University; the Yale University Library; the Library of Congress; the Pennsylvania State Library; the Moravian Library at Bethlehem, Pennsylvania; the Morgan Library, New York City; the New York State Library; the English Public Record Office and the British Museum. I wish that I could acknowledge the many others who contributed, but the list would seem endless. To them I express my sincere appreciation.

I am also grateful for a grant-in-aid from the Oberlaender Trust Fund of Philadelphia, Pennsylvania (Dr. Wilbur K. Thomas, Director), which permitted me to conclude satisfactorily my research in Ireland and England. This organization of American citizens also contributed toward the publication of this volume.

The errors, which I hope are few, are necessarily of my own making. The interpretation must be attributed to me only.

W. A. K.

TABLE OF CONTENTS

LIST OF ILLUSTRATIONS

KEY TO FOOTNOTE CITATIONS

B. M.—British Museum, London.

B. T. Jour.—the printed records of the Board of Trade Journal, published by the British Government.

Jour. B. T.—the transcripts of the Board of Trade Journal made for the Historical Society of Pennsylvania, and to be found in its library.

C. C.—Calendar of State Papers, Colonial, America and West Indies.

Doc. Hist.—*Documentary History of New York.*

Hist. Mss. Com.—Historical Manuscripts Commission Reports, published by the British Government.

H. L.—Huntington Library, San Marino, California.

H. S. P.—History Society of Pennsylvania, Philadelphia, Pa.

L. C.—Library of Congress, Washington, D. C.

Liv. Mss.—The manuscripts of Robert Livingston, first Lord of Livingston Manor, now in the possession of the estate of Johnston Livingston Redmont, New York City.

N. C. Col. Rec.—*Colonial Records of North Carolina.*

N. Y. Col. Docs.—*Documents Relative to the Colonial History of New York.*

N. Y. Col. Mss.—Manuscripts in the New York State Archives, Albany, New York.

N. Y. H. S.—New York Historical Society Library, New York City.

N. Y. S. L.—New York State Library, Albany, New York.

P. R. O.—Public Record Office, London.

S. P. G. Mss.—Society for the Propagation of the Gospel in Foreign Parts, London. Transcripts are to be found in the Library of Congress and in the New York Historical Society Library (Hawk's Transcripts).

Citations are given invariably by page rather than by document number, which method is followed occasionally in similar monographs.

CHAPTER I. THE CAUSES OF THE EARLY "PALATINE" EMIGRATIONS

SHIPLOADS OF German peoples, variously estimated from two thousand to thirty-two thousand,[1] arrived in London between May and November of 1709. A year earlier a small band of fifty had preceded them. As most of the latter and the greater part of the former group came from the Rhenish or Lower Palatinate, the name "Palatine" was applied indiscriminately to the rest of the immigrants, although they came from the neighboring territories as well.[2]

A contemporary pamphlet lists the home principalities as follows: the Palatinate, the districts of Darmstadt and Hanau, Franconia (including the area around the cities of Nuremburg, Baireuth and Würzburg), the Archbishopric of Mayence, and the Archbishopric of Trèves. The districts of Spires, Worms, Hesse-Darmstadt, Zweibrücken, Nassau, Alsace and Baden are also mentioned.[3] To this list Würtemberg must be added,

[1] John Stow, *Survey of the Cities of London and Westminister* (1720), II, 43 estimated the immigration of 1709 at two or three thousand; William Maitland, *History of London* (1756), I, 507 has twelve thousand as their number; a contemporary account in *Das verlangte nicht erlangte Canaan . . . oder Ausführliche Beschreibung von der unglücklichen Reise derer jüngsthin aus Teutschland nach dem Engelländischen in America gelegen Carolina und Pensylvanien. . . .* (Franckfurt und Leipzig, 1711), 113, hereafter cited as *Das verlangte nicht erlangte Canaan*, gives the total number who went to England as 32,468.

[2] "A Brief History of the Poor Palatine Refugees Lately Arrived in England" (July 18, 1709), in *Ecclesiastical Records of the State of New York* (Albany, 1901), III, 1782, hereafter cited as *Eccles. Rec.* Copies of the 1709 edition are in the British Museum and the National Library of Dublin. A 1710 edition may be examined in the Trinity College Library, Dublin. The name "Palatine" will be used below consistently in referring to all the German immigrants of this period, since it appears most convenient, if not strictly accurate.

[3] *Das verlangte nicht erlangte Canaan*, 99.

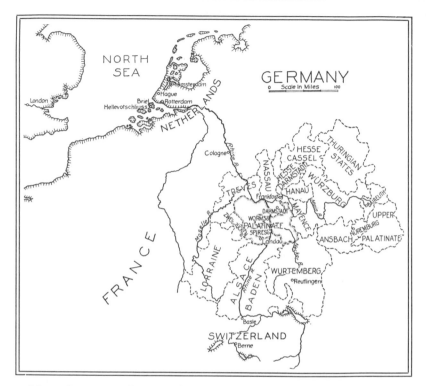

MAP OF RHINELAND, Germany, showing the sources of the Palatine Emigration.
The borders of the Rhenish Palatinate are slightly shaded.
Drawn by A. Cefola.

since a number of Palatines are known to have emigrated
thence, notably John Conrad Weiser. The area, from which
the emigration poured, extended along both sides of the Rhine
River and its tributaries, the Main and Neckar Rivers. It
extended roughly from the junction of the Moselle and the
Rhine south to Basle, Switzerland; and from Zweibrücken,
alongside Lorraine, as far west along the Main as Baireuth,
bordering the Upper (or Bavarian) Palatinate.[4]

Many causes were given for the unprecedented size of the
emigration. That most frequently mentioned was devastation

[4] See Map of Germany.

by war. The end of the Thirty Years' War left the people of the Palatinate prostrate. True enough a remarkable recovery from this visitation was achieved, due to the fertility of the soil and the co-operation of the ruler, but prosperity was short-lived; in the latter part of the seventeenth century the Palatinate was repeatedly the stamping ground of Louis XIV's armies. Marshal Turenne thoroughly devastated the province in 1674. Moreover, protracted disputes among the neighboring princes, remaining from the religious wars of the early part of the century, gave rise to continuous warfare, in one instance between the Archbishop of Mayence assisted by the Duke of Lorraine, and the Elector Palatine.[5] In 1688–9 partly to vent his malice against Protestants, the Grand Monarch had the Palatinate laid waste again. The military necessities following William III's "conquest" of England probably made this step necessary. At any rate over two hundred years later the Heidelberg ruins left by this invasion were described as "the most interesting ruins in Europe."[6]

During the War of the Spanish Succession, Marshal Villars crossed the Rhine unexpectedly in May, 1707, terrorized southwestern Germany, plundering and requisitioning freely on the Palatinate, Würtemberg, Baden and the Swabian Circle.[7] In September of the same year, the French retired across the Rhine, having, in the words of an angry colonel in the English army, "over-run the lazy and sleepy Empire and not only maintained a great army in it all the year, but by contributions, sent money into France to help the King's other affairs."[8] Not only was this invasion unnecessary from

[5] *Theatrum Europaeum*, XI, 344, 497; L. Häuser, *Geschichte der Rheinischen Pfalz* (Heidelberg, 1856), II, 629; N. M. Pletcher, *Some Chapters from the History of the Rhine Country* (N. Y., 1907), 94.

[6] J. G. Wilson, in *American Historical Assoc. Reports* (1891), 287.

[7] Townshend Mss. (*Hist. Mss. Com. 11th report*, Appendix), IV, 65, mentions "the plunder and the money they took by force from the good families of Strasbourg."

[8] C. T. Atkinson, "The War of the Spanish Succession, Campaigns and Negotiations," in *Camb. Mod. Hist.*, V, 418.

a military point of view but it was also a political blunder, for it united Germany against Louis.[9] But for the people living in the war zone, these invasions wiped out the fruits of many new and promising revivals, and discouraged further struggle for better living conditions.[10]

To the curse of devastation was added an unkind prank of nature, when at the end of 1708 a winter, cruel beyond the precedent of a century, set in to blight the region. As early as the beginning of October the cold was intense, and by November 1st, it was said, firewood would not burn in the open air! In January of 1709 wine and spirits froze into solid blocks of ice; birds on the wing fell dead; and, it is said, saliva congealed in its fall from the mouth to the ground.[11] Most of Western Europe was frozen tight. The Seine and all the other rivers were ice-bound and on the 8th of January, the Rhone, one of the most rapid rivers of Europe, was covered with ice. But what had never been seen before, the sea froze sufficiently all along the coasts to bear carts, even heavily laden.[12] Narcissus Luttrell, a famous English diarist of that day, wrote of the great violence of the frost in England and in foreign parts, where several men were frozen to death in many countries.[13] The Arctic weather lasted well into the fourth month. Perhaps

[9] A. Hassall, "The Foreign Policy of Louis XIV," in *Camb. Mod. Hist.*, V, 57.

[10] Abel Boyer, *The History of the Reign of Queen Anne digested into Annals 1709* (London, 1710), 166; hereafter cited as Boyer, *Annals*. Professor Julius Goebel, Sr., has performed a valuable service by publishing a collection of letters by a few emigrants of 1709. These letters clearly show that the bad economic conditions were largely responsible for their authors' emigration. "Briefe Deutscher Auswanderer aus dem Jahre 1709," in *Jahrbuch der Deutsch=Amerikanischen Historischen Gesellschaft von Illinois* (Chicago, Illinois, 1912), 124–189.

[11] R. N. Bain, "Charles XII and the Great Northern War," in *Camb. Mod. Hist.*, V, 600.

[12] *Mémoires . . . du . . . duc de Saint-Simon* (Paris, 1857), IV, 280; *Journal du Marquis de Dangeau* (Paris, 1857), XII, 303 *et seq.*

[13] Narcissus Luttrell, *Brief Relation of State Affairs* (Oxford, 1857), VI, 393, 399 under dates of January 8th and January 25, 1709.

the period of heaviest frost was from the 6th to the 25th of January. Then snow fell until February 6th.[14] The fruit trees were killed and the vines were destroyed. The calamity of this unusually bitter weather fell heavily on the husbandmen and vine-dressers, who in consequence made up more than half of the emigrants of 1709.[15]

Other influences almost as malign, though of a more chronic nature, were disturbing the inhabitants of the Rhine Valley. The splendor of Versailles had dazzled many petty rulers of Germany, who sought to emulate the gorgeous court life surrounding Louis XIV. The expenses of their lavish and arrogant living had to be met by heavy taxes on their subjects, often so exhausting as to leave the peasants themselves without bread. Naturally bitter feelings were aroused against the ruling class, who called themselves fathers of the people without exhibiting any traces of fatherly care for their welfare. The need for money to carry on war too made the taxes mount higher day by day. A letter from the Palatinate in 1681 mentioned that "Thousands would gladly leave the Fatherland if they had the means to do so," because of the French devastation and "besides this, we are now suffering the plague of high taxes."[16] Conditions did not improve during the next twenty-five years apparently, for an unbiased report from the Palatines waiting in Holland for transportation to England stated they came flying "to shake of the burdens they ly under by the hardshipps of their Princes governments and the contributions they must pay to the Enemy."[17] Therefore,

[14] Onno Klopp, *Der Fall des Hauses Stuart* (Wien, 1887), 215.

[15] *Journal of House of Commons*, XVI, 597; hereafter cited as *C. J.; Eccles. Rec.*, III, 1747, 1824; Public Record Office Mss., Colonial Office, 388/76, 56 ii, 64, 68–70, hereafter cited as P. R. O., C. O.; Friederich Kapp, *Die Deutschen in Staate New York* (New York, 1884), I, 19; Franz Löher, *Geschichte und Zustände der Deutschen in Amerika* (Cincinnati, 1847), 42; *Der Deutsche Pionier* (Cincinnati, 1882), XIV, 295.

[16] Letter of Henrich Frey, D. H. Bertolet, *The Bertolet Family* (Harrisburg, Pennsylvania, 1914), 173.

[17] Public Record Office, State Papers, 84/232, 248, hereafter cited as P. R. O., S. P.

oppressive feudal exactions by the petty rulers may be regarded as one of the underlying reasons for the emigration.[18]

Another cause suggested, and in general accepted in eighteenth century England, was religious persecution. Certainly religious conditions were of large importance in the early eighteenth century. To ingratiate themselves with benevolently inclined people, emigrants found it convenient to plead religious persecution. Friends of the immigration in England justified their help on religious grounds, while others fiercely attacked the authenticity of the rumored persecutions. The disagreement on this point has been perpetuated by descendants of that German stock, who are reluctant to forego a lustrous prestige equal to that of the Pilgrim Fathers.

What was the religious condition of the Germanies in 1709? *Cuius regio, eius religio*, established at the Peace of Augsburg (1555) and modified by the Treaty of Westphalia (1648), was still functioning. It recognized three churches: Catholic, Lutheran and Calvinist, and provided that the religion of the ruler should be the religion of the people. Under such conditions religious persecution might well exist. The belief that religious persecution was a cause is strengthened at first sight by the fact that the Elector of the Palatinate in 1709 was John William, Duke of Newburg, a Catholic.[19] There are no formal charges of persecution, however, about 1709.[20] Of course, this

[18] Library of Congress MSS., Archdale MSS. 1694–1706, 57, hereafter cited as L. C., Archdale MSS.; *Das verlangte nicht erlangte Canaan*, 21; "Brief History," in *Eccles. Rec.*, III, *1785 and 1794;* W. H. Bruford, *Germany in the 18th Century* (Cambridge, Eng., 1935), 39, 121.

[19] *The State of the Palatines for Fifty Years Past to This Present Time* (London, 1709), 3. A 1710 edition of this pamphlet is published in *Eccles. Rec.*, III, 1820. The copy of the 1709 edition is in the Widener Library of Harvard University.

[20] Reports of persecution by the Elector Palatine in 1709 refer to the Bavarian Palatinate and also to Silesia. Luttrell, *op. cit.*, VI, 464, 483. These accounts are not to be attributed to John William, Elector Palatine, of the Rhenish or Lower Palatinate, a different man. Also see *Monthly Mercury* (July, 1709), XX, 248.

might be due to the inexpediency of criticizing the Elector Palatine, an English ally in the War of the Spanish Succession then being waged. But by the same token, the Elector should have found it poor policy to affront his Protestant ally (England), by mistreatment of his own Protestant subjects.[21] John William had reigned since 1690. While there are reports of persecution in 1699,[22] were religious intolerance at that time the sole cause of the emigration, it should have driven away these German emigrants before 1709.

The disagreement on this point in the past, warrants a close examination of the religious composition of those immigrant groups in London. Of the first forty-one Germans of the 1708 immigration, fifteen were Lutherans and twenty-six Calvinists (or Reformed).[23] The fourteen others who joined the group in London were also Protestants. In their petition to the Queen this group, all Protestant, made no mention of religious persecution. They spoke though, of the French ravages in 1707 in the Rhine and Neckar Valleys.[24] For the 1709 immigration, four lists compiled in London exist of those who arrived from May 3rd to June 16th. Unfortunately no lists seem to have been made in London after that date, but for the 6500 Palatines then present these lists are informative and

[21] The relations between England and the Palatinate were excellent at this time. The Elector Palatine secured the support of the English at the Vienna Court (British Museum Mss., Ad. Mss. 15866, 90, hereafter cited as B. M.) and was supplying his troops for English and Dutch use. The English used eleven battalions of Palatine troops in Catalonia in 1709. P. R. O., S. P. 44/107, 221; S. P. 34/11, 154. In fact, on the occasion of the New Year in 1709 the rulers of England and the Palatinate exchanged greetings in their own handwriting, an unusually friendly proceeding. B. M., Add. Mss. 15866, 156.

[22] Eccles. Rec., III, 1453 et seq.

[23] Journal of the Commissioners of Trade and Plantations 1704-1708, 484; hereafter cited as B. T. Jour. The first Board of Trade report erred in referring to them as "These 41 poor Lutherans," Calendar of State Papers, Colonial America and West Indies 1706-8, 723; hereafter cited as C. C. In all cases the page, not the number of the document, is cited.

[24] Ibid., 720.

reliable. They were made by two German clergymen at the English court, John Tribbeko, chaplain to the late royal consort, Prince George of Denmark, and George Andrew Ruperti, minister of St. Mary's German Lutheran Church in Savoy. The 1770 families were distributed as follows: Lutherans, 550; Reformed, 693; Catholics, 512; Baptists, 12; Mennonites, 3. Almost one-third of the Palatines in London on June 16, 1709, were of the Catholic faith.[25]

Religious persecution by the Catholic Elector might drive out Protestants, but certainly not Catholics. It might still be held that the Protestants had fled from Catholic rulers and the Catholics from Protestant princes. Yet, on August 2, 1709, an English gentleman, Roger Kenyon, wrote to his sister-in-law that he had visited the Palatines on Blackheath, a commons seven miles southeast of London. He added that they "came over not on account of religious persecution, for most of them were under Protestant princes . . . ."[26] The real religious difficulties in Germany were those created by the clash of the various sects. Anton Wilhelm Böhme, pastor of the German Court Chapel of St. James and an influential friend of the Palatines at court, so advised a correspondent in Germany on May 26, 1710. Böhme mentions the desire of many people to seek a non-sectarian Christianity in Pennsylvania. The question which Böhme answered was whether it was deemed advisable that people, who on account of their conscience could no longer subscribe to any sect and therefore were tolerated almost nowhere, should carry out their desire to emigrate although they had no real certainty of God's will. In a fatherly fashion, Böhme advised them to examine their own conscience for the inner or motivating cause of such an important journey. Significantly, he wrote that many a man, after he had acquired flourishing acres in America, forgot the

[25] P. R. O., C. O. 388/76, 56ii, 64, 68–70. The first list, that of May 6th, is given in Appendix B, but not all the vital statistics in the list are included for reasons mentioned there.

[26] Kenyon MSS. (*Hist. MSS. Com., 14th Report*, Appendix), IV, 443.

religious motivation of his pilgrimage. Such people degener-
ated so far that they were more concerned with the cultivation
of their lands than of their souls. Böhme added that they stood
as so many monuments, warning others not to allow greed
to move them.[27]

Although Böhme strongly doubted the religious urge for
the new world, he also mentioned disagreement with, and
persecutions by, the authorities incited by religious zealots
and orthodox Churchmen. These, he held, should be suffered
for the sake of truth and the glorious blessing promised by the
Lord. The persecutions must not have been severe, for Böhme
confessed that he could not see how a Christian could, on
account of the oppression suffered up to then, leave his
fatherland.[28] The German divine dwelt at great length upon
the dangerous temptations of religious squabbles.

The theory, that religious persecution was a most important cause for these emigrations, has been impaired by Böhme's
letter. In his argument, he declared that only a very few of
these people, when they came to England, had provided themselves with a prayer-book or similar religious work. Fewer
still had a New Testament or Bible, and they would have remained without any were it not for the Queen's generosity.[29]
This fact lends support to other evidence. The Catholic
Elector Palatine John William had issued on November 21,
1705, a declaration promising liberty of conscience.[30] In 1707
a disinterested person testified to the sincere execution of the
declaration.[31] On the 27th of June, 1709, the Council of the

[27] *Das verlangte nicht erlangte Canaan*, 15–30.

[28] *Ibid.*, 24.

[29] *Ibid.*, 22. One of the few Bibles brought from Germany at that time
was that brought by Gerhart Schaeffer. This Lutheran Bible, published in
Franckfurt am Mayn in 1701, is still in the possession of descendants of the
Palatine Schaeffer, the Kingsley family of "The Rocks," Schoharie, N. Y.

[30] *Eccles. Rec.*, III, 1600.

[31] John Toland, *Declaration lately published by the Elector Palatine in favor
of his Protestant Subjects* (London, 1714), 4.

A Tranflation from the High-Dutch, *of a Declaration
made (by Direction from the* Elector Palatine) *by
the Proteftant Confiftory in the* Palatinate.

" WHereas it has been fignify'd to the Re-
" form'd Confiftory in the *Palatinate*, that
" feveral of the Families, who are gone down the
" *Rhine*, to proceed to *Penfilvania*, to fettle them-
" felves there, commonly pretend they are ob-
" lig'd to retire thither for the Sake of Religion,
" and the Perfecution which they fuffer upon that
" Account; and fince it is not known to any of
" the Confiftory, that thofe with-drawn Subjects
" have complain'd, that they fuffer'd at that
" Time any Perfecution on Account of Religi-
" on, or that they were forc'd to quit their
" Country for want of Liberty of Confcience, con-
" trary to his Electoral Highnefs's gracious Decla-
" tion of the 21ft of *November*, 1705. therefore, as
" foon as the Confiftory underftood that a Num-
" ber of Subjects were gone out Abroad to the faid
" *Penfilvania*, and that more were like to follow,
" they thought it necefſary to acquaint all the
" reform'd Infpectors and Minifters with it, to
" undeceive their Auditors, as alfo thefe with-
" drawn Peeple, and that they are not like to gain
" their End in all Probability, and to perfwade
" them againſt their withdrawing any farther;
" as alfo to the Intent to fhew the groundlefs Pre-
" tences of fuch Peeple to go out of the Country
" on Account of the faid Religious Perfecution.
" Which we do atteft hereby in favour of Truth.
" Done at *Heidleburg* the 27th of *June*, 1709.
    " L. S. The Vice-Prefident and Council of the
" Confiftory conftituted in the Electoral *Palatinate*.
    " *V. P. Howmuller, T. Heyles, H. Croutz, J. Clofter.
        Z. Kirchmejer. Schemal.*

A declaration of the Protestant Consistory in the
Palatinate, denying any religious persecution by the
Elector Palatine, June 27, 1709.
    Courtesy of the Pennsylvania-German Society.

Protestant Consistory in the Palatinate issued a statement denying the pretences of emigrants that they were persecuted.[32] Indeed, a colonial report of the Evangelical Lutheran Congregation in Pennsylvania made this statement, "Some may think that it is unreasonable to care for these people, as the most of them went into this distant part of the globe from their own irregular impulse, and without necessity or calling, because it no longer suited them to comply with good order in their native lands."[33] The plea was made then not to make the children born in America suffer for the error of their parents.

Indeed a dispatch from Holland in June, 1709, reported that the Palatines, Protestants and Catholics, "seem to agree all very well, being several of them mixed together husbands and wives of different religion or united by parentage." Further, they were "flying not so much for religion" as for other reasons.[34] Considering these facts it must be concluded that religious persecution was not an important cause for the 1708–9 Palatine emigrations. Religious disputes and squabbles may have contributed in a minor way. Due to the special conditions existing along the Rhine and in England, it was advantageous to pose as "poor German Protestants" persecuted for their faith. This will be discussed in greater detail below.

To devastation by war, oppression by petty princes imitating the "Sun Monarch," the destructive winter of 1708–9, and religious bickerings, may be added a desire for adventure so usual in the youth of any land. These causes created a dissatisfaction with their present lot, which only irritated another potent cause, that of land hunger. A number of Palatines in New York were overheard to remark, "We came to America to establish our families—to secure lands for our children on

[32] "Brief History," in Eccles. Rec., III, 1793.
[33] Hallesche Nachrichten (Oswald Trans., Philadelphia, 1881), II, 237.
[34] P. R. O., S. P. 84/232, 249.

which they will be able to support themselves after we die.''[35]
But all these causes themselves would perhaps have been insufficient to call forth such a great emigration of large families
with young children on their hands. How did the attraction
of the foreign shore come to them?

To those Germans dissatisfied with their lot, effected by
the conditions outlined above, came the enticing advertising
of English proprietors of the colonies in America. Pamphlets
extolling the climate and life in the New World were disseminated throughout the Rhine Valley. Agents for the proprietors entered into negotiations with interested parties.
Adventurers like François Louis Michel and George Ritter
engaged to bring companies of colonists.[36] Correspondence
was carried on between proprietors and prospective settlers.
All these activities were in the interests of Carolina or
Pennsylvania.

One of the Germans, Ulrich Simmendinger by name, migrated with these groups to New York;[37] and having lost his
two children in England, he and his wife, Anna Margaretta,
returned to their fatherland about 1717. Shortly thereafter he
published a little booklet,[38] giving an account of his experiences and containing a list of those people he had left behind
in New York. For this reason it is valuable in the study of that
emigration. Simmendinger says that assuredly his friends
would not think he made this hazardous trip for excitement
and adventure, particularly with his wife and children. His
resolution was made under the paternal necessity of providing

[35] *Documentary History of State of New York* (Albany, 1850), III, 658, hereafter cited as *Doc. Hist.*

[36] Townshend MSS. (*Hist. MSS. Com., 11th Rept.*, Appendix), IV, 63;
C. C., 1706–1708, 61.

[37] Listed as one of the Palatines remaining at New York, 1710, *Doc.
Hist.*, III, 564.

[38] Ulrich Simmendinger, *Warhaffte und glaubwürdige Verzeichnüss jeniger . . .
Personen welche sich Anno 1709 . . . aus Teutschland in Americam oder Neue Welt
begeben . . .* (Reuttlingen, ca. 1717). See Appendix F. below for list of families.

TITLE PAGE OF SIMMENDINGER'S *Warhaffte und glaubwurdige Verzeichnüss.* *Courtesy of New York Public Library.*

for his own wife and children. He says nothing of religious persecution. Simmendinger apparently emigrated then with the intention of enjoying a better competence because of aid expected from the British Queen.[39] He further states that in the year 1709, in response to the genuinely golden promises written by the Englishmen, many other families from the Palatinate also set forth to England in order to go from there to Pennsylvania.[40]

In regard to the "golden promises," it is worth noticing that a British parliamentary committee investigating the causes of the immigration reported: "And upon the examination of several of them [the Palatines] what were the motives which induced them to leave their native country, it appears to the committee that there were books and papers dispersed in the *Palatinate* with the Queen's picture before the book and the Title Pages in Letters of Gold (which from thence was called the Golden Book), to encourage them to come to *England* in order to be sent to *Carolina* or other of her Majesty's Plantations to be settled there. The book is chiefly a recommendation of that country."[41]

This work thus referred to might have been written by Kocherthal, as his book first appeared in 1706.[42] The Reverend

[39] *Ibid.*, 2–3. Simmendinger states this frankly. Frank R. Diffenderffer, "The German Exodus to England in 1709," in *Pa. Ger. Soc. Proc.* (1897), VII, 292, finds as one of the chief reasons for the emigration "the hope of bettering themselves."

[40] "Dann als Anno 1709, auff die lauter güldene versprechende Engelländische Schreiben/viele Familien aus der Pfalz . . . hinab nach Engelland/um von dar nach Pensylvaniam über zugehen." *Ibid.*, 2. Also, Friederich Kapp, *Geschichte der Deutschen Einwanderung in Amerika* (Leipzig, 1868), 86.

[41] *C. J.*, (April 14, 1711), XVI, 597.

[42] V. H. Todd and J. Goebel, *Christoph von Graffenried's Account of the Founding of New Bern* (N. C. Hist. Com. Pub., Raleigh, N. C., 1920), 14, conclude that the Golden Book is the same as Kocherthal's. This may have been true, but Simmendinger speaks of Pennsylvania. See also Christopher Sauer, *Pennsylvania Bericht* (1754), quoted in *Der deutsche Pionier*, XIV, 295–6.

Joshua Kocherthal,[43] described as a German evangelical minister, had not been to America at the time he published his book, but he had been in England to make inquiries about the colonies.[44] Did Kocherthal come to some agreement with important members of the ministry? Was he their agent or was he simply in the service of the proprietors of Carolina? No definite promises are made in his book but several passages, coupled with the Queen's picture and the gilded titlepage, might give the impression to the poor people into whose hands the book would come, that they might expect help from her, both in crossing the channel and after their arrival in England, in going to the colonies. One passage read, "Whereupon finally the proposal was made that the Queen be presented with a supplication to whether she herself would not grant the ships . . . But these proposals are too extensive to describe here, and yet it is hoped that through them the effort will not be in vain, although in this matter no one can promise anything certain . . . ."[45] That its effect was great can be judged by its circulation. This handbook for Germans was so much in demand in the year 1709, that at least three more editions were printed.[46] In fact, the book continued to

[43] This name has been spelled erroneously with a second K, "Kockerthal," by writers following documentary misspellings, apparently based on its pronunciation. The name appears on his tombstone in the Evangelical Lutheran Church, West Camp, N. Y. and uniformly in the British documents as "Kocherthal."

[44] Todd and Goebel, *op. cit.*, 13. Kocherthal may have been in communication with W. Killigrew, a gentleman much interested in Carolina, who in 1706 confidentially suggested to the British government that it buy out the Carolina proprietors through him at a low price, adding "I am in treaty with some thousand of Protestant People from foreign parts, who are desirous of to go thither when this affair is settled which naturally will increase the rent of the county and the customs by considerable for England." P. R. O., C. O. 5/306, 3 i; *C. C. 1706–1708*, 183.

[45] *Ibid.*, 15; Kocherthal, *Aussführlich und umständlicher Bericht von . . . Carolina* (4th ed., Franckfurt, 1709), 28, hereafter cited as Kocherthal, *Bericht*.

[46] Diffenderffer, *op. cit.*, 317; A copy of the 4th impression is in the Library of Congress.

Außführlich-und umständlicher
Bericht
Von der berühmten Landschafft

Carolina/

In dem
Engelländischen America
gelegen.
An Tag gegeben
Von

Kocherthalern.

Vierter Druck/
Mit Anhängen/ zweyer Engelischen
Authoren gethanen Beschreibung/ und eines
auff der Reyse dahin begriffenen Hochteutschen
auß Londen Benachrichtigung;
Nebst
Einer Land-Carte von Carolina ver-
mehrt.

Franckfurt am Mäyn/
Zu finden bey Georg Heinrich Oehrling/
Anno M DCC IX.

TITLE PAGE OF KOCHERTHAL'S *Aussführlich und umständlicher Bericht*
(4th edition). *Courtesy of the Library of Congress.*

TITLE PAGE of Böhme's *Das verlangte nicht erlangte Canaan* (1711), answering Kocherthal's *Bericht. Courtesy of Historical Society of Pennsylvania.*

have such an effect, even after Kocherthal had gone to New York in 1708, that Reverend Anton Wilhelm Böhme, a friend of the Palatines at court and previously referred to, felt called upon to contribute several letters for a pamphlet under the title, *Das verlangte nicht erlangte Canaan* ("The desired, not acquired Canaan"), directed specifically against Kocherthal's roseate description of Carolina.[47]

An interesting collection of manuscripts now preserved in the Library of Congress throws light on the problem pre-

[47] Todd and Goebel, *op. cit.*, 14. A copy is in the Historical Society of Pennsylvania Library in Philadelphia. M. H. Höen, who wrote the foreword, should be credited with editorship at least.

sented by Kocherthal's veiled promises. This collection, known as the Archdale Papers, contains correspondence of John Archdale, one of the proprietors of Carolina. As early as 1705, Archdale was arranging for a settlement in Carolina by what was called the High German Company of Thuringia. Polycarpus Michael Pricherbach, the German correspondent, writing from Langensalza in Thuringia, mentioned reading Richard Blome's *English America*, a description of the English possessions in the western hemisphere. This had been translated into German and published in Leipzig in 1697. Four deputies were sent over to London with the intention of visiting some english province in America. They met and talked with a Mr. Telner, who it seems represented the proprietors of Carolina. They then returned to Germany.[48] The plans probably miscarried as nothing was heard of the venture later.

However, two proposals, made by the High German Company of Thuringia, suggested to the proprietors of Carolina the kind of advertising to use with the greatest appeal in the Germanies. On September 2, 1705, the German Company asked the Carolina proprietors to announce "that all such as shall address themselves to them, After the first Transport (Seing it is needless at the first shiping over) and are not able to pay any monie for their passage, should be transported free by your Lordps without any payment as far as Carolina." This was to be repaid finally by years of service for the company in Carolina.

The second proposal was an inducement to be carried out only after the first transport had safely arrived in Carolina, "for what I am now going to say could not possibly be ventured sooner. There should be published by us and in our names, a short plain description of the good scituation and Conveniences of the Country, with the advantageous Conditions granted to us by the proprietors, there should also cir-

[48] L. C., Archdale MSS. 1694–1706, 122.

cumstancially be sett forth the great eveready proffetts that might be Expected from there, and subjoyned thereunto Expecially this clause, that a Poor Man hath only need to provide himself to come to London and then to pay nothing for his transport thence to Carolina because upon his address to the Lords Proprietors they would maintain and transport him to Carolina whereby nothing which might recomend and make this country should be past by or omitted. Such printed and published description to be authorized by a short preffase by the Lords Proprietors, would then by good friends, left behind be everywhere made known and there being now to God no doubt but that in these hard times in Germany . . .,''[49] colonization would be quickened.

In 1706 Kocherthal was not so particular as to require that he be settled in America first. He obliged the proprietors with his *Aussführlich und umständlicher Bericht von der berühmten Landschafft Carolina*. . . . The Queen was substituted for the Lords Proprietors as the kindly benefactor and veiled promises were made. The fulfillment of the Thuringian suggestion is apparent. What is not so evident, is Kocherthal's remuneration. Kocherthal never even visited Carolina, much less settled there. On his arrival in England in 1708, he appealed to the Queen for aid in accordance with his pamphlet's hints. It would seem that the author was sincere in writing of the Queen's help, which was anticipated, as quoted above. Kocherthal was well received by the English government but was sent to New York. This will be related below.

Similar advertising concerning Pennsylvania was also producing air castles for disheartened Germans. William Penn, who later founded Pennsylvania, made several visits to the Rhine country, one in 1677.[50] Penn discussed religious matters wit hmany Lutherans and Calvinists of the Rhine Valley. The

[49] *Ibid.*, 60 *et. seq.*

[50] Samuel M. Janney, *The Life of William Penn* (Philadelphia, 1852), 117 *et. seq.*, recounts Penn's journey in that year and especially his friendship with Princess Elizabeth of the Palatinate.

royal charter for Pennsylvania was granted in 1681. Shortly thereafter appeared in London a brief description of the new province: *Some account of the Province of Pennsylvania in America*.[51] Penn offered to sell one hundred acres of land for two English pounds and a low rental. He combined humanitarianism with business, for he advertised popular government, universal suffrage, and equal rights to all regardless of race or religious belief. Murder and treason were the only capital crimes; and reformation, not retaliation, was the object of punishment for their offenses. This book appeared in translation in Amsterdam the same year and its distribution in the upper Rhine country probably affected favorably the movement of Germans to Pennsylvania.[52]

Pennsylvania was the best advertised province and it was mainly due to the liberal use of printer's ink. No professional promoter or land speculator of the present day could have devised any scheme, which would have proved a greater success than the means taken by William Penn and his counsellor, Benjamin Furley, to advertise his province.[53] Various books were published for German consumption for over twenty years previous to the emigration of 1709.[54] Among them, Pastorious' *Umständige geographische Beschreibung* (detailed geographical description) of 1700 and Daniel Falckner's *Curieuse Nachricht von Pennsylvania* (curious news from Penn-

---

[51] Julius F. Sachse, *The German Pietists of Provincial Pennsylvania 1694–1708* (Philadelphia, 1895), 440; E. E. Proper, *Colonial Immigration Laws* (Col. U. Studies in History, Economics and Public Law, 1900, XII, no. 2), 46.

[52] Albert B. Faust, *The German Element in the United States* (New ed., N.Y., 1927), I, 32 *et. seq.;* H. L. Osgood, *English Colonies in the Eighteenth Century* (New York, 1924), II, 491; Sachse, *op. cit.*, 443 *et. seq.*

[53] J. F. Sachse, *Curieuse Nachricht von Pennsylvania (of 1702)*, (Phila., private ed., 1905), 8. Sachse calls it "The book that stimulated the Great German Emigration to Pennsylvania in the early years of the eighteenth century." Also see Sachse's account of literature used to induce German emigration, *Pa. Ger. Soc. Proc.*, VII, 175–198.

[54] See Sachse's list of some fifty reprints of title-pages, *Pa. Ger. Soc. Proc.*, VII, 201–256; *Das verlangte nicht erlangte Canaan*, 95.

PORTRAIT OF WILLIAM PENN. *Courtesy of Pennsylvania-German Society.*

sylvania) of 1702 were combined into a single work in 1704 by the Frankfort Company, for whom Falckner became attorney along with Benjamin Furley.[55]

One writer tells us that English agents were sent throughout the Palatinate to induce immigration, much in the same way as did our western railroad companies of a later date. These companies, having received large bounties in land from the government, sent agents throughout Europe to influence emigration so that their land grants might be settled and revenue-producing.[56] These early land agents, "Neuländer,"[57] or whatever they may be called, must have used to full advantage the reputation Penn and his colony had acquired in the Rhineland.[58] Simmendinger, quoted above, gave his expected destination as Pennsylvania. Luttrell reported foreign news on April 28th and May 12, 1709, of Palatines coming to England bound for Pennsylvania.[59] Penn's advertising was productive of good results at last.

Before the kind of help extended to the emigrants and the means employed by the British government can be understood, it is necessary that the position of England as the protector of the Protestant cause in Europe be understood. William of Orange with his wife Mary had taken the English throne from his father-in-law, James II, in 1688 to secure intervention by England and support for the Protestant cause on the continent against the encroachments of Catholic France.[60] As Louis XIV aged, he grew more intolerant. Counsels of moderation even by the influential Madame de Maintenon were unavailing. In 1685 the Edict of Nantes, granting religious toleration to

[55] Sachse, *Falckner's Nachricht*, 23–28.

[56] John M. Brown, *Brief Sketch of the First Settlement of the County of Schoharie by the Germans* (Schoharie, 1823), 5.

[57] Faust, *op. cit.*, I, 61.

[58] Kapp calls them "Speculators," and says they associated themselves with the Quakers. *Die Deutschen*, I, 20.

[59] Luttrell, *op. cit.*, VI, 434, 440.

[60] G. N. Clark, *The Later Stuarts 1660–1714* (Oxford, 1934), 143.

French Protestants, was revoked and persecution followed.[61] Many Huguenots, as the French Protestants were called, fled to England, Germany and the New World.[62] When William declared war on France in 1689, he published a "Proclamation for the encouraging French Protestants to transport themselves into this Kingdom," promising that they would not only have his royal protection but that he would also "so aid and assist them in their several trades and ways of livelihood, as that their being in this realm might be comfortable and easy to them."[63]

Queen Anne on her accession in 1702 continued, under the guidance of the Marlboroughs and their relatives, those policies on which was predicated her right to the throne.[64] The Second Hundred Years' War entered its second phase, the War of the Spanish Succession. In diplomatic discussions the English sought to secure religious and civil rights for the Protestants on the continent. They even considered proposing in the negotiations for peace at Geertruidenberg in 1708 that the change in a ruler's religion should not "influence the worship or revenues of his subject (wch is the most reasonable thing in the most), most of the evill effects proceeding from such a change of religion will be avoyded."[65] In other ways help was extended to foreign Protestants, such as those of Bergen and Courland, for example. At their petition collections were taken up in England under government auspices for

[61] A. J. Grant, "The Government of Louis XIV," in *Camb. Mod. Hist.*, V, 24; Viscount St. Cyres, "The Gallican Church," *ibid.*, V, 89.

[62] J. S. Burn, *History of the French, Walloon, Dutch and other Foreign Refugees Settled in England from the Reign of Henry VIII to the Revocation of the Edict of Nantes* (London, 1746), 18. The number of names of French origin among the Palatine emigrants (See Shipping Lists in Appendix) suggest that many were French refugees fleeing a second time.

[63] Paul de Rapin-Thoyras, *History of England 1661–1725*, trans. and continued by H. Tindal (London, 1744), XVI, 347.

[64] Clark, *op. cit.*, 212.

[65] B. M., Add. MSS. 28055, 425; P. R. O., S. P. 84/233, 38.

funds for building of churches.[66] When on June 12, 1709, a French Protestant petitioned Queen Anne in behalf of "a million persecuted protestants," she assured her petitioner, "she had already given her ministers abroad instructions concerning the same and will doe for them what else lies in her power."[67] There are other indications of a similar nature, which show that the Protestants looked to the English Queen to take care of their interests.[68]

At this time Queen Anne was especially susceptible to Protestant appeals. Queen Anne's consort, Prince George of Denmark, died on October 28, 1708, "to the unspeakable grief of the Queen."[69] Prince George was of German Stock,[70] a Lutheran, and had brought many of his countrymen and co-religionists to London. The Royal Chapel in St. James Palace (Lutheran) established in 1700, owed its existence to him.[71] The funeral sermon which the Reverend John Tribbeko preached in the Royal Chapel on November 21st emphasized the Prince's interest in the Protestant cause.[72] It probably softened the Queen's grief to act as the gracious benefactress of the oppressed co-religionists of her departed husband.[73] At any rate she took a great deal of interest in relieving the Palatines in 1709.

A more important question is how far the English Ministry was aware of the advertising activities and how far it coun-

[66] P. R. O., S. P. 44/108, 25 (1708–1709).

[67] Luttrell, op. cit., VI, 452.

[68] Townshend MSS. (Hist. MSS. Com. 11th Report, Appendix), IV, 52.

[69] B. M., Add. MSS. 15866, 135; Add. MSS. 6309, 27; Egmont MSS. (Hist. MSS. Com. 7th Report, Appendix), II, 232; Agnes Strickland, Lives of the Queens of England (Boston, 1859), XII, 189.

[70] L. Katscher, "German Life in London," in Nineteenth Century (May, 1887), XXI, 728.

[71] Ibid., 738.

[72] John Tribbeko, A Funeral Sermon on the Death of H. R. H. Prince George of Denmark (London, 1709), 27.

[73] C. B. Todd, "Robert Hunter and the Settlement of the Palatines," in National Magazine (February, 1893), XVII, 292.

PRINCE GEORGE OF DENMARK, royal consort of Queen Anne. *Courtesy of Pennsylvania-German Society.*

tenanced them. The English policies were predicated on the postulates of mercantilism accepted by seventeenth century Europe.[74] These mercantilist doctrines attached a high value to a dense population, as an element of national strength. It was even argued that colonies would weaken the parent country by lessening the population.[75] In this view of migration, England would benefit by, and the Rhine countries would lose, and perhaps oppose, the movement of peoples. It was said to be "a Fundamental Maxim in Sound Politicks, that the Greatness, Wealth, and Strength of a Country, consist in the Number of its Inhabitants."[76] The preamble of an English law of 1709 observed that "the increase of people is a means of advancing the wealth and strength of a nation."[77] The States General of Holland echoed "that the Grandeur and Prosperity of a Country does in general consist in a Multitude of Inhabitants."[78] The *Monthly Mercury*, a contemporary English publication, discussing Holland's new law, remarked that "The States [were] sensible of the Truth of the Maxim that the number of Inhabitants is the Strength of a nation. . . ."[79]

In pursuance of such aims, the English Parliament was bombarded with propaganda favorable to the naturalization of foreign Protestants. Under the heading "Some weighty considerations for Parliament," Archdale, the Carolina proprietor referred to before, wrote that 2,000 white people in Carolina were worth 100,000 at home. He argued that this

[74] Clark, *op. cit.*, 43; E. F. Heckscher, *Mercantilism* (London, 1935), II, 159.

[75] Proper, *op. cit.*, 74.

[76] [Francis Hare], *The Reception of the Palatines Vindicated in a Fifth Letter to a Tory Member* (London, 1711), 4, 37 *et. seq.* Hare was chaplain to the Duke of Marlborough.

[77] 7 Anne, c. 5, *Statutes of the Realm*, IX, 63.

[78] *The State of the Palatines*, 6; *Eccles. Rec.*, II, 1775 and 1830.

[79] *Monthly Mercury* (London, July, 1709), XX, 275; Josiah Child, *A New Discourse on Trade*, (1693 ed.), 154; Edgar S. Furniss, *The Labourer in a System of Nationalism* (Boston, 1920), 33.

was due to their use of English goods and the products they exchanged so favorably for England.[80] He went on, "the body of Europe is under a general fermentation . . . which will more and more persecute an uneasy body of Protestants . . . [who] opprest with taxes, drained of their wealth and lyeing in the jealous sight of popery, are growne so uneasy, as to be willing to transplant themselves under the English Government." A petition from a Pennsylvania German asked for a naturalization act for German Protestants, who although inclined to emigrate were under great difficulties from lack of it.[81]

William Penn was the author of a general naturalization bill for the colonies. In urging its approval to a member of the House of Lords, he pointed out "the interest of England to improve and thicken her colonys with people not her own."[82] But early in January, 1709, Penn wrote to James Logan in Pennsylvania, "Tho' we have here a bill for Naturalization in the House, and I think I never writ so correctly, as I did to some members of Parliament, as well and discoursed them on that subject, . . . it moves but slowly. . . . "[83]

Finally, giving way to the pressure, Parliament moved to encourage immigration and on February 5th, leave was given in the House of Commons to bring in a bill for naturalizing foreign Protestants. On the 28th the bill passed its first test vote on a motion to continue the old provision of the law, which lost 101 to 198. The bill was passed on March 7th by a vote of 203 to 77, but over the protests and opposition of the City of London, whose authorities wanted a clause inserted protecting their own rights to the duties paid by aliens.[84] On the 15th the bill was agreed to by the Lords 65 to 20. Royal

[80] L. C., Archdale MSS., 1694–1706, 151.

[81] Ibid., 70; On naturalization, see A. H. Carpenter, "Naturalization in England and the American Colonies," in Amer. Hist. Review, IX, 288–303.

[82] Huntington Library, H. M. MSS. 22285; hereafter cited as H. L.

[83] Penn-Logan Corres. (Memoirs of Historical Society of Pa., X), II, 323.

[84] Luttrell, op. cit., VI, 404, 408, 415, 417.

assent made it a law on March 23rd.[85] This was the first general naturalization law in England. It provided that the naturalized had to take the oath of allegiance, and partake of the sacrament according to the Anglican ritual before witnesses, who signed a certificate to that effect. In addition, all the children of naturalized parents were to be considered natural-born subjects.[86] The greatest benefit secured by the act was the right to purchase and hold land, which might be transmitted to one's children. Those naturalized were also permitted to take part in trade and commerce, usually forbidden to foreigners.[87]

Palatine or German immigrants were not particularly mentioned it appears. But Macpherson states, "This law was said to have been made with a particular view to the Protestant Palatines brought this year into England."[88] Certain it is that by the time the act was passed, the first wave of the emigration was already well on its way down the Rhine.[89] Still the news of the bill's consideration by the English Parliament may have reached prospective immigrants. That this act was a preparation for their coming, or even an added attraction for the immigration itself is highly probable. It would seem then, that the parties who urged and were successful in securing the passage of the naturalization law, were intimately connected with colonial projects in America. Men, such as Archdale and Penn, stimulated through agents and

---

[85] C. J., XVI, 93, 108, 113, 123, 131, et. seq.; Eccles. Rec., III, 1724, 1832; Paul Chamberlen, History of the . . . Reign of Queen Anne (London, 1738), 312.

[86] 7 Anne, c. 5, Statutes of the Realm, IX, 63.

[87] L. C., Archdale MSS. 1694–1706, 70.

[88] David Macpherson, Annals of Commerce (London, 1805), III, 6.

[89] The first contingent of the Palatines arrived in London about May 3rd (B. T. Jour. 1708–1714, 26). They were over six weeks, a few weeks at least, at Rotterdam awaiting transportation and the time needed to cross the Channel, in addition to the time spent on the way to Rotterdam, would certainly amount to two months. The Kocherthal party in 1708 needed two months to travel from Frankfurt to London. Eccles. Rec., III, 1729.

advertising a movement of people, who assured themselves that the British government had engaged to provide for them.

On the other hand the British authorities do not seem to have prepared for such a large immigration. In fact, the records of the Board of Trade and Privy Council may be searched in vain for evidence that the Palatine immigration was planned or at least expected and prepared for, other than by the general naturalization act just referred to. But this much is clear, the English government under Anne was embarking upon a mercantilist policy of colonial development, in which its population both at home and in the colonies was to be enlarged by stimulating and even subsidizing immigration from foreign shores.

Precedents existed for governmental controlled immigration for English dominions. In 1679, Charles II sent two shiploads of French Huguenots to South Carolina, in order to introduce the cultivation of grapes, olives and the silk-worm.[90] In 1694, Baron de Luttichaw petitioned for permission to import 200 Protestant families, some 1,000 persons, from the Germanies to his land in Ireland.[91] In 1697, King William offered a grant of 500 pounds to some Jamaica merchants to transplant men to Jamaica.[92] In 1706, Governor Dudley of Massachusetts Bay and New Hampshire, proposed that a colony of Scots be settled in Nova Scotia.[93] In the same year, Colonel Parke, governor of the Leeward Islands asked for "10,000 Scotch with otemeal enough to keep them for 3 or 4 months" to lead against [French] Martinique. He proposed to settle them there, if successful.[94] But reception of the Huguenots in England in Elizabeth's reign seemed to be the most applicable precedent, and it was strongly cited for that

[90] Proper, *op. cit.*, 81.
[91] *Cal. Treas. Papers 1557–1696*, 346.
[92] *C. C. 1696–1697*, 389.
[93] *C. C. 1706–1708*, 31, 234, 439.
[94] *Ibid.*, 356, 358.

purpose.[95] With the ambitious design of James II to unite all the colonies under one government, the resources of Parliament and the Crown were used to foster immigration.

In the reign of Queen Anne this idea took practical shape. Considerable sums of money were expended to assist Protestant refugees in making their way to England and the English colonies. For example, early in 1706 Secretary of State Hedges informed Governor Granville of Barbados concerning one Francisco Pavia and his family from Cadiz, whom "H. M. has not only bestowed her royal bounty upon . . . to transport them thither, but also recommended them to you, that you will give them all fitting countenance and assistance."[96] In the same year the Board of Trade at the behest of Secretary of State Hedges considered a proposal by François Louis Michel and George Ritter to settle some "4 or 500 Swiss Protestants . . . on some uninhabited lands in Pennsylvania or on the frontier of Virginia." The last stipulation called for transportation with their effects from Rotterdam at Her Majesty's expense. The Board of Trade approved the proposal, and made practical suggestions for carrying it out. Indeed, the Board did not even find fault with the suggestion that the government should pay the cost of transportation, which it estimated would be eight pounds per head.[97] This proposal was carried out under private auspices with a handsome subsidy. These efforts were due largely to political and commercial motives, and partly to the genuine interest which England took in championing the Protestant cause in Europe.[98]

Still such a program of colonial development[99] had to be

[95] [Hare], *op. cit.*, 4; "Brief History," in *Eccles. Rec.*, III, 1776.

[96] *C. C. 1706–1708*, 14.

[97] *Ibid.*, 62, 79.

[98] Proper, *op. cit.*, 74.

[99] An evidence of this program was the negotiation with Penn for the purchase of his government. By the summer of 1712, the terms of the surrender had been agreed upon, 12,000 pounds, payable in four years, with certain stipulations. Janney, *op. cit.*, 524.

pursued with caution to avoid diplomatic intervention. Not all governments were ready to rid themselves of an undesirable religious sect by arranging deportation to British America as the Swiss canton of Bern did in 1710.[100] Indeed, as a rule, princes were not disposed to permit their subjects to be enticed from their obligations to them.[101] For this reason open invitations apparently were not issued. It can be concluded that the large German emigration of the second decade of the eighteenth century was due in a general way to these causes: (1) war devastation, (2) heavy taxation, (3) an extraordinary severe winter, (4) religious quarrels, but not persecutions, (5) land hunger on the part of the elderly and desire for adventure on the part of the young, (6) liberal advertising by colonial proprietors, and finally (7) the benevolent and active co-operation of the British government.[102] The background and causes of the Palatine emigration have been described, but the manner in which the British government participated in the actual movement has still to be pointed out. In particular, how did the emigration gather momentum? This will be discussed in Chapter III. Chapter II will describe the small 1708 immigration, which blazed the trail.

[100] Indeed the Swiss authorities went so far as to ask the good offices of the British to prevent Dutch interference with the compulsory transportation of the Anabaptists through Holland. Letter from British Envoy Abraham Stanyan to Lord Townshend, April 5, 1710. *Magg Bros. Cat.*, No. 522.

[101] Todd and Goebel, *op. cit.*, 13. It appears probable that the emigrations under discussion caused the Elector Palatine to treat his subjects better, as the Duchess of Orleans wrote to her half-sister Louisa, Raugravine in the Palatinate, so that "When those who have gone to Pennsylvania hear about it they will quickly return." *Letters to Madam* (London, 1924), II, 25.

[102] Professor E. B. Greene is correct in his general conclusion as to the causes of this emigration. *Provincial America 1690–1740* (New York, 1905), 230.

CHAPTER II. THE SMALL PALATINE EMIGRATION OF 1708

SINCE THE founding of Germantown in Pennsylvania under the leadership of Francis Daniel Pastorius in 1683, no large groups of Germans had sought homes in the New World. Intermittently, individuals with their families may have made the voyage, but of larger movements there were none. Twenty-five years passed before another band of emigrants made their way down the Rhine on their way to America. The emigration of 1708 was the prelude to the later heavy German emigrations of the eighteenth century.

The leader of the band of emigrants of 1708 was the Reverend Joshua Kocherthal, referred to before as the author of a promising description of Carolina. Kocherthal had visited London two years earlier and canvassed the possibilities at that time. What arrangements were made and with whom is not known but that assurances of aid were given appears certain judged by the experiences of the little band. The group was originally composed of forty-one people; ten men, ten women, and twenty-one children,[1] ranging in age from six months to fifteen years. The heads of the families were Lorenz Schwisser, Henry Rennau, Andreas Volck, Michael Weigand, Jacob Weber, Jacob Pletel, Johannes Fischer, Melchior Gülch, and Joshua Kocherthal. One of the ten men was single, a young man of twenty-three, Isaac Türck by name. They came from the neighborhood of Landau in the Rhenish Palatinate and represented themselves as refugees of the war there.[2]

[1] P. R. O., C. O. 323/6, 56. Also, History Society of Pennsylvania Library Transcripts, B. T., Plantations General, VII, 54, hereafter cited as H. S. P. A fifteen year old girl was considered a woman evidently. B. T. Jour. 1704–1708, 482; C. C. 1706–1708, 722.

[2] N. Y. Col. Docs., V, 53; Doc. Hist., III, 543.

On February 16, 1708, Kocherthal and his party applied to the English consular representative at Frankfort on the Rhine for passes to England.[3] Mr. Davenant, the representative, refused to give them passes, money or recommendations, for fear of displeasing the Elector Palatine. Instead of aiding them immediately, he requested instructions from London. Mr. Boyle, one of the principal Secretaries of State, replied that though the desire of those poor people to settle in the plantations was very acceptable and would be for the public good, the Queen could by no means consent to Mr. Davenant's giving encouragement in any public way, either by money or passes to the Elector Palatine's subjects to leave their country without his consent.[4] If the emigrants received any aid in Frankfort, it was secretly given.

Reverend Kocherthal and his party continued on their journey, however. On the way down the Rhine they received many gifts of food, money and even clothing from those charitably disposed. Their progress from town to town must have attracted considerable attention and acted as valuable publicity for the English colonies. Kocherthal's confidence that the English government might provide the passage from Holland to England was well-founded it seems. In a letter, which was written from London, July 31, 1708, and appeared as a third appendix to the 1709 edition of his *Bericht*, Kocherthal stated, "the city council in Rotterdam gave us twenty-five florins [£4.3.4] and had us brought to Hellevotschliuss[5] at their own cost in a ship belonging to the city. At the Hague we obtained from the English envoy that a free pass was given us to England and so we were brought from Hellevotschliuss in Holland clear to Harwich in England without a penny's cost."[6]

[3] H. S. P., B. T. Plantations General, VIII, 53.

[4] *C. J.*, XVI, 597.

[5] Hellevotschliuss is about fifteen miles from Rotterdam on a large island close to the coast.

[6] Kocherthal, *Bericht* (1709), 28.

Immediately on his arrival in London, Kocherthal petitioned the Queen. This petition recited the cause of the emigration as the French ravages upon the Rhine and Neckar Rivers in 1707. In the judgment of the immigrants, so severe was the destruction that they could not possibly attain sufficient means of livelihood during the hard times, which still continued. Although Kocherthal requested a dwelling place in the English West Indies[7] and aid in establishing the colony, he did not mention royal promises.[8] This fact may mean little, however, since he was a man of singular tact, and charity was not to be secured by demands, at least not in the eighteenth century. At any rate, the petition was sent to the Board of Trade for advice as to the most proper place to settle the Palatines, as to transportation and as to the subsistence necessary to provide for them meanwhile.[9] The Secretary of State apparently already had decided to settle the Palatines at government expense. Whoever had promised Kocherthal aid, as related in his *Bericht* already referred to, was moving the authorities as expected. Since matters of importance were decided often by the ministers in informal meetings without record (a practice which was to develop into the cabinet system), it is not surprising that it is difficult to determine how or by whom this early decision to help the Palatines was secured.

Meanwhile the Board of Trade was considering the matter. On the 22nd of April, the Board had Kocherthal before it, to report in more detail the condition of his band. At this time he described their occupations as follows: "One is a joyner, another a smith, the others all versed in gardening, husbandry, planting, and tillage, and the women were versed in and

[7] The term "West Indies" appears to have been loosely used in the early eighteenth century to include the British colonies in the New World.

[8] H. L., H. M. MSS., 1403.

[9] *C. C. 1706–1708*, 720; P. R. O., S. P. 44/107, 14, 20.

understood the same business."[10] The Board recommended immediate aid for subsistence.[11] At the next session on the Palatines, the Board of Trade was advised by a Mr. Lodwick, who had resided in New York for about fifteen years, that New York was a poor place to send them. He said that all land in the province had already been granted, except land which lay forty or fifty miles from the Hudson River. The three Lutheran ministers, who resided in London, accompanied Kocherthal before the Board. They told the Board that they had read the testimonials giving a good character to the said minister and others, and they had no reason to doubt their truth. The religious beliefs of the forty-one persons were given as fifteen Lutherans and twenty-six Calvinists.[12] On May 10th, two warrants were issued for the distribution of money to the Palatines; one for one hundred pounds,[13] the other for forty shillings a day from April 15th past until their transportation to New York.[14]

On the same day the Queen approved an Order in Council, which was considered the following year as the royal sanction for the government venture into the manufacture of naval stores. The Order recited the condition of the refugees and the Board of Trade's suggestion of settlement in Jamaica or "Antego" (Antigua), where large tracts of land were ungranted and a great need of white people existed. The fear that the hot climate would adversely affect the Palatines led to the proposal that they "should be settled upon the Hudson River, in the province of New York, where they might be

[10] B. T. Jour. 1704–1708, 482. Among the six other families of Palatines who arrived in London shortly thereafter and joined the group were a stocking maker and a weaver; C. C. 1706–1708, 783; N. Y. Col. Docs., V, 53. See complete list in Appendix A.

[11] C. C. 1706–1708, 721.

[12] B. T. Jour 1704–1708, 483.

[13] P. R. O., C. O. 5/1049, 6; C. C. 1706–1708, 744, 745.

[14] P. R. O., C. O. 5, 67; In accordance with this order another 100 pounds was issued on June 10th, P. R. O., C. O. 5/1049, 69; C. C. 1708–1709, 35, 82.

[First Half]
Denization Papers granted to Kocherthal's Party of Palatines in London in May, 1708.
Courtesy of Pennsylvania-German Society.

[SECOND HALF]
DENIZATION PAPERS granted to Kocherthal's Party of Palatines in London in May, 1708.
Courtesy of Pennsylvania-German Society.

useful to this kingdom, particularly in the production of naval stores, and as a frontier against the French and their Indians." At the same time orders were issued to the proper authorities to provide 655 pounds for clothing, tools, etc., and to make the Palatines free denizens of the kingdom without charge.[15]

Before the departure for New York, Kocherthal acquainted the Board of Trade with the fact that fourteen more Germans (two from Holstein) had unexpectedly arrived and likewise desired to go to New York.[16] On the next day, May 28th, he presented a list of the new group.[17] The petition was considered favorably. In the meantime preparations went ahead for the settlement. Lists of tools and other necessaries were drawn up and submitted. The cost of the voyage was estimated at 333 pounds.[18] On the 28th of June Kocherthal submitted a complete roster of his company. The late-comers were Peter Rose and his wife, Maria Wemarin, a widow, and her daughter, Isaac Feber with his wife and son, Daniel Fiere with his wife and two children, and Herman Schüneman.[19] The other two Germans not listed had entered the services of Lord Lovelace,[20] the newly-appointed governor of New York. Their names are supplied from the list of May 28th, mentioned above, as Peter Hübertsen and his son Jacob, a lad of fifteen. On questioning, the Board learned that Kocherthal had made an agreement with the others to clear six acres of land for him the first year, to enable him to settle.

Reverend Kocherthal next petitioned for a salary as clergy-

---

[15] P. R. O., S. P. 44/107, 67; *C. C. 1706–1708*, 727; *Acts of Privy Council Col. 1680–1720*, 553.

[16] H. S. P., Jour. B. T., XX, 157; *Doc. Hist.*, III, 328; *Eccles. Rec.*, III, 1703

[17] *B. T. Jour. 1704–1708*, 496; *C. C. 1706–1708*, 738; *N. Y. Col. Docs.*, V, 44; P. R. O., C. O. 1049/57, 139. Peculiarly only thirteen people are listed, the name of Herman Schüneman being absent. This is supplied from the list of June 28th.

[18] *C. C. 1706–1708*, 744, 757, 783.

[19] *N. Y. Col. Docs.*, V, 53.

[20] H. S. P., Jour. B. T., XX, 222.

man, but the Board of Trade "found no precedent of a salary being settled here upon foreign clergymen in the Plantations, only that at New York the French Minister there has a salary of twenty pounds out of the Revenue." But the Board recommended that Governor Lovelace grant him a reasonable portion of land for a glebe and that twenty pounds be allowed Kocherthal for clothes and books. This was accordingly done.[21] For these favors, Kocherthal thanked the Board of Trade in a letter from New York, dated February 15, 1709.[22]

About the middle of October, 1708, the Palatines sailed with Lovelace for New York, leaving behind them the family of Melchior Gülch (also known as Gilles or Hilg). His wife was ill with a "cancer of the breast," which the surgeons were hopeful of curing in three or four months. During this period the family was supported by the government. But Frau Gülch died, and on April 19, 1709, Melchior petitioned for an order to the Navy Board for transportation to New York.[23] The voyage of the main party with Governor Lovelace in 1708 occupied over nine weeks. On board the Palatine ship, the *Globe*, two children were born to German families and were baptized by Kocherthal September 14th and November 28th.[24] Governor Lovelace landed at Flushing, Long Island. He wrote immediately on December 18th, "Our winter sets in very hard, the Ports and Rivers are full of Ice; I am in pain for the Germans and Recruits on board the *Globe* they wanting water, and the Weather not permitting us to assist them. This coast is so terrible in the Winter I think no Ship ought to be sent

[21] P. R. O., S. P. 44/107, 87; *C. C. 1708–1709*, 34, 61; *N. Y. Col. Docs.*, V, 63; *Doc. Hist.*, III, 543.

[22] *C. C. 1708–1709*, 222; *B. T. Jour. 1708–1714*, 67.

[23] *Ibid.*, 120, 184, 281; *B. T. Jour. 1708–1714*, 23.

[24] Kocherthal Records, 4. A MS. record in the possession of St. Paul's Evangelical Lutheran Church at West Camp, N. Y. This has been translated and published in *Olde Ulster, a biographical and historical magazine* (Kingston, N. Y., 1907), III, 54. Another translation is J. C. Krahmer, *The Kocherthal Records* (St. Johnsville, N. Y., 1931).

PORTRAIT OF GOVERNOR FRANCIS LOVELACE. *Courtesy of Pennsylvania-German Society.*

hither from England after August at fartherest . . . ."[25] The Palatines spent the winter in New York City. Two more children were baptized there on January 23rd and February 23rd.[26]

Governor Lovelace gave the Palatines land on the west side of the Hudson River about fifty-five miles north of New York City. The settlement was made at the mouth of Quassaick Creek.[27] Lots of from one hundred to three hundred acres were divided among the settlers, fifty acres per person. In pursuance of Lovelace's instructions, five hundred acres

[25] *N. Y. Col. Docs.*, V, 67.

[26] Kocherthal Records, 4.

[27] Mr. Ralph A. Weed, for years President of the Historical Society of Newburgh Bay and the Highlands, now deceased, collected considerable material on this Palatine settlement, which was "boxed and not available" for this study.

were granted to Kocherthal for a glebe, and an additional two hundred and fifty acres for his family.[28] This settlement was the beginning of Newburgh, New York. The Palatine colony was to have been a frontier settlement, but Newburgh was fully a hundred miles from Albany, beyond which the frontier began. The Palatines, it had been suggested by the Board of Trade and echoed by the Privy Council, were to make naval stores, but no plans or preparations for that work were made.

During the administration of Lovelace, the Palatines at Newburgh were well taken care of. The allowance of nine pence per day for each person supplied them with food and other necessities. But Lovelace's administration was short. He died on May 6, 1709, "having never had a well day in his government." He had contracted a cold on the voyage over, which probably developed more serious complications. Pity the plight of Lady Lovelace, for one son died before his Lordship and the young Lord passed away a fortnight later.[29] Up to the time of his decease, Lovelace had expended two hundred and two pounds, seventeen shillings and eight pence in behalf of the Palatines, which sum was certified to by Kocherthal and Schüneman.[30] At the beginning of 1711, Lady Lovelace had not yet received the money due her on this account.[31] But before 1715 her husband's successor in the governorship, Colonel Robert Hunter, had reimbursed her out of the quit-rent fund of the colony with a sum somewhere between 400 and 500 pounds.[32]

Soon after the death of Lovelace the Palatines were in actual want of provisions. They petitioned the Council of

[28] N. Y. Patent Books, VIII, 333; N. Y. Land Papers, V, 142, VI, 39, 57 and 188; N. Y. Council Minutes, XI, 89; Doc. Hist., III, 572.

[29] N. Y. Col. Docs., V, 81. New York Historical Society, Hawks Transcripts of London Society for Propagation of the Gospel Records, I, 154, hereafter cited as N. Y. H. S.

[30] C. C. 1708–1709, 459.

[31] Cal. Treas. Papers 1708–1714, 233.

[32] C. C. 1714–1715, 307.

New York on May 26th, to provide for them as the Queen had intended. Colonel Nicholson, a colonial official with influence, who was in the province to take part in the 1709 expedition against Canada, testified to the intentions of the British government subsidy.[33] The Council thereupon requested Colonel Thomas Wenham to support the Germans until the expiration of the year as ordered, or until Her Majesty's desire became known. This request was made necessary by the lack of revenue in the province and by the colonial government's great debts.[34]

At the same time charges were made that nineteen of the forty-seven Germans in the settlement had turned "Pietists" and had withdrawn from communion with the minister and the others. A committee of the Council investigated these charges and was of the opinion on June 21st, "that nothing of the aligations suggested against those called 'Pietists' have been proved before them. . . ." Accordingly their subsistence allowance, which had been withheld on that account, was restored to them. This religious dispute indicated at least that the members of the settlement were not in complete harmony with each other. Another cause for discord appeared, when Melchior Gülch arrived from London. He brought a variety of joiner's tools and other supplies, including a barrel of lime, and two grindstones. The Germans by a common division took possession of all the tools. On April 29, 1710, Gülch asked for an order against them to secure the joiner's sets, which he claimed had been given to him for his own possession, for his son, and for an apprentice.[35]

Near the end of June, Kocherthal found himself in financial straits. He was dissatisfied with the means afforded for his settlement. He therefore determined to return to England and

<hr />

[33] Colonel Nicholson had been consulted by the Board of Trade in London with reference to the Palatine settlement. *B. T. Jour. 1704–1708*, 496.

[34] *Doc. Hist.*, III, 545.

[35] *Ibid.*, 551.

personally to plead his cause with the Queen or her government. On June 29th Kocherthal most humbly implored Colonel Ingoldesby, Lieutenant-Governor of the province, then acting governor, to procure free transportation for him on one of Her Majesty's ships.[36] Having secured passage, on August 18th, he further requested Ingoldesby to give him a testimonial of the "civil life and behavior" of himself and his group since his arrival, inasmuch as this would very much contribute to the happy success of his mission.[37] Kocherthal did not return to London in order to lead the 1710 emigrants, as has been asserted.[38] He was unaware of the developments over there. He undertook his journey to secure further help from the Queen, principally for himself.

During his short residence in New York Kocherthal had contracted a debt of thirty pounds, among the items being house-rent, firewood, a table, a bedstead, a chest, three stools, candles and household goods. Other expenses were for teaching English to his children, and a physician and nurse for his wife's illness. While he had been assigned seven hundred and fifty acres of land, he had not received the capital to work it, as he desired. He had not found matters as pleasant as he had anticipated in his *Bericht*. He therefore determined upon the voyage to London, which cost him an additional twenty-five pounds, to be secured from the Queen or her government.[39]

After Kocherthal's departure for London, the settlement's benefactor, Colonel Wenham, died and again the German colonists were in dire want. On September 23, 1709, they petitioned the Lieutenant-Governor and the Council in the hope

[36] *Ibid.*, 546.

[37] N. Y. Col. MSS., LIII, 108.

[38] C. B. Todd, "Robert Hunter and the Settlement of the Palatines," in *National Magazine* (February, 1893), XVII, 292; Todd, "The Story of the Palatines," in *Lippincott Magazine* (March, 1883), XXXI, 244; B. M. Brink, "The Palatine Settlements," in *N. Y. State Hist. Assoc. Proc.* (Albany, 1912), XI, 139.

[39] P. R. O., C. O. 5/1049, 155.

that they might provide a gentleman, willing to support them with their allowance, until it expired on January 1st. By October 10th, the Palatines had obtained two men willing to provide the ready payment of the remainder due them, one hundred and ninety-five pounds and three shillings, Colonel Nicholas Bayard and Mr. Octavius Conradus. The arrangement was made, however, only after the Germans had entered into a penal bond fully to repay the money, should it not be received from the Royal Treasury within twelve months. The Council, approving of this, agreed to certify the amount to the Lord High Treasurer as they had done for Colonel Wenham.[40]

At all events, Kocherthal returned to London, and on December 27, 1709, he addressed the Board of Trade in a clever fashion. He drew up a paper on the subject of viticulture in America. He wrote that he had corresponded ''with all such persons as have had the least experience in that affaire, and have actually undertaken a journey over the whole Continent.'' Kocherthal asserted that the planting of vineyards could ''be the most proffitable labour which the new-comers there could ever desire, and more advantageous to this Kingdom than the America sugar or tobacco trade.'' After raising a series of questions and answering them, he concluded that ''It would in a short Time evidently appear That the English America is full as fit and capable for the said nursery and Wine Trade as any other Part or Place in the Whole Universe.''[41] To this attractive dissertation, Kocherthal attached an abstract of letters, which it appeared were received by him from ''friends,'' concerning his maintenance in New York. In this way he brought to the attention of the authorities what he desired, and even argued for it without appearing to do so.

[40] *Doc. Hist.*, III, 547 *et seq.*

[41] *C. C. 1708-1709*, 565; P. R. O., C. O. 5/1049, 155. Today the hills bordering the Hudson River are covered with grape-vines. Not Reverend Kocherthal, but a prohibition experiment two hundred years later was responsible for the industry.

These extracts are most interesting, since they present some idea of what was considered necessary to set up a small plantation in 1710.

For such a modest enterprise over five hundred pounds were required. These are some of the items: to clear the ground for the house and barn, ten pounds; building a house, one hundred and eighty pounds; a barn, seventy pounds; two negro slaves to do the work, one hundred and twenty pounds; a wagon, cart, plow and (h)arrow, twenty pounds; three horses, four cows and two hogs, twenty pounds; (as it would take over a year to produce) subsistence for a family of seven, a man, woman, three children and two slaves, eighty pounds. To these items, Kocherthal added twenty pounds for incidentals and the seventy pounds he needed for immediate expenses and debts.[42]

Another "friend" apparently wrote Kocherthal that this sum of money would not suffice or be paid him in London. This "friend" advised Kocherthal to resign his seven hundred and fifty acres and petition Her Majesty for half of the money, three hundred pounds. This sum could then be used to pay Kocherthal's debts in New York and the expense of living there for another year. He could in the meantime cast about for another place of living and leave at the end of that time. A third "friend" cautioned Kocherthal to "take care to discharge his debts, otherwise his possessions would certainly be seized and his children sold for servants."

One of Kocherthal's "friends" wrote, "As to the Report Wee have had That there are so many High Germans in London Who are to come hither I doe look upon this to be false, But if the same be True There are 5 Dutch Ministers in the province, and the English Minister in Albania [Albany] the Reverend Mr. Barkley doth Sufficiently understand the

[42] A gift of this kind could be expected by Kocherthal only if he felt that in justice something further was due to him for services rendered, perhaps in writing the *Bericht*, that most favorable description of Carolina, which he never visited.

High dutch Tongue. . . ."[43] It is difficult to understand how the decision of Secretary of State Sunderland on November 4th, which will be discussed later, to send more Germans to New York, could have reached the colonies and comments returned to England by December 27th.

Kocherthal's connection with the 1709 migration is that of a press agent. It was his *Bericht* of 1706, which encouraged many of his fellow-countrymen to consider the New World. His example in 1708, and especially the reception he and his band received at the hands of the English government, pointed the way for others to follow. An account of the aid, that could be expected by others and was received by Kocherthal, was added as a third Appendix to his *Bericht*, and disseminated in the Rhine Valley. The four impressions, made in 1709, are indicative of the demand for the pamphlet and of its influence in encouraging emigration.[44] But Kocherthal's accidental presence in London, late in 1709, has misled students of this movement to attribute to him a mythical leadership, even asserting that his return to England was for that purpose.

Kocherthal apparently received some aid from funds voted by Parliament in connection with the large Palatine immigration of 1709. At any rate he returned to New York and resumed his labors with his fellow-countrymen. But it does not appear that he was provided with the capital for the plantation he envisioned. His history and that of the Newburgh Palatines merged with that of the large immigration of 1709 and will be discussed later in a chapter on the dispersal of the Germans in New York. Meanwhile the various causes of Palatine emigration treated in Chapter I, were giving pause to many disheartened and dissatisfied Germans in the Rhine country. The well-established fact that Kocherthal had followed the course laid out in his *Bericht*, gave further impetus to a movement of population, which for its brief intensity was incredible in that age. Let us follow the 1709 emigration from the Rhineland to London.

[43] P. R. O., C. O. 5/1049, 155.
[44] B. M., Strafford Papers, Add. MSS. 22202, 130.

CHAPTER III. THE 1709 EMIGRATION IN ENGLAND

SCARCELY HAD the harsh winter season of 1708–9 begun to relax its hold in February, when various inhabitants of the Rhine Valley hopefully began their preparations to go to England. These consisted mainly of gathering up their few possessions and securing a recommendation from the local authorities.[1] One of these documents has survived during these two centuries. Gerhart Schaeffer, preparing to emigrate in 1709, secured the following certificate of good character from the Mayor and the clerks of court of Hilgert Dorf, in Hesse-Nassau: "He has lived with us in Hilgert Dorf with his housewife for 24 years and has conducted himself well and honestly, so that all his neighbors regarded him as a faithful neighbor and were entirely satisfied with him, and the neighbors would have been much pleased if it had been God's will that he should remain longer here." It was signed by the Mayor, duly sealed and witnessed.[2]

The passage down the Rhine to Holland took from four to six weeks. This journey was beset with many delays and inconveniences. Fees and tolls were frequently demanded.[3] On the other hand philanthropic assistance was not lacking. Along the river the Palatines were presented with money and food by pious countrymen, many of whom regarded the pilgrims with envious eyes, wishing they too might be seeking their fortune in the New World. Bread, meat, butter and cheese and even an occasional gift of clothing brightened the

[1] Simmendinger, *op. cit.*, 2.

[2] The original remains in the possession of Schaeffer's descendants, the Kingsley family, of The Rocks, Schoharie, N. Y.

[3] Gottlieb Mittelberger, *Journey to Pennsylvania* (Philadelphia, 1898), 18. This refers to later years, but earlier conditions were worse.

[FIRST HALF]
LETTER OF RECOMMENDATION OF GERHART SCHAEFFER, a Palatine emigrant, May 26,
1709. *Courtesy of the Kingsley Family*, Schoharie, New York.

[Second Half]
LETTER OF RECOMMENDATION OF GERHART SCHAEFFER, a Palatine emigrant, May 26, 1709. *Courtesy of the Kingsley Family*, Schoharie, New York.

slow journey.[4] Ever present too must have been the fear that the authorities would halt them temporarily for some trifling matter, as often occurred, or turn them back definitely, as frequently threatened.

While the pioneer groups were preparing for emigration along the Rhine and its tributaries the Neckar and Main Rivers and beginning to gather in numbers, unidentified individuals approached the British authorities in their behalf late in December, 1708. The first British official reference to the 1709 Palatine immigration came from James Dayrolle, British Resident at the Hague. It was an undated and unsigned document in French entitled, "Memorial relating to the Poor Protestants from the Palatinate." When Dayrolle enclosed it in a dispatch of December 24, 1708, he said, "It was brought to me from the German post office. How it came thither and from whence I know not." The memorial read: "There arrived in this place a number of Protestant families, traveling to England in order to go to the English colonies in America. There are now in the neighborhood of Rotterdam almost eight or nine hundred of them, having difficulty with the packet boat and convoys." After describing these emigrants as composed of poor families of vigorous people, fleeing persecution and oppression in the Palatinate, the memorial concluded with an appeal to Dayrolle: "My Lord, you are humbly supplicated to procure passage and transportation to England out of the benevolence and charity of the Queen."[5] The unknown author of the memorial seems to have anticipated the arrival in Rotterdam of the Palatines by over three months, for it was not until April 19th that Dayrolle reported about nine hundred Palatines at Rotterdam.[6] Meanwhile nothing appears to have been done in London with the exception of the first general naturalization act as related in Chapter I.

[4] Kocherthal, *Bericht*, 77.
[5] P. R. O., S. P. 84/232, 7.
[6] P. R. O., S. P. 84/232, 188.

Although Davenant, the English representative at Frankfort in the Palatinate had been ordered in 1708 not to give any public encouragement, money, or passes to emigrants (as was related in Chapter II), Dayrolle at the Hague in the Netherlands was under no such restrictions. Beginning on March 29, 1709, and at intervals thereafter, he reported to London the granting of passes to sixty or a hundred families at a time.[7] On the same date Dayrolle informed London of the general naturalization act under consideration by the Dutch and that undercover moves were being made to have the French recognize such naturalization,of French refugees. But the result was reported of course to be uncertain.[8] Dayrolle apparently feared that the Dutch might induce the emigrants to remain in the Netherlands to the loss of Great Britain and her colonies. How groundless this fear turned out to be will soon be apparent.

But Dayrolle was a zealous official, determined to secure these "strong and laborious people" for his own country. By April 19th, the number of Palatines at Rotterdam was about nine hundred persons and more were expected. Dayrolle suggested that the transports bringing troops from England to the Low Countries, to fight against the French in the War of the Spanish Succession, might return to England with the Palatines. He further related to Secretary of State Boyle, "I have acquainted the Duke of Marlborough with it, and his Grace is likewise informed of that poor people's circumstances, wanting some assistance to get over, and he has promised to move Her Majesty in their behalf."[9]

Marlborough was the dominant personality in Queen Anne's government, not only as the military genius of his age and the leader of the alliance against France, but also be-

[7] P. R. O., S. P. 84/232, 157, 184, 188.

[8] It should be remembered that the English in the first decade of the 18th century grudgingly admired the economic progress of the Dutch and such references were well calculated to inspire English action of a similar nature. The English naturalization law was adopted on March 23rd. (See Chapter I).

[9] P. R. O., S. P. 84/232, 188.

cause of his family connections. His brother George had dominated the Admiralty until 1708; his son-in-law, Sunderland was the leading Secretary of State; his friend, Godolphin, was the head of the Treasury; and his wife was believed to be supreme over the Queen.[10] Marlborough as minister plenipotentiary was present at the Hague with Lord Townshend to negotiate peace terms at Geertruidenberg. Dayrolle wisely consulted the Duke, for the mention of his interest was enough to move Boyle to present the matter to Queen Anne.[11] With the Queen's approval, orders were issued to the transport ships as Dayrolle had suggested, that is, to return laden with Palatines.[12]

Late in April four transports carried 852 Palatines to London, their subsistence on the voyage being supplied by private charity secured in the Low Countries.[13] In fact, many contributions had to be made to keep the refugees alive. Among others the United Baptists at Amsterdam solicited funds for the Palatines of their faith, many of whom had started from Switzerland.[14] In the same month, the burgomasters of Rotterdam appropriated 750 gilders (c. 75 pounds) for distribution among the destitute emigrants.[15] When some

[10] W. T. Morgan, "The Ministerial Revolution of 1710 in England," in *Pol. Sci. Quarterly* (June, 1921), XXXVI, 195.

[11] Since the calendar of the Marlborough family papers indicated material dealing with the Palatines (Marlborough MSS., *Hist. MSS. Com.*, *8th Report*, Appendix, 47), permission was sought of the family for access to the papers. The request was refused, the only instance of unwillingness to co-operate experienced in the course of this research. Fortunately, the public archives contain enough correspondence to make sufficiently clear Marlborough's official connection with the immigration. The family papers might have indicated a financial interest in the Carolina venture as a motive for Marlborough's co-operation, but this is to be doubted judged from the casual way in which he came to be concerned in transporting the Palatines to England.

[12] B. M., Add. MSS. 15866, 166; P. R. O., S. P. 104/74, 83; S. P. 44/108, 59.

[13] P. R. O., S. P. 87/4, 265. This group is evidently the band of 852 Palatines as noted in the first London Relief Lists of May 6, 1709, compiled by Messrs. Ruperti and Tribbeko; P. R. O., C. O. 388/76, 56 ii.

[14] H. S. P., J. F. Sachse, Dutch Transcripts, April 8, 1709.

[15] Resolutions and Dispositions of Burgomasters of Rotterdam, III, 121.

of the Palatines visited Dayrolle on May 6th, he informed them of the order to use the army transports to carry them to England. He was told then that the Elector Palatine had published an edict forbidding emigrants to leave. Two boats laden with Palatines were seized on the Rhine River and the emigrants were imprisoned. Nevertheless, Palatines arrived daily in Rotterdam after escaping by land.[16]

But when the convoy arrived on May 10th it was learned that only one ship had been ordered to receive Palatines. As a thousand were now awaiting transportation, there was keen disappointment. Dayrolle went to Marlborough, "Who will order it possible, that care may be taken to have them all shipp'd."[17] Since 900 more Palatines arrived in Rotterdam within one week, Dayrolle had Mr. Cardonnel, Marlborough's secretary, write on May 10th to Secretary Boyle "upon that subject."[18] Cardonnel at Marlborough's order suggested that Dayrolle manage the transportation of the Palatines, making the necessary agreement for their transportation and subsistence in their passage to England.[19]

Anticipating the authorization of this plan from London, Dayrolle with the approval of Cardonnel appointed two Dutch merchants, Hendrik van Toren and John Suderman, to supervise the loading and sailing of the emigrants.[20] These men advised Cardonnel from Rotterdam on the 11th of May that the convoy would sail for England before the orders from London could possibly arrive. They therefore asked him

[16] P. R. O., S. P. 84/232, 218.

[17] P. R. O., S. P. 84/232, 222.

[18] P. R. O., S. P. 84/232, 229; C. J., XVI, 597.

[19] P. R. O., S. P. 84/232, 222.

[20] P. R. O., S. P. 44/107, 249. Jan van Gent, another Dutch merchant, replaced Suderman early in June as one of the two Commissioners supervising the embarkation at Rotterdam. Both van Toren and van Gent were men of fine reputation and seem to have been motivated by Christian charity, being members of the Anabaptist Church. They received no remuneration but on the contrary censure from London before they finished their work. P. R. O., S. P. 84/232, 267; S. P. 84/232, 525.

to seek Marlborough's[21] authorization for transporting and subsisting the Palatines at the government's expense to prevent the loss of opportunity for shipping at the next sailing. Their letter concluded with the statement that, "The charity Her Majesty [Queen Anne] shows toward the poor and the inclination which my Lord Marlborough made appear to help those Germans, gives us hopes that his Grace will be pleased to give a favorable answer to our representation."[22] The reply came promptly on the same day, "His Grace is willing you should proceed to the Embarkation of the poor Palatines as soon as you are sure the Convoy is ready to sail and supply them with provisions during their passage upon the best terms not exceeding 4 d. a day." The merchants were also ordered to check carefully the masters of the vessels employed in the service and transmit the names of every person put on board with their age.[23] In pursuance of this order 1283 persons were shipped on May 12th.[24]

On the next day Mr. Cardonnel wrote to the Secretary of the Treasury concerning Marlborough's authorization for the embarkation, "the convoy being ready to saile, his Grace has thought fit, not to loose any time, to give orders for shipping them off so that you may soon expect to hear of them on your side where you will know best what is to be done with them." Mr. Tilson, the secretary, was further instructed to communicate the matter to the Treasurer so that money would be made available to Dayrolle at the Hague for payment of the mer-

[21] It has appeared to be necessary to describe in some detail the connection of Marlborough to the emigration, since earlier writers, considering the report of the Parliamentary Investigating Committee in 1711, have been quite at a loss to do so.

[22] P. R. O., S. P. 87/4, 265.

[23] Lists of Embarkation were kept but without the notation as to age which was requested. These lists, published for the first time, are in the Appendix C. to this book, where their nature and value are discussed.

[24] P. R. O., T. 1/119, 6; S. P. 84/232, 239.

chants' claims for transporting the people.[25] On May 17th, Cardonnel wrote to Mr. Tilson again on the subject of the Palatines, this time at more length. He began, "you will have seen by my last letter the direction my lord Duke has thought good to give in relation to the poor Palatines. In consequence of them, there are about 1300 embarkt and I believe sail'd by this time."[26]

From London on that same date Secretary of State Boyle sent the following letter to Mr. Dayrolle authorizing the transportation of the Palatines at government expense. "Upon what you mentioned in yours of the 21 Inst. N. S.[27] concerning the great number of German Protestants, now lying at Rotterdam, which want to be transported hither; and upon a representation from Mr. Cardonnel, by order of the Duke of Marlborough of the best method for taking care of them, Her Majesty has commanded me, to signify her pleasure to you, that you should take the Transportation of the Said Poor German Protestants into your care, and make an agreement on the best terms you can for providing the necessary Transports there, and subsisting those people in their passage to England. My Lord Treasurer has likewise her Majesty's directions to order Mr. Brydges, the Paymaster, to write Mr. Sweet at Amsterdam, To supply you with such sums of money as the service may require."[28] At the Hague, Dayrolle acknowledged the receipt of the order on May 24th, mentioning that at that time about 2000 more Palatines were at

[25] P. R. O., S. P. 87/4, 267.

[26] P. R. O., S. P. 87/4, 158.

[27] It should be noted that the Julian calendar was in use in England until 1752, while the Gregorian calendar was generally followed on the continent. There was at this time eleven days difference between the calendars, thus Dayrolle's letter of May 21st New Style was written on the English date, May 10th Old Style. This letter was later used (in 1711) by a Parliamentary committee investigating the Palatine immigration, as the basis for charges against Marlborough and his son-in-law Sunderland.

[28] P. R. O., S. P. 104/74, 85; S. P. 44/107, 229; B. M., Add. MSS. 15866, 170.

Rotterdam, awaiting the sailing of the convoy some five days later.[29]

Marlborough's interest in the emigrants and his influence in England were most helpful in securing the English government's aid. It should be clear furthermore that for the subsistence at the government's expense of the second party of Palatines sent on May 12th Marlborough was personally responsible, since he issued the order anticipating the approval of London which did not arrive until May 24th. But the British government with the Queen's approval had authorized the use of the returning army transports as early as April 23rd. It is apparent too, that in May the London authorities regarded the transportation of the Palatines as an extended project, for Secretary Boyle instructed Dayrolle concerning "such further [Palatine] accounts as you shall send me from time to time for that service."[30]

The Palatines continued to arrive in Rotterdam in increasing numbers. Early in June, the arrivals numbered about a thousand a week.[31] This rate was maintained until late in July, when strenuous efforts to stop the emigration were beginning to take effect. On June 14th, Dayrolle informed London that "upon the continuation of H. M. Bounty or any other encouragement, you may have half Germany if you please, for they are all flying away not only from the Palatinate, but from all other countrys in the neighborhood of the Rhine. . . . The expenses may be great but are necessary, if you are in want of these people for the Plantations, as my Lord Townshend seems to be of opinion you are, otherwise they must perish where they come to lye at Briel."[32] Most of the Palatines were quite poor. They were encamped outside Rotterdam in a most miserable condition. A number of shacks

29 P. R. O., S. P. 84/232, 239.
30 P. R. O., S. P. 104/74, 88; B. M., Add. MSS. 15866, 172.
31 P. R. O., S. P. 84/232, 259.
32 P. R O., S. P. 84/232, 268.

covered with reeds were all the shelter they had from the
weather.[33] Marlborough and Lord Townshend, his fellow
ambassador, each contributed 50 pounds to help care for
them.[34] All dispatches to England describing the Germans
emphasized their need. The great number of children among
them was also pointed out.[35]

In the meantime the shipping of the Palatines was being
pushed with all despatch possible. Provisions were given to
the Palatines while on board ship, and for six or eight days
for the crossing.[36] The bargain for subsistence and transportation was made by Mr. Cardonnel with the two Commissioners
van Toren and van Gent at 4 stivers a day for each subsisted
and 40 stivers for each transported, roughly 4 d. and 3 s. 4 d.
respectively.[37] As early as May 17th the Dutch Admiralty had
been requested to aid in the embarkation. Even the packet
boat carrying dispatches between England and the continent
was to carry Palatines who presented themselves, bearing a
note or pass from Dayrolle.[38] A month later, Dayrolle proposed that men-of-war be dispatched to convoy ships, as they
could be secured at Rotterdam for transport purposes.[39]

By June 8th, the Commissioners van Toren and van Gent in
Rotterdam had shipped over 6,000 Palatines at the expense of
the British government.[40] As the emigrants continued to
arrive in great numbers, Dayrolle began to have qualms concerning the expense. On June 1st, he wrote that, "They tell
me the whole Palatinate is ready to follow them poor and
rich, so that you will please to let me know what is her
Majesty's pleasure in case the numbers augment in that

[33] P. R. O., S. P. 87/4, 184.
[34] P. R. O., S. P. 84/232, 480.
[35] P. R. O., S. P. 87/4, 186; S. P. 84/232, 249.
[36] P. R. O., S. P. 44/107, 242; T 1/119, 72.
[37] P. R. O., S. P. 84/232, 259.
[38] P. R. O., S. P. 87/4, 158, 160.
[39] P. R. O., S. P. 84/232, 273.
[40] P. R. O., T 1/119, 10, 26, 72.

manner."[41] On June 7th, after pointing out the number of Palatines reported on the way to Rotterdam, he finished, "you may judge how far the expense may go." On the 10th, he asked for further instructions.[42] Meanwhile in London on June 7th and June 10th, Secretary of State Boyle sent dispatches to Dayrolle, ordering him "to continue the same methods in taking care of the poor Palatines, as you have hitherto done, till further orders."[43] But on June 14th, Dayrolle again emphasized the great expense and asked Boyle for particular directions, "How far to go with money for subsisting them on their passage." A few days later, Dayrolle promised to follow directions, "till new orders" were received, but he wanted instructions about the extraordinary expenses.[44]

At last, on June 24th, Boyle sent orders to Dayrolle to send over only those Palatines at Rotterdam upon receipt of his letter. The immigrants were coming "over so fast" that it was impossible to care for them and dispose of them, and "the success of the whole matter may happen thereby to be disappointed." A further restriction was then added, "And as there are many papists mix'd among them you are for the future to allow none to come over but such as are Protestants."[45] Dayrolle had reported the presence of a great many Roman Catholics on June 1st, but Marlborough had told him, "there was no great inconveniency, to let them go with the rest."[46] The difficulty in discriminating was great, and the Catholic Palatines were a problem left for the London authorities to handle.

On the 25th of June, Dayrolle wrote that he could not understand the instructions issued by the Treasurer to his

[41] P. R. O., S. P. 87/232, 248.
[42] P. R. O., S. P. 84/232, 259, 261.
[43] P. R. O., S. P. 104/74, 88, 89; B. M., Add. MSS. 15866, 174, 175.
[44] P. R. O., S. P. 84/232, 267, 273.
[45] P. R. O., S. P. 104/74, 90; B. M., Add. MSS. 15866, 176.
[46] P. R. O., S. P. 84/232, 249.

representative at the Hague to "pay only such as are actually on board ready to come over, and no more than what will be necessary to bring them hither."[47] On the 29th, he moved to stop several thousand Palatines on their way down the Rhine River. He sent some back to give warning to the rest. He also ordered that an advertisement be inserted in the *Gazette* of Cologne, notifying the people that no more would be received. In his report to London on July 1st, Dayrolle asserted he would not concern himself any further in the affairs of the Palatines, unless he received further orders to do so. He was impelled to point out though that "if once the warr be finished, very few of this people will abandon their country and you may loose the opportunity of having them." He also enclosed several proposals for settlement which he had received.[48] Nevertheless, on July 5th, when Dayrolle reported the sailing of 2,776 Palatines the day before, he mentioned the presence of 500 more at Rotterdam, "who must shift for themselves, as well as they can, if you don't send me new orders."[49] He was informed that his advertisement had caused the several thousand on the Rhine to turn back. But the following week, this information was found to be false. About 1,200 Palatines then at Rotterdam sent deputies to Dayrolle, begging his intercession with the British government in their behalf. Failing to persuade them to return home, he agreed to write but gave them no encouragement.[50]

While these events were taking place in the Netherlands, Boyle wrote from London, complimenting him on his actions in preventing further immigration. Upon this information, as it appeared, that no more Palatines would be arriving in Rotterdam destined for London, orders were given to ship the 500,[51] referred to in Dayrolle's letter of July 5th. But Dayrolle then found that the Palatines awaiting transporta-

[47] P. R. O., S. P. 84/232, 300.
[48] P. R. O., S. P. 84/232, 305, 309.
[49] P. R. O., S. P. 84/232, 320.
[50] P. R. O., S. P. 84/232, 325.
[51] P. R. O., S. P. 104/74, 90, 91; B. M., Add. MSS. 15866, 178, 180.

tion numbered 2,000.[52] At a loss for action, he questioned Boyle on July 15th, "I can not avoid sending all or none at all. My Lord Townshend is of the opinion, Her Majesty will not be displeased, if I provide transports for the whole number not being possible for these people to retire to their own country."[53] Boyle replied immediately on the 19th, "if the 2000 you mention in this letter are not embarked, when mine comes to your hands, you must have nothing to do with any of them."[54] But his order was too late, for on July 18th, 1,433 Palatines sailed for London.[55] Dayrolle wrote this fact the next day, the very day that Boyle in London was forbidding the embarkation. These immigrants were certainly fortunate that the days of electrical communication had not yet appeared. Dayrolle expected trouble, for he excused himself, saying that he had acted by the advice of Lord Townshend.[56]

Still there were Palatines arriving in Rotterdam. Dayrolle advised Boyle late in July that the good people of that city thought of sending them over at private expense without passes and perhaps without convoys, which he could not prevent.[57] On August 12th, he reported that about 1,000 had sailed under those conditions, 250 of them having had sufficient funds to pay their own way.[58] On the 23rd, Secretary Boyle instructed Lord Townshend to request the Dutch to prevent any further embarkation.[59] On the 26th, Boyle ordered Dayrolle to inform them, that any more Palatines sent to England would be returned.[60] He replied reassuringly that since the summer was over, few of them would come.[61]

[52] P. R. O., S. P. 84/232, 333.

[53] P. R. O., S. P. 84/232, 337.

[54] P. R. O., S. P. 104/74, 92.

[55] P. R. O., T. 1/119, 79, 82.

[56] P. R. O., S. P. 84/232, 343.

[57] P. R. O., S. P. 84/232, 349.

[58] P. R. O., S. P. 84/232, 383.

[59] P. R. O., S. P. 104/74, 95; B. M., Add. MSS. 15866,185.

[60] P. R. O., S. P. 104/74, 94; B. M., Add. MSS. 15866, 187.

[61] P. R. O., S. P. 84/232, 41.

The warnings to the Dutch authorities seem to have had little effect however for the immigration was not stopped. Though the Dutch had passed a general naturalization act on July 18, 1709, N.S.,[62] they apparently wanted to rid themselves of these poor emigrants, who had become a serious charge against their charitable resources. During August the authorities of Rotterdam sent notices up the Rhine, attempting to halt the emigration. For eight days, Messrs. van Toren and van Gent were despatched in two yachts paid for by the town authorities.[63] On August 24th, the town authorities of Brielle, the seaport for embarkation, asked financial support from Rotterdam for the Palatines, "their poor-purse being exhausted." They even threatened to send the emigrants back to Rotterdam.[64] From Rotterdam two days later the burgomasters replied, reciting their own difficulties and their efforts to extricate themselves. They offered to join Brielle in seeking help from the States General, the national assembly of Holland.[65]

When Dayrolle formally requested the States General to order their College of Admiralty not to allow any more Palatines to be transported to England, they replied that they could not prevent those already in the Netherlands from crossing to England, but that they would order their ministers at Cologne and Frankfort to warn the people not to come for that purpose.[66] This was done accordingly, and their ministers acknowledged those orders on September 13th and 15th

[62] P. R. O., S. P. 84/232, 338; *The State of the Palatines*, 7. There was much dissatisfaction with this naturalization law, since it gave the Jews and Roman Catholics the same benefit offered to Protestants, who felt they should be shown preference. P. R. O., S. P. 84/232, 360.

[63] Resolutions and Dispositions of Burgomasters of Rotterdam, III, 126, 127.

[64] Letters to Burgomasters of Rotterdam 1707-1713, XXIII (August 26, 1709).

[65] Letter Book of Burgomasters of Rotterdam, X (August 26, 1709).

[66] Record of Resolutions of the States General of the United Netherlands, 1709, II, 348; P. R. O., S. P. 84/232, 480.

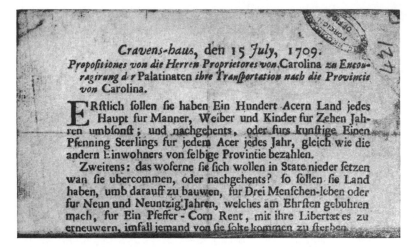

Cravens-haus, den 15 *July,* 1709.
Propofitiones von die Herren Proprietores von Carolina zu Encou-
ragirung d r Palatinaten *ihre Transportation nach die Provincie*
von Carolina.

ERftlich follen fie haben Ein Hundert Acern Land jedes
Haupt fur Manner, Weiber und Kinder fur Zehen Jahren umbfonft ; und nachgehents, oder furs kunftige Einen
Pfenning Sterlings fur jedem Acer jedes Jahr, gleich wie die
andern Einwohners von felbige Provintie bezahlen.
Zweitens: das woferne fie fich wollen in State nieder fetzen
wan fie ubercommen, oder nachgehents? fo follen fie Land
haben, umb darauff zu bauwen, fur Drei Menfchen-leben oder
fur Neun und Neuntzig Jahren, welches am Ehrften gebuhren
mach, fur Ein Pfeffer - Corn Rent, mit ihre Libertæt es zu
erneuwern, imfall jemand von fie folte kommen zu fterben

CIRCULAR ADVERTISING CAROLINA, distributed to the Palatines aboard the transports in Rotterdam in August, 1709. *Courtesy of the British Public Record Office.*

respectively. The Dutch authorities were most concerned with the possibility of their being saddled with the care of the stranded emigrants.

In the meantime, Dayrolle was confronted with a provoking incident. He had failed early in September to stop the sailing of several transports laden with Palatines, but he learned that someone in England was encouraging the movement despite his advertisement against the emigration. Then late in August an unknown gentleman, who had come accompanied by a servant from Harwick (England) on the packet boat, went aboard the transports laden with Palatines. After distributing some charity funds, he passed out thousands of circulars, which he desired them to send to their friends in Germany.[67] These circulars, about 3″ by 6″ in size, were entitled, "Propositions of the Lords Proprietors of Carolina to encourage the Transporting of Palatines to the Province of Carolina." The propositions, dated July 15th, offered (1) a hundred acres of land for each man, woman and child, free

[67] P. R. O., S. P. 84/232, 415.

from quit-rent for ten years, and thereafter to pay one penny per acre annually (2) if they would settle in towns now or later, to lease them land for building and improvement for the term of three lives or ninety-nine years, which should expire first at a pepper-corn rent, with the privilege to renew in case the lives died.[68] Dayrolle could not discover who the gentleman was, but he offered the suggestion, "'Tis probable those tickets came from the Proprietors of Carolina or from some disaffected people."[69] Boyle immediately called a meeting of the Lords of the Committee of Council and he wrote, "It is possible orders may be given for sending them back again."[70] On September 9th, he acquainted Dayrolle with the results of the Council meeting. Although the landing of more Palatines could not be prevented, they would not be cared for at public expense, until those already in England could be provided for.[71] Dayrolle went further than that, for he informed the Palatines embarking at Rotterdam, they would be sent back from England.[72] Indeed, 2,257 Roman Catholic Palatines were sent back to Rotterdam with a present of 5 gilders each late in September.[73]

Nevertheless, there were 1,500 more emigrants at Rotterdam desirous of reaching England.[74] They even considered sending deputies to England to petition the Queen for her assistance. On September 28th, the Palatines at Rotterdam sent a heartrending petition to Secretary Boyle, in which they related how they had been enticed to leave their homes by what they just learned to be false promises in Queen Anne's name. As they had spent most of what they had to subsist on

[68] P. R. O., S. P. 84/232, 421. These proposals had been made to the Board of Trade in London on August 11th to encourage the Palatines there to settle in Carolina. C. C. 1708–1709, 445.

[69] P. R. O., S. P. 84/232, 423.

[70] P. R. O., S. P. 104/74, 95; B. M., Add. MSS. 15866, 189.

[71] P. R. O., S. P. 104/74, 96; B. M., Add. MSS. 15866, 190.

[72] P. R. O., S. P. 84/232, 444.

[73] P. R. O., T. 1/119, 93, 98, 136–153; S. P. 84/232, 467, 480.

[74] P. R. O., S. P. 84/232, 467.

their journey, they with their wives and children would perish of hunger unless admitted to England. In their deplorable condition they ate their "bread in tears." They begged him to relieve them "from a continual agony."[75] Nevertheless, on October 11th, Secretary Sunderland refused their petition, although the Queen was touched by their misery. He pointed out "the great clamour that such numbers doe raise in the time of scarcitie, and the great load and expense it is on the government." The British government also felt certain that should it vary from its resolution to admit no more, there would be no end to the immigration.[76] But on the same day, Dayrolle at the Hague wrote to Sunderland that 1,100 Palatines had sailed several days earlier, "notwithstanding all my endeavors to prevent it."[77]

The following week, Sunderland informed Dayrolle of their arrival in the Thames River and ordered an investigation, for inquiry pointed to Mr. Henrick van Toren under Dayrolle's authority, "forcing the Palatines to sail for England, even though some of them had hired their passage in boats, to return home."[78] Dayrolle after an investigation found that the officials of Rotterdam, desiring to rid their city of the Palatines who would not return home, had Messrs. van Toren and van Gent ship them "with what moneys I know not." Dayrolle could not prevent it, but he thought that van Toren and van Gent were motivated only by the most charitable considerations.[79] Dayrolle was not so innocent though, for in a letter of November 5th to Messrs. van Toren and van Gent, he wrote, "My sending the quantity [of Palatines] you imbarqued lately has been disapproved, tho my intentions were good." He wished them success, if one of them went to England to make representations as they intended, but "for

[75] P. R. O., S. P. 84/232, 449.
[76] P. R. O., S. P. 104/74, 97; B. M., Add. MSS. 15866, 192.
[77] P. R. O., S. P. 84/232, 495, 517.
[78] P. R. O., S. P. 104/74, 97, 98, 99; B. M., Add. MSS. 15866, 193, 194, 195.
[79] P. R. O., S. P. 84/232, 525.

my own part, I dare not write anything more on that subject nor meddle in it."[80]

Late in October, when explaining the sailing of the last party "against" his orders, Dayrolle remarked that there would be no more except a few left behind, but "I am informed that a great many intend to come next summer, if not timely prevented by some notification in Germany made in Her Majesties name, not being possible to dissuade them by any other authority."[81] Following his suggestion, a Royal Proclamation was drawn up, printed in German and distributed widely in the Rhine Valley. It declared that no more people would be received in England, much less supported. All those Germans, who arrived since the first of October were to be sent back to Germany at the first opportunity. All who intended to emigrate were warned that such attempts would assuredly fail, unless they had means of their own to support themselves.[82]

Summarizing the numbers of the Palatine immigration of 1709 to England, the records show that

852	sailed late in April and arrived			early in May
1,283	"	May 12th	" "	about May 19th
2,926	"	May 31st	" "	June 6th
1,794	"	June 10th	" "	June 16th
2,776	"	July 4th	" "	July 11th
1,433	"	July 17th	" "	July 24th
c. 1,000	"	August 6th	" "	August 13th
c. 1,082	"	October 11th	" "	October 18th

13,146 are mentioned in the official correspondence.[83] It is

[80] P. R. O., S. P. 84/232, 529.

[81] P. R. O., S. P. 84/232, 536.

[82] *Das verlangte nicht erlangte Canaan*, 10, 92; Diffenderffer, *op. cit.*, 15.

[83] This table is compiled from the following sources: P. R. O., C. O. 388/76, 56 ii; T. 1/119, 6–10, 27, 65, 72, 82; S. P. 87/4, 265; S. P. 84/232, 239, 320, 383, 495, 517. For information concerning the first six lists of emigrants, see the Appendices B and C. There were no lists kept of the last two groups noted as sailing in August and October, since they were supplied with funds obtained from private charitable sources in Holland.

quite probable however that the number reached 13,500, since quite a few of the Palatines were sent by the packet boat or by regular shipping at their own expense or by charity funds after the official transportation ceased on July 18th. Small groups going in this way may have sailed without mention in the official correspondence.

Of the probable number of 13,500, who were able to reach England, 2,257 Roman Catholics were sent back late in September, as related before. On January 20th, 1710, Boyle notified Dayrolle that about 900 Palatines who desired to return home were to be sent shortly and that they should have his best efforts to speed them on their way.[84] So on March 3rd, 1710, he received Dayrolle's report of their safe arrival.[85] Late in March of the next year (1711) 618 Palatines, all Roman Catholics, were returned to the Netherlands. They were given five gilders each as a parting present to speed them on their way home.[86] This seems to have been done by the British government for all the Palatines returned to the continent, and it was a gesture much admired in the Netherlands.[87] More than 3,000 Roman Catholics were sent back in all, if Simmendinger's estimate is correct.[88] With more than 3,500 returned, there were left about 10,000 of the 13,500 estimate, still to be accounted for. What did the British authorities do with them?

In London, the citizens were amazed. In three months more than 11,000 alien people had arrived in their midst. London was not so large a city that many thousands could be poured into it conveniently without notice. The government was hard put to provide shelter and food for them. The squares, the taverns, all the refuges of London were crowded

[84] P. R. O., S. P. 104/74, 100; B. M., Add. MSS. 15866, 197.

[85] P. R. O., S. P. 104/74, 101; B. M., Add. MSS. 15866, 199.

[86] P. R. O., T. 1/132, 165, 170. This debarkation list of Palatine families is included in Appendix D.

[87] P. R. O., S. P. 84/232, 480.

[88] Simmendinger, op. cit., 3.

with Palatines. In addition, 1,600 tents were issued by the Board of Ordnance[89] and encampments were formed on Blackheath on the south side of the Thames, at Greenwich, on the Thames, just north of Blackheath, and at Camberwell,[90] a suburb of London, about two miles from St. Paul's. Others found quarters near the Tower, in St. Catherine's, Tower Ditch, Wapping, Nightingale Lane, East Smithfield and their neighborhoods. Barns and cheap houses were rented for them at Kensington, Walworth, Stockwell and Bristol Cansey.[91] The large rope-houses at Deptford were utilized for shelter for many of the Palatines, while others were disposed of by the care of charitable persons in Aldgate and Lambeth.[92] About 1,400 were lodged in the large warehouse of Sir Charles Cox, who had offered it gratis.[93] The crowded condition of these places of shelter made them unhealthy. The Board of Trade was informed of this and strove to remedy the difficulty; certainly the Board and the English Whigs[94] in particular deserve a great deal of credit for their sympathetic treatment and generosity, in the early stages of the immigration. At any rate, surgeons were sent among the Palatines and efforts were made to lessen their discomfort by securing additional quarters.[95]

The Germans evidently expected that immediately on arrival in England, they would be dispatched in a body across the sea; but no one stood ready to carry out such a program.

[89] P. R. O., S. P. 44/108, 93; B. M., Strafford Papers, Add. MSS. 22202, 105; "Brief History," in *Eccles. Rec.*, III, 1786.

[90] Marlborough MSS. (*Hist. MSS. Com., 8th Report*, Appendix), 47; *State of the Palatines*, 7; Boyer, *op. cit.* (1709), 167; B. T. *Jour. 1708–1714*, 37.

[91] "Brief History," in *Eccles. Rec.*, III, 1786; also 1741.

[92] Stow, *op. cit.*, I, 43; *Cal. Treas. Papers 1708–1714*, 153.

[93] Diffenderffer, *op. cit.*, 297. Since he allowed them to remain until they were sent to Ireland and elsewhere, thus losing revenue in the seasonal period of the use of the warehouse, he was given as compensation 100 guineas by the government on February 9, 1710.

[94] [Hare], *Canary Birds Naturaliz'd in Utopia* (London, 1709).

[95] See Minutes of Palatine Commissioners' Meeting in *Eccles. Rec.*, III, 1740 *et seq.; C. C. 1708–1709*, 296.

The Palatines were almost entirely dependent upon the government to keep them from starvation. The first 852 were allowed a total of 20 pounds per day,[96] which amounted to less than six pence each for men, women and children. But the expense was a great burden on the government, particularly in war-time. Godolphin wrote to Marlborough, June 24, 1709, "I hope you will not think it necessary to send an express with news, our exchequer being so low at present; as to the extraordinary number of poor Palatines who come over every day, they are a very great burthen upon the Queen."[97] In fact, on June 14th, the subsistence of the Palatines was costing the government 80 pounds a day.[98]

Shortly after June 1st, the Ministry hit upon the expedient of raising money by public subscription. Letters were sent to the leading financial organizations, requesting voluntary contributions, for example to the Bank of England and the East India Company.[99] On June 7, 1709, the Justices of the Peace for the County of Middlesex sent a petition to the Queen asking for authority to take up a collection in their county for their Palatines. The Queen not only granted the desired authority, but also extended it to the public generally throughout the kingdom.[100]

A proclamation was issued June 28, 1709, for the collection of alms and a board of commissioners was appointed to handle the funds and "to perform every matter and thing . . . necessary and convenient for the better Employment and Settlement of the said poor Palatines." The commissioners named were nearly a hundred in number and included the great dignitaries of the kingdom.[101] The collection was carried out largely

---

[96] B. T. Jour. 1708–1714, 36.

[97] Private Corres. Duchess Marlborough (London, 1838), II, 338.

[98] C. C. 1708–1709, 343.

[99] P. R. O., S. P. 44/108, 92.

[100] Boyer, Annals (1709), 167; Luttrell, op. cit., VI, 453, 454, 474.

[101] Ibid., Appendix III, 35 et seq.

LONDON: Printed for J. Baker, at the Black-Boy in Pater-Noster-Row. 1710.

CONTEMPORARY WOODCUT, showing the Palatines encamped on Black-heath outside London. *Courtesy of the Widener Library, Harvard University.*

through the organization of the Established Church. The various bishops wrote letters to the clergy of their dioceses during the first week of July, and advanced all kinds of arguments for, and refuted some against, the policy of relieving these "poor German Protestants."[102] The letter of the Bishop of Oxford is particularly noteworthy in that he attached a postscript, "I think it would much forward this service if you could prevail with some of the chiefest of your parishioners to accompany you when you go to collect the charity of the rest."[103] On one impulse or another the Whigs vied with one another to contribute to the fund, the Duke of Newcastle alone donating 500 pounds,[104] and the large sum of 19,838 pounds, 11 shillings was collected.[105]

The Palatine camps were a source of wonder to the London

[102] *Ibid.*, Appendix III, 42. Bishop William Nicolson wrote from Carlisle to Bishop Wake of Lincoln, "The Palatine briefs are not yet arrived in the North. And when they do come they'l find charity very cold in these parts. I should be thankful for one of your printed letters, since I am wholly in the dark, as to the sum and substance of the affair. Some comfort it is to find, by your information that the numbers of Papists amongst those people are not so great as was said." Christ Church, Oxford, Wake MS., August 29, 1709.

[103] *Ibid.*, Appendix III, 53. The method suggested is still in vogue today among clergy as the best known method to produce results.

[104] Portland MSS. (*Hist. MSS. Com., 13th Report*, Appendix), II, 207.

[105] *Eccles. Rec.*, III, 1753.

populace.[106] Every Sunday crowds would gather and the Palatines became the focus of curiosity-seekers. They capitalized
this by making toys of small value and selling them to the
multitudes who came to see them. One account of the Palatines states, "They are contented with very ordinary food,
their bread being brown and their meat of the coarsest and
cheapest sort, which, with a few herbs, they eat with much
cheerfulness and thankfulness. On the whole, they appear to
be an innocent, laborious, peaceable, healthy and ingenuous
people, and may be rather reckoned a blessing than a burden
to any nation where they shall be settled."[107] An interesting
incident, which is at the same time illustrative of the hardi-
hood of these people, is the one related by a contemporary
diarist, Luttrell, September 13, 1709, "A wager of 100 pounds
was laid last week, that a German, of 64 years' old, should
walk in Hide Park 300 miles in 6 dayes, which he did within
the time, and a mile over."[108]

The conditions among the Palatines were certainly very
bad. Bread was never known to have been so dear[109] and the
government allowance was insufficient to sustain them properly. They were obliged to beg on the streets of London and
this begging was done principally by the married women.[110]
Philanthropists of the day distributed both money and supplies among the needy Palatines. One shopkeeper, a Quaker,
cut up several wagon-loads of cloth during eight consecutive

[106] R. Palmer wrote to Ralph Verney in the country, "The case of the
Palatines is all our domestic talk." August 17, 1709, Verney MSS. (Hist.
MSS. Com., 7th Report, Appendix), 507.

[107] The State of the Palatines, 27; Eccles. Rec., III, 1831.

[108] Luttrell, op. cit., VI, 488.

[109] Gilbert Burnet, History of His Own Times (2nd ed., Oxford, 1833), VI,
38 says that bread sold at double the ordinary price; Das verlangte nicht
erlangte Canaan, 15. A Royal Proclamation was issued on October 24th, putting in execution the old laws against forestalling and regrating of corn,
Robert Steele, ed., Catalogue of Tudor and Stuart Proclamations 1485–1714
(Oxford, 1910), 530.

[110] C. J., XVI, 596.

days. Another gave shoes, while a third distributed shirts.[111]

But the novelty of the presence of the Palatines soon wore off for the London populace and an uglier attitude, due to the tight economic conditions, set in.[112] The poorer classes of the English people said the Palatines came to eat the bread of Englishmen, and reduce the scale of wages. The latter, it was alleged, had already fallen from 18 pence to 15 pence per day, where the Palatines were encamped.[113] Even the native beggars felt that the Queen's bounty should belong to them.[114] The shopkeepers were also opposed to the newcomers for fear that their trade might be harmed by the competition of unenfranchised foreigners.[115]

The Palatine encampments were occasionally attacked by London mobs. Upon one occasion about 2,000 infuriated Englishmen, armed with axes, scythes, and smith hammers, were said to have made an attack upon the Palatine camp and struck down all who did not flee.[116] When settlements of Palatines were attempted, riots occured in some localities. Juries were prejudiced. Nothing "that was said upon oath by the witnesses [was] sufficient to gain any verdict at Sundrich but in Justification of the Rioters."[117] Many times were the Palatines threatened and mobbed, much to the Queen's chagrin.[118]

This feeling against the Palatines was exhibited even among the "better" people of England. It seems to have been rooted in a fear of contamination by prevalent contagious

[111] *Das verlangte nicht erlangte Canaan*, 108; *The Piety and Bounty of Great Britain, with the Charitable Benevolences of her Loving Subjects toward the Support and Settlement of the Distressed Protestant Palatines* (London, 1709).

[112] *Ibid.*, 8.

[113] Burnet, *op. cit.*, V, 439; *Das verlangte nicht erlangte Canaan*, 111.

[114] *A Song in Praise of Begging or the Beggars Rival'd* (1710); Burnet, *op. cit.*, VI, 38.

[115] [Hare], *Reception*, 30.

[116] *Das verlangte nicht erlangte Canaan*, 108.

[117] P. R. O., S. P. 34/11, October 13, 1709.

[118] P. R. O., S. P. 44/108, *passim*.

diseases. On July 15, 1710, Lady Pye wrote to Mrs. Abigail Harley of someone's fine daughter having died of smallpox. She added, "The notion with some people is that the Palatines brought in this very ill kind [of smallpox]."[119] On August 23, 1709, Mr. John Floyer wrote to Lady Dartmouth at Blackheath, "I wish you the recovery of your health, and a better neighbor than the Palatines, who I fear have infected your pure air. Our country has loads of them and call them gypsies not knowing the language and seeing their poor clothes."[120] One writer says that the English hatred of the Palatines shows only their great dislike for aliens, which was proverbial.[121] On the other hand, the Palatines were not a people of little spirit. They soon came to resent this attitude of the English and met it in kind. *Hearne's Collections* (August 26, 1709) contains an account of 40 Palatines in the neighborhood when three or four Englishmen, drinking a pot or two of ale, "made some Reflections upon the Receiving of these People into the Kingdom; which, being heard by one of the Palatines, he gave a hint to his Companions, and they all immediately came into the Room and beat the persons in a very rude and inhuman manner."[122]

Meanwhile the Palatines had little employment, and the pressing problem was what to do with them. The efforts to settle the Palatines began with the first official letter after their arrival. In this letter, the Earl of Sunderland, writing to the Board of Trade, on May 3, 1709, indicated the government's desire according to the prevailing mercantilist views to encourage immigration. The Queen had been informed of the arrival of some hundreds of German Protestants and expected more from the Palatinate with the intention of settling in the

[119] Portland MSS. (*Hist. MSS. Com., 15th Report*, Appendix), IV, 549.

[120] Dartmouth MSS. (*Hist. MSS. Com. 15th Report*, Appendix), III, 147.

[121] C. B. A. Kent, *Early History of the Tories* (London, 1908), 434.

[122] C. E. Doble, ed., *Remarks and Collections of Thomas Hearne* (Oxford Hist. Soc., 1885–1906), II, 239.

English plantations in America. "Her Majesty was convinced however, that it would be much more advantageous to Her Kingdom, if these people could be settled comfortably here instead of sending them to the West Indies." Such a result would be a great encouragement to others to follow their example. The addition to the number of her subjects would in all probability produce a proportionable increase of their trade and manufactures. The Board of Trade was ordered to take the matter under consideration and report as soon as possible the proper method and the part of England most feasible for it.[123]

Two days later, Sunderland had ordered the Board of Trade to inquire into their numbers and condition, and to report what was needed for their support, until they were either settled in England or sent to the plantations.[124] Pursuant to this request the Board of Trade asked two German ministers resident in London to carry on the inquiry. These men were John Tribbeko, chaplain of his late R. H. Prince George of Denmark, and George Andrew Ruperti, minister of the German Lutheran Church in the Savoy.[125] They reported to the Board on May 9th, that the Palatines were in dire straits. A number of them were ill for want of necessary sustenance. Many were almost naked. They were "pakt up in such great numbers, we have found very often 20 to 30 men and women together with their children in one room."[126] Tribbeko and Ruperti drew up from time to time the four Palatine lists, which are a valuable source of information today.[127] But

[123] Sunderland added that since most of the immigrants were "husbandmen and labouring people," it should be easier to dispose of them to the advantage of the public. P. R. O., S. P. 44/108, 66; *B. T. Jour. 1708–1714,* 26; *Eccles. Rec.,* III, 1733; *C. C. 1708–1709,* 290.

[124] P. R. O., S. P. 44/108, 67; *C. C. 1708–1709,* 295; *Eccles. Rec.,* III, 1734.

[125] *Eccles. Rec.,* III, 1736.

[126] P. R. O., S. P. 44/108, 72; *C. C. 1708–1709,* 296.

[127] P. R. O., C. O. 388/76, 56 ii, 64, 68–70. For a discussion of these lists see Appendix B.

the crowds of people were soon beyond their best efforts, and they had to ask for help.[128]

Most of the Palatines were farmers and vine-dressers, that is, over half of the first four groups to arrive in London as noted by Messrs. Tribbeko and Ruperti. The rest were distributed in some 35 other trades, the next highest number of occupations being about 90 carpenters and about 75 textile workers. The lists included about 12 schoolmasters and three surgeons.[129] Some of the Palatine vine-dressers, "encourag'd by their friends abroad in Pensilvania," brought vine plants with them for a new start in the plantations.[130] The last group to leave Rotterdam for England was described as "for the most part tradesmen."[131]

The continued arrival of many Palatines and their inability to support themselves began to worry the Ministry deeply. On the 15th of May, Sunderland commanded the Board of Trade to "make what dispatch you can to report. . . ."[132] By August 6th, the Lord Treasurer had written to the Board "to make a proposal for the speedy disposing of them, in such manner as may soonest lessen the expense the Government is now at for their subsistence."[133] At the same time, he commented on the "slow steps that are made towards [the] settling of them."

One of the schemes projected was to settle 10,000 Palatines on the Rio de la Plata, in South America. A regiment would have been necessary to protect them, however, and the calculated expense of over 200,000 pounds was prohibitive. Another project called for a settlement in the Canary Islands. The proposer did not mention that the Spaniards were to be driven out, but as they were an obstacle, this project was not given consideration.[134]

[128] C. C. 1708–1709, 370.
[129] P. R. O., C. O. 388/76, 56 ii, 64, 68, 69.
[130] P. R. O., S. P. 87/4, 158.   [131] P. R. O., C. O. 84/232, 480.
[132] Ibid., 300; Eccles. Rec., III, 1738.   [133] Ibid., 444.
[134] "Brief History," in Eccles. Rec., III, 1789.

The Board of Trade received a proposal from the Society of London for Mines Royal to employ the strongest of the Palatines in the silver and copper mines of Penlyn and Merionethshire, Wales.[135] The merchants of Bedford and Barnstable, concerned in the Newfoundland fishery, offered to employ 500 Palatines in their industry.[136] A project for settling some of them in Herefordshire and Gloucestershire, proposed by the Marquis of Kent, Lord Chamberlain, was also considered by the Board of Trade. The last project, it was found, would entail a cost of 150,000 pounds, if all were settled at the proposed rate; hence it was abandoned.[137] A proposal was also made for repeopling with Palatines the islands of Nevis and St. Christopher in the West Indies, which had recently been attacked by the French.[138] Colonel Daniel Parke, Governor of the Leeward Islands, who made the suggestion, was sorely provoked with Sunderland because it was not accepted.[139]

An attempt was then made to settle the Palatines throughout England by offering three pounds per head to the parishes which would be willing to receive them, the government to pay the expense of sending them to the respective places.[140] The bounty was taken in some instances and the immigrants, finding themselves uncared for, returned to London again. Some of their experiences are interesting. One Palatine, who had been a hunter, was, to his great disgust, required to take care of swine. Sixteen families were sent to the town of Sunderland, near Newcastle in Yorkshire. They expected grants of land, but were made day laborers. Another group was given a half pound of bread a day per person, a pound of salt a week,

---

[135] B. T. Jour. 1708–1714, 41, 42, 47; C. C. 1708–1709, 307, 322, 370.

[136] Luttrell, op. cit., VI, 496.

[137] H. S. P., Jour. B. T., XXI, 138; B. T. Jour. 1708–1704, 44, 47; C. C. 1708–1709, 343, 360.

[138] Luttrell, op. cit., VI, 420, 422, 454.

[139] C. C. 1710–1711, 96.

[140] B. T. Jour. 1708–1714, 60; Verney MSS. (Hist. MSS. Com., 7th Report, Appendix), 507.

but no meat or vegetables.[141] Many of the Palatines, too poor to return or for other reasons, probably stayed. The plan to locate the Palatines in England was earnestly attempted. Sunderland wrote a letter, among many others, to the Mayor of Canterbury, asking him to receive and permanently locate some of them. This letter, referred to the town magistrates, was answered by the observation that they could not comply with the request, as their own poor were a heavy burden.[142] Liverpool received 130 but they drifted away as soon as the government support had been exhausted.[143] The Justices of Peace of East Riding, Yorkshire, agreed to accept Palatines, but the authorities of Nottinghamshire regretted that they could do nothing to assist them.[144] Some Palatines were also settled in Chester.[145]

Captain Thomas Ekines of the English Navy came forward with a proposal that 600 of the Palatines, about 150 families, should be settled in the Scilly Islands,[146] a small group off the southwest coast of England. Sunderland thought well of the project, and on September 21st and October 2, 1709, two transports were sent down the Thames with 450 Palatines on board, well provisioned and supplied.[147] The inhabitants of the Island of Scilly, learning of the venture, protested that they could not earn a living themselves on that meager haven, and so these people were never sent to their destination, but after remaining on shipboard three entire months, were again set on shore on December 30th of the same year. They eventually

[141] *Das verlangte nicht erlangte Canaan*, 111.

[142] P. R. O., S. P. 44/108, 87; S. P. 34/13, June 17, 1709; *B. T. Jour. 1708–1714*, 314.

[143] P. R. O., S. P. 44/108, 155; *Das verlangte nicht erlangte Canaan*, 110.

[144] P. R. O., S. P. D. 34/11, 47, 60.

[145] Corporation of City of Chester MSS. (*Hist. MSS. Com., 8th Report,* Appendix), 395.

[146] Portland MSS. (*Hist. MSS. Com., 13th Report*, Appendix), II, 207.

[147] P. R. O., S. P. 44/108, 151, 162, 168, 188.

found their way back to Blackheath. The cost of this miserable failure was some 1,500 pounds.[148]

A merchant was reported to have made a contract to send 500 families to Barbados.[149] It does not seem to have been carried out, but 500 Palatines were settled in the Bahama Islands in 1717.[150] It is not clear however that they were part of the 1709 immigration. In 1722, Charles Carrington, of New Providence, describing Nassau to the Board of Trade, wrote, "about 14 miles west of Nassau is Palatyne town, inhabited by Palatines, an indolent, laizy tribe and good for little."[151] On the other hand, when Governor Phemey wrote to Lord Cartaret in 1723, he said, "The remaining Palatines are now by my assistance in a very flourishing condition. . . . They are a very industrious people and I could wish for a great many more of them."[152] Several proposals were made to the Board of Trade to settle some Palatines in Jamaica. These were very seriously considered,[153] but the ambitious plans drawn up proved to be too costly, and the climate was adjudged too warm for the emigrants. It does not appear that any settlement of importance was made,[154] although a few Palatines may have been sent there. Luttrell noted, August 3, 1710, that, "Letters from Jamaica tell us that the Palatines designed for that place are safely arrived there, and disposed of to the advantage of that island."[155] A contemporary account reads that those of 16 families sent to Sunderland, who

[148] C. J., XVI, 598.

[149] The State of the Palatines, 8.

[150] C. C. 1717–1718, 29.

[151] P. R. O., C. O. 23/2, 75; C. C. 1722–1723, 60.

[152] P. R. O., C. O. 23/13, 147.

[153] P. R. O., C. O. 137/8, 451; C. O. 5/908, 76; C. C. 1708–1709, 657–872 passim; C. C. 1710–1711, 53, 58.

[154] C. C. 1710–1711, 244; C. C. 1716–1717, 337.

[155] Luttrell, op. cit., VI, 613; also see 422, 454, 455. Luttrell may be confusing Jamaica with New York as even the continental colonies were often loosely referred to as the West Indies.

had tried to run away in the night, were sent finally to Jamaica as slaves.[156]

Disappointed and disillusioned, 150 of the able-bodied young men enlisted in the British army and were sent to serve in Lord Galloway's regiment then on duty in Portugal,[157] and some 18 or more apparently enlisted in Lord Hay's regiment, according to Luttrell.[158] We are told that 322 entered the military service and that 141 children were "purchased by the English," which means most probably that they were apprenticed perhaps for a price.[159] At least 56 of the young people became domestic servants.[160]

The large number of Catholics in the Palatine immigration has been mentioned before, but it will be remembered that the Queen was saving only "poor German Protestants." The Catholic Palatines in London, and in Rotterdam, awaiting transportation, were given their choice of becoming "poor Protestants" to be saved by the Queen, or of returning to their homes along the Rhine.[161] Many of the Germans were devout people, as the contemporary accounts indicate, yet some found it convenient to change their religion.[162] Those who refused were ordered to return to Germany.[163] About September 6, 1714, several thousand Catholic Palatines, preparing to go

[156] *Das verlangte nicht erlangte Canaan*, 110.

[157] *Eccles. Rec.*, III, 1831.

[158] Luttrell, *op. cit.*, VI, 494.

[159] *Das verlangte nicht erlangte Canaan*, 112.

[160] *Ibid.*

[161] Simmendinger (*op. cit.*, 3) stated "Catholischer Religion/ehe sie auf der Königen Anmuthen ihren Glauben changiren wolten/ wieder nach Hauss umgekehret. Dieser Catholischen Ruck=Reise aber/öffnete uns in Roterdam über 5. wochen lang still gelegenen Reisenden/den Passnach Engelland . . .;" Boyer, *Annals* (1709), 168.

[162] "Several of the poor Palatines who came lately over, and were papists, have renounced that religion, and more of them 'tis expected will doe the like." (August 6, 1709), Luttrell, *op. cit.*, VI, 473.

[163] "The Papish Palatines who came hither are ordered to goe home, having passports for the same." (September 15, 1709), Luttrell, *op. cit.*, VI, 489.

home again, petitioned the Queen. They said they had been encouraged to leave their homes, having a promise for the free exercise of religion, which was now denied them. Accordingly, they requested the Queen out of her goodness and justice to pay their expenses home.[164] Their request was granted. Records show that more than 2,000 were returned, and the costs were paid by the government.[165]

A sad commentary must be made upon an incident which occurred on August 17, 1709. Secretary of State Boyle wrote to the Secretary of War, Sir Robert Walpole, that the resolutions of the commissioners for returning the Palatines to Germany had been laid before the Queen. She ordered that "you do take care, that some commission officer do go among the Palatines and try whether any of the Papists will enter into Her Majesty's service in Portugal."[166] Although the Papists were not welcome to stay in England, they were quite acceptable in Her Majesty's armed forces. In the midst of all the flurry and confusion attendant on the distribution and settlement of the Palatines, Secretary Sunderland learned to his disgust that the Board of Trade could not meet, since a majority of its members were out of town. So, on October 5, 1709, orders were issued commanding their immediate return to consider "matters of moment which require despatch." Two weeks later, on the 19th, a standing order was sent to the Board of Trade, requiring them to have a quorum of members in constant attendance.[167] To say the least, this is an interesting example of the inefficiency of British colonial officialdom in the eighteenth century.

[164] Doble, *op. cit.*, II, 446.

[165] "Mr. Doben and Sir Thomas Janssen, concerning Palatines shipped off to Holland, some 2000 and upwards, desire Mr. Dayrolle who is to prepare a list and may have orders to take care of supervising, and allowing 5 guilders a head, and deducting for such as do not appear." P. R. O., S. P. 11/36 (September 16, 1709).

[166] P. R. O., S. P. 44/107, 267.

[167] P. R. O., S. P. 44/108, 156, 157.

In the crowded quarters and with meager sustenance, the Palatines had fallen prey to fevers and plagues. Death wrought havoc in their ranks in spite of their hardiness. It is not known how many died in their encampment at Blackheath and elsewhere in London, but the number must have been nearly a thousand.[168] With all reasonable calculations and deductions made, it seems probable that the descendants of several thousands of the Palatines are among the English population today.

Now when the fruits of Penn's advertising campaign were finally ripening, where was Penn's proposal to take the Palatines off the hands of the government? Unfortunately, Penn was in no financial position to send the Palatines to his colony in 1709. He had suffered a nine months' imprisonment in 1708 for a 10,500 pound debt dishonestly claimed by former friends.[169] Penn was finally released from his debt to the Fords, but his expenses were heavy and his province was under mortgage to friends, who had aided him. Indeed for some years he had been negotiating with the British Ministry for the sale of his proprietorship.[170] This undoubtedly accounted for the small part taken by Penn in disposing of the Palatines in London in 1709.

From the difficulties described in this chapter it should be evident that the British government did not plan for this large Palatine immigration in 1709. It prayed for immigration as a general blessing, but this avalanche of people was like a flood instead of rain. The government's strenuous efforts to stop the movement and the generous attitude it maintained stood in sharp contrast to the conduct of the proprietors of English

[168] *Das verlangte nicht erlangte Canaan*, 113; Goebel, "Briefe" in *op. cit.*, 187.

[169] Janney, *op. cit.*, 508. The Board of Trade's efforts to settle in 1708 the Pennsylvania-Maryland boundary dispute were delayed by Penn "being under restraint." *C. C. 1706–1708*, 711.

[170] *Ibid.*, 509, 522, 525. The colony was mortgaged for 6,600 pounds in 1708. Penn asked 20,000 pounds of the British government for the surrender of his rights. P. R. O., C. O. 5/1265, 208; *C. C. 1720–1721*, 208.

colonies, who were largely responsible for the emigration. The proposals to settle the Palatines discussed so far were for the most part discarded in favor of more promising ventures. Proposals to send Palatines to Ireland, Carolina and New York were in the latter category, and the large bands of emigrants transported there justify special attention to their adventures.

CHAPTER IV. THE IRELAND AND
NORTH CAROLINA SETTLEMENTS

HARD PRESSED by the problem of disposing of so many immigrants, the Ministry turned in all directions for suggestions. On July 7, 1709, the Council of Ireland, with Joseph Addison among them, proposed to the Queen that a number of Palatines be sent to Ireland to strengthen the Protestant cause there,[1] and late in August, 794 families were sent there. They were taken in wagons to Chester, where they embarked for Ireland.[2] The first groups landed between the 4th and the 7th of September, others came during October. In January, 1710, the total number of Palatines in Ireland was 3,073, of whom 1,898 were adults, and 1,175 were under fourteen years of age.[3] The transportation charges amounted to 3,498 pounds, 16 shillings and 6 pence.[4]

A committee of ten Irish gentlemen, supporters of the Protestant cause, were organized as the Commissioners for Settling the Poor Distressed Palatines in Ireland.[5] On their arrival, the Palatines were temporarily lodged in Dublin and received for subsistence 18 pence a week for each person above fourteen years of age and 12 pence for each under that age.[6]

[1] Marlborough MSS. (*Hist. MSS. Com.*, *8th Report*, Appendix), 47; B. M., Add. MSS. 35933, 15.

[2] Luttrell, *op. cit.*, VI, 474; *The State of the Palatines*, 7; P. R. O., S. P. 44/107, 264, 265.

[3] B. M., Add. MSS. 35933, 18, 27; Add. MSS. 17677 DDD, 242; Add. MSS. 22202, 130; P. R. O., T. 1/119, 91; S. P. 44/107, 297.

[4] *C. J.*, XVI, 596. The Commons Journal report is misleading in that it gives 3,800 as the total number of Palatines in Ireland. Greene, *op. cit.*, 231, went to the other extreme in his statement that "a few Palatines were sent to Ireland but the great majority were sent to America."

[5] B. M., Strafford Papers, Add. MSS. 22202, 130.

[6] B. M., Add. MSS. 35933, 18; P. R. O., T 1/119, 100, 104, 123.

To finance the arrangements, the Crown appropriated 15,000 pounds of its revenues in Ireland to be paid in three years at 5,000 pounds a year. Early in 1710, an additional 9,000 pounds were set aside under similar arrangements.[7] Charitable collections secured 409 pounds, 18 shillings and 6¼ pence more for the fund.[8] The appropriation of such sums of money by the government aroused the speculative interest of the Irish landlords. Their Irish tenants did not possess a capital of 24 pounds per family of four,[9] neither did the Irish tenants have the financial backing of the Crown. As a result, the Palatines were distributed in lots varying in size from one family to 56 families. The 43 gentlemen, who became their landlords by a draw, were to settle the Palatines on their lands.

The Commissioners wrote to them shortly thereafter to learn how they proposed to settle the families assigned to them and at what rates. As to the financial arrangements, the landlords were expected to give "a cheaper Bargain" than they gave others. The Commissioners suggested that the landlords might agree to receive the customary proportion of corn towards the plowing and seed, which they were to furnish. For the other necessaries such as horse, cart and cows, the landlords were expected to be satisfied with one-third of the subsistence allowance, until the allowances could be secured in larger advances.[10] The Irish landlords were urged to consider the satisfaction in doing a generous Christian act, the security for themselves in settling so many Protestant families on their estates, and the contribution they would be making towards strengthening the Protestant interest and safety of

[7] *C. J.* XVI, 596; Thomas Somerville, *History of Great Britain during the Reign of Queen Anne* (London, 1798), 527.

[8] B. M., Add. MSS. 35933, 18; Stair MSS. (*Hist. MSS. Com., 2nd Report*, Appendix), 231.

[9] Palatine Pamphlet, no title, printed in Dublin by Andrew Crooke, 1710, 3, Harvard Library, gift of J. P. Morgan, hereafter cited as *Crooke's Pamphlet.* This pamphlet is a general letter written by the Commissioners for Settling the Palatines to prospective landlords.

[10] *Ibid.,* 2.

the country.[11] In concluding their letter to the Irish gentlemen, the Commissioners promised that should any Palatines refuse the contracts offered, they would be stricken off the list of those receiving Her Majesty's bounty. A declaration in "High Dutch" was to be distributed to this effect among the Palatines.[12]

Arrangements were made and 533 families, composed of 2,098 men, women and children, were dispersed over the countryside. The Commissioners for Settling the Palatines assured the Lords Justices of Ireland early in 1710 that all care had been exercised in their settlement. Many of the landlords were said to have been at great charge to themselves in providing habitations, firing and other conveniences for the Palatines. The lands set apart for the Palatines were assigned to them at easy rates, often a third less in rent than similar lands were let to other tenants.[13]

Notwithstanding the kind entertainment the Palatines met with, to the professed surprise of the Commissioners many of the Palatines left their settlements, returned to Dublin, and took ship for England. In fact, 232 families had returned from Ireland to England by November 25, 1710, and in the next two months, 52 more families sailed for England in spite of attempts to stop them.[14] On February 15, 1711, only 188 of the 533 families distributed over the countryside were still on the lands allotted them. Over 300 of the families were in Dublin, where a great many of the men had been employed in the building of a government arsenal nearby. When the arsenal was completed, they lived on the royal allowance without apparently troubling to find employment.[15]

[11] Nicholas Tindal, *Continuation of Mr. Rapin's History of England* (5th ed., London, 1763), XVII, 215; Somerville, *op. cit.*, 527.

[12] *Crooke's Pamphlet*, 4.

[13] B. M., Add. MSS. 35933, 12, 17.

[14] A proposal was made to send those Palatines back to Holland, who returned from Ireland. P. R. O., S. P. 34/13, 14.

[15] B. M., Add. MSS. 35933, 13, 18.

Of those Palatines who left their settlements, many stole away without giving their landlords any notice. The Commissioners reported, according to the best information they could get, the Palatines thought that the lands in Ireland were to be rent free. Many of them could not be persuaded to the contrary. The more turbulent Germans stirred up the others with stories of better treatment accorded to those Palatines still in England. A worthless fellow-countryman, who had lived in Ireland several years before, victimized the Palatines by pretending to act as an agent for them in London. Many of the Palatines, it appeared, intended to live on Her Majesty's allowance in Ireland till peace was made and then go back to Germany.[16]

The Commissioners for Settling the Palatines in Ireland were not unprejudiced in their account of the Palatine ingratitude. Over half of them had become landlords of the Palatines. They were interested parties in informing the Lords Justices that the Palatines had been well treated and generously provided for. Three of the returning Palatines examined in London said that they left because of the hard usage they received from Commissary Hinch, Mr. Sweet (one of the landlords], and others. They charged that they had not received their subsistence. They claimed that after application to the Lord Lieutenant of Ireland, they received subsistence, but for one week only. They had even paid their own passage to England, although Mr. Hinch had offered them ten shillings each to leave Ireland. They corresponded with each other and met at Dublin for the return voyage.[17]

It seems probable that a number of the Irish landlords were not above taking advantage of their Palatine tenants, who spoke another tongue and were in a somewhat hostile country. The native Irish tenants, Catholic in faith, were not inclined to welcome Protestants, who might secure their lands on more favorable terms and they seized every oppor-

[16] *Ibid.*, 19.   [17] *C. J.*, XVI, 596.

tunity to abuse the Palatines. As no other arrangement seems to have been made, it appears probable that the Palatine allowances were turned over to the Irish gentlemen to distribute to their tenants, and under such arrangements the Palatine tenants might receive very little of the allowance granted them. After all, it would be too much to expect a people such as these, with eyes on the New World and its golden promises, to be satisfied with even favorable terms among the meager opportunities of Ireland. It was none too prosperous for most Irishmen themselves.

However that may be, the return of increasing numbers of the Palatines to England soon caused apprehension there in 1710. On the 10th of May, the Commissioners for the Palatines in England sent a representative, one Mr. Crockett, to Ireland to persuade the Palatines to remain while they drew their comfortable maintenance, but notwithstanding Mr. Crockett's good intentions and excellent abilities, he had little success.[18] The attempts to hold them in Ireland failed, because as Chief Justice Broderick said, neither the officials nor the landlords had power to stop the Palatines, who were a free people.[19] On one occasion, having boarded a ship to persuade a number of the Palatines not to return to England, Mr. Crockett was threatened and narrowly escaped being thrown into the sea. The Irish Commissioners even offered to transport to Hamburg those Palatines who desired to leave. They had no acceptances. The Germans seized their first opportunity to steal away to England, still with the hope of settling in the English colonies in America.

Consequently, the Irish Commissioners, having discussed the situation with Mr. Crockett, drew up a memorial on July 25th. This representation addressed to Thomas, Earl of Wharton, the Lord Lieutenant of Ireland, reviewed the futile attempts at settlement of the Palatines to that date, and recom-

[18] B. M., Add. MSS. 35933, 12; C. J. XVI, 596.
[19] C. J. XVI, 596.

mended that the Crown allow 40 shillings a year to each Palatine family for twenty-one years. This was to be offered as an encouragement for them to stay in Ireland. The money remaining from the original appropriations would be necessary to provide cattle, household stuff, tools and subsistence until the Palatines should provide for themselves.[20]

There the matter rested. On October 14, 1710, the Irish Commissioners requested the Lords Justices of that country to obtain Her Majesty's answer, since no reply to their proposal had been received. This inaction was due to the Ministerial Revolution, then taking place in England. Harley and his associates through intrigue were engaged in ousting the Whigs from office, and government affairs had to await the outcome of their machinations. Many officials were removed from office after the change of Ministry. The Earl of Wharton was replaced by the Duke of Ormond as Lord Lieutenant of Ireland.[21] "Perfectly a stranger to the whole transaction," Ormond requested from the Irish authorities a full report and opinion on the matter.[22] On December 12th, the new Secretary of State, Dartmouth, issued an order to stop the continued return of Palatines from Ireland to England. The Commissioners for Settling the Palatines in Ireland drew up on February 15, 1711, at the request of the Lords Justices, a detailed report of the Palatine affairs. On that day, 2,051 Palatines remained in Ireland. Of the original appropriation of 24,000 pounds for their support and settlement, 10,319 pounds was left but this sum, the Commissioners reckoned, would be exhausted by July 2, 1712. They then repeated their proposal for the annual allowance of 40 shillings for twenty-one years, "which is intended towards the payment of the Rents they shall set under. . . ."[23]

[20] B. M., Add. MSS. 35933, 15.
[21] Morgan, "The Ministerial Revolution of 1710," in *loc. cit.*, XXXVI, 209.
[22] B. M., Add. MSS. 35933, 16.
[23] *Ibid.*, 20.

The Irish Commissioners further requested that the Palatines be obliged to declare whether they would accept the arrangement or not. Those who would accept were immediately to enter into covenants as other tenants did with their landlords. Those who refused were to be sent to their own country or elsewhere at the first opportunity. Finally, the Commissioners had reports from the gentlemen who had retained several of the Palatines on their lands, that they would be obliged to return the Palatines to Dublin by March 15th, unless the 40 shillings per annum allowance were made. On the 28th of March, 1712, the English government approved the grant to each family of 40 shillings annually for seven years. It was estimated that 263 Palatine families of 978 persons still remained in Ireland then, but by the time the Irish Commissioners heard of the grant (August 11, 1712), nine more families had departed. With this additional support, the 254 families were all settled in the country.

Near the close of September, 1712, Sir Thomas Southwell sent 130 Palatine families down to his estate in the County of Limerick,[24] where ten other families had remained. Southwell rented them land at almost half of what it could bring, and supplied them with cash and other necessaries. It was stated in June, 1714, when Southwell petitioned the king for 200 pounds due him, that had he not advanced the money, "the last ninety Families wou'd have left the Kingdom."[25] Southwell expressed himself as reluctant to seize the possessions of the Palatines, but he would be compelled to do so unless the Crown reimbursed him. However, on September 1, 1716, the Lord Lieutenant of Ireland successfully supported Southwell's claims to the British Treasury for a Palatine debt, which had grown to 557 pounds.[26]

[24] They settled principally at Court Matrix, Killiheen, Ballingarrane and Pallaskenry, and then spread out to the locations given in Appendix I.

[25] B. M., Add. MSS. 35933, 24.

[26] *Ibid.*, 25.

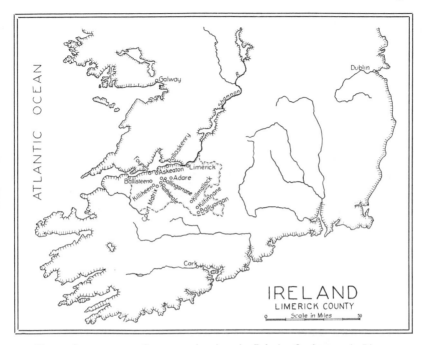

Map of Southwestern Ireland, showing the Palatine Settlements in Limerick County. The borders of Limerick County are slightly shaded.
Drawn by A. Cefola.

The Palatines were reported as having employed themselves very industriously in raising flax and hemp. At that time the Commissioners recommended that a minister be secured to read to them the liturgy of the Anglican Church, to which the Palatines readily conformed. The Commissioners further suggested that an agent who understood the German language be appointed to see that the Palatines were not misused by their landlords or by their Irish neighbors.[27] Since a number of the Germans received the sacrament within the time set, looking toward naturalization (under the law which had been repealed in 1711), without taking through ignorance the oath of allegiance required, the Commissioners recommended their case be presented to Parliament for remedy.

[27] *Ibid.*, 27.

The Palatines were favored by fortune with the accession of the Hanoverian George I to the British throne in 1714. Since his accession was a continuation of the precious Protestant succession to the throne, the government naturally was even more disposed to support the Protestant cause, especially in Catholic Ireland. Indeed, the "poor German Protestants" were likely to receive special favors from a king who was so German that he could not speak English. On June 15, 1715, an order was issued to continue the 40-shilling grant to each Palatine family for the remainder of the seven-year term, expiring March 28, 1719. In addition, on August 12, 1718, the general annual allowance of 624 pounds was ordered to be continued for 14 more years on the expiration of the former grant.[28]

Incidentally, this settlement of Palatines in Ireland was made against a background of distrust of the Irish Catholic population. Fear, that Ireland would be the base for an attempt on the part of the Stuart pretender James III to win back the throne of England, swayed the authorities. In Limerick, where the Palatines remaining in Ireland were eventually established, there had been a serious scare in 1702. The Roman Catholics were rumored to be forming an army. As a result in the next year an act was passed by the Parliament of Ireland, expelling all Roman Catholic residents of Galway and Limerick, unless they gave sufficient assurance of allegiance to the Queen and her successors.[29] Similar rumors continued to haunt the authorities in the next ten years. Consequently, the introduction of Protestant settlers in Limerick County was particularly fortunate from the view-point of those in power. All those able to bear arms were enrolled in the Free Yeomanry of the country and were known as "The German Fusiliers" or "True Blues." Each man was supplied with a musket called a "Queen Anne" with which to protect him-

[28] *Ibid.*, 29.
[29] P. Fitzgerald and J. J. McGregor, *The History of Limerick* (Dublin, 1827), II, 455.

self and his family.[30] At the same time an educational and religious program for conversion of the Irish Roman Catholics was seriously considered.[31]

As late as 1758, the Palatines still had their separate settlements in Ireland. On the afternoon of February 23rd of that year, John Wesley "rode over to Court Mattress [Court Matrix], a colony of Germans, whose parents came out of the Palatinate fifty years ago. Twenty families settled here, twenty more at Killiheen, a mile off; fifty at Balligarane, about two miles eastward; and twenty at Pallas [Pallaskenry], four miles further."[32] In 1745 Wesley found the Palatines without pastors and completely demoralized but he soon remedied that condition. The Germans became staunch Methodists, which many of them still remain. In 1760, five or six families, including Philip Embury and his cousin Barbara Heck, came to New York. It was here in 1766 that Barbara helped found the Methodist Church of this country by insisting that cousin Philip preach against worldliness.[33] Arthur Young, in his *Tour of Ireland*, nearly 70 years after the settlement, found three villages of about 70 Palatine families. "For sometime after they settled they fed upon sour crout, but by degrees left it off, and took to potatoes. . . . Their industry goes so far, that jocular reports of its excess are spread: in a very pinching season, one of them yoked his wife against a horse, and went in that manner to work and finished a journey at plough. The industry of the women is a perfect contrast to the Irish ladies in the cabins, who cannot be persuaded on any consideration, even to make hay, it not being the custom of the country. . . ."[34]

[30] William Crook, *The Palatines in Ireland* (London, 1866), 251.

[31] B. M., Add. MSS. 35933, 21.

[32] John Wesley, *Works* (1st Amer. ed., New York, 1831), IV, 3.

[33] W. W. Sweet, *Methodism in American History* (New York, 1913), 54.

[34] He was nevertheless of the opinion that the Palatines had done far less than the Irish peasant would have done if they had received half the encouragement. Arthur Young, *Tour in Ireland* (Dublin, 1780), 76.

As late as 1830, another traveler wrote that "The elders of the family preserve, in a great degree, the language, customs, and religion of their old country, but the younger mingle and marry with their Irish neighbors . . . they are at present, as regards both their customs and traditions, only a relic of the past; and yet one so strongly marked and so peculiar, that it will take a long time before all trace of the Fatherland is obliterated."[35] Johann Kohl in his *Travels in Ireland* in 1842 did not visit the settlements personally, but was informed in the neighborhood, that they could still be distinguished from the rest by the names of "Palatines."[36] But when William Beidelman, once Lieutenant-Governor of the Commonwealth of Pennsylvania, visited Ireland in the closing years of the nineteenth century, he found no trace of any German dialect in the Palatine neighborhoods in Limerick. The language had died out, only German names remained. Some of these had so changed as to make their origin scarcely recognizable. Mr. Beidelman found that the descendants of the Palatines had so intermarried with the Irish population, that their descendants were more Irish than German.[37]

A visit to the area of Palatine settlements in Limerick County in 1934 confirmed much of this. Some Palatine descendants have forgotten their origin. One prominent descendant in replying to a question about German customs, countered with the query, "Were the Palatines Germans?" It is estimated by various individuals of these so-called Palatines that about 700 of them are still living in Limerick County.[38] These

[35] Robert Montgomery Martin, *Ireland Before and After the Union with Great Britain* (2nd. ed., London, 1848), 191.

[36] Johann Georg Kohl, *Travels in Ireland* (London, 1844), 76.

[37] William Beidelman, *The Story of the Pennsylvania Germans* (Easton, Pennsylvania, 1898), 73.

[38] See the list of families in Appendix I. For much of this information I am particularly indebted to Mr. Julius Sheppard, a prominent Palatine of Ballingarrane with a particularly keen mind. I also must express my appreciation of the fine courtesy and help extended to me by the Methodist minister Reverend A. Reilly, of Adare, Limerick County, Irish Free State.

estimates made independent of one another are remarkable for their general agreement. But it should be noted that many of the Palatines remaining are descendants of mixed unions, that is, with Irish and English in the last generation or two. The adult generation today is largely the ninth in Ireland. Still some are pure Palatine stock and their heavy cast German countenances can be distinguished from the population generally. Careful inquiry has established the complete loss of the German tongue as far back as the seventh generation in the country, that is, about 1860. One Palatine nearly eighty years of age claims that his grandparents knew German, but this was rare. The same individual asserts that his grandfather died at the age of 110. In fact, another Palatine's aunt, still alive (1935), counted 102 years of existence.

Today there is no bad feeling or prejudice between the Irish and the Palatines, other than the general lack of sympathy between Catholic and Protestant. But the Palatines consider themselves Irish and the conclusion is evident that they have been assimilated thoroughly. However, this seems to have been accomplished only in the last three generations. Before that mixed marriages with the Irish were rare and German was probably still their language. In fact, one Palatine's parents were double first cousins, and this was considered rather common. Were there any truth in the prejudice against close marriages, these Palatine descendants should show degeneracy, but the healthy ruddy stock left with marked signs of longevity goes far to show otherwise, when the stock is good to begin with. On the other hand, there are at least two families showing marked feeble-mindedness. In more recent times, the prosperous Palatines are held in high regard in the county and many a native Irishman will ask his Palatine neighbor for his opinion of the price to be asked for his cattle at the county fair.

It may be recalled that Arthur Young estimated the number of the Palatines at 700 in 1776. It would seem that the

Palatine population has not increased, but this is not true. As the native Irish generally have contributed to the population of the world, old and new, so have the "Irish Palatines." Many of the Palatines recall members of their families who emigrated 50 years ago or even more recently to Australia, Canada, United States (Boston, Chicago, New York, and even as far west as Oregon), and various parts of Ireland. This is particularly true of the Switzers, who may be found in various parts of Ireland, in Queens County and Dublin as well as in Limerick County. Here is a typical case. Alexander Jordon, Sr., a French Huguenot, married Mary Smith of Palatine descent. Of the eleven children which blessed that union, one is in New York, U. S. A., one in Reading, England, one in Brighton, England, three in Belfast, Ireland, one in West Africa, two in Limerick and two are dead.

But the natural increase in population has been adversely affected, it is apparent, within the last two generations. Most of the Palatines can recall large families of a dozen or more children, one in fact of two dozen, 17 of whom lived to adulthood. But small families are the rule today. One Palatine, of the ninth generation had two children himself; he was one of four children but his grandparents on his father's side had 13. Of course, inquiries were out of order, but the inference was obvious from certain remarks that the small families were a matter of choice, rather than due to any decline in the fertility of the stock. It should be remembered in this connection that it has been in these last few generations that mixed marriages with the Irish and other stock have become common rather than exceptional. These small families are probably not to be attributed to close in-breeding.

Of German customs there are none. Sourcrout is unheard of and other Pennsylvania German customs have no foothold in Limerick County. That great quencher of German thirst, beer, is not popular and even the cider for which the district was noted some years ago has lost its popularity. I did notice an old home-made cider press now resting after more than a century of use. John Wesley and his successors have done a thorough job. The Palatines are today a monument to the good influence of a strict but honest discipline. It must also be noted that some of the Palatines have become Catholic, and this is attributed by the Protestant clergy to the influence of the mixed marriages. I sought in vain for the remnant of a German custom. This failure to find one and the assimilation are to be explained largely by the fact that no further immigration of Germans took place. Here under adverse conditions, national antipathy in the beginning, religious hostility, and economic bitterness, assimilation was delayed for about a century and a half. But then it came fast and with surprising completeness. However, it is well to keep in mind that the Irish themselves have been fairly Anglicized too, at least, to adopting the English language.

What is left, surprising as it may be, is a remnant of the manorial system set up by these Palatines. Early travelers have not commented upon this institution, and hence one is unprepared for a common with grazing rights and arable land rotating annually in use among the shareholders. These are not found among the Irish and are a survival of the first settlement of great interest. In both Court Matrix and Killiheen, a town-land near it, is to be found a meadow for a field held in common. About thirteen families still hold rights in Court Matrix and about twelve in Killiheen. The number of cattle one can graze on the common depends upon the amount of land held in the arable land, and originally each share was eight acres and carried with it one or two "collop." A "collop" was grazing for one cow or two yearlings. Today over these commons there are ninety to a hundred cattle grazing. The arable land is rotated every year, the holders receiving different lands until the whole parcel has passed completely through their hands when they begin to repeat the order all over again.

Two Views of the Commons at Court Matrix, Ireland, showing the balks (in the right foreground) still used to separate the plots of land.

One custom was still recalled. That was the custom of the Palatines of having their own Burgomaster, who judged their disputes. In later years he was known as "the King of the Palatines." The last really to hold that title was James Teskey and that was over 60 years ago. Several have been referred to since then by that title but apparently only in a facetious manner. Here again is proof that assimilation occurred about the middle of the nineteenth century, for only then would the Palatine descendants be ready to allow the natives to settle their affairs, that is, when they felt themselves to be natives too.

The Palatine woman is still the typical hard-working German *frau*, although she would not recognize the word. As one of my companions remarked somewhat derisively, "They would not think of having a maid, and do all the work themselves." Hard-working, whether in the household or in the field, they are helpmates to the core. They still pickle and preserve large quantities of fruits and vegetables, and in this they are the marvel of their neighbors.

Their prosperity too is well recognized in the country. Frugality has concealed much of their wealth, but that which is evident is sufficient to excite the friendly envy of the Irish neighbors. One of them exclaimed, "I can't understand these Palatines. I work as hard as they do, but I can't keep up with them" financially. In the early days the Palatines planted their potatoes in plowed drills and plowed them out. They were thus able to use only one-third the dung used by the Irish, who planted their potatoes in four-row ridges with spades. The Palatine farmers appear to be the first to build silos in Ireland. These practices would seem to indicate that there was a sound personal basis for their prosperity aside from the government aid, though Arthur Young thought that these improvements were solely due to the fact that the Palatines were given long leases.[39]

[39] Young, *op. cit.*, I, 178.

Professor Cunningham was too severe when he quoted with apparent approval a parliamentary speech of 1748, "The poor Palatines . . . were found to have neither industry nor ingenuity."[40] When Professor Cunningham held that the Palatines were successful almost as much because of the terms on which "the land was leased as to any special characteristics among the settlers,"[41] he was stating one view of the case. Not only were the government subsidies of great help, but they were also quite necessary under the uniformly unfriendly conditions. That important factor may be recognized without derogatory conclusions to the people of any nationality. What is now evident, is that the Palatine descendants have continued their prosperity and have won through even under adverse conditions so apparent in the Ireland of today. What is even more convincing, is the general approbrium and approval of the Palatine people held throughout Limerick County by other elements of the population.

Turning to another large settlement of Palatines, we find that a party of Palatines was sent to North Carolina. The efforts of the Carolina Proprietors to populate their colony, culminating in the advertising pamphlet by Kocherthal, have been described, and it has been noticed that Kocherthal's account of Carolina was an important cause of the 1709 emigration. The Lords Proprietors of Carolina were, it seems, among the first to make proposals to the Board of Trade. As early as July 16, 1709, the Proprietors made "proposals to a committee of Council to take all the Palatines here from 15 years to 45 years old, and send them to their plantation; but her Majestie to be at the charge of transporting them, which will be above 10 pounds a head."[42] On July 28th, they ordered that the advertisement printed in the *Gazette* concerning the

[40] William Cobbett, *Parliamentary History of England* (London, 1813), XIV, 139 hereafter cited as *Parlia. Hist.*

[41] William Cunningham, *Alien Immigrants in England* (London, 1897), 250–253.

[42] Luttrell, *op. cit.*, VI, 465.

Palatine immigration, "be printed in High Dutch, for the use of the poor Palatines and the rest of the Germans."[43] On August 11th, they proposed to give 100 acres of land for each man, woman and child, free from any quit-rent for ten years. After ten years, the quit-rent was to be one penny an acre annually. They offered to lease land to the Palatines for the term of three lives or ninety-nine years.[44] These were the same terms as offered in the small circular which was distributed among the Palatines while still in Rotterdam.

These proposals had not been accepted when another group of promoters from Switzerland joined the Proprietors of Carolina in the project. A religious schism had split the town of Bern, and the party of Mennonites, or Anabaptists as they were known in England, were forced to emigrate.[45] They negotiated through a former citizen of Bern, Franz Louis Michel, with the proprietors of Pennsylvania and Carolina. Indeed, some arrangements for land in Pennsylvania had already been made. William Penn, a year later, on April 4, 1710, wrote to Lord Townshend at the Hague asking him to aid in the free passage through Holland of a company of 50 or 60 Switzers under one "Mitchell," who had contracted with him for lands.[46]

Michel was also interested in developing silver mines in the colonies. He enlisted in the latter enterprise Christopher von Graffenried, of an aristocratic family of Bern, a man of pleasing personality, but burdened with debt. The mining project appealed to him as a means of building up his fortune and in 1708, he secretly left Switzerland, having engaged a small party of miners to follow him on his call.[47] According-

[43] "List and abstracts of documents relating to South Carolina [also North Carolina] now existing in State Paper Office, London," in *S. C. Hist. Soc. Coll.* (Charleston, South Carolina, 1857), I, 179.
[44] *C. C. 1708–1709*, 445.
[45] The Mennonites were the followers of Menno Simons, an early Dutch Anabaptist.
[46] Townshend MSS. (*Hist. MSS. Com., 11th Report*, Appendix), 63.
[47] Todd and Goebel, *op. cit.*, 223.

ly, in 1709 Graffenried was in London awaiting the development of his mining plans. The delays were annoying. His
partner, Louis Michel, was occupied with negotiations for
the Swiss settlements. On April 28th, Graffenried came to an
agreement with the Proprietors of Carolina, for the purchase
of 10,000 acres of land[48] on or between the Neuse and Cape
Fear Rivers or their branches in North Carolina. The purchase
price was 10 pounds for each thousand acres. It was further
agreed that 100,000 acres were to be reserved to the company
for 12 years, if they desired to purchase additional land. The
terms were to be at the above mentioned rate, provided the
land was taken up within seven years. After that period, the
company would have to pay according to the custom prevailing there. One member of the company was to be made a
Landgrave, and was to purchase 5,000 acres at the customary
quit-rent.[49] By July 14, 1709, Graffenried had joined with
Michel in his settlement project, for on that date he and
Michel explained to the Board of Trade their proposal to
settle Swiss Protestants in Virginia.[50]

The men and women of the 1709 Palatine immigration
began to arrive, as already described, in large numbers early
in May, and the British government was hard pressed to
provide for them. At this juncture, English friends of Graffenried, some of high rank, advised him not to lose so favorable
an opportunity to attain desirable settlers on his lands. He
was assured that if he would take a considerable number of
the Palatines to America, the Queen would not only grant
him the money for their passage, but in addition would make
a good contribution for them. The good contribution as a
matter of fact amounted to almost 4,000 pounds.[51]

Consequently, Graffenried hastened to conclude his ar-

[48] C. C. 1708–1709, 432, 443, 461.
[49] N. C. Col. Rec., I, 707.
[50] C. C. 1708–1709, 425.
[51] Todd and Goebel, op. cit., 224.

rangements with the Proprietors of Carolina. He paid 50
pounds for 5,000 acres on August 4, 1709, and was made a
landgrave.[52] On the 3rd of September, Graffenried, Michel
and the Proprietors entered into another arrangement. Under
this agreement, 10,000 acres were granted to Graffenried and
his heirs, for the settlement of Palatines.[53] Michel, who was
to purchase 35,000 acres, actually contented himself with one
fourteenth of that area.[54] From these arrangements, it is apparent that the direction of the company's affairs had passed
into the hands of Graffenried.

Late in September, 40 or 50 families of Palatines petitioned
that they might be transported with the Swiss now going to
North Carolina,[55] and on October 10th, the Commissioners
for the Settling of the Palatines permitted Graffenried and
Michel to pick out 600 Palatines, about 92 families, to go to
Carolina with them. They chose young, healthy and industrious people of various trades. On the 21st, 50 more persons
were accepted.[56] Each emigrant received 20 shillings worth of
clothes from the government, which also paid their passage,
amounting to 5 pounds, 10 shillings each.[57]

Preparations for the settlement in Carolina were now under
way. The Lords Proprietors sent to Carolina two letters of
instructions with regard to the Palatines. These were sent on
September 22, 1709, the first letter being addressed to Christopher Gale, Receiver General of North Carolina. It directed
him to supply "Graffenried with such necessaries and provisions of ours for the poor Palatines at such rates as you
received them, taking and forwarding his receipt for the
same." The Proprietors intended in this way to extend two
years' credit to the new settlement. The second letter went to

[52] N. C. Col. Rec., I, 717.
[53] C. C. 1708–1709, 719.
[54] N. C. Col. Rec., I, 718.
[55] Acts Privy Council Col., II, 614.
[56] Marlborough MSS. (Hist. MSS. Com., 8th Report, Appendix), 47a.
[57] N. C. Col. Rec., I, 986; Trinity College Hist. Pub., IV, 65.

the "Governor or President and Council and Assembly, of North Carolina." It may be taken as a statement of British colonization aims. The Proprietors stated, "We being extreamly desireous that the good of our Province should by all means be promoted, and being sencible that nothing can more effectually contribute thereto than by encreasing the number of the inhabitants and planters, who by their labour and industry may occupy the soil and improve the produce thereof, we have therefore given all reasonable encouragement to some families of poor Palatines to come and settle amongst you, . . . we do earnestly recommend them to your care."[58]

Graffenried, according to his own account, took great pains in preparing for the settlement in Carolina. A supply of all kinds of necessary tools was collected. Good food was provided for the voyage. Twelve Palatines were appointed foremen among the people and the whole group was placed under the supervision of three colonial officials bound for Carolina, the Chief Justice, the Surveyor General, and the Receiver General. When all arrangements had been made, Graffenried had the Commissioners for the Settling of the Palatines inspect the arrangements on the ships. Finally in January, 1710, the Palatines sailed for America, [59] Graffenried remaining in England to await the arrival of Michel with his Swiss Anabaptists. Because of rough winds and storms, the ships were driven off their course, and arrived in Virginia, thirteen weeks later.

The Palatines were in poor condition. They were overcrowded, which contributed to the sickness and death of many on the voyage. They were unaccustomed to the salt food. When they finally landed, many could not restrain themselves; several died from drinking too much fresh water and overloading themselves with raw fruits. Others died of fever. The band had lost more than half its members before it was settled.[60]

[58] C. C. 1708–1709, 471.
[59] Trinity College Hist. Pub., IV, 66.
[60] Todd and Goebel, op. cit., 225; N. C. Col. Rec., I, 909.

One ship, carrying the best of the supplies, was plundered at the mouth of the James River by a French privateer.[61] The Palatine party was next transported 20 miles overland, and then shipped across Albermarle Sound to the Neuse River. Here Surveyor General Lawson placed them on the south side of the point of land along the Trent River, in the very hottest and most unhealthy locality—this, Lawson appears to have done for his own advantage, as it was on his land or what he later sold as his land[62]—and there the Palatines lived until fall, when Graffenried arrived.

The Swiss portion of the settlement was meeting with great difficulties. The first group left Bern on March 8, 1710. A number of the group were men who had been imprisoned for their Anabaptist beliefs. They were really being deported to America. When they reached the Low Countries, the Dutch intervened in favor of the victims of the religious persecution. All of the prisoners were freed, but some of them continued on their way.

Meanwhile, Graffenried and Michel, on May 18, 1710, signed the contract with Georg Ritter and Peter Isot, by which they legally became members of the Bern Land Company.[63] The enterprise was founded on the 17,000 acres actually purchased and 12 years' option on 100,000 acres. Permission was also given to take up land above the falls of the Potomac, which would however, be held of the Crown, subject to the Governor of Virginia. The exact amount paid for the land was 175 pounds. Aside from these land grants, the Bern Company had mining rights in Carolina, Virginia, Maryland and Pennsylvania. The stock of the company, consisting of 7,200 pounds, was divided into twenty-four shares

[61] *C. C. 1710–1711*, 114.

[62] Todd and Goebel, *op. cit.*, 226.

[63] This group had petitioned the British government on June 28, 1709, for lands and financial aid to settle about 500 Swiss Protestants in Virginia. *C. C. 1708–1709*, 398; P. R. O., S. P. 44/108, 106. The contract is given in full in Todd and Goebel, *op. cit.*, 292 *et seq.*

of 300 pounds each. No one person could hold more than one share, but it was not all paid in. Michel was credited with a share to pay him for his discoveries which he claimed to have made and for the 2,500 acres he had turned into the society. One share was credited to Graffenried for his 5,000 acres and his work with the Palatines; and Georg Ritter had a share for expenses already incurred, which left only 6,300 pounds to be paid in. When the contract was signed, others had not contributed their amounts, having until September, 1711 to pay; hence it is impossible to determine how much Graffenried had on hand to support himself and his colonists. The report written months later (in May, 1711) indicates a shortage of 2,400 pounds which should have been raised in some manner. Graffenried, at that time, had spent 2,228 pounds, a part or all of which he had borrowed. The shortage of 2,400 pounds would have covered this and left a little besides. It is very likely that the keeping of the contract would have saved his colony.[64]

Graffenried and the Swiss arrived in Virginia on September 11, 1710,[65] carrying a letter from the Queen to the governor of Virginia. It would seem, too, that the more firmly established colony of Virginia was expected to aid the new settlement nearby. After paying his respects to the Virginia authorities, Graffenried proceeded to the Palatine settlement on the Neuse and Trent Rivers in North Carolina. He found his settlers in misery and wretchedness almost indescribable. They had been compelled to give their clothes and whatever else they possessed to neighboring settlers for food. Most of the colonists were enfeebled by ill health. The aid promised Graffenried and ordered by the Lords Proprietors was not forthcoming.

It seems that Graffenried against his inclination was forced to take a hand in the political struggle raging in North Carolina. In 1708, Edward Tynte had been appointed Governor

[64] Todd and Goebel, *op. cit.*, 47.
[65] Graffenried sailed from Newcastle early in July. *Ibid.*, 366.

of South Carolina with instructions to deputize Edward Hyde[66] over the northern colony. Until Hyde should arrive, Tynte left in charge Colonel Thomas Cary, a former South Carolina merchant. Unfortunately for the affairs in North Carolina, Tynte died during the summer of 1710 without signing Hyde's commission and administering the oath. Cary, in control of the government and its finances, refused to yield it to Hyde.[67] He also disregarded the instructions of the Proprietors with regard to the Palatines. Graffenried was finally forced openly to take Hyde's part.[68]

He had to use his credit to secure flour from Pennsylvania and other supplies from Virginia. Having provided temporarily for his settlers, he busied himself with the planning of a new town on the land originally designated. With the Surveyor General and his clerk, Graffenried laid out broad streets and houses well separated one from the other. Three acres of land were marked for each family. The village was divided to resemble a cross. In the center a lot was set aside for a church. Meanwhile a good number of Palatines and Swiss began to fell timber to build houses. Every family was given its own plot of ground, so that they could clear it, build their cabins, and prepare their soil for planting and sowing. The settlement was occupied and soon took on the appearance of prosperity. In eighteen months, Graffenried could boast that the Palatine settlement had made more progress than the English inhabitants had in four years. From a combination of the River name, *Neuse*, and *Bern*, the home city of the Swiss, including Graffenried and Michel, the settlement was named New Bern.[69]

Graffenried also had "a private and very exact treaty with the Palatines, which was projected, examined and agreed upon beforehand by the Royal Commission, too ample to be

[66] This Edward Hyde should not be confused with Edward Hyde, Lord Cornbury, one time Governor of New York.
[67] *C. C. 1711–1712*, 33.
[68] Todd and Goebel, *op. cit.*, 57, *et seq.*
[69] *Ibid.*, 71, 378.

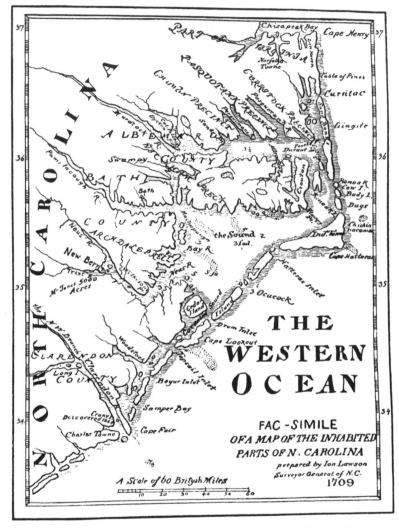

MAP OF NORTH CAROLINA, simplified and retouched to show the Palatine Settlement at New Bern in 1710. *Courtesy of Pennsylvania-German Society.*

inserted here more than in summary: 1st, My colonists owed me fidelity, obedience and respect, and I owed them protection. 2d. I was to furnish each family for the first year a cow and two swine and some utensils, reimbursement to be made after 3 years. 3d. I was to give to each family 300 acres of land and they were to give me for quit-rent two pence per acre, and I on the other hand was to be responsible for the 6 pence per 100 acres acknowledgment toward the Lords Proprietors."[70] This contract was feudal in character. All that was needed was to make its provisions hereditary upon the descendants of the settlers as the title of Landgrave was to be hereditary for Graffenried. That the latter actually exercised authority was evident, for he incurred the enmity of a Palatine blacksmith by sentencing him to a day's log-sawing for using foul language. Some of the Palatines rebelled and left the settlement. Before they could be brought to terms, the Tuscarora Indians made a serious attack on the white settlement.

Despite Graffenried's fair treatment of the Indians, New Bern was subject to Indian attacks in the war which suddenly broke out in 1711. Houses were burned, household furniture destroyed, cattle were shot down and about seventy Palatines were murdered and captured.[71] Graffenried himself narrowly escaped a horrible death, when he and Lawson, the Surveyor-General, were captured. They were liberated temporarily, but Lawson insisted on quarreling with one of the Indian chiefs. As a result, they were both condemned to die. Graffenried saved himself by claiming an exemption as "King of the Palatines."[72] His claim was allowed, but Lawson was tortured to death. Before his release in October, Graffenried was forced to arrange a treaty of neutrality for the Palatines in case of war between the Tuscororas and the English.[73] It came too late however, for all the splendid promise of the settle-

[70] Ibid., 69.
[71] N. C. Col. Rec., I, 927 et seq.; Todd and Goebel, op. cit., 82.
[72] Ibid., I, 992.   [73] Ibid., I, 935.

ment was brought to naught by that first attack of the savages. The leaders of the settlement considered moving to
Virginia or Maryland. Graffenried set out by water to get aid
from the governor of Virginia. A sloop was loaded there with
provisions and military supplies with the help of a prominent
colonist, Colonel Pollock, but the sloop never reached New
Bern, for due to carelessness it caught fire, resulting in the
total loss of the supplies. A larger sloop or brigantine was
sent after much delay.

The end of the Indian troubles brought the Germans little
relief. Graffenried exercised one of the rights of a lord over his
dependent tenants and permitted the settlers to leave the
settlement for two years to work for the English planters. His
partner Michel duped him concerning the silver mines he had
supposedly found in Pennsylvania. Heavily in debt, Graffenried's creditors, including Pollock, became impatient. His
slaves were taken and held for their master's debts and almost
penniless, his settlement in need, the mining project an
illusion, his partner faithless, Graffenried retired to Virginia
on September 20, 1712. There he remained until spring among
his friends, trying to get help. On Easter, April 16, 1713, he
began his return to England by way of New York. He reached
London about September 13th.[74]

In London, Graffenried could obtain no help. Neither the
British government nor the Lords Proprietors were inclined
to risk any money. A disappointed Graffenried could explain
it later only by the deaths of the Queen and the Duke of
Beaufort, one of the Carolina Proprietors, which had occurred
on August 1st and July 25th respectively in 1714, while he
was in Bern.[75] The party of miners, however, for whom
Graffenried had arranged in 1709, were awaiting him in
London. Under J. Justin Albrecht some 40 miners had set out
from Germany with naive faith in the good fortune awaiting
them in America after securing passage there from London.

[74] *Ibid.*, II, 58.   [75] Todd and Goebel, *op. cit.*, 94, 257.

Graffenried had written to them from Carolina, relating the all-too-evident uncertainties, among which was the fact that no mines had yet been discovered. But he was himself so wrapped in hope that he was ill-fitted to write counsels of prudence; he had advised the chief miner and a few others to come for a reconnaissance, if they felt disposed. Accordingly, Albrecht had gathered his company together and had managed to reach London.[76]

Hard pressed himself, Graffenried did the best he could for the miners, who refused to turn back. Finally, he found two merchants trading to Virginia, who agreed to advance the transportation and subsistence of these Germans above what they possessed, provided Governor Spotswood of Virginia would accept them and pay the ship captain the amount due him. As the governor had recommended Graffenried to a Colonel Blankistore with regard to mines in that colony, this recommendation was used to forward the arrangement. In April, 1714, the miners arrived in Virginia, where they were well received by Spotswood and founded the settlement of Germanna on the Rapidan River, a branch of the Rappahannock. For the governor they built and operated iron works about 10 miles northeast of the present town of Fredericksburg.[77]

Graffenried remained in England only 4 or 5 weeks and then began his journey home, reaching his family in Bern, November 11, 1713. The members of the Bern Company refused to carry out the agreement. Graffenried was too poor to sue for breach of contract. He tried but failed to interest others in the project, and finally he had to abandon his colony.[78]

Before he departed from Carolina, Graffenried had assigned the Palatines' land to Colonel Pollock as security for the loans previously extended to him, though the land was probably

[76] *Ibid.*, 257.

[77] Faust, *op. cit.*, I, 178; William J. Hinke, "The First German Reformed Colony in Virginia," in *Jour. Presbyterian Hist. Soc.* (Philadelphia, 1903), II.

[78] *Ibid.*, I, 94.

worth only 200 pounds, while the debt amounted to 700 pounds. On February 10, 1715, Pollock wrote in to Graffenried at Bern, asking him to pay 700 pounds at London and keep the title to the land he had taken up.[79] Pollock wrote a severely critical fashion but to no avail.[80] In Graffenried's own account of the failure the accusations are so universal as to raise the presumption that he too was remiss. At least, he did not deal fairly with the Palatines, who never secured titles to the land they had taken up with him.

The Palatines at New Bern had in the meanwhile managed to survive. On November 6, 1714, they petitioned the Council, stating that they were unprovided with the lands, stock and other necessaries promised them and that they were reduced to great want and poverty by the Indian war. They asked that they might be granted permission to take up 400 acres of land for each family at the rate of 10 pounds per 1,000 acres, and be allowed two years to pay for it.[81] Nothing seems to have been done. On March 29, 1743, the Palatines at New Bern requested titles for the land, but Cullen Pollock, the son of Thomas, produced his father's patent and the Palatines' petition was dismissed.[82] In 1747, another petition was drawn up by the Palatines. This was sent to the Privy Council Committee for Plantation Affairs and at length, on March 16, 1748, the government issued orders to Governor Johnston to give the settlers the equivalent of the lands of which they had been dispossessed in 1743, free of quit-rent for 10 years. The colonial assembly was to provide for the expenses of surveying and granting the titles.[83] This was done, and the Palatines were moved to the frontier. Meanwhile other Germans had begun to move into North Carolina from Pennsylvania following the natural highway of the Great Appalachian valley. By 1750, German immigrants had settled in the counties, Craven, Jones, Onslow and Duplin.

[79] N. C. Col. Rec., II, 166.
[80] Todd and Goebel, op. cit., 97.   [81] N. C. Col. Rec., II, 46.
[82] Ibid., IV, 632.   [83] Ibid., IV, 868, 873, 954, 967.

CHAPTER V. THE BRITISH NAVAL STORES PROBLEM AND THE ORIGINS OF THE NEW YORK SETTLEMENT SCHEME

ABOUT SEVEN years before the 1709 Palatine immigration to England, the British authorities began to have serious and continuous trouble with a foreign monopoly. This foreign monopoly, established by the Crown of Sweden, controlled the supply of naval stores, that is to say, tar and pitch. Naval stores as a general term includes masts, and ship timber of all kinds as well as tar, pitch, rosin and hemp, and even iron in some of its manufacture. Here the term will be used particularly in referring to tar, pitch and other resinous products of the pine tree.

England was well on her way to the undisputed empire of the sea, which she held after the War of the Spanish Succession,[1] and she was in serious need of a reliable supply of naval stores. As there appeared to be no other source of supply for them in sufficient quantities, the Swedes determined to make the most of their advantage and charged exorbitant prices; this was especially true in the first two periods of the Second Hundred Years' War. During both the War of the League of Augsburg (1689–1697) and the War of the Spanish Succession (1702–1713) Swedish tar not only rose to profiteering prices but was obtainable only under other disadvantageous conditions. A brief history of the Swedish Tar Company, or Stockholm Tar Company as it was also known, is necessary to the proper understanding of the British naval stores problem.

The first company was organized in 1654. Fourteen years of complaints against its irregular proceedings by both England and Holland followed. In 1668 bad management finally

[1] A. T. Mahan, *Influence of Sea Power upon History 1660–1783* (8th ed., Boston, 1894), 224.

forced the first company's failure and the trade was open until 1672. The second company lasted only eight years. It was dissolved in 1680 by the Crown, for its inefficient service to Sweden during the war with the Elector of Brandenburg. Sweden at this time was allied with France in the second war of conquest against Holland. The trade was once again free until 1689 when another group of merchants with influence at court secured the monopoly.[2]

Having intimated in its petition that foreigners were enjoying the advantages of the trade in naval stores, the Stockholm Company hit directly at the freight carriers *par excellence*, the Dutch. It sold its commodities indifferently to all nations except to Holland. To that country, the company reserved for itself the right to export, and it sold there at such high prices that the Dutch began to encourage the manufacture of naval stores in Muscovy and Norway. The result was a large quantity of Swedish tar, constantly on hand, which had to be offered at reasonable prices.

The greatest objection of the contemporary English economists of the seventeenth century to the traffic in naval stores was that most of this trade had been carried in the ship-bottoms of other countries. Sir Josiah Child, in his famous mercantilist work, *The New Discourse on Trade*,[3] devoted several pages to a discussion of this phase of the Baltic trade. Two hundred Baltic ships were coming to England and yet not one English ship had been built for the Baltic trade between 1651 and 1668. From 1697 to 1700 only half the Baltic trade was carried in English bottoms, and in the case of Norway, "from Michaelmas [September 29], 1691 to Mich'as 1696, there were entered on the Customs House at London 1,070 foreign ships from those parts and but 39 English."[4]

[2] P. R. O., C. O. 5/3, 37 ii.

[3] Sir Josiah Child, *New Discourse on Trade* (1693 ed.), 83, 93, 94, 143, 157. The first edition appeared in 1692.

[4] R. G. Albion, *Forests and Sea Power* (Cambridge, Massachusetts, 1926), 158. This is a scholarly treatment of the timber problem in supplying naval stores for H. M. Royal Navy.

The interest of the English in securing this trade then, was in the freight as well as in the security of the naval stores supply. Dr. Albion quotes an Englishman as saying, "Freight is the most important raw material which we possess."[5] One writer expressed it, "Losing that trade was putting a number of ships out of employment, and, consequently, paying our neighbors for work, while our people were unemployed."[6] In addition to these considerations, about 1680, a duty of over fifty per cent. had been laid on English woolens by Charles XII and by 1700 English merchants had been virtually forced out of the Swedish dominions by a series of harsh discriminations. Professor Cunningham puts "the cart before the horse" when he states, "Eventually the Government adopted the policy of looking to our plantations in North America for the supplies of timber and naval stores, which were needed to supplement British deficiencies, so that less care was taken to foster the Baltic trade, while a decrease in the demand for English cloth contributed to their decline."[7] In reality, as Professor Albion shows, the Baltic trade, having been closed to the English merchants, brought the unfavorable state of affairs to a head and resulted in decisive action to remedy the situation.[8]

As a result of the Swedish tariff, England exported to Sweden much less than she imported from there, the balance of trade being unfavorable to her to the extent of more than 200,000 pounds annually.[9] From 1697 to 1700, the average adverse balance for England in the trade with Norway and Denmark was 36,672 pounds; with the East Country, 154,539 pounds; and with Russia, 53,368 pounds.[10] This situation, in

[5] *Ibid.*, 158.
[6] Quoted by E. L. Lord, *Industrial Experiments in the British Colonies of North America* (Baltimore, 1898), 56.
[7] William Cunningham, *The Growth of English Industry and Commerce* (Cambridge, England, 1912), II, 236.
[8] Albion, *op. cit.*, 159.
[9] Osgood, *op. cit.*, I, 495.
[10] Macpherson, *op. cit.*, II, 719.

an age controlled by principles of mercantilism, was considered highly undesirable.[11] The Northern War (1700–1721)
between Sweden and Russia moreover changed the situation
for the worse. The frequent Muscovite invasions of Finland,
where the best and largest quantity of naval stores had been
made, caused that province to fall very short in its deliveries.
The limited supply was reflected in the Swedish rise in prices.
The Tar Company's directors also seized the occasion not to
sell tar or pitch for England unless it was loaded in ships
belonging to them and at the freight rates demanded. In the
years 1701 and 1702, the English merchants engaged in that
trade were unable to secure the quantity needed by the Royal
Navy. It was learned, however, to the anger of the British
authorities, that France had received a quantity.[12] No de-
ficiency was more embarrassing to England than this need of
naval stores which a rival power could and did withhold from
her at will.

Early in 1703, the directors of the Swedish Tar Company
announced that in the future they would not sell any more
naval stores at Stockholm, no matter who wanted them or
where they were to go. All tar and pitch was to be sent on the
company's account and was to be purchased from its factors
abroad. The commissioners of the British Navy sent many
complaining letters on the subject to the proper authorities,[13]
but protests and diplomatic representations failed to remove
the determination of the Swedish merchants to sell in London
only.[14] Finding a satisfactory agreement was impossible, the
British envoy at Stockholm, Dr. Robinson, in 1703, suggested
the development of the resources of the colonies in these com-

[11] Cunningham, op. cit., II, 580–2, says that mercantilism aimed primarily at increasing relative national power through a process of maintaining population and the development of English resources, colonial and
domestic, to make England self-sufficient.

[12] P. R. O., C. O. 5/3, 37 ii.

[13] P. R. O., C. O. 388/12, 76.

[14] P. R. O., C. O. 5/3, 37 ii.

modities, even though it might cost a third more to bring them across the ocean. This was in harmony with the principles of mercantilism and had great weight in determining the ministerial policy.[15]

The British government was not entirely ignorant of the resources of America in these respects. The letters of Edward Randolph, Surveyor General of Customs in America, subsequent to 1691, referred to the resources of the colonies in general in pitch, tar, rosin and hemp, as well as in timber for ships. In 1698, he had observed in New York "abundance of tar brought down Hudson river to be sold at New York."[16] Beginning about 1687, the growing interest in the possibility of securing England's badly needed naval stores from her American colonies had been apparent in the effort of a number of merchants to secure charters of incorporation for their production. Efforts were also made by individuals or associations of merchants who wished to undertake their importation under contract with the government. Sir Matthew Dudley made a proposal of this kind in 1688 and again in 1702.[17] Although the organization of a joint stock company was discouraged by governmental requirements,[18] the government itself was not indifferent to the importance of imperial development along these lines.[19]

The Treasury Board and others began to seek comparisons between the cost of the continental supply and the probable

[15] Osgood, *op. cit.*, I, 495; Lord, *op. cit.*, 57 *et seq.* See also the comprehensive Report of Board of Trade to the Queen (Feb. 14, 1710), *C. C. 1710–1711*, 45 *et seq.* Justin Williams, State Teachers College, River Falls, Wisconsin, has pointed out the influence of the crisis in 1702–1703 in determining the bounty policy in his manuscript "English Mercantilism and Carolina Naval Stores, 1705–1776," which it has been the author's privilege to read.

[16] *C. C. 1699*, 106.

[17] *C. C. 1693–1696*, 297; Osgood, *op. cit.*, I, 497.

[18] A statute of 1697 (8 and 9 William III, C. 20 and 32) restricted the number of stockholders in any company to 100 in order to limit speculation in shares. The government itself in making contracts usually required that security should be offered for the performance of the agreement.

[19] *C. C. 1696–1697*, 53; Lord, *op. cit.*, 19.

cost of colonial naval stores. This was particularly true as soon as the first colonial war was under way.[20] Colonel Benjamin Fletcher, Governor of New York, reported in August, 1693, that tar was produced there for 12 pounds per last, that is, per 12 barrels. The Navy Board considered that too high, since they usually contracted for it at the rate of 11 pounds, 12 shillings and 6 pence. They admitted, however, that due to the "loss of three of the Years Tarr Ships and the scarcity of it in Towne," they had to pay fully 13 pounds per last. A report in the Navy Office for January 30, 1694, showed that in 1693, pitch was 50%, tar 100%, and hemp about 30% higher than before the war (1689). References were also made during these years to the probable production of naval stores in the colonies in general, and particularly to the great resources of Carolina in this respect.[21]

On January 22, 1694, the Privy Council ordered that notice be given upon the Exchange that all proposals for the importation of naval stores from the colonies would be considered with a view to give "all fitting encouragement to the undertakers."[22] Lists of specifications with blank columns for the insertion of bids were sent out.[23] The result of this activity was the acceptance by the King's Council, March 29, 1694, of a proposal made by Sir Henry Ashhurst and Sir Stephen Evance, who agreed to import a ship-load of naval stores, including timber from New England, provided the government would pay on sight their bills for cost, interest and other charges. They agreed to permit the King to make whatever allowance for their profit he thought their pains and hazard might deserve.[24] A Navy Board invoice of June 10, 1696, records the fulfillment of the contract.[25]

[20] P. R. O., C. O. 324/5, 327, 331, 340; C. C. *1693–1696*, 226, 243.

[21] C. C. *1693–1696*, 509, 511; Osgood, *op. cit.*, I, 496; Lord, *op. cit.*, 5.

[22] P. R. O., C. O. 324/5, 329; C. C. *1693–1696*, 241.

[23] P. R. O., C. O. 324/5, 339.

[24] P. R. O., C. O. 324/5, 340, 362.

[25] P. R. O., C. O. 324/8, 372.

In that year, at the instigation of the New England colonial agents, the Navy Board sent John Bridger and two others (William Partridge and Benjamin Jackson) to investigate the possibilities of production of ship timber and to instruct the colonists in the making of tar and pitch.[26] The commissioners were not very well qualified; Bridger, an English ship-builder, had had considerable experience and was probably the best-fitted of the three.[27] The New Hampshire assembly was induced to urge the inhabitants to sow hemp as a test of the capacity of their soil to yield that product, but the results were disappointing.[28]

The three commissioners inspected the woods of New England to some extent and experimented with the Finnish method of making tar. Bridger was hopeful enough to state that he could supply the demand of England for these commodities from that section, but his colleague, William Partridge, called attention to the scarcity of labor and resultant high wages as serious obstacles to the enterprise.[29] In their report of their survey of New England with a view to the production of naval stores, Partridge and Jackson in 1699 proposed that the government send over at its expense "a sufficient number of poor families to settle in compact towns in convenient places and that they be encouraged, by giving them small lots of land as aforesaid, who on account of their being transported at the King's charge, may be obliged to attend the service in the woods at a reasonable rate. For doubtless there are many poor families in England, that would be willing to come upon such terms, not being able to trans-

[26] *Acts of Privy Council Col. 1680–1720*, 303; *C. C. 1697–1698*, 537. A Mr. Furzer was also sent but he died in Barbados on the way over. *C. C. 1697–1698*, 241.

[27] Osgood, *op. cit.*, I, 499.

[28] *C. C. 1699*, 9.

[29] *Ibid.*, 10, 428, 449; *C. C. 1700*, 72. When the Board of Trade was reconstituted in 1697, "the obtaining of naval stores from the Plantations [was] particularly committed to their attention." *C. C. 1696–1697*, 542.

port themselves." They recommended this for several reasons. First, the people of New England were not to be diverted from their modes of livelihood to which they had been long accustomed. Then too, the French, making encroachments on New England, were now claiming land to the Kennebec River, the best part of which was most fit for naval stores. It was pointed out that these lands on the Kennebec River were the best in the province for the production of naval stores and the commissioners could "see no reason to doubt" but that the government "may be well supplied and from hence with those commodies [rosin, pitch and tar] in a very short time as with timber."[30] Jackson had gone so far in a previous letter as to suggest that there was a "design to supply the French King with naval stores" from that region.[31]

The specimens of tar and pitch sent to England by the commissioners were pronounced inferior by the dockyard officers,[32] but Lord Bellomont, then Governor of New York, and the Board of Trade were of the opinion that the dockyard officials were merely unduly prejudiced against products from a new source.[33] The Navy Board's criticism of the quality and crude methods of production of naval stores was severe and certainly unfavorable to the policy of encouraging their importation.[34] Incidentally the Board probably secured more profit for themselves by allotting contracts to private parties.[35] Indeed in 1711, the Commissioner of Accounts discovered some frauds in supplying the Navy with naval stores.[36]

Bridger had an enthusiastic ally in Richard Coote, Earl of Bellomont. Bellomont had dwelt in his letters from New York to the Board of Trade on the resources of the colonies in

[30] P. R. O., C. O. 5/908, 213 *et seq.*
[31] P. R. O., C. O. 5/860, 41; *C. C. 1697–1698*, 537.
[32] *C. C. 1700*, 66.
[33] *Ibid.*, 566, 682.
[34] Osgood, *op. cit.*, I, 502; Albion, *op. cit.*, 243, 251.
[35] Albion, *op. cit.*, 247.
[36] Gibson, *Memoirs of Queen Anne* (London, 1729), 102.

general, in timber and other materials for naval stores.[37] Realizing that the chief obstacles were labor supply and high wages, he proposed the employing of independent companies of soldiers, increased to 1,000 men. Additional pay, with land grants and a small subsidy at the end of seven years, would, he thought, be sufficient inducement and would result in protection for the frontier.[38] As no one in authority would assume the responsibility for expending the money required, this particular scheme came to naught.[39] While Bellomont's plan was not considered favorably, the Colonial State Papers show that his letters aroused among the officials a general interest in the subject of colonial naval stores. Between the offices there were numerous exchanges of views on this subject during the few years which followed 1700, and these included many references to the letters of the New York governor.[40] On October, 4, 1700, the Board of Trade made a representation on naval stores to the Privy Council, largely based on Bellomont's letters. Other merchants came forward with proposals to import naval stores from the plantations for the Royal Navy.[41] The commissioners for executing the office of Lord High Admiral reported favoring the encouragement of several proposals ''without exclusion to others who shall desire to follow the like trade.''[42] Indeed, it appears that other forces were working in the same direction to encourage colonial production of naval stores. These were the prospects of another war with France shortly and the monopolistic attitude of the Stockholm Tar Company previously described.

Late in 1702 Bridger sent to England a quantity of hemp and tar which had been produced in New England under his supervision. On February 18, 1703, the officers of the rope-

[37] N. Y. Col. Docs., IV, 501, 587, 707; C. C. 1699, 257 particularly.
[38] Osgood, op. cit., I, 503.
[39] C. C. 1697–1698, viii.
[40] Osgood, op. cit., I, 503.
[41] P. R. O., C. O. 324/8, 272–278.
[42] P. R. O., C. O. 324/5, 335.

yard at Woolwich certified to the quality of these samples.[43] In the same year Thomas Byfield and several associates, who had been in a joint stock company in general trade with Pennsylvania, petitioned for a charter to enable them to import naval stores from Carolina. It was already known that large quantities of pitch and tar were procurable from that region. The law officers and customs board suggested restrictions which were not acceptable to Byfield and his partners, and so the project failed.[44]

During the later months of 1703 under orders from Sir Charles Hedges, one of the principal Secretaries of State, the Board of Trade considered prices at which naval stores could be imported from America and the amount procurable. It had before it proposals to furnish colonial naval stores for the government by Sir Matthew Dudley, Thomas Byfield, John Bridger and others. But since the petitioners balked at providing security for the carrying out of their contracts or required governmental financing as well as a grant of monopoly, the Board decided that the plantations could not furnish all that was needed, and proposed instead that a bounty be given to off-set the high freight.[45] Accordingly in 1704, when the Stockholm Tar Company was enforcing its most obnoxious commercial restrictions against the English, the growing discontent with the unfavorable Baltic balance of trade and the precarious dependence on the Northern Crowns found expression in "An Act for encouraging the Importation of Naval Stores from America." Bounties of 4 pounds per ton for tar and pitch, 3 pounds per ton for "Rosin or Turpentine," 6 pounds per ton for hemp were offered and the Navy was to have preemption of all such articles within twenty days of their arrival in England.[46] This act, put into force in 1705, also

---

[43] P. R. O., C. O. 324/8, 276.

[44] Osgood, *op. cit.*, I, 505; *C. C. 1704–1705*, 393.

[45] P. R. O., C. O. 5/3, 137, 145; C. O. 324/8, 278; Lord, *op. cit.*, 60 *et seq.*

[46] Albion, *op. cit.*, 250; Osgood, *op. cit.*, I, 506.

forebade the cutting of small "Pitch Pine and Tar trees, not being within any Fence or actual Inclosure, under the growth of twelve inches Diameter."[47]

Definitely, then, the policy had become one of active and direct governmental subsidy. The reasons given in the preamble of the act are enlightening. It states that the colonies were protected with the design of being useful to England. The manufacture of naval stores, if encouraged, would employ and increase English shipping, and the naval stores could be exchanged for woolen and other manufactures from England. This exchange would relieve England of purchasing naval stores from foreign countries with money or bullion.[48] The system of bounties was devised to serve a threefold purpose. The development of the outlying parts of the empire would free the mother kingdom from a dangerous dependence upon foreign countries; the energies of the colonists absorbed in producing raw materials would be safely diverted from manufactures;[49] and the Baltic lands would lose a monopoly which enabled them to exploit the market. Mercantilism permeates the policy.

It is also evident that in the early eighteenth century the woolen interests were the interest of the dominant group. Their protection is carefully and continuously provided for. For example, the Board of Trade in its report to the Queen upon the Swedish pitch and tar monopoly on February 14, 1710, recommended the encouragement of naval manufactures in the colonies for the further reason of its "good effect in drawing off your Majesty's subjects inhabiting the Plantations from woollen, linen, and other manufactures."[50] The protection of the woolen interests appears repeatedly. On May 29,

[47] 3 and 4 Anne, C. 10.

[48] Albion, *op. cit.*, Appendix A, also contains this preamble.

[49] An excellent discussion of the manufacturing problem in the northern colonies is Curtis Nettels, "The Menace of Colonial Manufacturing, 1690-1720," in *The New England Quarterly* (April, 1931), IV, 230.

[50] *C. C. 1710-1711*, 48.

1705, the Privy Council considered a report of the Board of Trade which claimed that woolen goods of all sorts from England could find a colonial market "in as much as those people have been induced by proper encouragements to desist from carrying on and working that manufacture in America, and in lieu thereof have applied themselves to the produce of pitch, tar and other naval stores, of which considerable quantities are now arrived, in barter whereof the woollen manufactures of England will be readily accepted of."[51] A report of the customs officials to the Lord High Treasurer, on January 7, 1707, intimated optimistically "they understood that since the inhabitants of New England had applied themselves to the produce of naval stores, the woollen manufacture was greatly interrupted and it would in all probability be wholly left off."[52] They also stated that if the premium were not interrupted, all sorts of naval stores would be imported from New England equal to the best imported from Sweden and Norway.

Caleb Heathcote, a colonial merchant and a member of the New York Council, wrote in 1709 to the Board of Trade, referring to former urgent correspondence, "my proposal was to divert the Americans from going on with their linen and woolen manufactories . . . so far advanced . . . that three-fourths of the linen and woolen, especially of the coarser sort they use, is made among them."[53] His apprehension probably led him into some exaggeration. These reports of colonial manufacturing, however, stimulated the Board of Trade to consider some means of providing the northern colonies with a staple, comparable to tobacco and rice in the southern colonies.

In 1705 Bridger was appointed Surveyor of Woods in the colonies. His commission stated that, "we are desirous that our

[51] *Acts Privy Council Col. Unbound Papers*, 47.
[52] *Cal. Treas. Papers 1702–1707*, 482.
[53] Dixon Ryan Fox, *Caleb Heathcote* (New York, 1926), 155; P. R. O., C. O. 5/1050, 74, 537.

Dominions be furnished with pitch, tar and hemp and other naval stores from the Plantations, and applications [have] been made to us by divers merchants and traders to the Plantations that a person expert in the producing and fabricating such stores should be sent to those parts. . . ."[54] Bridger took up the work in New England, and there inaugurated the "Broad Arrow" policy.[55] He proceeded to his task with a great deal of vigor and for the next few years the Board of Trade had many complaints and reports from the zealous government official.[56] Several reports are especially noteworthy. Bridger wrote on March 9, 1708, "I last summer got the government to print directions and have been in most parts that make tarr in this Province, and have instructed and encouraged them to making of Tarr . . . But they want an example, saying let us see you do what you have directed, and if we see that answers, then we will proceed." On the 13th he further wrote, "New York I know and upon Hudson River there is pitch pine enough to supply England with tar."[57] On July 6th Bridger was "well assured that at New Yorke there would be great quantitys of tar made there, if I was there to instruct them."[58]

In this atmosphere of official encouragement toward the colonial naval stores industry, the small company of 55 immigrants, led by Kocherthal, were sent to New York with the newly-appointed Governor Lovelace, as authorized by the Order in Council, to manufacture naval stores and protect the frontier.[59] Neither preparations nor plans for the manufacture of naval stores were made for this group. These settlers were rather the recipients of a gracious government charity. What

[54] *C. C. 1704–1705*, 732.
[55] The "Broad Arrow" was the system of marking trees as reserved for the use of the Royal Navy.
[56] *C. C. 1706–1708, 1708–1709, passim.*
[57] *Ibid.*, 698, 704.
[58] *C. C. 1708–1709*, 20.
[59] *Cal. Treas. Papers 1708–1714*, 37; *Acts Privy Council Col. 1680–1720*, 553.

was the immediate origin then of the government settlement project in which a large part of the 1709 immigration engaged?

On February 27, 1705, John Chamberlayne, agent for the Massachusetts Bay Colony, and Secretary of the Society for the Propagation of the Gospel, sent to Charles Montagu, Lord Halifax, prominent Whig politician and financier,[60] an interesting proposal from an anonymous friend. It suggested "as an addition and advantage to the Crown of England, That a Colony of Scotchmen may be permitted to take and settle the territory of Canada on such terms as may be honourable for the Crown and Encouraging for the Scotch to undertake such a design." It further proposed that this settlement enter into terms with the British government to supply it with naval stores.[61]

The following quotations from the manuscript give an excellent idea of the conditions which called forth the proposal. "If her Majestie, The parliament of England, and the Gentlemen Com^rs for providing Stores for the Navy were Sensible of the great advantage it would bee to the Crown to take and Settle Nova Scotia and Le Acada with a Colony of Suitable people whose Buiseness should be to provide Stores, it is very probably that the Navie of England might in a little time have large Stores from thence upon Reasonable Terms, which may be provided with the Manufactury of England and spare the vast Sums of Ready money which they are forced to disburse to foreigners for the supply of her Majesties Navie . . . . Naval Stores may be provided by English Manufactures and English Shipping, whereas they are now bought from Sweden, Norway, etc. with money and in foreigne ships . . . the Queens Navy may be furnisht from her own plantations in Time of Warr, when a Dependence upon foreigne States for Stores would bee precarious."

[60] G. F. Russel Barker, "Charles Montagu," in *Dictionary of National Biography* (London, 1894), XXXVIII, 221.

[61] B. M., Egerton MSS. 929, 90 *et seq.*

In the last statement of the proposal the anonymous proposer seems to foretell the government policy, which found expression in the Canadian expeditions of 1709 and 1711.[62] He wrote that "the New England Plantations cannot be effectually Secured till the French are dispossest of Nova Scotia, Le Cada and Canada either by force or by Treaty of peace." The paper, which was endorsed "Proposals for a supply of Naval Store from America," was left in the possession of Halifax and apparently remained fresh in his mind. For directly subjoined to the original proposal is another one without date or signature, but in the writing of Lord Halifax.[63] This document is endorsed at its conclusion, "Proposal for a colony on Kenebeck River," the same location Partridge and Jackson had recommended so highly as a possible source for naval stores. The occasion for his lordship's proposal apparently was the 1709 Palatine immigration,[64] for the formation of a society "for Encouragine and Employing the poor Palatines" was planned. Although no record in the Board of Trade papers indicates its presentation, it may well be that the settlement plan for the manufacture of naval stores was passed on to Sunderland, the Secretary of State, and another prominent Whig. This theory is reasonable, since such a prominent personage as Halifax, a member of the Whig Junto in the time of William III, would be unlikely to work through the ordinary channels of government procedure.

That the plan was seriously considered by Halifax is indicated by the corrections and additions also in his handwriting. The plan was for a private venture into the manufacture of naval stores with some very interesting features. All

[62] See William Thomas Morgan, "Some Attempts at Imperial Co-operation during the Reign of Queen Anne," in *Trans. Royal Hist. Soc.*, 4th series (London, 1927), X, 171–194.

[63] B. M., Egerton MSS. 929, 96; B. M., Add. MSS. 28055, 316.

[64] Halifax was one of the Commissioners for Receiving and Disposing of the money to be collected for the subsistence and settlement of the poor Palatines, Boyer, *Annals*, Appendix III, 40.

persons investing money were to have an allowance of 8 per cent per annum interest. The Palatines, who would be investing their labor, were to have credit given to them proportionable to their ability to work at the rate of 3 shillings per day for an able man. But out of this allowance was to be taken all provisions and necessaries furnished to them. The governor and all other officers belonging to this colony were to be chosen by the members of the society, the votes being proportionable to their holdings of stock. For the more orderly government of the Palatines and for the more easy adjusting of their accounts, the Palatines were to divide themselves into several groups. The chiefs of these groups were to have credit in the books of the company for those under their care, and were to account for them.[65]

For the encouragement of the undertaking the British government was to contract to buy all naval stores that the Society would deliver for seven years, at such rates and prices to be agreed upon with the Lord Treasurer after the next session of Parliament. A very interesting feature was the provision for division of profits. Those arising from the sale of naval stores, cultivating the land, improving the fishery, or any other way, were to be divided annually among the members of the Society in proportion to their stock, acquired by money or labor. This scheme which appears to be so equitable in its treatment of capital and labor, at least in theory, was passed by for a public venture into industry. The plan seems to have foundered on the provision, "That Her Majesty do advance a sum of money by way of Imprest for such stores as they shall deliver." The Ministry probably felt too that were any profits to accrue from the Palatines, such money should go toward repaying the heavy expense defrayed by the government in the transportation and subsistence of those people.

[65] Several features of this plan were taken over and adapted for the government project to manufacture naval stores, described in chapters VI and VII.

At any rate, among the various expedients suggested in the Board of Trade sessions on the subject of the Palatines, the German ministers said that many were of the same country as those gone to New York with Lord Lovelace and had expressed a desire of being transported there.[66] On August 24th the members of the Board, with the Chancellor of the Exchequer among them, considered the settling of some Palatines upon the Hudson River in New York, and agreeing, sent two representatives to the Lord High Treasurer.[67]

The first of these representations of August 30th was concerned with the plans to settle Palatines in Jamaica, but the second was an alternative suggestion that should the Jamaica plan be considered too expensive, then the Palatines might be sent to New York. They declared, "If it be thought advisable that these poor people or any part of them be settled on the Continent of America, We are of opinion that such settlement, especially if made at H. M. charge should be in Provinces under H. M. immediate government, and we know no place so proper as Hudson's River on the Frontier of New York. . . ." The Board proposed the same easy conditions as were accorded the Palatines under Governor Lovelace in 1708. Indeed, the Board suggested further that the Palatines might encourage vine husbandry in Virginia.[68] However, during most of the time from July 30th to November 10th the Board of Trade concerned itself exclusively with the consideration of Jamaica as the better possibility.

But the Commissioners for managing the affairs of the Palatines (appointed as related in Chapter III) had been receiving and sifting many proposals for the settlement of these Germans. As the members of the Ministry were members of the Commission, that body really exercised through them a great deal of authority. So it is with little surprise that we find

[66] B. T. Jour. 1708–1714, 26.
[67] Ibid., 65, 72.
[68] C. C. 1708–1709, 452; Eccles. Rec., III, 1796.

that on November 4th Sunderland's secretary notified the Commissioners of Transport to prepare two men-of-war as convoy for 3,000 Palatines to be sent to New York. The Commissioners for managing the affairs of the Palatines had already entered into a contract with several merchants for transportation of that large group of emigrants.[69] The warships were to be ready by December 15th and orders were issued to Sir John Norris in command of the convoy to "take care of the ships with the Palatines as far as his and their way shall lie together."[70]

Meanwhile the Board of Trade was informed of the action taken. On November 11, 1709, it received a letter from Mr. Pringle, Sunderland's secretary, enclosing a letter "from the Earl of Sunderland to the President of the Council of New York, about making provision for the Palatines that are to be sent thither, desiring the said letter may be sent by the first opportunity, which was done."[71] Sunderland's letter of November 10th informed the President of the Council of New York that 3,000 of the Palatines were to be sent to New York within a month and reassured him that the expenses of the settlement would be taken care of in England.[72] On November 29, 1709, Sunderland referred to the Board of Trade for consideration a proposal from Colonel Robert Hunter, who had just been appointed to the governorship of New York and New Jersey on September 9th,[73] relating to the settlement

[69] P. R. O., Adm. 1/4093, 137.

[70] P. R. O., Adm. 1/432, 518, 519.

[71] B. T. Jour. 1708–1714, 88, also 89. In regard to Pringle, see Luttrell, op. cit., VI, 391. The authorization for this project was the Order in Council of July 29, 1707 issued with reference to the Palatines led by Kocherthal. Acts Privy Council Col. 1680–1720, 553.

[72] C. C. 1708–1709, 515; Eccles. Rec., III, 1808.

[73] P. R. O., S. P. 44/108, 147; N. Y. Col. Docs., V, 91; C. C. 1708–1709, 463; Acts Privy Council Col. 1680–1720, 801. For information on Hunter's life consult C. H. Manners, "Robert Hunter," in Dictionary National Biography (New York, 1891), LXIII, and R. L. Beyer, "Robert Hunter Royal Governor of New York; a Study in Colonial Administration," a manuscript dissertation at the University of Iowa (1929).

PORTRAIT OF CHARLES SPENCER, Earl of Sunderland. *Courtesy of Pennsylvania-German Society.*

of some Palatines at New York. Sunderland requested swift action.[74] As Governor-elect, Hunter had attended a Board meeting with Mr. Champante, New York's colonial agent, just one week before Sunderland's letter to the Board of November 29th. Curiously enough, nothing was then said of his proposal.[75] If Hunter had such a proposal, why was it not made at that time? Sunderland had decided on New York at

[74] *B. T. Jour. 1708–1714*, 98.   [75] *Ibid.*, 93.

least by the 4th of November, and so on the 29th he introduced "Hunter's" proposal to the Board. Sunderland probably
evolved the scheme from previous suggestions and then used
Hunter to sponsor it.

Color is lent to this belief by Hunter's statements on the
30th, "Having Received orders to lay before your Lordships
what I had to offer in relation to the 3,000 Palatines to be sent
to New York, and the imploying of them there:—it being
now resolved that these people shall be Imployed in Naval
Stores, and good assurances had of a Fond requisite for setting
of them to work that way. . . ."[76] Significantly he also stated,
"Kenebeck River in the northern part of New England is
beyond all dispute the most proper place for that purpose.
. . ."[77] The plan of Lord Halifax for a private society to manufacture naval stores was endorsed "Proposal for a colony on
Kenebeck River." There is a strong presumption that this was
the origin of the plan for a settlement to manufacture naval
stores under governmental operation. The Board of Trade
occupied itself solely with "Hunter's" proposal and in three
days had approved the proposition as outlined by him, and
was returning the same to Sunderland in a report.[78] This was
remarkable speed for that time and organization.[79]

Colonel Hunter feared that the Palatines might leave the
naval stores project or be decoyed into the proprietary
colonies. He therefore requested that the Palatines be placed
under contract. On December 20, 1709, the Board of Trade
received, "A letter from the Earl of Sunderland of yesterday's

[76] N. Y. Col. Docs., V, 112; DuPré, Hunter's commissary, in 1711, said,
"Colonel Hunter being upon his departure for his Government did readily
engage in a design to carry and settle at New York . . . ," B. M., Harleian
MSS. 7021, 279.

[77] C. C. 1708–1709, 538.

[78] B. T. Jour. 1708–1714, 98; C. C. 1708–1709, 550.

[79] H. E. Egerton, Short History of British Colonial Policy (London, 1897),
116, gives a good brief account of the poor organization. He calls the results "motion without progress."

date, signifying her Majesty's pleasure that this Board do advise with Mr. Attorney General about drawing up an instrument to be signed by the Palatines to be sent to New York with Colonel Hunter, for holding them to the terms proposed by the representation of this Board of the 5th instant." Colonel Hunter was present and presented the draught of such an instrument. The Board did as it was ordered.[80]

In regard to the Palatine contract, the Ministry evidently felt it must protect itself against the threatening attack of the Tory opposition. Bellomont's scheme for manufacturing naval stores by soldier labor had largely failed because no one would assume the responsibility for paying their passage to New York. The solution of this difficulty was found in Hunter's proposal for the Palatine manufacture of naval stores in New York and the application of the proceeds to the reimbursement of the government for the passage, etc. The plan was in the nature of an indenture, making the Palatines indentured servants until they had repaid the government. The government was to direct this work for repayment and no time limit for the required service was set. In this respect the contract was most unfair; certain it is that none of the other Palatine groups were treated in this manner. By its terms the Palatines could have been kept in perpetual serfdom,[81] by simply charging more for expenses than the naval stores profits could repay.

In this fashion the British authorities embarked on a venture in government manufacture, similar to the *manufactures royales* of France for the production of cannon, arms and other articles. Most of the French governmental industries produced luxury goods, such as lace, tapestry, paper, glassware, etc., for the use of the court at Versailles.[82] But in England the greatest reliance of the government for industrial

[80] *B. T. Jour. 1708–1714*, 106; *C. C. 1708–1709*, 560 *et seq.*

[81] See the contract, *N. Y. Col. Docs.*, V, 121; P. R. O., C. O. 5/1049, 144.

[82] Heckscher, *op. cit.*, 188, 191.

and commercial ventures was the private company.[83] If this governmental industry for the production of naval stores in New York had succeeded, the English might well have followed the example set by the French.[84] This is not assuming that the economic development of the last two hundred years would have been different, for it is difficult to believe that the age of laissez-faire coming in the closing decades of the eighteenth century could have been resisted. Rather, a robust group of government industries might have hampered its whole-hearted acceptance.

The choice of the colony itself was not a bad one, for the New York frontier was woefully weak and a strategic thrust by the French would have cut the English colonies into two. The settlers at Albany had been slightly diminished by the raids of King William's War and worst of all the Five Nations of Indians, which formed the great bulwark against the French, had been reduced from 2,800 to 1,321 fighting men.[85] Of this number, the Senecas, who numbered about half, were said to be in the interest of the French.[86] The French were aware of the point of weakness. Frontenac, governor of Canada in 1697, wrote that the "capture of New York would

[83] *Ibid.*, p. 221. Heckscher points out the total absence among the English of industrial establishments similar to the French. The Palatine naval stores industry was an exception to his generalization. For the English reliance on joint-stock companies, see W. R. Scott, *Constitutions and Finances of English, Scottish and Irish Joint-stock Companies to 1720* (Cambridge, England, 1912), III, *passim*.

[84] A similar proposal for the establishment of a royal town to be called Augusta and to be settled by the some 500 families for the manufacture of naval stores was made by Thomas Coran in 1713 and approved by the Board of Trade. *C. C. 1712–1714*, 222; Miss E. L. Lord discusses the proposal, *op. cit.*, 51 *et seq.*

[85] *C. C. 1697–1698*, xi, 381, not 387 as noted on page xi; *N. Y. Col. Docs.*, III, 817; W. T. Morgan, "The Five Nations and Queen Anne," in *Mississippi Valley Historical Review* (1926), XIII, 173 *et seq.*; A. H. Buffinton, "Albany Policy and Westward Extension," in *Mississippi Valley Historical Review* (1922), VIII, 348.

[86] L. C., S. P. G. MSS. A-5, CLXXVI; N. Y. H. S., Hawks Trans., I, 228; *N. Y. Col. Docs.*, V, 174.

contribute much more to the security of his colony . . . [and] would be much more easily effected than the capture of Boston. . . ."[87] The New York frontier had not been materially strengthened by 1709.[88]

The projected settlement to manufacture naval stores under government operation was a logical culmination of two pressing difficulties or problems. The naval stores problem as outlined immediately above could be solved by manufacturing in the colonies, if cheap labor could be provided. In 1709 the government was urgently looking for means to employ the Palatines who were encamped round about London at heavy expense to the government. The settlement appeared to be an answer to both problems. The scheme itself grew out of a plan, which was originally made for a settlement of Scots, and then revised for a stock company. The Ministry preferred to have the government attempt to regain some of this expenditure in behalf of the Palatines, especially since even under private operations subsidies were demanded. An added incentive was the need for the development in the northern colonies of a staple desirable to England to pay for more English manufactures, for at the turn of the century New York exported to England only 27,567 pounds worth of goods to 356,024 pounds worth for Barbados.[89] Indeed, a most illuminating recent study emphasizes this reason as the decisive consideration in motivating the naval stores policy.[90] Also the New York frontier

[87] P. F. X. de Charlevoix, *History of New France* (London, 1902, J. G. Shea, trans.), V, 70; See also Morgan, "Five Nations," in *loc. cit.*, 169, *et seq.*

[88] Peter Wraxall, *Abridgment of Indian Affairs* (Cambridge, Massachusetts, 1915, C. H. McIlwain, ed.), 61 *et seq.; C. C. 1708-1709*, 316.

[89] H. S. P., B. T. Plant. General, IX, 39. Also see *N. Y. Col. Docs.*, V, 616.

[90] C. P. Nettels, *The Money Supply of the American Colonies before 1720* (Madison, Wisconsin, 1934), 155, 156. Chapter V is particularly effective in its treatment of colonial naval stores as a colonial return for English manufactures. Professor Nettels corrects Beer's interpretation of English policy as mainly concerned with the colonies as a source of raw materials, emphasized instead the prime consideration of markets for English goods. English mercantilism wanted the colonies, as Professor Nettels puts it, to buy English goods, paying with products the English needed, and using English shipping.

had to be strengthened, and too, the colonial authorities were not averse to the Royal colony becoming more profitable. These factors led to the diversion of the Palatines who had emigrated with the intention of settling in Pennsylvania or Carolina.

On January 11, 1710, the Board of Trade received Sunderland's letter inclosing the Queen's approval of the proposal to settle the Palatines in New York.[91] On the 26th additional instructions, relating to the Palatine settlement, were sent to Colonel Hunter.[92] Preparations were rapidly pushed forward, though much more slowly than Governor Hunter anticipated, for as will presently appear he did not sail as early in 1710 as he had expected.

[91] *B. T. Jour. 1708–1714*, 111.

[92] *C. C. 1710–1711*, 23; *N. Y. Col. Docs.*, V, 160; P. R. O., C. O. 5/1231, 3.

CHAPTER VI. A GOVERNMENT REDEMPTIONER SYSTEM

THE PREPARATIONS for the largest single emigration to America in the colonial period[1] were pushed forward with all possible speed. As related in the preceding chapter, Colonel Hunter personally gave the Board of Trade an account of the New York naval stores proposal on November 30th. At the same time he suggested the various requisites for the settlement. Four persons sufficiently instructed in the methods of making naval stores were to be sent along to teach the trade and supervise the work. Commissaries, clerks of stores, and other officers with sufficient funds would be needed. A number of cauldrons and other tar-making necessaries would have to be supplied in England.

As the housing situation in New York appeared to be very uncertain and some time would elapse before the Palatines could build huts for themselves, it was suggested that at least 600 tents be sent. Since the prople were "to be planted on the Frontiers it will be absolutely necessary they be armed with 600 Firelocks & Bayonetts at least, from Her Majesty's Stores here, and a proportionable quantity of powder and shott . . . ."[2] A quantity of hemp seed was also to be taken along to provide immediate work in its sowing.

The next day, December 1st, Hunter again appeared before the Board with several problems on the proposed settlement. On what lands were the Palatines to be planted? In what manner were the lands to be granted to them, and in what proportions and under what reservations? Would it not be advisable that the Palatines "be servants to the Crown for a

---

[1] Karl Frederick Geiser, *Redemptioners and Indentured Servants in the Colony and Commonwealth of Pennsylvania* (New Haven, 1901), 29.

[2] *N. Y. Col. Docs.*, V, 113.

certain Term, or at least 'till they have repaid the Expences the Crown is at in setting them to work, and subsisting them. . . ?''[3] The governor estimated that twelve iron kettles, twelve ladles and tunnels to each kettle, would be sufficient for the tar-making. As for instructors in the trade, he remarked, ''There being no great Mystery in these manufactures, I believe Mr. Bridger with such as he can bring along with him, if ordered will be sufficient to instruct them.'' The plan in simple form provided that the government was to transport and settle the Palatines in New York at its own expense. The Palatines were to make naval stores for the government in return for the money spent in their behalf.

In their report of December 5th on Hunter's proposal, the Board of Trade appeared very optimistic. They observed, ''that one man may make by his own labour six tunns[4] of these [naval] Stores in a Year; and we have been informed that a number of men assisting each other may in proportion make double that quantity; so that supposing 600 men be imployed in this work, they make produce 7000 Tuns of these goods a year, and if in time a greater quantity should be made there, than shall be consumed in your Majesty's Dominions, We hope the overplus may turn to a very beneficial Trade with Spain & Portugal.''[5]

They expected the government premium of four pounds per ton of tar imported from the colonies would cover the freight charge. The Commissioners sent over by the Navy Board in 1696 had reported that tar could be secured in New England at five pounds a ton. The Board therefore held that the tar to be manufactured by the Palatines might be sold as cheaply as that from the northern countries. Nevertheless, they concluded, ''should the American Tarr be something Dearer, Yet it is the Interest of this Kingdom to have the same paid for in Woollen and other Manufactures from hence;

[3] *Ibid.*, 114; *C. C. 1708–1709*, 540.
[4] A tun contained eight barrels.
[5] *Doc. Hist.*, III, 640.

whereas that from the Northern Crowns is bought with ready money." The Board of Trade proposed that Mr. Bridger, Surveyor-General of Her Majesty's woods in America and at that time in New England for a period of four years, be ordered to repair to New York with three or four persons skilled in manufacturing naval stores. Annual salaries of 200 pounds in New York money were to be allowed to each. The officials, such as commissaries and clerks as outlined by Hunter, were also approved. To these the Board added a few others. Supervisors were to live among the Palatines, "to over-see and keep them at Work."[6]

To handle the London end of the venture, an agent or factor was to be appointed by the government. His duties were to remit "such summs of money as your Majesty shall from time to time judge proper to be remitted to New York" for subsistence and to receive and sell all naval stores consigned to him on account of the Palatines. The factor was then to dispose of the naval stores to the Commissioners of the Navy at the market price, or to other merchants if necessary. If purchased for the Navy the bills were to be made out in the usual manner. The factor was to be under the government's immediate orders, receiving the usual factorage fees for his services. After all expenses had been deducted, the profits were to be taken by the government as payment of the money expended in settling the Palatines in New York.[7]

In their report the Board of Trade also tried to answer two of the questions propounded by Hunter. The question as to whether it would not be advisable to make the Palatines "servants to the Crown for a certain Term" was not mentioned. As to the manner and terms of settlement, the Board thought that the Palatines might be planted in a body or in different settlements wherever the governor found it most proper. The

[6] N. Y. Col. Docs., V, 119. See Doc. Hist., III, 561 for a more detailed plan of Governor Hunter of a later date.

[7] Ibid., 120; Doc. Hist., III, 642.

governor was to grant without fee or reward forty acres per person to each family, after they had "repaid by the produce of their labour" the expenses of their settlement. The usual quit-rents were to commence and be payable seven years after the said grants.[8] The Board advised that the Palatines be "Encouraged to settle and work in partnership, that is 5 or more families to unite and Work in Common."

In reply to the question as to the lands on which to settle the Palatines, the Board of Trade suggested the large tracts of land recently returned to the Crown, being the extravagant grants vacated by an Order in Council on June 26, 1708.[9] These lands in the Mohawk and Hudson Valleys of New York had been granted ten years earlier by Governor Fletcher, just before he had been replaced, to a number of colonial gentlemen, including Nicholas Bayard, Godfrey Dellius, Captain Evans and Caleb Heathcote,[10] whose brother was governor of the Bank of England.

When late in the seventeenth century Lord Bellomont became governor of New York, he favored another faction of the landowning class.[11] On March 2, 1699, the New York assembly passed an "Act for vacating, breaking and annulling several Extravagant Grants of land made by Colonel Benjamin Fletcher, late Governor of the Province." Upon being referred to the colonial authorities in England, no immediate action was taken on the act, this being the usual slow manner of procedure.[12] When Viscount Cornbury became governor in 1702 the assembly suffered either a change of heart or political complexion, for on November 27th they passed an act, repealing the above act together with several others. This likewise received no attention in England until July 29, 1707, when a Committee of the Privy Council recommended the approval

[8] *Doc. Hist.*, III, 639.
[9] *Eccles. Rec.*, III, 1812; *N. Y. Col. Docs.*, V, 117.
[10] *N. Y. Col. Docs.*, V, 117; *Eccles. Rec.*, III, 1685.
[11] *C. C. 1698*, 914.
[12] *Ibid.*, 483.

of the first act and the disallowance of the later one.[13] The reasons why the Committee considered it "absolutely necessary the said grants be vacated" are indicative of the more active colonial policy and the awakened interest in the colonies as a source of naval stores. "A strong argument urged for vacating these grants is, that great Quantities of Masts and other timber fit for Naval Stores, grow upon the lands thus granted away, which cannot be Regained to the Benefit of the Crown, till the Grants are vacated." That neither satisfactory rents nor other obligations to cultivate and improve the lands had been secured were other objections. Other reasons offered in justification of the annulment were the appeasement of the just claims of the Indians and the encouragement of further settlement.

Consequently, a new policy was proposed of granting not more than 2,000 acres to any one person, and at an annual quit-rent of two shillings and six pence for every hundred acres. At least three acres for every fifty acres taken up had to be settled or cultivated within three years under penalty of forfeiture of the grant.[14] The vacating of the "Extravagant Grants" became a new threat to the land-owning class in colonial New York. Most of them had received their grants under similar conditions and circumstances. It was objected in the argument before the Board of Trade, that such proceedings "would render the Properties of all lands uncertain and precarious." Indeed such procedure might conceivably have bolstered up the governor's attempts to maintain the prerogative of the Crown. It was argued in 1707, "That if the power of Revoking grants be left to a Governor, Council and Assembly, the Governor may have the choice of so many of the Council, and have such an influence in having his own

---

[13] *Acts Privy Council Col. 1680–1720*, 553. The annulment of the extravagant grants was approved in the same Order in Council which authorized the settlement of Kocherthal's Palatines in the colony of New York at public expense.

[14] *C. C. 1706–1708*, 513.

Creatures returned to be of the Assembly, that he may at any time Act arbitrarily & unjustly in such Revocations." Of course, the real obstacle to such a development was the impossibility of securing an assembly in New York opposing its own class interests, that of the landed aristocracy. The larger landowners were acutely aware of the danger and their efforts to protect their holdings can be observed in Livingston's case and in the passage of the Naturalization Act of 1715, as will appear later in our story.

These "Extravagant Grants" had been the only land available in New York upon which to settle the new Palatine immigrants of 1708; for in that year, in its report on the settlement of Kocherthal's party, described in Chapter II, the Board of Trade urged the confirmation of the Vacating Act for that purpose.[15] That the Board should suggest these lands again for Hunter's scheme was to be expected. The lands in the Mohawk Valley and those in Schoharie were known to have an obstacle for transportation in the waterfalls at Cohoes. This defect was not considered any hindrance to settling the Palatines there, should there be no other more convenient site in the province. The selection of the site was distinctly left in the hands of the governor, Colonel Hunter.[16]

The Board of Trade, having made no recommendation as to making the Palatines covenanted servants, was to hear further from Colonel Hunter on the subject. On December 19th, Secretary Sunderland wrote to the Board that Hunter had proposed a contract to hold the Palatines "from falling off from the employment designed for them, or being decoy'd into Proprietary Governments."[17] At the same time the Board received a draft of such a covenant from Hunter. This was referred to the Attorney-General, James Montague, for his

[15] *Acts Privy Council Col. 1680–1720*, II, 552.

[16] *N. Y. Col. Docs.*, V, 118. See pictures of Cohoes Falls, *Doc. Hist.*, III, 638.

[17] H. S. P., Jour. B. T., XXI, 315; P. R. O., S. P. 44/108, 186.

opinion,[18] and on the 21st he returned it with a few corrections and additions.[19] This covenant was executed at Plymouth a few days before the Palatines sailed from England.[20]

The covenant stated that in consideration of the large sums advanced by the government "toward the transporting, maintaining and settling" of the Palatines for their employment in the production of naval stores, the Palatines for themselves, their "heirs executors and administrators" contracted to settle on lands assigned to them by the government and continue resident upon those lands. On no account or manner of pretense were the Palatines to quit or desert without leave of the governor. They agreed to employ their utmost power and that of their respective families in the "production and manufacturing of all manner of naval stores." It was further agreed "that as soon as we shall have made good and repaid to her Majesty, her heirs and successors, out of the produce of our labors in the manufactures we are employed in, the full sum or sums of money in which we already are or shall become indebted to her Majesty," the governor shall grant "40 acres to each person free from all taxes, quit-rents or other manner of services for seven years."

No time limit to the length of service was specified, but it is apparent that these Palatines were indentured servants of the British government and that they were to be employed in manufacturing naval stores until the profits had not only paid their expenses, but also repaid the Queen for their transportation and settlement. The Palatines seriously impaired their liberty of action, for they entered into contract to obey

[18] *C. C. 1708–1709*, 561; *B. T. Jour. 1708–1714*, 107.

[19] P. R. O., C. O. 5/1049, 144; B. M., Harleian MSS. 7021, 279; in *Eccles. Rec.*, III, 1814, the parentheses are the Attorney-General's additions. The deletions he made have been omitted. Line seventeen on page 1815 should have parentheses before "without leave" and after "so doing and;" *N. Y. Col. Docs.*, V, 121 was taken from an Entry Book. It gives the additions of the Attorney-General in italics but carries the words deleted without any indication, as though they were parts of the document.

[20] B. M., Harleian MSS. 7021, 284.

the governor and work for the government until it was repaid. This is a unique example of a governmental redemptioner migration.

On the 11th of December, Hunter pressed Secretary Sunderland to secure for the use of the Palatines the 600 tents and 600 firelocks with bayonets and ammunition necessary "upon account of their being to be planted on the Frontiers, where they will be much exposed if unarmed." The next day Sunderland wrote to the Duke of Marlborough, the Master-General of Ordnance, requesting him at the Queen's command to secure an estimate of the cost from the Board of Ordnance. Perhaps the fact that he was the Duke's son-in-law permitted his personal desires being stated for he wrote in addition to the Queen's commands, "These poor people being now upon their Departure it is necessary no time should be lost, wherefore I desire your Grace will direct this Acct. to be sent as soon as may be."[21] On the 17th, the Board of Ordnance wrote to the Duke that at Sunderland's request, they had made an estimate of the supplies. The cost was 1,479 pounds and 12 shillings sterling. They stated at the same time that they had not yet received the 913 pounds due for the loss and damage of the tents for the Palatines encamped on Blackheath and Camberwell.[22] In fact, 9,348 pounds worth of supplies had been laid out by the Ordnance department without parliamentary provision for the same. The equipment was ordered for the Palatines.[23]

The Society for the Propagation of the Gospel in Foreign Parts, a voluntary missionary organization, had troubled itself with finding a suitable minister for the Palatines.[24] The Bishop of London had concluded a letter of December 9th to Mr. Chamberlaine, the Secretary of the Society, "Dutch Minister I have none for the Palatines, neither know I where

[21] P. R. O., S. P. 44/108, 177, 222.
[22] P. R. O., S. P. 44/108, 185.
[23] Cal. Treas. Papers 1708–1714, 148.
[24] Eccles. Rec., III, 1718, 1811.

to find any.''[25] Several of the Palatines petitioned the Society to retain one John Frederick Haeger in this capacity.[26] Upon Reverend Haeger's agreeing to Anglican ordination by the Bishop of London, he was appointed by the Society at an annual salary of fifty pounds, with the usual fifteen pounds in addition, allowed him for books.[27] The Society for the Propagation of the Gospel was interested in the spread of the Anglican faith, and in this respect, it was an important factor in the attempts to assimilate the Germans.

On December 21st, Hunter made arrangements with the Lord Treasurer for the remittance to New York of 8,000 pounds sterling for the Palatine settlement.[28] John Raynor, Attorney-General to New York, requested that the arrears of his salary be paid out of the quit-rent fund, since he would suffer a great loss in fees due to the grants of land to be made to the Palatines without fees.[29]

Meanwhile, Mr. Henry Bendysh, who acted as secretary to the Commissioners for Collecting for and Settling of the Palatines,[30] had made the necessary arrangements for transportation, as related in Chapter V. On December 17th, he informed Godolphin, the Lord High Treasurer, that he had executed charter-parties with commanders and owners of ships to carry about 3,300 Palatines to New York at five pounds, ten shillings per head.[31] This was a low rate, indeed, since Luttrell had noted that transportation to Carolina was above ten pounds,[32] and Böhme had specified seven pounds as the price of passage to Pennsylvania or Carolina.[33] The charges

[25] Society for the Propagation of the Gospel in Foreign Parts MS., 82, hereafter cited as S. P. G. MSS.

[26] *Eccles. Rec.*, III, 1813.

[27] *Ibid.*, 1817.

[28] *Cal. Treas. Papers 1708–1714*, 150.

[29] *C. C. 1710–1711*, 37.

[30] For his services Bendysh later received 1,000 pounds. *Cal. Treas. Papers 1714–1719*, 114.

[31] *Ibid.*, *1708–1714*, 149.

[32] Luttrell, *op. cit.*, VI, 465.   [33] *Das verlangte nicht erlangte Canaan*, 11.

for transportation were to amount to between 18,000 and 19,000 pounds sterling besides demurrage, a compensation for delay above the time agreed upon.[34] The captains and their owners agreed to have their ships ready to take the Palatines and their goods on board between the 25th and 29th of December. They agreed to be at the buoy of the Nore about fifty miles from London on or before the 2nd of January, wind and weather permitting. Mr. Bendysh on his part agreed to have a convoy at that time and place to proceed "without Stopping at any Port or Place in England." The demurrage due, upon failure to observe these conditions, was at the rate of eleven shillings and six pence per ton per month for the ships, and six pence per day for each Palatine.[35]

The ten ships were in the Thames at the specified time. The Palatines were taken on board, but when seven of the ten ships reached the Nore on the 2nd of January, the convoy refused sailing orders.[36] For the delay, which ensued the ship-owners and commanders received demurrage and the total cost of the transportation to New York reached the sum of 25,854 pounds, 15 shillings and 8 pence sterling. This sum was paid by the end of October, 1710.[37] On January 26, 1710, Sunderland sent Hunter "Additional Instructions," which empowered him to carry out the project to manufacture naval stores in accordance with the Board of Trade representation to the Queen of the previous December 5th.[38]

Accounts have varied as to the time Hunter sailed for New York. Conrad Weiser wrote in his Journal, "About Christmas Day we embarked. . . ."[39] Luttrell noted in his diary on December 29, 1709, "Colonel Hunter designs, next

[34] *Cal. Treas. Papers 1708–1714*, 149.

[35] P. R. O., C. O., Admiralty Class 1/4283.

[36] *Ibid.*

[37] *Cal. Treas. Papers 1708–1714*, 148, 206.

[38] P. R. O., C. O. 5/1231, 3; *N. Y. Col. Docs.*, V, 160.

[39] Weiser Diary, in *Americana* (New York, September, 1913), VIII, 797; also in *Olde Ulster* (Kingston, New York, 1906), II, 203.

PORTRAIT OF GOVERNOR ROBERT HUNTER, the authenticity of which has been
questioned. No other portrait of him is extant.
Courtesy of the New York Public Library.

week to embark for his government at New York, and most of the Palatines remaining here goe with him to people that colony."[40] Cobb argued in his account that the departure took place toward the end of January, 1710.[41] Diffenderffer, writing for the Pennsylvania German Society, said they sailed in March.[42] The *London Gazette* noted, April 7, 1710, that ten ships were ready to sail with Palatines from Portsmouth for New York under convoy.[43] In a report to Robert Harley, then Secretary of State, June 18, 1711, James DuPré, commissary at New York for Hunter and who sailed originally with Hunter, stated that all the Palatines embarked in December, 1709, but did not start until April 10, 1710.[44] The demands for demurrage made by the owners of the vessels also show that the fleet did not finally leave Plymouth, further west along the southern coast of England, until April 10th.[45] The Palatine transports had moved along the coast of England, touching Portsmouth and Plymouth during the early months of 1710 and finally sailed on April 10th. The Palatine accounts of a long voyage may be reconciled to this revision of the date. They were on board ship for six long months and the sufferings of the Palatines were terrible, for misery seems long in duration. Indeed, one of the Palatine ships had to return to port and sailed again later.[46]

Probably because of the low transportation rate, the people were closely packed in the ships. Many of them suffered from the foul odor and vermin; some below deck could neither get fresh air nor see the light of day. Under such conditions the

[40] Luttrell, *op. cit.*, VI, 529.

[41] Sanford Hoadley Cobb, *The Story of the Palatines* (New York, 1897), 125; Osgood, *op. cit.*, I, 513 also accepted this time.

[42] Diffenderffer, *op. cit.*, 319.

[43] *London Gazette*, No. 4676.

[44] B. M., Harleian MSS. 7021, 280.

[45] P. R. O., Admiralty Class 1/4283. A. L. Cross, *Anglican Episcopate and the American Colonies* (New York, 1902), 91 has a typographical error, 1713 should read 1710.

[46] The *Berkley Castle*, N. Y. Col. Docs., V, 166.

younger children died in great numbers. The last letters before sailing, written at Portsmouth during April, reported eighty deaths in one ship and one hundred sick in another.[47] Good healthy food was not provided and its lack no doubt added to the general unhealthy conditions. Soon the fleet was ravaged by ship-fever. Modern science has traced this malady, now known as typhus and recognized as more deadly than typhoid,[48] to such carriers as infected fleas and body lice. Crowded in those foul holds with little or no provision for the most elementary sanitation, the immigrants were decimated by this dread disease. From their misery indeed, the disease took on a rather sad distinction, since it became known to the doctors of that day as the "Palatine fever."[49] A petition made later in New York by one Thomas Benson, a surgeon, for reimbursement for medicine stated that on his ship 330 persons had been sick at one time.[50] How welcome must the call of land in sight have sounded to these early immigrants!

The first ship to arrive was the *Lyon*, which touched New York on June 13, 1710, Governor Hunter's ship and several others following the next day.[51] One, the *Herbert*, was wrecked on the east end of Long Island on July 7th,[52] and the last did not arrive until August 2nd.[53] A letter from Hunter to Lord Godolphin, the Lord Treasurer, and dated October 24, 1710, stated that of the 2,814 Palatines who had started, 446 had

---

[47] *Das verlangte nicht erlangte Canaan*, 9; Emil Heuser, *Pennsylvanien im 17 Jahrhundert* (Neustadt, 1910), 66.

[48] Watson Davis, "Typhus in the New World," in *Current History*, XXXIV, 94; "Diary of a Voyage from Rotterdam to Philadelphia in 1728," in *Pa. Ger. Soc. Proc.*, XIX, 17.

[49] A. Matthews, "The Word 'Palatine' in America," in *Nation* (Cambridge, Massachusetts, 1904), LXXVIII, 125.

[50] *Doc. Hist.*, III, 558, December 26, 1710. This document is now missing from the Albany Archives. *Cal. N. Y. Hist. MSS. Eng. 1664-1776* (Albany, 1866), II, 375.

[51] *N. Y. Col. Docs.*, V, 551; *B. T. Jour. 1708-1714*, 178.

[52] *Doc. Hist.*, III, 559; *N. Y. Col. Docs.*, V, 166.

[53] B. M., Harleian MSS. 7021, 280; *Doc. Hist.*, III, 559.

died before the end of July. Thirty little newcomers joined on the way over,[54] restoring a portion of the loss.

The arrival of nearly 2,500 immigrants, rumored to be laden with disease, was no small matter to the New York city of the second decade of the eighteenth century. A census was taken June 5, 1712, and showed 4,846 free inhabitants and 970 slaves in the city.[55] No wonder the New York City Council protested the reception of any Palatines within the city, saying it would endanger the health of the inhabitants and deter the country people from coming in as usual.[56] The Palatines were therefore landed and encamped on Nutten Island, now known as Governor's Island, which apparently preceded Ellis Island as an immigrant station or "gateway to America." Three doctors were to report upon the condition of their health. On June 16, 1710, a scheme for governing these Palatines was hastily formulated. The Council also issued a proclamation to prevent extortionate prices of bread and provisions on account of their presence.[57]

In their tents on Governor's Island, the Palatines were in a miserable condition. Typhus was still ravaging them.[58] These weakened people, lamenting the loss of their relatives, were forced to settle down and care for the sick and dying. Two doctors, John Christopher Kurtz and John Philips Rüger, were in constant attendance.[59] Hunter reported to London on July 24th that about 470 Palatines had died on the

[54] B. M., Add. MSS. 17677 DDD, 624. In 1720, however, the Palatines themselves estimated that about 4,000 were sent over and 1,700 died on board, or at their landing. See their petition to the Board of Trade, *N. Y. Col. Docs.*, V, 553. The statement is an estimate made ten years later and hence is exaggerated.

[55] N. Y. Col. MSS., LVII, 180.

[56] *Minutes of the Common Council of City of New York* (New York, 1905), II, 408; *Doc. Hist.*, III, 552.

[57] *Doc. Hist.*, III, 552, 554 *et seq*.

[58] *C. C. 1710–1711*, 119; L. C., S. P. G. MSS. A-6, XLIV.

[59] N. Y. Col. MSS., LIV, 192; *Cal. N. Y. Hist. MSS. Eng. 1664–1776*, II, 373.

voyage and during the first month in New York.[60] The emigrants were slow in recovering their health after their wretched passage from England. Peter Willemse Romers, a coffin-maker, was the chief benefactor, for in 1711 he petitioned for 59 pounds, 6 shillings sterling in payment for 250 coffins used for the burial of Palatines during the summer of 1710.[61]

Many children were left orphans. The problem of caring for them was solved by apprenticing them. According to the records seventy-four were apprenticed by Hunter from 1710–1714,[62] among them being John Peter Zenger, who later became famous in American history for his fight for freedom of the Press. Unfortunately, Hunter did not stop with orphans; he also apprenticed children whose parents were still living, and in this way separated families. John Conrad Weiser lost a son, George Frederick, in this manner and there were other cases, causing many a heartache. The petition of the Palatines of 1720 lists this as one of their chief grievances.[63]

Meanwhile, Hunter was attempting to locate a suitable tract for the settlement of the Palatines. Four tracts in New York, part of the vacated "Extravagant Grants," had been considered as possibilities while the Palatines were still in England. One was on the Mohawk River above Little Falls, fifty miles long by four miles wide (around Herkimer and German Flats); another, between twenty-four and thirty miles in length on the Schoharie River; a third, on the east side of the Hudson River, twelve miles long by seventy miles wide. A fourth was also considered, on the west side twenty miles by forty miles long. When the Board of Trade recommended to the Council the settlement of Kocherthal's party in New York in 1708, it pointed out that these lands would be at the

[60] N. Y. Col. Docs., V, 167; Doc. Hist., III, 559.

[61] Doc. Hist., III, 568.

[62] Ibid., 553, 566.

[63] Eccles. Rec., III, 2168; Doc. Hist., III, 425.

disposal of the government for that purpose, if it approved the New York law invalidating those "extravagant grants" made by Colonel Fletcher as suggested by the Board on July 29, 1707.[64] Accordingly, on June 26, 1708, the Council approved the New York act annulling those grants,[65] and consequently these lands were available for settlement by the Palatines. No grant was specifically made in the contract signed by the Germans. On the contrary, the matter was left to the discretion of the governor.

Concerning one of the tracts, the Schoharie grant, which Governor Fletcher had given to Colonel Bayard, an interesting legend arose. A number of the Palatines later became dissatisfied with their situation. Some of them realized that they were to be exploited, and probably in the discussion among themselves in justification of their opposition, the story of the Indian grant of Schoharie took shape. Years after the New York troubles, Conrad Weiser wrote in his Journal, "For the Indian deputies who were in England at the time the German people were lying in tents on the Black moor [Blackheath] had made a present to Queen Anne of this Schochary that she might settle these people upon it."[66] The elements of truth in the legend are easily recognized. The Schoharie lands had been one of the four tracts mentioned by the Board of Trade as possible sites for the naval stores experiment with German labor. Five Indians had been taken to England in 1710 by Peter Schuyler, Mayor of Albany, as a publicity scheme to interest the government in another attempt to take Canada after the failure of 1709. The references to both these facts apparently became confused in the heated Palatine discussions, and finally, they fused into several sentimental and touching accounts of the pity aroused in the savage breast by the

[64] *Doc. Hist.*, III, 542; *Eccles. Rec.*, III, 1703.

[65] *N. Y. Col. Docs.*, V, 48, 141.

[66] Weiser Diary, in *loc. cit.*, 797. The Palatine petition to the Board of Trade on August 20, 1720 quoted the Indians as saying that they had given the land to Queen Anne for the Palatines. *Eccles. Rec.*, III, 2169.

wretched condition of the Palatines on Blackheath, as related in later histories.[67]

Unfortunately for the legend, the New York Palatines boarded their transports between December 25th and 29th, 1709. From then on until April 10, 1710, the ships were moving along the southern coast of England or awaiting convoy there.[68] The five "Indian Sachems" sailed from Boston early in February, 1710, and did not arrive in London until April, where they had an audience with the Queen on the 17th.[69] The Queen and all England had been imposed upon, for "Hendrick the great prince that was so honored in England cannot command ten men, the other three were not sachems."[70] Although the Five Nations thanked Governor Hunter for the fine treatment accorded the "natives of the Mohogs' nation,"[71] the latter were disgraced and never again were they admitted to Indian Councils.[72]

Cobb, the most extensive writer on the Palatines, has attempted to prove this legend by Governor Hunter's statement to the Board that he had sent men to "survey the land on the Mohaques River, particularly the Skohare, to which the Indians have no pretence."[73] The next four words, "being Colonel Bayard's Grant,"[74] not considered by Mr. Cobb,

[67] Cobb., op. cit., 107; Kapp, Die Deutschen, I, 24; Löher, op. cit., 43; M. R. Diefendorf, The Historic Mohawk (New York, 1910), 59; W. W. Ellsworth, "The Palatines in the Mohawk Valley," in N. Y. Hist. Assoc. Proc. (1915), XIV, 295.

[68] P. R. O., Admiralty Class 1/4283.

[69] P. R. O., C. O. 5/1049, 157; Luttrell, op. cit., VI, 571; C. C. 1710–1711, 40, 78; Morgan, "The Five Nations and Queen Anne," in Loc. cit., XIII, 179 et seq.

[70] L. C., S. P. G. MSS. A-5, CLXXVI; N. Y. H. S., Hawks Trans. of S. P. G. MSS., I, 228; Doc. Hist., III, 899.

[71] C. C. 1710–1711, 495. Hunter called them in 1713 "men of no consideration or rather the most obscure amongst them." C. C. 1712–1714, 158.

[72] "Colden Letters," in N. Y. Hist. Soc. Coll. (1868), 200.

[73] Cobb., op. cit., 132.

[74] N. Y. Col. Docs., V, 167.

indicate why Hunter felt that the Indians had no claim to Schoharie, but they were not convenient to the historian's thesis. Bayard's grant was part of the so-called "extravagant grants" of Governor Fletcher, which were annulled by the New York assembly with the approval of the English government as mentioned before.

Governor Hunter himself was mistaken however, in his opinion about the Indians, for they at first refused to allow the men to survey the land.[75] This is not surprising, for the Board of Trade had mentioned in its recommendation of Schoharie on December 5, 1709, that the land was "claimed by the Mohaques, but that claim may be satisfied on very easy terms."[76] Hunter investigated their claims and found at Albany instructions to the authorities to restore their right and title to the lands in question. Hunter therefore acknowledged their claim.[77] In a conference with Hunter at Albany on August 22, 1710, the Indian Hendrick, apparently the only genuine sachem on the trip to England, said, "We are told that the great queen of Great Brittain had sent a considerable number of People with your Ex^{cy} to setle upon the land called Skohere, which was a great surprise to us and we were much Disatisfyd at the news, in Regard the Land belongs to us. . . . Nevertheless since Your Excell^{cy} has been pleased to desire the said land for christian settlements, we are willing and do now Surrender . . . to the Queen . . . for Ever all that tract of Land Called Skohere. . . ."[78] In reply, Governor Hunter accepted the land in the Queen's name, promising them a suitable reward.

The Indian gift of Schoharie was made then at Fort

[75] *Doc. Hist.*, III, 560.

[76] P. R. O., C. O. 5/1121, 472; *N. Y. Col. Docs.*, V, 117.

[77] *C. C. 1710–1711*, 223.

[78] N. Y. H. S., Misc. Coll. of MS. on Indian Affairs. Livingston, as Commissioner of Indian Affairs, omitted the report of this conference in sending the series to England, *C. C. 1710–1711*, 834. Hunter however told the Board of Trade, *Ibid.*, 223.

Albany, August 22, 1710, to the Queen for Christian settlements, referring apparently to the Palatines. It was given to please Governor Hunter, and perhaps in fear that he would take it anyway. Certainly the gift was not inspired by the wretchedness of the Palatine immigrants, and there existed no obligation on the part of Governor Hunter to settle the Palatines there. He had no orders from the Queen to do so. Schoharie was only one of several tracts suggested as available because of the annullment of the "extravagant grants," "In case there be not found an opportunity of doing it more conveniently in some other part of that Province."

Bridger, who was to instruct the Palatines in tar-making, was sent to judge the possibilities of Schoharie. He reported it as good land but in no wise fit for the object in hand, that of making naval stores, as there was no pitch pine there.[79] The distance from New York City was also considered, but the real conflict seemed to have been in choosing between good farm land for the Palatines or proximity to the necessary pine trees to make naval stores.[80] The specific purpose of the settlement was to make naval stores and Hunter was to select the spot of settlement according to the contract; while he realized the difficulties of securing good farm land adjacent to pine lands "being good for nothing," he was determined to "accomplish the great Design," and for that the pine trees were the prime requisites.

One writer has said it was possible that Bridger may have spoken in the interest of Robert Livingston, a known specu-

[79] C. C. 1710–1711, 253; N. Y. Col. Docs., V, 168.

[80] Ibid., 140; Osgood, op. cit., I, 499, states, "The problem was a complex one for the conditions affecting the production of hemp differed wholly from those which related to pitch and tar. . . ." This same incompatability applied to all land necessary for other farm products of consequence. H. D. House, New York State Botanist, in a letter to the author on March 26, 1927, stated, "The pitch pine . . . undoubtedly formed at that time a major portion of the forest upon the sandy and gravelly areas, and in general upon the areas of poor, sterile, or rocky soil. . . ."

lator,[81] who sold the land used for the Palatine settlement to Hunter. Such a charge, in relation to the selection of the site of settlement, supposes that Bridger reported falsely in regard to the absence of pitch pine in Schoharie. Color is lent to this version by a statement in 1707 of Mr. Champante, the New York colonial agent. He was arguing for the annulment of the "extravagant grants" of Governor Fletcher, one of which was the Schoharie lands to Nicholas Bayard. He said, "a strong argument against the grants is that they contain great quantities of timber fit for masts and naval stores."[82] This statement, however, included the Mohawk lands and others as well as the Schoharie and may perhaps be regarded as probably inaccurate, so far as it relates to Schoharie.

Fortunately, science has developed sufficiently to be able to shed some light upon the subject. An authority on New York botany states, "it is extremely unlikely that pitch pine ever occurred in Schoharie in any abundance for the reason that geographical formation in that section is chiefly limestone and glacial drift, upon which pitch pine does not grow in any abundance and upon the limestone formations and resulting soils pitch pine was never found." He adds, "there may have been a limited amount of pitch pine along the Mohawk, since at the present time there are some scattered clumps of that tree in that region."[83] Accordingly, Bridger's statement seems verified by present day scientists. Hunter, through his representatives before the Board of Trade on December 1, 1711, did not base his decision against settlement at Schoharie upon the lack of pitch pine. The first reason— conflicting, it will be seen, with his earlier statement on the matter—was that "the Purchase thereof from the Indians was not clear." Other reasons were the difficulty of defending

[81] Jeptha R. Simms, *Frontiersmen of New York* (Albany, 1882), I, 107; hereafter cited as Simms, *Frontiersmen*.

[82] *Acts Privy Council Col. Unbound Papers*, 61.

[83] H. D. House, New York State Botanist, in a letter to the author, April 11, 1927.

Courtesy of Pennsylvania-German Society.

it from the French and Indians and the presence of a sixty-foot waterfall on the river below the proposed site.[84] This waterfall, however, had been adjudged no serious obstacle before Hunter sailed from England.[85]

At any rate, the governor thought it advisable to look for lands nearer at hand, as near as possible to a navigable river and pine lands. A tract of land of 6,300 acres on the west side of the Hudson River, about ninety-two miles from New York City, was in the possession of the Crown.[86] It had formerly

[84] B. M., Harleian MSS. 7021, 280; *C. C. 1711–1712,* 174.

[85] The Board of Trade said, "We do not see that this objection will be any hindrance to the seating them there." *N. Y. Col. Docs.,* V, 117.

[86] B. M., Harleian MSS. 7021, 280; *C. C. 1710–1711,* 261; *Ibid., 1711–1712,* 174; *N. Y. Col. Docs.,* V, 290.

been granted to Captain Evans by Governor Fletcher, and had recently been resumed as one of the "Extravagant Grants." This land was used for the settlement of the Palatines and the experiment in naval stores manufacture. In addition, Hunter on Bridger's recommendation entered into an agreement with Robert Livingston, Commissioner of Indian Affairs, for another tract on the east side of the Hudson River near the former Evans tract. On September 29th, 6,000 acres were purchased with the liberty of using the pitch pine neighboring the tract on Livingston's land.[87] The price was 266 pounds of English money, which amounted to 400 pounds in colonial currency.[88] The friendship between Hunter and Livingston was an interesting development. Both were of Scotch descent and had need for each other. Only once did Hunter question Livingston's loyalty to himself, but one doubt, arising at the time of Colonel Nicholson's visit of investigation in 1711,[89] did not long affect the tie.

Livingston's holdings were indeed not without criticism by colonial officials. Governor Bellomont had written to the Board of Trade on November 28, 1700, of other "Extravagant Grants" not made by Governor Fletcher, but equally worthy of investigation. Besides van Rensellaer's and Nichols', he named Livingston's, "of 16 miles long and 20 or 24 broad."[90] In another letter a year later he wrote, "Mr. Livingston has on his great grant of 16 miles long and 24 broad, but 4 or 5 cottages as I am told, men that live in vassalage under him and work for him are too poor to be farmers. . . ."[91] How Livingston must have welcomed the Palatine settlements!

Livingston's sale of 6,000 acres was surprising in view

[87] Livingston Family Ms. of original indenture in possession of Johnston Livingston Redmont Estate of New York City, with other valuable colonial manuscripts; hereafter cited as Liv. MSS. Also, *Doc. Hist.*, III, 644.

[88] *N. Y. Col. Docs.*, V, 170, 172.

[89] Dominion Archives, Ottawa, G. B. Patent Rolls 1702–1760, I, 31.

[90] *N. Y. Col. Docs.*, IV, 791.

[91] *Doc. Hist.*, III, 629.

of the fact that his deeds called for only 2,600 acres.[92] But still more surprising was the result of the survey made just before Governor Hunter issued a confirmatory grant to Livingston, giving his manor representation in the assembly in 1715. On October 20, 1714, the deputy Surveyor found that Livingston Manor contained 160,240 acres, for which Livingston paid annually twenty-eight shillings current money quit-rent.[93] A recent authority on New York land laws has termed such quit-rent as not unusually low, since the lands were undeveloped.[94] It was precisely the fact that such large grants were undeveloped and often remained so for many years, which caused the British authorities to object to such "extravagant grants" and to demand two shillings, six pence sterling for every hundred acres.[95] In return for the confirmatory grant and the privilege of sending a representative to the colonial assembly, Livingston entered the assembly as representative of his manor, and he helped Hunter in his administrative difficulties. He was of assistance in securing a friendly assembly, which held office for many years. When Hunter was to leave, as Speaker of that assembly Livingston lauded his friend in high terms and thus contributed to the reputation of Hunter as the best governor of New York in colonial history. In consideration of the so-called bargain price for the land, a contract was also drawn up by the Chief Justice of New York and every precaution was taken to protect the Crown's interests. Livingston agreed to furnish one-third of a loaf of bread (4¼ pence size) and one quart "ship's beer" (a very low grade of beer) to each person daily.[96]

[92] *Ibid.*, 616, 621, 622, 624.

[93] *Ibid.*, 690, map.

[94] Julius Goebel, Jr., *Some Legal and Political Aspects of the Manors in New York* (Baltimore, 1928), 17.

[95] *C. C. 1706–1708*, 513.

[96] *Ibid.*, 653. Livingston had also been accused in 1700 of being concerned with Captain Kidd, the pirate, as well as in frauds as collector of excise at Albany (*Ibid.*, 629). These charges were not proved, however.

Hunter also purchased for the use of the Palatines a tract of neighboring land from one Thomas Fullerton, who was in the Custom Service of Scotland. He paid relatively more for this tract of 800 acres, saying that Fullerton could expect no profit from the Palatines' presence as was the case with Livingston.[97] Fullerton gave Hunter power of attorney to dispose of the same. This tract was almost opposite the purchase made from Livingston and seems for that reason to have been well selected. It is apparent that three tracts of land were used for settlement, although quite often only the two large tracts are referred to.[98]

Early in October the movement of the Palatines to the manor began, the cost of this transportation being 200 pounds.[99] The land was surveyed and five towns were marked out, three on the east side of the river and two on the west side.[100] Here the Germans cleared the ground and built themselves huts, each one according to his knowledge and ability.[101] Later a number of smaller settlements appeared. In June, 1711, there were seven villages inhabited as follows: (on the east side) Hunterstown, 105 families; Queensbury, 102 families; Annsbury, 76 families; Haysbury, 59 families; (on the west side) Elizabeth Town, 42 families; George Town, 40 families; and New Town, 103 families. The total number of Palatines on the Hudson was 1,874.[102] A large number of

[97] *Ibid.*, 661.

[98] *Ibid. 1710–1711*, 261, 484.

[99] B. M., Harleian MSS. 7021, 283; *Doc. Hist.*, III, 652. Fullerton's land was claimed by Dirk Wessel by means of the Sockerman patent, but as the latter grant was later, it was not allowed. Liv. MS. letter of April 6, 1711.

[100] *Doc. Hist.*, III, 668.

[101] Simmendinger, *op. cit.*, 3.

[102] *Doc. Hist.*, III, 668. On the east side, Germantown remains to mark these settlements; on the west side, West Camp (New Town), Evesport (Elizabeth Town), at Smith's Landing (George Town). Other Palatines settled at Katsbaan (King's Town), Rhinebeck, and Kingston. *Olde Ulster*, II, 203; III, 116, 225, 229.

the Palatines, it will be seen, remained in New York City. This group numbered about 350 in 1710[103] and about the beginning of 1713, 83 Palatines in 23 families still remained there.[104] Most of these were widows with families, though a few were employed in the governor's gardens.

[103] *Ibid.*, 562 *et seq.*

[104] Simmendinger, *op. cit.*, 12.

CHAPTER VII. THE GOVERNMENT TAR INDUSTRY IN OPERATION

As the Palatines arrived in Livingston Manor, Livingston provided food, tools, tent-poles and other necessities. He also furnished storage for their supplies, for all of which he made proper charges.[1] The Palatines were then allotted small plots of land to build their huts. The lots for houses and small gardens were about forty feet in front and fifty feet in depth.[2] The huts were made of rough logs, the cracks plastered with mud, and each was built according to the builder's own ideas. When the last group was sent from New York to be settled on Fullerton's tract, instructions were sent to Livingston to lay out the lots somewhat wider than the others, but not to make it too apparent.[3] The Palatines were not to receive the forty acres promised each, until they had fulfilled their contracts.

From November 10, 1710, until the following March 8th, 78 barrels of flour, 19 barrels of salt pork and 22 bags of bread were distributed among the Palatines on the west side settlements.[4] They were also given fresh pork and beef. The food supplies were doled out in this fashion: bread, beer and salt for every day, beef or pork for three days a week, and fish or a quantity of butter, cheese, flour or peas for the other four days in the same quantities usually allotted soldiers being transported.[5] Many fat cattle were purchased from neighboring farmers and at one time (in January, 1712), seventy cattle were slaughtered for the Palatines' larders.[6] During the first two

[1] N. Y. Col. MSS., LVII, 124a.
[2] B. T. Jour. 1708–1714, 226.
[3] Liv. MS., letter of April 14, 1711.
[4] N. Y. Col. MSS., LIV, 174.
[5] P. R. O., C. O. 5/1085, 67.
[6] N. Y. Col. MSS., LVII, 124b, LIV, 57.

years it would appear that the immigrants were supplied with enough food to keep body and soul together, if not free from care. It was not until July 13, 1711, that the commissary on Livingston Manor felt assured of enough supplies on hand not to worry;[7] and we may therefore express no surprise that the storehouse was robbed early in January of 1711.[8] In April the people on the west side unavailably asked for permission to make their own bread, for reasons unmentioned, but probably well-founded.[9]

In 1711 many things quite necessary for the proper settlement of the Palatines were still wanting. Among the items listed as immediately needed we may note, steel for mending edged tools, three sets of smithy tools, three pairs of millstones, sixteen whipsaws, warehouses, and a church on each side of the river. Other essentials were plow shares, pitch and dung forks, iron for horseshoes, nails and harness for horses.[10] As for the spiritual needs of the Palatines, besides Reverend Kocherthal, a German minister named John Frederick Haeger, served the Hudson River settlements. Haeger had been employed by the London Society for the Propagation of the Gospel to preach to the Germans and incidentally convert them to the Church of England.[11] This he endeavored to do, but only with great difficulty. He strove to hold them together in one church, but bickering between the Lutherans and the Reformed began as soon as they landed in America.[12] Haeger was responsible for the building of a schoolhouse in Queensbury early in June, 1711.[13] He petitioned the governor in 1715, and in 1717 he obtained a license to build a church, but the

[7] *Doc. Hist.*, III, 672.

[8] Liv. MS., letter of January 7, 1711.

[9] *Ibid.*, letter of April 29, 1711.

[10] N. Y. Col. MSS., LIV, 98a.

[11] L. C., S. P. G. MSS. A-6, XLV; A-9, IV; A-15, 5; A-10, 181.

[12] *Ibid.* A-6, XXI.

[13] N. Y. Col. MSS., LV, 29b; LVIII, 57a.

building lagged for several years.[14] The Society for the Propagation of the Gospel incidentally was much interested in assimilating the Germans in a generation at least.[15] But the Germans, unmindful of this concern for the next generation, continued to multiply, for Reverend Haeger baptized 61 children and married 101 couples from July, 1710 to July, 1712.[16] Kocherthal was performing similar services for the Lutheran settlers.[17]

The organization, which was to manage the business of manufacturing naval stores for the British Royal Navy, was military in character. This was to be expected, since the organizer[18] was a military man who had seen active service under Marlborough. Colonel Hunter, of course, was in charge, subject only to orders from London. Under him were assorted groups of officials, whose salaries and incidental expenses amounted to 1,800 pounds sterling annually. George Clarke, then Secretary of the Province, was listed as Treasurer and Commissary of Stores. The tentative salary was 200 pounds sterling which does not appear to have been paid.[19] Robert Lurting, deputy commissary, was not active so far as appears in the colonial records that remain, but he received a salary of 100 pounds colonial currency, which equalled 66 pounds, 13 shilings and 4 pence sterling. The duties of these two officers seemed to be concerned with the securing of various supplies such as meats, which were often obtained from New York City. Another Commissary of Stores was to receive 250 pounds colonial currency (166 pounds, 13 shillings, 4 pence sterling),

[14] L. C., S. P. G. MSS. A-12, 341.

[15] Ibid. A-7, IX. The efforts of the Society were not successful, for in 1836 a description of the Palatine settlements holds that "German largely prevails among the older inhabitants but their children are educated and converse in English." Thomas F. Gordon, Gazeteer of the State of New York (Philadelphia, 1836), 695.

[16] Ibid. A-8, 31, 158.

[17] Kocherthal Records MS. shows 35 baptisms from 1710 to 1712 and 100 marriages during the same period. See Olde Ulster, III, 32, 92; IV, 24, 56.

[18] N. Y. Col. MSS., LIII, 160b.

[19] B. M., Harleian MSS. 7021, 285; N. Y. Col. MSS., LIV, 98a.

James DuPré, who had served as commissary for the Palatines in London, holding this position in the New York project.[20] He had two assistants, Jean Cast, a Frenchman, and Andrew Bagge, at salaries of 60 pounds (New York currency) annually. Cast had charge of the supplies given the settlers on the east side of the Hudson River, on the Livingston Manor, while Bagge had charge of the supplies on the west side of the river.[21] John Arnoldi served as "Phisitian General," at the annual salary of 100 pounds (New York currency). Salaries were also specified for two surgeons, two overseers, two clerks or schoolmasters, six captains, six lieutenants, two messengers and four nurses. It does not appear that these positions were regularly occupied.[22] The captains and lieutenants were appointed, however, as a manuscript, partly burned, preserves eight of their names.[23] Seven listmasters, Palatines, were appointed, one for each village; these were to keep the rolls of their villages and aid the tar instructor in handling the Palatine labor. They were, for Hunterstown, John Peter Kneskern; for Queensbury, John Conrad Weiser; for Annsbury, Hartman Windecker; for Haysbury, John Christopher Fuchs; for Elizabeth Town, John Christopher Gerlach; for George Town, Jacob Manck; and for New Town, Phillip Peter Grauberger.[24]

In May of 1711 a rebellion of some three or four hundred Palatines gave excuse for a more stringent military rule. A secret association had been formed among the Palatines, who did not intend to remain on Livingston Manor. Hunter met them and tried to reason with them, but they stubbornly demanded that they should receive "the lands appointed them by the Queen" in the Schoharie Valley. Some of the Palatines,

[20] *Doc. Hist.*, III, 561.
[21] N. Y. Col. MSS., LIV, 174.
[22] *Ibid.*, LV-LIX, *passim.*
[23] *Ibid.*, LIII, 160b. The fire of 1911 in the State Building was responsible for the damaged condition of the document.
[24] *Ibid.*, LV, 100; LVII, 124b; *Doc. Hist.*, III, 672.

more violent, cried that "they would rather lose their lives immediately than remain where they" were. "To be forced by another contract to remain on these lands all their lives, and work for her Majesty for the ships use, that they will never doe." The Palatines charged that they were cheated by the contract. They did not believe that it was the same contract which Cast had read to them in their own language in England. They said that it had then provided, that seven years after they had forty acres per person given them they were to repay the Queen with hemp, masts, tar, and pitch. They also declared that, were they not allowed their contract, three or four men would go to England and lay their case before the Queen.[25]

Hunter put them off until he was reinforced by a military detachment of seventy men from Albany. He then disarmed the Palatines in each village and they were at his mercy. Realizing this, the deputies submitted and the people asked for pardon and seemed again willing to work.[26] The fact of the matter was, as Hunter himself admitted later to the Board of Trade, the Palatines had forced the governor to "abscond" for fear that they would capture his person.[27] Hunter appeared to be slow in forgiving the affront.

As a result of the disorders, he revoked all Palatine military commissions and put the people entirely under the command of their overseer and the officials. They were to be treated "as the Queen's hired Servants," which they were. Determined to prevent the recurrence of such disorders in the future, Hunter issued a commission establishing a court over the Palatines on June 12, 1711, with Robert Livingston as the president and six other commissioners, Jean Cast, Richard Sackett, Godfrey Wulfen, Andrew Bagge, Herman Schüneman and the commanding officer of the detachment of soldiers

[25] *Doc. Hist.*, III, 664.
[26] *Ibid.*, 667.
[27] *B. T. Jour. 1718–1722*, 195, August 9, 1720.

placed at the manor.[28] But the court was full of dissension. Cast wrote to Hunter, July 13, 1711, "The President of the Court, who in view of the public interest, ought to be the least in the Board on account of his private interests, makes no scruple of despising and treating with indignity a colleague who, with a good intention, confers a pleasure on the people, which the other does not find to his advantage. . . ."[29] The court had power to punish the Palatines for all "Misdemeanors, Disobedience or wilfull Transgressions" by confinement or corporal punishment, not extending to life or mutilation.[30] Hunter evolved a scheme for employing the Palatines and it was one of close supervision, with the ever-present threat of punishment as the incentive to keep the people at work.[31]

The subsistence supplies of the Palatines were principally bread, meat and beer; the bread and the beer were supplied by Livingston at New York rates, subject to alteration should the assize of New York change.[32] The Palatines were not permitted to make their own bread.[33] Meats might be sent up the river from New York[34] or secured by Livingston from the neighboring Dutch farmers.[35] The Commissaries of Stores meticulously used certificates and receipts for the stores received and issued. Masters of sloops, who carried supplies to Messrs. Cast and Bagge, on their respective sides of the river, had to sign for the articles they carried, and upon their delivery of the goods, the commissaries certified to that effect.[36] Every month or two, Cast certified the amount and quality of the bread and beer delivered by Livingston for the use of the Palatines.[37]

[28] N. Y. Col. MSS., LV, 100; *Doc. Hist.*, III, 669 *et seq.*
[29] *Doc. Hist.*, III, 673.   [30] *Ibid.*, 669.
[31] *Ibid.*, 678.   [32] *Ibid.*, 655.
[33] Liv. MS., letter of April 29, 1711.
[34] *Ibid.*, March 10, 1711.
[35] N. Y. Col. MSS., LIV, 57.
[36] *Ibid.*, 191a and b.   [37] *Ibid.*, 19a and b.

Livingston also served the settlement well in his readiness to give cash, when needed.[38] He kept a detailed account of these disbursements, which he then collected from Secretary Clark, the treasurer, sometimes after a great deal of argument.[39] Among the items, every six months, was that of forty-five pounds, two shillings colonial currency for storage of supplies and two chambers for the use of the commissary.[40] In addition, Livingston claimed a salary of 258 pounds colonial currency as an Inspector of the Palatines from August 24, 1710, to March 25, 1713.[41] When Richard Sackett, a nearby farmer, came to direct the work, he depended to a large degree on Livingston to supply his wants. He especially wrote short orders for cash or supplies for Palatine workers.[42]

Dissensions existed between the commissaries. Andrew Bagge wrote to Livingston concerning Cast, "as other affaryr[s] are keep from my knowledge soe must this. His privat peck [pique] to me ought not to interfere with the Publick" business. Since Cast could not understand English, Bagge was unable intelligently to converse with him, and was probably jealous of the reliance the governor placed upon Cast. At any rate, the bickerings referred to were serious obstacles to a business-like issuing and accounting for provisions.[43]

The Palatines were given their supplies in a very irregular fashion. In the rough drafts of the accounts remaining, occasionally two to five days' subsistence were given as one item. The Palatines were supplied for days or perhaps a week at a

[38] *Ibid.*, LVIII, 48e, 62a-d.

[39] *Ibid.*, 107, 108a; LIX, 36; LV, 27; Liv. MSS., letters of March 10th and 27th, 1711.

[40] *Ibid.*, 17.

[41] *Ibid.*, LIX, 37.

[42] *Ibid.*, LVII, 169b.

[43] Bagge wrote further, "and untill he letts me know what quantity of Beere each family have rec'd:, and how much they are to have either quarterly or otherwise, my notes signifyes noething. . . ." Liv. MS., letter of January 7, 1712.

time. All of them did not receive the same articles in equal amounts, especially since frequently there was not sufficient goods to be distributed to all. The final draft of the subsistence account is too regular to be strictly accurate. The decrease in numbers of from one to ten is indicated in a steady loss. It would appear that the number of deaths was noted and the daily account was then calculated on the basis of so many less the previous totals.[44]

These subsistence accounts were kept in a "ledger," as it was called though it was really a day-book, in which so many days' subsistence was charged to someone as it was issued. This "ledger" had cross references to a "journal," which would be called a ledger today, made up of the alphabetical list of Palatine families with their charges.[45] The accounts, based on the regular subsistence allowances of six pence per day for adults and four pence, all in sterling, for children under ten years of age, were not accurate. Hunter himself admitted on two occasions, that all other miscellaneous expenses, such as the salaries of the officers, came out of the Palatines' meager subsistence allowances.[46] Indeed, since the Palatines were to repay the subsistence allowed to them, it can be concluded that they were also bearing the cost of the miscellaneous expenses as well as the officers' salaries.

Another direct source of dissatisfaction was the subsistence furnished. The food supplies furnished by Livingston were alleged to be deficient in amount and inferior in quality,[47] despite Cast's certification to the contrary. In those days this was almost sure to be the case with farmed contracts. The

[44] N. Y. Col. MSS., LVI, 97, 98b. Bagge complained in January, 1712 that he could not keep an exact account. Liv. MS., January 9, 1712.

[45] The "journal" and "ledger" are P. R. O., C. O. 5/1230 and 1231 respectively. The summary of the "Subsistence Lists," taken from the "journal," are published below in Appendix E., with certain modifications explained there.

[46] N. Y. Col. Docs., V, 342, 449; C. C. 1711–1712, 305.

[47] Osgood, op. cit., I, 514.

contract was well drawn and Livingston could certainly have been required to furnish good food, and it seems that Cast took care that Livingston did not gain too much from the transaction. Yet in spite of their best intentions and efforts the service of supply apparently left much to be desired.

Cast wrote to Hunter, May 1, 1711: "The experience of the tare [weight marked when empty] of the Barrels is very incorrect, and that such deception causes the people not to take the flour in barrels according to the Tare, but ordinarily to return the barrels to me that I may make a new tare, led me to make a bet with Mr. Robert Livingston, Jun[r] that a barrel, tared 17 lbs., weighed 20 lbs. I was universally censured for making such a wager. But when the Barrel was emptied and well shaken and cleaned, it weighed 21 lbs. tare. Judge, Sir, what a loss of flour this is. I sent Mr. Bagge 20 barrels today . . . and requested him to investigate the cheat. The 18 barrels are tared 16 lbs., 1 barrel 17 lbs. and one 19 lbs. I would make another bet that not one of them runs below 20 lbs. tare. It is too palpable a fraud to mark so many at 16 lbs. Mr. Bagge will not fail to advise you how the tare turns out."[48] Again on July 13, 1711, Cast wrote the governor in complaint of Livingston, "But since the reconstruction of our Board, I have found that his design has ever been to obtain the management of all the supplies for the People, and had I not had the foresight to demand a declaration from the general commission he would have seized it altogether and had made Mr. Meyer his clerk whom he would have got to do what he could not get me to do—that is, everything that may content his cupidity."[49]

As for the supplies of meat Hunter simply bought much of it in New York and salted it well before sending it up the river. As time passed, and Hunter's credit with it, the meat apparently became worse. In a letter of May 1, 1711, Cast wrote to Hunter, "I have received the 20 barrels of Pork

[48] *Doc. Hist.*, III, 660.   [49] *Ibid.*, 674.

which I distributed among the people at this side and supplied all with some to the 10th of May. . . . I never saw salted meat so poor nor packed with so much salt as this Pork was. In truth one eight of it was salt."[50] Some two months later, Cast wrote again to Hunter, "Whatever little I may receive, I only hope that the meat which is brought me will be of good quality. For however submissive the people are at present . . . I could not avoid arranging with the listmasters to induce the people to take the meat last sent me. I shall be in despair should I have again to receive any such. . . . I beg you, sir, to attend to it and relieve the people as much as possible from salted provisions." But even with such food, orders had been given to retrench in distributing it, which meant even less of that. In the same letter, Cast said, "It is less difficult to retrench bad than good food. But he must also bear in mind that this is carrying things to extremes."[51]

In the first year in New York, Governor Hunter had spent 21,700 pounds sterling on the Palatines. Of this sum, 19,200 pounds went for subsistence at the rate of 1,600 per month. At that time DuPré, the Commissary of Stores, was sent to London to secure an additional 15,000 pounds sterling a year for two years, when, it was asserted, the venture would not only be self-supporting but would be repaying the large sums invested.[52] Instead of securing the grants, DuPré was busily occupied, defending Hunter and Livingston from the attacks of the Earl of Clarendon, formerly Governor Cornbury of New York.[53] On arriving at New York in 1710 Hunter had helped Cornbury to escape his creditors, and when the noble lord

[50] *Ibid.*, 659.

[51] *Ibid.*, 672. July 13, 1711. On July 30, 1712, retrenchment of beer was ordered by issuing it "only to the men that work and not for their familys." N. Y. Col. MSS., LVII, 191a; *Doc. Hist.*, III, 682.

[52] B. M., Harleian MSS. 7021, 282; P. R. O., C. O. 5/1050, 33; H. L., L. O. MSS., 7.

[53] *N. Y. Col. Docs.*, V, 289; *C. C. 1710–1711*, 172, 389; Liv. MS., December 11, 1711.

departed, July 31, 1710, he wrote a note to Hunter, telling him how much he appreciated his help and that it would be a pleasure to be of service to him at any time.[54] When the time came however, within a year, Cornbury, then Lord Clarendon, forgot his obligation to Hunter in his hatred for Robert Livingston.[55] Clarendon wrote, March 8, 1711, to Secretary of State Dartmouth that it was unfortunate that Hunter had fallen into Livingston's hands and that, were any more outlay made, it would only contribute to Livingston's further wealth.[56] The Board of Trade apparently favored Hunter and desired to go ahead,[57] but the Treasury was apathetic with sad results for the governor as we shall see.

Meanwhile Hunter was also having difficulty with the only competent instructor in the manufacturing of naval stores available. Having aided in the selection of a suitable tract, Bridger secured Hunter's permission to return to New England until spring, when he would be needed again. In the spring of 1711, he refused to return to New York. Hunter charged him with unfaithfulness.[58] A recent writer, nevertheless, gives Bridger a high commendation for his years of faithful service in the colonies, stating that "actuated by the interest of the Navy, which he had previously served as a shipwright, he did more than any other man to inaugurate the Broad Arrow policy."[59] Why did Bridger leave Hunter and his project and

[54] *Ibid.*, 406.

[55] H. L., L. O. MSS., 11. Livingston, who bitterly opposed Cornbury in New York, wrote to England, describing Cornbury's weakness for promenading in women's attire and his Lordship's day "after dinner till twelve at night" as spent at the bottle. *Cal. Treas. Papers 1702–1707*, 512. Clarendon's animosity might also be attributed to Hunter's dismissal of Sheriff Anderson, despite Clarendon's strong recommendation of him. *N. Y. Col. Docs.*, V, 406; I. N. Phelps Stokes, *Iconography of Manhattan Island* (New York, 1928), IV, 472.

[56] *N. Y. Col. Docs.*, V, 195.

[57] H. L., H. M. MSS., 1642; *C. C. 1712–1714*, 170.

[58] *C. C. 1711–1712*, 98.

[59] Albion, *op. cit.*, 243.

refuse to return from New England to instruct the Palatines? It might have been because of the influence of someone who did not wish the project to succeed. Hunter insinuated to the Board of Trade on January 1, 1712, "how basely Mr. Bridger has endeavor'd to betray this service, he has since wrote to me that it was not by his own will that he absented himself, he best knows whose will determined him to soe black a purpose. . . ."[60] It is explained more probably by Bridger's requests for his traveling expenses, which the Board of Trade referred to Hunter to pay, and which, it appears, he referred back to the Board. At least, Bridger wrote, "I have apply'd to Col. Hunter, who refuses me travailing charges."[61] This he followed with insinuations to the Board of Trade, July 23, 1711, which seem tainted with an ambition of his own: "I am told that the victualing of the Palatines and not the raising of naval stores induced a general to undertake an affair he was wholly ignorant of." He then made a proposal to manufacture naval stores in New England with soldier labor, providing he was made lieutenant-governor of New Hampshire.[62] On September 12, 1711, Hunter complained that Bridger refused to return to the Palatine settlement, "pretending want of sufficient encouragement,"[63] although Hunter had recommended to the Board of Trade that he be granted an additional salary.

[60] *C. C. 1711–1712*, 194. Hunter hinted that this was Francis Nicholson, in New England in 1711 for the expedition against Canada. *N. Y. Col. Docs.*, V, 449; *Doc. Hist.*, III, 675. Colonel Nicholson arrived at Boston June 8th, 1711, *C. C. 1711–1712*, 38. In "Androborus," a drama in manuscript undoubtedly written for private enjoyment, Hunter describes Nicholson as a potential enemy, Widener Library, Cambridge, Massachusetts. In 1715 he referred to him as that "Teazer Nicholson," *C. C. 1714–1715*, 306. Also, see *N. Y. Col. Docs.*, V, 449.

[61] *Ibid.* 1708–1709, 20, 259, 693; *Ibid.* 1710–1711, 253, 524; *B. T. Jour. 1708–1714*, 227.

[62] *Ibid. 1711–1712*, 25.

[63] *Ibid.*, 98. As early as February 19th, 1711 the Board was assuring Bridger of an increase in salary for his work with the Palatines. *C. C. 1710–1711*, 369; also, *C. C. 1714–1715*, 303, 306.

It is fairly clear that in their rivalry for leadership in the important enterprise of naval stores production, for the prestige and honor that would come from such success, these two officials had gone beyond indifference to a sharp antipathy in their relation to each other. Bridger, who had been advocating a development of such a manufacture on a large scale in the colonies for thirteen years before 1709, now doubtless felt that Hunter had stolen his fire. On the eve of the new venture in New York, Bridger had sent a proposal from New England in regard to naval stores, for on January 16, 1710, the Board wrote to Bridger, "We have had under our consideration the method proposed by you for encouraging the making of tar and pitch in New England." The Board then stated that as 3,000 Palatines were to go to New York under Hunter, Bridger was to receive further information in that matter upon Hunter's arrival.[64] In short, as one writer put it in commenting on Bridger's action against Caleb Heathcote's proposal of 1705, "Bridger seemed a rather jealous official."[65] Of Heathcote's proposal to produce naval stores in New York and build a ship, Bridger wrote, "I do, with the result of my own experience, say it is impossible and he cannot performe any one thing he aims at."[66] This jealousy and the possibility of seeing another man take the credit for the accomplishment of his dream of supplying England's needs for naval stores in the colonies probably hastened the rupture between him and Hunter, if it did not altogether account for it.

The manufacturing of tar in 1711 was held up by the second Canadian Expedition (1711). Hunter was intensely engaged in the gathering of provisions and military forces.[67]

[64] *Ibid.* *1710–1711*, 10.

[65] Fox, *op. cit.*, 153. Heathcote proposed to build government frigates at New York, out of naval stores from there, thus saving the costs of shipment to England.

[66] *C. C.* *1706–1708*, 54. Heathcote also submitted this proposal to Hunter in 1712, who sent it on to the Board of Trade, *Ibid.* *1711–1712*, 242.

[67] *Ibid.* *1711–1712*, 97, 100.

In July Bridger wrote to the Board of Trade that the Palatines would not work; a number of them were to go on the expedition against Quebec.[68] Two months later Hunter acquainted Bridger at Boston, "that I have employed the Palatines in preparing the Trees this Summer under the direction of Mr. Sackett however the Season drawing nigh for barking again if you think fit you may come and give them your directions. . . ."[69] Since the preparations for the expedition required a great deal of Hunter's time and effort as well as that of some 300 of the most able-bodied Palatines,[70] the tar business on the Hudson River suffered accordingly.

Richard Sackett, whom Hunter placed in charge as instructor of tar-making, was a local farmer who claimed to have lived three years in the "Eastern countries" among the manufacturers of tar. Hunter reported that he gave a very rational account of the method of preparing the trees.[71] Therefore, Bridger who had manufactured both tar and hemp satisfactory to the Navy Board,[72] was superseded by Sackett, whose knowledge and experience, to say the least, was doubtful. Mr. Sackett took charge with energy. About 100,000 trees were barked, a special preparation necessary before the tar burning could take place.[73] A foot-bridge was built across Roeloff Jansens Kill, a creek just above Livingston's gristmill, not far from its junction with the Hudson River.[74] Of the bridge, Hunter wrote, "I have made the best bridge in all North America over the river between the pine woods and

[68] *Ibid.*, 25; N. Y. Col. MSS., LV, 112.

[69] N. Y. Col. MSS., LVI, 18b.

[70] *Ibid.*, LV, 112; *B. T. Jour. 1718–1722*, 207. The Palatines thought by taking Canada to make Schoharie safe for their settlement there in the future. The memory of the sack of Schenectady (1690) was scarcely twenty years old. *Doc. Hist.*, III, 658.

[71] *C. C. 1710–1711*, 485.

[72] P. R. O., C. O. 324/8, 276.

[73] *C. C. 1711–1712*, 97.

[74] *Doc. Hist.*, III, 673, 679.

their settlements. . . ."[75] Carpenters were put to work on
storehouses and barrels under a plan whereby they received
two shillings a day, half in cash from Livingston, and the
other half in credit on their accounts.[76] As early as June 16,
1711, Sackett was using horses and wagons rented from
Livingston to bring in tar knots for making tar. Casks were
also collected by the teams.[77] At the same time Sackett was
having a cart made and on the 19th he purchased two horses
for ten pounds for use in the works.[78]

Early in July, the commissioners for the governing of the
Palatines made arrangements to hasten the production of tar
barrels. The listmasters of the Palatine towns were required
to appoint thirty-six men every Monday to take their turn
in aiding the coopers. Delinquents were to be reported and
punished. The listmasters were also cautioned to "take care
their people do not stragle again, that if they want to go to
work in the Harvest, Leave shall be given them provided it
may be known whether [whither] they goe, that they may
be sent for upon occasion."[79]

The detachment of soldiers held in readiness to enforce
the decrees of the commissioners was not conducive to better
feeling on the part of the Palatines. For the most part husbandmen and vine-dressers, they were dissatisfied with their
work and their location. They disliked to work in gangs and
under rigid supervision.[80] There was no incentive to work
hard to pay back the funds spent on them; they sought only
to receive the forty acres each of soil for their settlement.
They remarked to one another that they had come to America
"to secure lands for our children on which they will be able
to support themselves after we die, and that we cannot do

[75] C. C. 1711–1712, 99.
[76] N. Y. Col. MSS., LVII, 27b.
[77] Ibid., LV, 28g, 101.
[78] Ibid., 28a, 29d; Ibid., LVI, 177.
[79] Doc. Hist., III, 671.
[80] Osgood, op. cit., I, 514.

here.''[81] The Palatines worked but manifestly with repugnance, and merely temporarily.[82] Perhaps the repairing of the iron bolts on "the prison door" twice in one year had some significance,[83] for the Palatines were to be punished for laxness and the listmasters were reprimanded on occasion.[84]

The reports on the progress of the manufacturing were nevertheless promising. On June 6, 1711, Hunter wrote from Albany, "Our Tarr work goes on as we could wish God continue it. . . . We shall be at a losse for Casks in a little while for we go to work with the Knots. I have however sett all hands to work. . . ."[85] "That no hands may be idle we employed the boys and girls in gathering knotts whilst their fathers were a barking, out of which hee [Sackett] had made about three score barrells of good tarr, and hath kills ready to sett on fire for about as much more soe soone as he getts casks ready to receive it."[86] Pork barrels were used of necessity but they were not satisfactory.[87] Another group of interesting items in the Palatine receipts, preserved in the colonial records, are those given for "6 gallons of Rum for use of the Palatines at work in the Tarr work." It was required not only in the winter months such as January,[88] but also in the mild weather of June and July.[89]

The defection of Bridger and the appointment of Sackett as tar instructor caused uneasiness in England, and the Board of Trade began to inquire into the method of manufacturing naval stores. The reports secured were so divergent,[90] that

[81] *Doc. Hist.*, III, 658.

[82] *Ibid.*, 659.

[83] N. Y. Col. MSS., LVIII, 63e.

[84] *Doc. Hist.*, III, 670, 671.

[85] H. S. P., Greer Coll., Governors of the Colonies MSS., I, June 6, 1711.

[86] *C. C. 1711–1712*, 98.

[87] N. Y. Col. MSS., LV, 43.

[88] *Ibid.*, LVIII, 61a.

[89] *Ibid.*, 61e; H. S. P., Greer Coll., Governors of the Colonies MSS., I, June 6, 1711.

[90] *C. C. 1710–1711*, 369.

the Board decided to ask the British representative in Russia as to the method of manufacturing tar there. The representative, Mr. C. Whitworth, advised the Board from Riga that he knew nothing about the methods, but that he would inquire as soon as he arrived in Petersburg.[91] In April, 1712, he described the "Method of Preparing Tar in Muscovy." The fir trees were barked in the month of October (not in the spring) from the bottom eight feet high, except for a strip three or four fingers broad, which was left up the north side. In this condition the trees were to stand at least for a year,[92] and better still, for two or three years. The turpentine settled in the barked parts during this period.

When ready for use, the tree was cut down, usually in winter for the convenience of sledways. The part, which was barked, was cut off, carried to the place where it was to be burned, and split at full lengths into billets about the thickness of an arm. Laid in piles six feet high, a computation of the tar which it was to yield could be made. The slow heating or sweating was then done in a kiln very similar to that of charcoal burning, except that more care had to be taken to prevent leakage and a trench had to be provided to tap the tar from the kiln.[93]

The Board noted immediately that the Muscovy method was somewhat different from that of Mr. Sackett, and they forwarded the account to Hunter with that comment.[94] In the spring, Sackett barked the north quarter of the tree's circumference about two feet; in the fall, the south quarter about two feet, four inches; the second spring, the east quarter

[91] P. R. O., C. O. 5/1050, 36.

[92] The excellence of this method, the depriving of the trees of their bark and felling them the following year, has been recently approved and might be profitably applied in the U. S. Thomas Gamble, ed., *Naval Stores, History, Production, Distribution and Consumption* (Savannah, Georgia, 1921), 13.

[93] P. R. O., C. O. 5/1050, 40.

[94] *C. C. 1711–1712*, 298. Hunter attributed the differences to climate. *N. Y. Col. Docs.*, V, 348.

about two feet, eight inches; and the second fall, the remaining quarter, approximately three feet. The cutting down of the trees, the splitting into billets and the sweating process were the same as in the Muscovy method.[95]

Sackett's method was not productive of results. Not more than 200 barrels of tar, if that, were produced from all the trees prepared.[96] It would appear that Sackett had not barked the trees sufficiently when the sap was flowing toward the roots. Furthermore, the inner bark either had not been removed in sufficient quantities or with proper care. To the latter was attributed the lack of success. Hunter at first justified Sackett's procedure in 1712, attributing the difference to the heat of the sun, "I myself have observed that where by mistake the trees have been first rinded on the side where the sun's heat had most influence, the ground near it was filled with turpentine drained by it from the tree." After tests three years later,[97] Hunter was "at a loss for the true cause of the disappointment from the trees prepared for tar, knowing nothing of the art . . . what I chiefly guess to be the cause of the miscarriage is this, that the trees being barked by an unskilful and unruly multitude were for the most part pierced in the inward rind contrary to strict directions by which means they become exhausted by the suns heat in the succeeding summer during which they stood,[98] after the time appointed and proper for felling of them, many of them are good but not in the quantity that will answer the expence and labour. . . ."[99] It was ten

[95] *Ibid.*, 98. It may be noted in passing that the colonists, generally without instructions, extracted their tar almost entirely from fallen trees and pine knots. The use of this unprepared wood may account for the "burning" quality of the colonial product complained of by the Navy Board.

[96] *Eccles. Rec.*, III, 2169.

[97] *N. Y. Col. Doc.*, V, 348, 450, 472.

[98] But North Carolina planters in 1730 made tar from "Light wood," that is, the trees which had fallen to the ground from decay, the turpentine having been removed from the cavities for three years. Gamble, *op. cit.*, 16.

[99] *N. Y. Col. Doc.*, V, 479.

years later that, Governor Spotswood of Virginia claimed to have convinced the Board of Trade that tar could not be made with the class of labor available in the plantations. He then urged that tar burners be brought from Finland for the purpose.[100]

Cobb suggested that the failure occurred because the pine trees of the Hudson could not produce tar and pitch in profitable quantities.[101] Other writers have followed this view.[102] Cobb pointed out of course that a different pine, the Georgia pine (*pinus palustris*) was used successfully in the Carolinas to produce tar and pitch, but he hinted that the New York workers attempted to use the white pine (*pinus strobus*) which is unfit for the tar industry. He admitted the presence in New York of the pitch pine (*pinus rigida*), a tree abundantly supplied with resin needed for the production of naval stores, but argued that it did not occur in sufficient size or forests to permit an expensive settlement in Hudson district for that purpose.[103] Cobb suggested further to support his argument that Bridger discovered his mistake and for that reason absented himself from the foredoomed settlement. This view is most improbable, for Bridger undoubtedly was well acquainted with the difference between white pine and pitch pine, since he was marking the best of the former in New England with the "Broad Arrow," reserving them for masts to be used by the Royal Navy and he used the latter to make tar and pitch, as described earlier.[104] Moreover, there were sufficient reasons, already pointed out in this study, for Bridger's defection. As for Cobb's argument that the pitch pine was not found in forests of sufficient quantity, Bridger wrote to the Board of Trade and Secretary of State in London that he had

[100] Osgood, *op. cit.*, II, 333.

[101] Cobb, *op. cit.*, 171.

[102] For example, see Mary Riggs Diefendorf, *The Historic Mohawk* (New York, 1910), 62.

[103] Cobb, *op. cit.*, 173.

[104] *C. C. 1710–1711*, 142; *N. Y. Col. Docs.*, V, 169.

Pitch Pine.
Pinus rigida.

REPRODUCTION OF PITCH PINE, *pinus rigida* (⅔ natural size) from F. A. Michaux, *North American Sylva*, 1819 ed., II, 287.

"view'd several great tracts of pitch pine proper for making tar and pitch,"[105] and he had selected the Livingston Manor site.

Was Bridger trustworthy in choosing the tract on Livingston Manor? Did he deliberately establish the government industry in country barren of the pitch pine and ensure its failure? The botanist Andrew F. Michaux, who in 1807 traveled this country and observed the forest trees, noted the presence of pitch pine in abundant quantities in sandy soils and mountain ridges along the Atlantic coast, and in such cases it was compact, heavy and surcharged with resin,[106] necessary for the production of tar and pitch.[107] In a letter to the author in March, 1927, the State Botanist H. D. House wrote that,"the pitch pine (*pinus rigida*) undoubtedly formed at that time a major portion of the forest upon the sandy and gravelly areas, and in general upon the areas of poor, sterile, or rocky soil throughout the Hudson Valley and north to Lake George. It is still one of the commonest and most conspicuous trees on this type of soil throughout the region, withstanding better than white pine ground fires, etc."[108] As the Palatines claimed the lands were almost barren,[109] and there are certainly hills on Livingston Manor several miles from the river, we may safely conclude that there was at least sufficient pitch pine present some miles back of the Hudson to provide the project with a good beginning,[110] and further, that Bridger was honest in his choice of a location, for the disagreement with Hunter had not yet occurred.

[105] *Ibid.*, 253, 261.

[106] F. A. Michaux, *The North American Sylva* (Philadelphia, 1817), I, 151.

[107] The pitch pine (*pinus rigida*) has been successfully used for the production of tar, pitch and turpentine. Romeyn B. Hough, *The American Woods* (Lowville, New York, 1891), Pt. II, 42.

[108] H. D. House, New York State Botanist, letter of March 25, 1927.

[109] *Doc. Hist.*, III, 708, map on 690; *Eccles. Rec.*, III, 2169.

[110] The Earl of Clarendon, formerly Lord Cornbury and governor of New York, denied that pine forests were to be found on Livingston Manor, but his animous against Livingston and Hunter incidentally are reflected in the entire letter of March 8, 1711. *N. Y. Col. Docs.*, V, 196.

While the tar manufacture still promised so much, on March 1, 1712, Hunter distraught with a problem growing more difficult every day, wrote to the Board of Trade, "Your Lordships may guess at my uneasiness having heard nothing from your Lordshipps since last summer neither have I advice of the Paym't of any of my Bills on account of the Palatines, but I go on with work as if I had, having as your Lordships well know her Majesty's Commands to that Effect. I wait with great impatience for your Lordships commands. . . ."[111] But Hunter's bills of exchange continued to return to him with legal protests. One protest related that the clerk at the Treasury had answered, "He knew not of any orders touching the payment" of the said bill. Another clerk had replied that the bills "must be kept till the Lord Treasurer should give Direction about them, which would be suddainly. . . ." A third gentleman at the Treasury answered that the Lord Treasurer was not in and had not left any orders, touching the payment of the bill, "but believes the same will be paid."[112]

This state of affairs was due to the Ministerial Revolution of 1710, referred to on an earlier page, in which the Tories superseded the Whigs through bedchamber politics and influence. Upon the Tories' accession to office in 1710, the condemnation of all Whig projects was politically necessary to maintain the Tories in power. The Palatine immigration, so distasteful to the native English poor,[113] became a valuable political weapon and any national advantages accruing therefrom were sacrificed to the political exigencies of the moment.[114] The Tories pretended that the whole affair of the Palatines was a design against the Established Church,

[111] N. Y. Col. MSS., LVII, 102, 107.

[112] *Ibid.*, 29, 57, 148a.

[113] *Parlia. Hist.*, VI, 999; Gibson, *op. cit.*, 83.

[114] Somerville, *op. cit.*, 367 thought that "a more shocking example of political rancour can hardly be imagined;" Abel Boyer, *Political State of Great Britain* (London, 1711), 422 mentions "the great noise the business of the Palatines made [in 1711] both in the Parliament House and without doors."

to increase the numbers and strength of the Dissenters.[115] Queen Anne strongly favored the High Church party, as did the Tories generally. Hence, this charge that the Palatines strengthened the Low Church or Protestant party, probably gained the Queen's sympathy for the opposition and lost for the Whig Ministry the Queen's approval of their policy in regard to the Palatines.[116] At any rate, Dr. John Arbuthnot, Anne's Tory physician, represents her as becoming aware later of this Palatine immigration having been foisted upon the Established Church, as a sort of opiate to keep it acquiescent to the Whig Ministry's tolerant religious policy.[117] Old sectarian rancors of the seventeenth century were not yet forgotten; the Glorious Revolution had left them deep in party politics. Hence, despite considerations which we might expect to see more largely emphasized, such as the possible inexpediency of supporting such an immigration in a time of war depression, the issue was fought out in some degree on religious grounds. Francis Hare, Whig pamphleteer, defended the reception of the Palatines almost entirely along these lines, citing the reception of the French and the Flemish immigrants in Elizabeth's reign as a precedent.[118] The official documents as well as the Whig propaganda in favor of the Palatines, invariably referred to them as "Poor German Protestants," although it has been shown that nearly a third were of the Catholic faith.

A parliamentary investigation was conducted in 1711, with the design "to load the late administration with all that was possible."[119] The investigation did reveal that up to

[115] W. T. Morgan, "The Ministerial Revolution of 1710 in England," in *loc. cit.*, XXXVI, 188, 210; Kapp, *Die Deutschen*, I, 26, calls it a plot; Burnet, *op. cit.*, VI, 39.

[116] Gibson, *op. cit.*, 73.

[117] Dr. John Arbuthnot's "Law is a Bottomless Pitt," Pt. III, in G. A. Aitken, *Later Stuart Tracts* (*An English Garner*, E. Arber, ed., London, 1877–80), 349–352.

[118] [Hare], *The Reception, passim.*

[119] Burnet, *op. cit.*, VI, 39.

April 14, 1711, over 100,000 pounds had been expended upon the Palatines in various ways.[120] The House of Commons passed two resolutions: first, "That the inviting and bringing over into this kingdom of the Palatines, of all religions, at the public expence, was an extravagant and unreasonable charge to the kingdom, and a scandalous misapplication of the public money, tending to the increase and oppression of the poor to this kingdom and of dangerous consequence to the constitution in church and state; second, That whoever advised the bringing over the poor Palatines into this kingdom, was an enemy to the Queen and kingdom." It was proposed to lay the blame on Sunderland because of his letters to the Board of Trade, ordering it to consider plans for settlements, but this was put off from time to time, and delayed by adjournments until the matter was quietly dropped.[121] An insinuation was also directed against Marlborough because of the letter from his secretary Cardonnel of May 21, 1709, described in chapter III. As the 1709 emigration had been under way for several months before that date, the attempt to saddle Marlborough with the rôle of instigator was hardly to be taken seriously. As the report indicated, the result of the letter was that the Lord Treasurer ordered "Mr. Sweet at Amsterdam to supply him with such sums of money as that Service shall require."[122] The responsibility of Marlborough for the shipping of the Palatines at government expense has already been disclosed. Of course, Mr. Dayrolle and Lord Townshend also shared in the responsibility. But since the arrangement had been authorized by the government with the Queen's approval, there was little the Tories could do about it, except make political capital during the election of 1711. The change in administration as a result of that

[120] *C. J.* XVI, 598. The act of naturalization of 1709 was repealed (February, 1712) as a result of this investigation, *ibid.*, 472; XVII, 75; *Parlia. Hist.*, VI, 1088.

[121] *Parlia. Hist.*, VI, 1001; Burnet, *op. cit.*, VI, 39.

[122] *C. J.*, XVI, 597. This correspondence has been described in Chapter III.

election was to have an adverse effect on the naval stores project in New York. On the very day that Hunter landed in New York, June 14, 1710, Sunderland, the Whig Secretary of State responsible for the New York venture, had been dismissed in favor of Harley.[123] As late as October 31, 1712, the other new Secretary of State, Lord Dartmouth, wrote to Hunter with assurances of the remittances being speedily answered, and though it brought him "New Life,"[124] it left him in a state of suspense.

Several incidents are significant as pointing to the conclusion that the failure to support the venture was purely political. Hunter was still pleading without success for financial support when he received his commission as Brigadier, for which he thanked Lord Bolingbroke, one of the leading Tory Secretaries of State, in a letter dated October 31, 1712.[125] Apparently the Tory Ministry did not disapprove of Hunter and perhaps regretted the political necessity that left him in such financial straits. It must be remembered too, that although a Whig and friendly to Marlborough, Hunter had a strong friend in the Tory, Dr. Arbuthnot, the personal physician of Queen Anne.[126]

In great uncertainty and yet with hope, the governor continued to provide subsistence for the Palatines until September 12, 1712. A few helpless widows and orphans were taken care of until the 23rd. The total expenditure was 32,144 pounds, 17 shillings and 2 pence sterling. Of this sum, the greater part of which was secured on Hunter's credit, he received 11,375 pounds: 10,000 pounds, the parliamentary

[123] William Frederick Wyon, *History of Great Britain during the Reign of Queen Anne* (London, 1876), II, 209.

[124] *N. Y. Col. Docs.*, V, 353. Dartmouth had been a member of the Board of Trade and was present when it approved the venture on December 5, 1709, *B. T. Jour. 1708–1714*, 99.

[125] *C. C. 1712–1714*, 85.

[126] *N. Y. Col. Docs.*, V, 453; "The Colden Letters," in *N. Y. Hist. Soc. Proc.* (1868), 196.

appropriation made in 1709 for the encouragement of the production of colonial naval stores, intended for the payment of the bounty on tar and pitch; and 1,375 pounds, secured by the sale in 1715 of various supplies left from the unsuccessful venture. Therefore, from the Palatine accounts there was due to the governor about 20,769 pounds sterling.[127]

By 1715 Hunter's finances were in very bad shape. His credit was exhausted because of the debt he had made himself responsible for in connection with the Palatine subsistence, and he had not received his salary as governor, which was then five years in arrears. The New York assembly was disputing the right of the Crown to appoint a salary for the governor out of the revenues of the province.[128] When Hunter reported the situation to the Board of Trade, it recommended to the Ministry that Parliament pass an act establishing an independent support for the governor of New York. Although the Ministry approved the bill for presentation to Parliament, Hunter's friends decided to drop the matter, fearing that, if the New York governorship became more attractive by reason of Parliamentary support, the political plum might go to someone with more influence than Hunter.[129]

Having suffered the desperate situation for four years and failing aid from England, Hunter came to terms with the assembly in 1715. It had been pressing him for the unconditional approval (contrary to his instructions) of a general naturalization bill, which would legalize certain deficiencies in the colonial land-titles (see the terms of the act given in Chapter VIII), even offering him a present of several thousand pounds for his assent. Hunter finally agreed to the passage of the bill in return for a five years' appropriation for the gov-

[127] P. R. O., C. O. 5/1085, 67. These figures vary slightly from the figures presented by the New York agent to the Board of Trade in 1717. *C. C. 1717–1718*, 117. Also, *C. C. 1714–1715*, 340; *N. Y. Col. Docs.*, V, 462.

[128] *N. Y. Col. Docs.*, V, 481; *B. T. Jour. 1708–1714*, 228.

[129] *B. T. Jour. 1708–1714*, 228; *C. C. 1714–1715*, 306.

ernment's expenses.[130] Most of the debts outstanding against
the provincial government, including the governor's arrears
in salary, were also paid at the same time. This relieved the
pressure upon the governor and it soon appeared that his
friends in England had not deserted him either, for they
secured the permission of the Ministry to present a bill to
Parliament for reimbursing Hunter for his expenditures in
behalf of the Palatines.[131] It was unsuccessful however, as
Parliament adjourned before it could be properly pressed for
enactment.[132] The appropriate time for approaching Parliament was never found apparently, for in 1722 Hunter petitioned for the grant of islands in the Delaware River as payment for the money due to him. [133] Two years later he had
his report of the Palatine accounts audited and certified by
government officials and on November 15, 1727 he presented
a petition, with the auditor's report attached, to the King.[134]
Evidently the petition was unsuccessful, for later Hunter's
son and heir, Thomas Orby Hunter, presenting a memorial
requesting the Manor of Crowland in Lincolnshire, said that
no part of the claim had been satisfied.[135]

In 1716 the Board of Trade, under the Whig Ministry of
George I, was favorable to a continuation of the naval stores
industry. But although Hunter was of as firm opinion as ever
that "this country contains pine woods enough to answer
the uses of all the navigation of England," and that the
industry was beneficial, he refused to take it up again. "After
the disappointments I have met with I cannot advise the
renewing the project until we have persons skilled & prac-
tised in the method of preparing the trees in the country

[130] N. Y. Col. Docs., V, 416.
[131] Ibid., 481.
[132] C. C. 1717–1718, 192.
[133] Acts Privy Council Col. 1680–1720, 775.
[134] P. R. O., C. O. 5/1085, 67.
[135] P. R. O., Gifts and Deposits 8/73 (no date).

from whence we have that commodity, for I doubt all others are but pretenders." [136]

The colonial naval stores industry was developed nevertheless, especially in the Carolinas, under the encouragement of the government bounty of four pounds per ton. By 1715 the total barrels of tar and pitch imported into England from the plantations nearly equalled the importations from Europe. [137] In 1718 the plantations sent England 82,084 barrels, which were seven times the amount secured from the continent. Accordingly, colonial naval stores were produced successfully under the bounty system without the need for a government industry similar to Louis XIV's workshops. The settlement failed because of the lack of continued financial support by the English government, because of an unwilling labor supply under frontier conditions, and perhaps, because of poor management and incapable instruction in the methods of manufacturing naval stores.

[136] N. Y. Col. Docs., V, 479; Professor Osgood (op. cit., II, 515) was mistaken in stating that by 1714 all thought of continuing the production of naval stores was abandoned.

[137] Appendix B, Lord, op. cit., 142.

CHAPTER VIII. THE PALATINE SETTLEMENTS ON THE FRONTIER OF THE OLD WEST

Governor Hunter could not believe that the project would be allowed to fail for lack of financial support from England, but his discouragement increased with the passing months. The Palatines, who had never received the full subsistence for which they were charged, petitioned the governor for more supplies.[1] Eight days later the blow fell. Although the pine trees had received their last preparation, staves prepared for barrels, the magazine almost finished, and a road nearly completed between it and the pine forest, the enterprise was halted.[2] On September 6, 1712, Hunter gave orders to Cast to inform the Palatines that they would have to subsist themselves until further orders, his credit being exhausted. They were to hire themselves out if they could. They might go anywhere in New York or New Jersey, both under the jurisdiction of Hunter, but they had to secure a ticket of leave and register their destination. If they attempted to leave without these formalities, Cast was ordered to raise the hue and cry for them and imprison them until further orders.[3] The purpose of these conditions was to keep the Palatines in readiness upon the first public notice to return to work, as specified in the covenant.[4] This notice reached the Palatines about the middle of the month. The last day of the government subsistence for most of the Palatines was September 12th.[5] The Palatines were taken by surprise and ex-

[1] *Eccles. Rec.*, III, 2169. The order "to retrench in the article of beer" was issued late in July. Liv. MS., letter of July 30, 1712.

[2] *N. Y. Col. Docs.*, V, 347.

[3] *Doc. Hist.*, III, 683.

[4] *N. Y. Col. Docs.*, V, 347.

[5] P. R. O., C. O. 5/1085, 67.

perienced some anxiety as to their ability to survive the winter.[6]

Many of the Palatines scattered about the neighborhood of the settlements, seeking employment to provide themselves and their families with food during the coming winter. Some remained in the settlements where they had been placed by Hunter. During that winter without government aid their suffering was particularly pitiful. Their minister Reverend Haeger wrote to the Society for the Propagation of the Gospel on July 6, 1713, that "they boil grass and the children eat the leaves of the trees. I have seen old men and women cry that it should almost have moved a stone. [Several] have for a whole week together had nothing but welsh turnips which they did only scrape and eat without any salt or fat and bread."[7] Haeger had given what little he had so that he was in no better condition. Worse yet there was no hope of any alteration in their condition. Within the next five years many Palatines moved elsewhere. Several went to Pennsylvania, others to New Jersey, settling at Hackensack, still others pushed a few miles south to Rhinebeck, New York, and some returned to New York City, while quite a few established themselves on Livingston Manor itself. The last group had to accept Robert Livingston's terms and they were soon heavily in his debt.[8]

The more restless among them, who resented their condition of serfdom, immediately bethought themselves of the legendary Schoharie when they were thrown on their own resources. On October 31, 1712, Hunter wrote to the Board

---

[6] Kapp, *Die Deutschen*, I, 44.

[7] L. C., S. P. G. MSS. A-8, 189.

[8] *C. C. 1720-1721*, 180; Simmendinger, *op. cit.*, Appendix (see lists in Appendix F); Liv. MS., "Debt List of Palatines living in the Manor of Livingston," December 28, 1726. The Palatines who lived in the original settlement also fell into Livingston's debt but for more modest accounts. Liv. MSS., "Debt List of the Palatines living in the four villages in the Manor of Livingston," December 26, 1718, also January 1, 1721.

SCHOHARIE, New York, showing Old Fort Museum on the extreme right. *Courtesy of the Pennsylvania-German Society.*

of Trade relating that "some hundreds of them took a resolution of possessing the land of Scoharee & are accordingly march'd thither have[ing] been buisy in cutting a road from Schenectady to that place. . . ."[9] The governor was far from pleased at this removal without negotiation but was in a poor position to interfere, "it being impossible for me to prevent this;" in other words, Hunter thought of preventing it but of course saw no logical way of do so, since he could no longer subsist them.

It also appears that Hunter bore a real animus against the troublesome Palatines, especially those who had settled in Schoharie between September 12th and October 31, 1712, some forty or fifty families. In March, 1713, he remarked in a letter to Livingston, "Since nothing can restrain the madness of that people [the Palatines], I'm afraid I must apply an extraordinary severity."[10] On May 11, 1713, he wrote to the Board of Trade that he had used "all means imaginable to keep the Palatines together . . . but many are gone of their own heads to settle at Scoharee and the frontier."[11] Two months later he wrote concerning the deprivation of "those who run to Scohare."[12] The governor had been bothered so much by the Palatines, attracted by the storied claims of the Schoharie Valley, that he had become irritable on the subject.

The Palatines who intended to settle in Schoharie Valley first sent a number of deputies to make arrangements with the Indians there. The Indians were easily persuaded to sell the land to the deputies.[13] The fact is that they parted with their claims to the same lands on three separate occasions, once when Nicholas Bayard had purchased it about 1695, again by gift to Governor Hunter for the government as was related

[9] N. Y. Col. Docs., V, 347.
[10] Liv. MS., letter of March 30, 1713.
[11] N. Y. Col. Docs., V, 364.
[12] Ibid., 366.
[13] Weiser Diary, 15, in loc. cit., VIII, 798; Olde Ulster, II, 202.

earlier in this paper, and now to the deputies for the Palatines. The land-title difficulties which the Germans encountered were partly due to such uncertain memory of the savages, who were not averse to selling their claims as often as they could get an offer.

The procedure by which title to land was secured was well established by this time. One had to apply to the Governor in Council for a license to purchase from the Indians a tract of a certain number of acres in a particular locality. Fees of 20 shillings to the Governor, 6 shillings to the Clerk of the Council, in addition to 1 shilling, 6 pence for reading the petition in Council and 6 pence for filing it (all in colonial currency) were necessary. Then the purchaser made his deal with the Indians for a deed in English, practically always with the aid of "fire-water." After securing the Indian deed, the prospective patentee applied to the Governor and Council for a survey of the grant, and received a warrant of survey for a fee of 6 shillings. In the period of the early eighteenth century, these surveys were quite carelessly made and the land taken in was invariably many times larger than specified. A patent was then granted by the Governor and Council for the following fees in colonial currency: Clerk of Council, 3 shillings for drawing up a warrant or order for the patent; Attorney-General, 10 shillings for drafting the patent; Secretary of the Province, 30 shillings more or less for engrossing, sealing and recording; and the Governor, various amounts depending upon the size of the grant.[14] From this description of the method of securing title, it should be apparent that the Palatines engaging for land in Schoharie were buying trouble for themselves by their ignorance of procedure. It should be clear moreover how necessary the Governor's good will was for success in securing title.

Upon the return of the deputies from Schoharie about 150 families moved the same autumn (1712) to Albany and Sche-

[14] Ruth L. Higgins, *Expansion in New York with Especial Reference to the 18th Century* (Columbus, Ohio, 1931), 30; *N. Y. Col. Docs.*, V, 511.

nectady.[15] Here in Schenectady, Conrad Weiser told us his father stayed during the winter with Johannes Meynderton. He also related that bread was extraordinarily high but that the inhabitants were very liberal to the Germans. If Weiser's Journal has been read aright, it was in Schenectady that the Indian Quaynant visited his father and as a result Conrad was sent to live with the Indians about the end of November. It also appears that fifty families could not wait for spring but cutting a rough road from Schenectady to Schoharie in two weeks, they settled there for the winter throwing up rough shelters. With the help of the Indians they weathered the cold winter but with great suffering. How different the experience of these hardy pioneers contrasted with that of our complaining Matanuska Valley settlers sent to Alaska last year (1935).

At this time Governor Hunter sent orders, forbidding their settlement in Schoharie. Nevertheless, in March, 1713, the remainder of the 150 families joined their friends at Schoharie, traveling with roughly-made sledges through snow three feet deep.[16] The emigrants settled in seven villages, named as we are told for the deputies who made the arrangements with the Indians. The most northern village, Kniskerndorf, of which there are no remains today, was opposite the village of Central Bridge, nearly opposite the point where Cobleskill Creek empties into Schoharie River. Two miles south was Gerlachsdorf, of which there is no vestige left. Two miles further south was Fuchsendorf, later called Fox Town, where the Old Fort Museum of Schoharie now stands. Schmidsdorf, later called Smith's Town, is marked today by the little railroad station at Schoharie. Brunnendorf, later

---

[15] Weiser Diary, 15, 17, 21, in *loc. cit.*, VIII, 797. Weiser gives 1713 as the date of the migration but it is apparent from Governor Hunter's letters already cited that this movement took place in 1712. It is also plain from the diary, for Weiser gave 1713 as the year when the government subsistence was stopped, also an error.

[16] Kapp, *Die Deutschen*, I, 56; *Eccles. Rec.*, III, 2170.

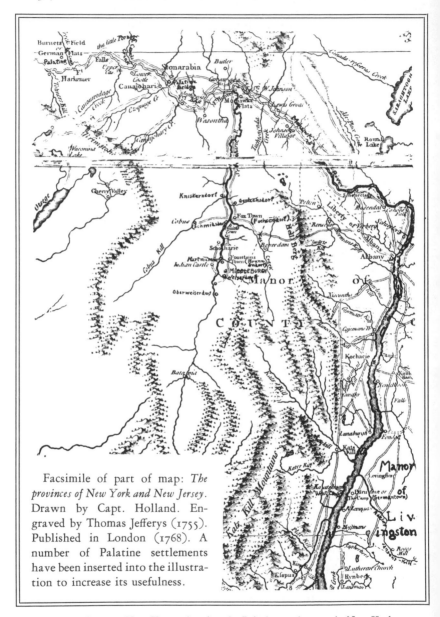

Facsimile of part of map: *The provinces of New York and New Jersey.* Drawn by Capt. Holland. Engraved by Thomas Jefferys (1755). Published in London (1768). A number of Palatine settlements have been inserted into the illustration to increase its usefulness.

MAP OF CENTRAL NEW YORK, showing the Palatine settlements in New York.
Courtesy of New York Historical Society.

known as Fountaindorf or Waterstown, was around the site now occupied by St. Paul's Lutheran Church in Schoharie. The last three mentioned were in what is now the incorporated village of Schoharie and were all three within a radius of one mile. Two and a half miles southwest of Brunnendorf was Hartmansdorf, of which an iron marker is the only indication now. Two miles further south was Weiserdorf on the edge of the present town of Middleburgh. Oberweiserdorf, a split off from Weiserdorf some years later, was the most southern settlement about three miles away.[17] In its early days Weiserdorf was supposed to have forty small rude huts, built of logs and earth, with bark for roofing and with skins covering the doorways.

The exact numbers moving to Schoharie do not appear in the records, but on October 26, 1713 Governor Hunter reported to an investigator of British projects in America, Colonel Nicholson, that 1,008 Palatines were in the Hudson River settlements, 500 in Schoharie Valley and about 500 among the various planters.[18] In 1718 a report of the Palatine ministers places 224 families of 1,021 persons along the Hudson River and scattered areas, while 170 families of 580 persons were in Schoharie.[19]

The first year in Schoharie (1713) was one of bitter struggle for the Palatines. Conrad Weiser in his Journal related how one borrowed a horse and another a cow. Someone else borrowed harness and a plow. Hitching the horse and cow together they broke up so much land that in 1714 they had almost enough corn for their needs. Meanwhile they often went hungry or appeased their appetites with wild

[17] See map of New York. Weiser Diary, 17, in *loc. cit.*, VIII, 797. The locations of these villages is based on information secured from Mr. Chauncey Rickard, the director of the Old Fort Museum, Schoharie, New York. The German word *dorf* means village or town. Also see John Heustis French, *Gazeteer of the State of New York* (8th ed., Syracuse, New York, 1860), 601.

[18] *C. C. 1712–1714*, 263.

[19] *Doc. Hist.*, I, 693.

potatoes and strawberries which grew in abundance and which the Indians had recommended to them. For flour, Weiser said they had to go 35 or 40 miles, presumably counting to and from Schenectady, where on credit a bushel or two might be obtained. This journey, starting early in the morning, took all day, and then after their business was completed in the town, they make the return trip, lasting throughout the night. Women as well as men undertook the trip. Weiser wrote too of the pain and tears of the hungry ones awaiting their return. If they went to Albany, the journey took three or four days.[20]

But there were silver linings in the dark clouds of adversity. The charity of the good people of Schenectady has been referred to. In addition records tell us of several occasions in 1713 when the Dutch Church of New York sent supplies for the Palatines in Schoharie. In July of that year the communicants of the Dutch Church sent to Albany 80 bushels of corn, fifty pieces of rookspeck (smoked pork), weighing about 500 pounds, 100 pounds of bread and six pounds of money for the purchase of flour. The Palatines were glad to go to Albany to receive these items and carry them home from there.[21] Hunting and fishing completed their scanty larder. Judge John M. Brown, in his *History of Schoharie*, largely based on tradition and published in 1823, wrote that Lambert Sternbergh of Gerlachsdorf purchased a skipple (three pecks) of wheat and sowed it in the fall of 1713. The yield of this most carefully cultivated wheat was said to have been 83 skipples.[22] But whatever the truth of the amount, we may be sure that it was most preciously treated and preserved. Within a few years regular over-day and night trips

---

[20] Weiser Diary, 23, in *loc. op.*, VIII, 798; Simms, *Frontiersmen*, I, 129.

[21] J. Munsell, *Annals of Albany* (Albany, 1856), VII, 236.

[22] J. M. Brown, *op. cit.* (Schoharie, New York, 1823), 10; Jeptha R. Simms, *History of Schoharie County* (Albany, 1845), 52, hereafter cited as Simms, *Schoharie*.

were made to Schenectady to have the grain ground into flour at the grist-mill there.

The Palatines had not been permitted to bring to Schoharie the tools supplied them by the government in the Hudson Valley settlements. Indeed, they feared they might be charged with theft. Consequently, they were hard-pressed to fashion substitutes with which to start building their settlement. In the old Fort Museum at Schoharie are many relics of pioneer life in the Schoharie Valley and from these we can secure a fair idea of the difficulties of the settlers and the courageous way in which they met them.[23] One settler fashioned a shovel from a log end, painstakingly hollowing it out. Another used the branches of a tree for a fork to be used in hay-making. A maul was made from a heavy knot of wood, the protruding branch being used as a handle. A mortar for grinding corn was made by taking a log two feet high, and cutting a hole 12 inches in diameter about 18 inches to 20 inches deep into one end. The sides at the top remained about an inch thick. A cornbread mixer was constructed by nailing together two half logs, after the edges joined together had been cut by two spheroid holes of about 8 inches in diameter. The hole of the mixer was about 10 inches deep while the depth of the log itself measured 14 inches. Iron gouges had to be secured to bore holes and the process of furnishing their huts with articles of convenience must have been quite laborious.

Their furniture must have been very crude for the time of the men was occupied in clearing the land and securing food, while the women had not only their household duties to perform but farm work as well. A split log with four stout sticks set in for legs was their table. Crude stools made in the same manner or rough sections of logs completed the furnish-

[23] Much of this information on early life is derived from an examination of the Old Fort Museum relics so courteously and effectively explained by Mr. Chauncey M. Rickard, the director of the Museum.

ings. These first huts apparently lacked fireplaces; cooking was done in stone ovens out of doors, built for the use of several neighboring families. As soon as more permanent dwellings could be built of log and stones, the fireplaces, so necessary in winter, were made by attaching a stone chimney to the outside wall and preparing a small stone floor and stone sides for fire protection. A bar across the fireplace and chains for hanging the pots gave the *hausfrau* a feeling of domestic security so desirable to these wanderers. Kitchen utensils were next acquired. Rocking chairs were the height of luxury and a prized possession in the settlements. As the years passed these early homes came to have benches with backs, solid tables and well-made chests, artistically decorated in bright colors and carrying Biblical verses in German worked into the design.

The earliest artificial light used by the Palatines were pitch pine knots. Tallow dips were scarce, necessitating rising at dawn and retiring at dusk. As the cheap clothing of kerseys, nap-shag and flannels, provided for the Palatines by the British government, wore out, the skins of the deer and beaver were fashioned into breeches, skirts and caps as protection from the elements. Shoes, excepting the moccasin, were made of heavy leather studded with iron clips for hard wear, and fastened with a buckle, or tied with leather thongs near the top.

The Palatines had large families as a rule, the children often numbering close to twenty or more, but the mortality was exceptionally high. The maidens married quite young, increasing their fecundity. The Palatine women were generally robust and strong, for within one week of their arrival in Schoharie Valley four children were safely born.[24] Difficulties were encountered in entering the sacred bonds of matrimony. Since the preacher was an infrequent visitor,

[24] Simms, *Schoharie*, 51; Simms, *Frontiersmen*, I, 127. The children were named Catharina Mattheus, Elizabetha Lawer, Wilhemus Bauch, and Johannes Erhardt.

couples sometimes neglected the ceremony itself, but their marital faithfulness was well enough established to be proverbial.

Conrad Weiser's Journal tells us that "Here the people lived for a few years without preacher, without government, generally in peace. Each one did what he thought was right." Of course, part of this orderly conduct was due to the respect held by the people for their listmasters, placed over them in

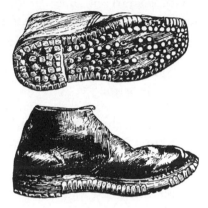

PALATINE SHOES
Courtesy of Pennsylvania-German Society.

the Hudson River settlements and who retained their authority in Schoharie too.[25] Elderly John Conrad Weiser, a magistrate in old Würtemberg in Germany, was perhaps the most eminent as well as the most fiery leader.

Governor Hunter in opposing their settlement in Schoharie,[26] probably feared that once there, they would never return to the manufacture of naval stores along the Hudson. He comforted himself somewhat as he told the Board of Trade that the Palatines at least strengthened the border, and that the Palatines "at Schoharee may be imploy'd in working in the vast pinewoods near to Albany, which they must be

[25] Weiser Diary, 27, in *loc. cit.*, VIII, 799.
[26] *Eccles. Rec.*, III, 2146, 2170; *C. C. 1712–1714*, 82.

obliged to doe they having no pretense to possession of any land but by performing their part of the contract relating to that manufacture."[27] In June, 1714, Hunter was interested in renewing the project. He had Sackett test the trees to see if they would do, observing, "If the trees answer I'll fall to work at my own Cost."[28] In August he informed the Board of Trade, "The trees are now ready for manufacturing, and I want nothing but money to imploy hands to made a very considerable quantity of tarr, having had the trees tryed which for the most part answer expectations."[29] Perhaps Hunter expected to drive the Palatines back into the Hudson Valley settlements.

Conditions were improving when in the summer of 1714 a colonial gentleman of prominence, Nicholas Bayard, visited the Palatines at Schoharie. He gave out that to every house-holder who would describe the boundaries of the land held, he would issue a deed in the name of Queen Anne. Tradition has described him as a royal agent.[30] This cannot have been the case, since he had no official connection at the time. In fact, Governor Hunter composed about that time an unpub-lished farce in three acts called "Androboros" in which Bayard is castigated in no uncertain terms.[31] Bayard belonged to the colonial opposition to the governor. His intentions with regard to the Palatines are unfortunately not clear. But, a consideration of his background[32] suggests that Bayard, whose grandfather had once purchased the Indian claim to Schoharie and whose patent had been disallowed by the Colonial and British authorities as an "extravagant grant"

[27] C. C. 1712–1714, 82; N. Y. Col. Docs., V, 347.

[28] Liv. MS., June 15, 1714.

[29] N. Y. Col. Docs., V, 380.

[30] Simms, Frontiersmen, I, 145.

[31] Widener Library, Cambridge, Massachusetts, Hunter MS., "Andro-borus," 14, 20, 27; Higgins, op. cit., 53.

[32] Mrs. A. P. Atterbury, The Bayard Family (Baltimore, 1928), 16. The elder Nicholas Bayard died in 1707.

in 1708, was trying to save something of his relative's investment. In 1710 he had petitioned that either the charges and fees be refunded or that the former grant be confirmed.[33] He may even have envisioned an appeal to London for a confirmation of the patent as Captain Evans, another dispossessed grantee, was doing.[34] Had the Palatines accepted his deeds and claimed the land from him, his case would have been materially strengthened as he could point then to improvements and settlement, the lack of which was a strong argument against the original grant.

Regardless of his intentions, Bayard was taken for a representative of Hunter and barely escaped the settlements with his life under the cover of darkness. He was besieged in John George Smith's house by an angry mob and shots were exchanged. Escaping after nightfall to Schenectady, Bayard sent word that if any would appear before him there, acknowledge him and name their boundaries, they should still receive a free deed and a lasting title.[35] How galling this experience must have been to Bayard and how it consequently must have pleased Hunter, but at the same time warned him of the temper of these German settlers.

The Palatine tradition has it that Bayard then sold the Schoharie title to five citizens of Albany. This may refer to his grandfather's Indian title, which had been voided as described in Chapter VI, for the Albany partners, who belonged to the governor's party in the colony, received their patent from Hunter on November 3, 1714.[36] This grant included 10,000 acres of Bayard's vacated grant upon which the Palatines were settled. The patentees were Myndert Schuyler,

---

[33] *Cal. N. Y. Land Papers* (Albany, 1864), 97.

[34] *C. C. 1720–1721*, 28. The Board of Trade recommended to Secretary of State Craggs that Evans be given an equivalent grant elsewhere, and issued orders accordingly. *Eccles. Rec.*, III, 2194.

[35] Simms, *Schoharie*, 61.

[36] N. Y. Patent Books, VIII, 74; *Cal. N. Y. Land Papers*, 110; N. Y. Land Papers, VI, 26, 80; N. Y. *Council Minutes*, XI, 245.

Peter van Brugh, Robert Livingston, Jr., John Schuyler and Peter Wileman. When Lewis Morris, Jr., and Andrus Coeman surveyed these lands for the Five Partners, they found that the flats of Fox Creek and a large part of Kniskerndorf had been omitted. These lands they secured for themselves and joined forces with the Albany group. The Five Partners therefore became the Seven Partners.[37]

The Palatines were called upon in 1715 to purchase, lease or vacate their land. Hunter claimed (in 1720) that at his instance favorable terms were extended to the Palatines, offering the land free from all rent for ten years, and after that on only a very moderate quit-rent.[38] They refused, and grew violent. When Adam Vrooman, a resident of Schenectady, tried to settle on land in Schoharie which he had secured by purchase from the Indians in 1711 and government patent in 1714,[39] they tore up his fences and pulled down the stone walls of his home. The Palatines evidently thought that the land was theirs. When warnings failed to drive out Vrooman's son, he was pulled from a wagon and beaten. When Vrooman reported these incidents to Governor Hunter, he also informed him that John Conrad Weiser and several others spoke of going to Boston, intending to sail for England.[40]

Upon this information Hunter issued a warrant for the arrest of John Conrad Weiser.[41] Apparently attempting to serve this warrant a sheriff from Albany, named Adams, came into the Schoharie Valley. No sheriff of the name of Adams has been listed in the Civil List of the time, but Judge Brown who related this story in his *History of Schoharie*, informed Mr. Jeptha R. Simms, the historian of our New York

[37] Simms, *Schoharie*, 60.

[38] *Eccles. Rec.*, III, 2146.

[39] N. Y. Patent Books, VIII, 92; N. Y. Land Papers, VI, 13, 37, 64; N. Y. *Council Minutes*, XI, 267; Simms, *Schoharie*, 55. Vrooman's Indian deed is in the Old Fort Museum, Schoharie, N. Y.

[40] *Doc. Hist.*, III, 687; N. Y. Col. MSS., LX, 3, 20.

[41] *Ibid.*, 688; N. Y. Col. MSS., LX. 26.

frontier, that he had heard the story from Mr. Adams' own lips.[42] Perhaps Adams was deputized for the occasion. If so, it was most unfortunate for him, for the Seven Partners greatly underrated the bravery of these people. Adams, conscious of his own honorable intentions, passed up through the valley and made a halt at Weiserdorf. No sooner had he explained his business and attempted the arrest than a mob appeared. The women of that generation, it would seem, possessed Amazonian strength. Under the direction of Magdalena Zeh, a self-appointed captain, they took the sheriff into their hands and dealt rather harshly with him. He was knocked down, and inducted into various places where the sow delighted to wallow. After receiving many indignities in the neighborhood of Weiserdorf, Adams was placed upon a rail and ridden through several settlements. Finally, he was deposited on a small bridge across a stream along the old Albany road, a distance from the starting point of between six and seven miles, quite a lengthy journey for such a conveyance. The captain then seized a stake and laid it over the sheriff's person until two of his ribs were broken. He was rescued a little later and eventually recovered.[43]

Matters rested thus for two more years. Then in 1717 Hunter ordered that John Conrad Weiser, together with three men from each village appear before him. He told them that he expected orders from England to remove them to another region, unless they came to an agreement with the owners of the land. They protested that they had built their homes and had made improvements. Hunter agreed to send twelve men to estimate the value of their improvements and reimburse them, but he failed to carry out his promise. Meanwhile they were not to plow the land. Needing food that

[42] Simms, *Frontiersmen*, I, 150, Brown, *op. cit.*, 13. No sheriff of Albany County was named Adams until 1840. E. A. Werner, *N. Y. Civil List for 1886*, 455.

[43] Brown, *op. cit.*, 12; Simms, *Frontiersmen*, I, 146, *et seq.*

winter, they sent deputies requesting permission to plow, and being refused, they disregarded the orders altogether.[44]

In 1718 the Palatines sent John Conrad Weiser, William Scheff and Gerhart Walrath[45] to London to ask for justice. They sailed from Philadelphia, but, were robbed of their money by pirates. The ship had to put into Boston for new supplies, and upon reaching London the Palatine deputies were imprisoned for debt. By that time Hunter himself had returned to London to recoup his fortune. He falsely claimed that the Palatines had taken possession of lands in Schoharie already granted to others.[46] He pointed out that the proprietors had offered them easy terms—no rent for ten years and thereafter only a moderate rent. His suggestion that they be removed to other lands on the frontier was adopted. The Palatines' deputies were not in agreement themselves as to what should be done.[47] This and their lack of financial resources lent feeble opposition to the influence of Hunter. Walrath, homesick, sailed for New York but died before reaching his destination. Toward the close of 1721 Schef returned but he too died soon —in his case within six weeks of his homecoming. At last in November of 1723 John Conrad Weiser came back to New York still unreconciled to the government's proposals.[48]

Colonel Hunter's successor, Governor William Burnet was ordered to settle the Palatines on some suitable lands.[49] In 1721 Burnet gave a number of the Palatines license to purchase land of the Mohawks provided that it was at least

[44] *Eccles. Rec.*, III, 2171; *Doc. Hist.*, III, 713.

[45] *C. C. 1720–1721*, 102. The letter of attorney sent by the Palatines in the autumn of 1719 gives us Walrath's name as Gerard, but it appears on the Subsistence List and in Simmendinger's List as Gerhardt.

[46] *N. Y. Col. Docs.*, V, 552.

[47] *Ibid.*, 574; *Eccles. Rec.*, III, 2177.

[48] Weiser Diary, 39, 43, in *loc. cit.*, VIII, 800. Before his return Weiser had carried the fight unsuccessfully to the highest authorities, the Lord Justices. *C. C. 1722–1723*, 311.

[49] *N. Y. Col. Docs.*, V, 582.

forty miles above Fort Hunter and at least eighty miles from Albany. He explained to the Board of Trade that he had made this condition in order to have the frontier extended. He also stated as evidence of the good will now prevailing that some Palatines had actually taken leases from the Seven Partners.[50] In 1722 Burnet purchased land in the Mohawk Valley (Burnetsfield) for the Palatines but they were slow in responding to his offers. About sixty families wanted to settle apart from the others and as they had been "most hearty for the government," Burnet permitted them to settle between Fort Hunter and Canada.[51] The leader of this group was John Christopher Gerlach. They petitioned for a patent in March, 1722, then realizing that they had to do their own purchasing from the Indians, they made the necessary arrangements.[52] On October 19, 1723, the Stone Arabia patent was issued to twenty-seven persons. It contained 12,700 acres about two or three miles back from the Mohawk River. The annual quit-rent of 2 shillings, 6 pence per hundred acres and customary conditions were made. This settlement developed into Palatine Bridge and the town of Palatine.[53]

Tradition has it that in 1723 fifteen families of the Palatines removed to the Tulpehocken district just east of the Swatara Creek in Pennsylvania. They migrated at the invitation of Sir William Keith, Governor of Pennsylvania, who invited them on the occasion of his visit to attend an Indian conference in Albany in 1722. The Pennsylvania records confirm the fact that Governor Keith invited them then. In truth the Pennsylvania records suggest further that several Palatines from New York settled in Pennsylvania "about 1717."[54] As Weiser wrote in his Journal, "the people received

[50] C. C. 1720–1721, 468; N. Y. Col. Docs., V, 634.
[51] Eccles. Rec., III, 2196; C. C. 1722–1723, 168.
[52] Cal. N. Y. Land Papers, 120, 138, 195, 196.
[53] N. Y. Land Papers, VI, 138; Cal. N. Y. Land Papers, 120.
[54] Pennsylvania Archives, 2nd series, VII, 78, 94; N. Y. Col. Docs., V, 677.

Map of Eastern Pennsylvania, showing Tulpehocken (Wormelsdorf) settled by the Palatines. *Courtesy of Pennsylvania-German Society.*

news from the land at Swatara and Tulpehocken in Pennsylvania. Many of them came together, cut a way from Schoharie to the Susquehanna and brought their goods there and made canoes and journeyed down to the mouth of the Swatara Creek and drove their cattle overland in the spring of 1723. Thence they came to the Tulpehocken settlement; later others followed and settled there, at first without permission of the owner of the land or company, or from the Indians from whom the people had not yet bought the land."[55] It seems

[55] Weiser Diary, 45, in *Loc. cit.*, VIII, 801.

that other Palatines preceded the 1723 emigrants from Schoharie to Pennsylvania, for a letter written in Albany on October 16, 1720, stated that some of the Palatines had gone
"to [the] Philadelphia government, where they think they
fare best."[56] But since Weiser wrote in his Journal that the
settlement in the spring of 1723 was the beginning of the
Tulpehocken settlement, it does not appear that the earlier
group settled there.

The Palatine settlements at Womelsdorf in the Tulpehocken region made the Indians restless and caused the colonial authorities of Pennsylvania great concern.[57] Several other
groups are said to have followed the 1723 emigrants. In 1725
there were thirty-three families settled there[58] and fifty more
families expected. These moved in 1729 and among them was
the family of Conrad Weiser, who served Pennsylvania and
the colonies generally as a valuable intermediary with the
Indians.[59] The elder John Conrad Weiser did not move to the
Pennsylvania frontier with the first families as he had often
threatened to do in earlier days. In 1726 he entered into an
agreement with John Van Kampen of Huntington County,
New Jersey to procure an Indian deed for land on the west
side of the Delaware River.[60] The attempt to secure this land
apparently failed, for Weiser later joined his son in Womelsdorf near the Swatara Creek in Pennsylvania.

Taking advantage of the offer made by Governor Burnet
to settle the rest of the Palatines on the twenty-four mile
tract above Little Falls, the family of Johan Jurgh Kast obtained in June, 1724, a patent for 1,100 acres. The patent included the usual reservations and required 27 shillings, 6

[56] C. C. 1720–1721, 180.

[57] Pennsylvania Provincial Papers, III, 51.

[58] Col. Rec. of Pa., III, 352. See lists of names in Appendix G.

[59] Daniel Häberle, Auswanderung und Koloniegründungen der Pfälzer in 18ten
Jahrhundert (Kaiserlautern, 1909), 94.

[60] Cal. N. Y. Hist. MSS., II, 497.

THE CONRAD WEISER HOMESTEAD, Womelsdorf, (Tulpehocken) Pennsylvania. *Courtesy of Pennsylvania-German Society.*

pence for annual rent.[61] One of the Kasts was also included in the nearby Burnetsfield patent, granted a year later. Another group of Palatines settled west of the same falls on lands offered by the Governor. This land was purchased from the Indians by John Conrad Weiser and other Palatines on July 9, 1722.[62]

The Burnetsfield patent, granted April 13, 1725, assigned one-hundred-acre lots to some ninety individuals. Some received their land all in one place, while others had thirty acres in the river bottoms between the Mohawk River and the West Canada Creek just before it joins the Mohawk, and seventy acres in woodland back of the river. As in the other patents they were required to pay the customary quit-rent.[63] The meadow lands south of the river were later known as the German Flats while the village opposite was called Palatine village and later Herkimer after the German-American general who won fame in the Revolutionary War. At last these Palatines occupied land to which they had undisputed possession. The Burnetsfield community prospered until the French and Indian War threatened the New York frontier.

In 1731, 8,000 acres, known as the Canajoharie patent, were granted to certain members of the colonial aristocracy.[64] These lands as well as certain others granted a little earlier were located in the present towns of Minden and Canajoharie. Palatines who early settled on these lands rented them from the Indians. There was considerable dispute between the Indians and the several colonial patentees in which the London authorities eventually intervened because of charges of fraud.[65] A compromise was finally effected in 1768 mainly

[61] N. Y. Land Papers, IX, 75, 76; Cal. N. Y. Land Papers, 173.

[62] N. Y. Col. Docs., V, 634; N. Y. Land Papers, VIII, 168; Cal. N. Y. Land Papers, 171.

[63] N. Y. Land Papers, IX, 22, 48, 174; Cal. N. Y. Land Papers, 166, 169, 182; N. Y. Patent Books, IX, 139, 165.

[64] N. Y. Patent Books, XI, 53; N. Y. Land Papers, 89, 103, 112, 122.

[65] N. Y. Col. Docs., VI, 851, 1017, 1178; VII, 671, 876.

through the good offices of Sir William Johnson, the great
colonial trader of central New York and the Palatines eventually purchased the lands they were occupying.[66]

In similar ways other groups of Germans heeded the call
of the new lands and the frontier was pushed westward.
About 1710 a company of Palatines, in faith Mennonites,
settled "toward the River Susquehanna" in Pennsylvania.
Palatines continued to arrive in that colony in increasing
numbers. For example, in 1717 one hundred "sold themselves
for servants to Pennsylvania for five years." About 400 more
were in London, awaiting disposition[67] when in 1717, the
registration of immigrants was required by the Pennsylvania
colonial authorities.[68] On September 14, 1727, a ship from
Holland arrived in Philadelphia with 400 Palatines. It was
then said a much greater number would follow.[69] This commanded the attention of the governor and council of Pennsylvania, who demanded a declaration of allegiance to the King
and fidelity to the proprietary government.[70] In fact in the
following year, John Penn, one of the heirs of William Penn,
considered the advisability of prohibiting or restricting the
German immigration.[71]

The stream of *Deutches Volk* ran rather steadily to Pennsylvania. Writers touching on this subject have attributed the
apparent preference for Pennsylvania to New York or other
colonies, to the harsh treatment of the Schoharie settlers.[72]

[66] *Ibid.*, VII, 850; VIII, 70, 78, 92, 94.

[67] *C. C. 1717–1718*, 29.

[68] *Minutes of Provincial Council of Pennsylvania*, III, 29.

[69] H. S. P., Pennsylvania Misc. Papers, Penn and Baltimore MSS., 1725–
1739, 27.

[70] *Minutes of Provincial Council of Pennsylvania*, III, 283; Samuel Hazard,
Register of Pennsylvania (Philadelphia, 1828), II, 203.

[71] *Pennsylvania Magazine of History*, XXVII, 378.

[72] Faust, *op. cit.*, I, 105; Bolton and Marshall, *Colonization of North America*
(New York, 1920), 319; Greene, *op. cit.*, 180, 230; M. W. Jernegan, *American
Colonies* (New York, 1929), 308; Proper, *op. cit.*, 39; Beidelman, *op. cit.*, 60;
Cobb, *op. cit.*, 108.

In this they follow the statement by the Swedish traveler, Kalm, who in 1748 wrote, "I am told of a very different reason which I will mention here [Kalm then describes the ill treatment, such as loss of land] . . . The Germans not satisfied with being themselves removed from *New York*, wrote to their relations and friends and advised them, if ever they intended to come to America, not to go to New York, where the government had shown itself so unequitable. This advice had such influence, that the Germans, who afterwards went in great numbers to North America, constantly avoided *New York* and always went to *Pennsylvania*. It sometimes happened that they were forced to go on board such ships as were bound to New York; but they were scarce got on shore, when they hastened on to *Pennsylvania* in sight of all the inhabitants of *New York*." [73] Kalm himself was careful to mention that he had been told this. [74] The last sentence, indeed, has the flavor of a story told for effect.

But Kalm was not satisfied with that, for his next sentence was, "But the want of people in the province [New York] may likewise be accounted for in a different manner." He then attributed the lack of settlers in New York to the large landowners and their reluctance to sell even at high prices. New York governors had made similar comments in earlier days. Governor Dongan called attention to the small number of immigrants who entered the province after its capture from the Dutch. [75] Governor Bellomont wrote in 1700, "The

[73] Peter Kalm, *Travels in America* (Warrington, England, 1770, Forster Trans.), I, 271.

[74] Kalm remarked about the importance of the French as neighbors in preserving the colonial loyalty. He made the startling prophesy in 1748 as told him by colonial gentlemen, which was fulfilled in 1776–1783, "that the *English* colonies in *North America*, in the space of thirty or fifty years, would be able to form a state by themselves, entirely independent of *Old England*," *op. cit.*, I, 265. This is an early evidence of what Professor Jernegan has recently referred to as "the Movement for Independence." *Amer. Hist. Rev.*, XXXVI, 503.

[75] Proper, *op. cit.*, 39.

people are so cramp'd here for want of land, that several families within my own knowledge are remov'd to the new country (a name given by them to Pennsylvania and the Jersies) . . . What man will be such a fool to become a base tenant to Mr. Dellius, Col. Schuyler, Mr. Livingston (and so he ran through the whole roll of our mighty Landgraves) when, for crossing Hudson's river, that man can for a song purchase a good freehold in the Jersies."[76] On October 2, 1716, Governor Hunter advised the Board of Trade that, "it is apparent that extravagant tracts of land being held by single persons unimproved is the true cause that this province does not increase in number of inhabitants in proportion to some of the neighboring ones."[77]

Nevertheless, Hunter too had allied himself with the speculators and the large landowners. The Schoharie grant was given to the Seven Partners, young gentlemen, sons of the landed aristocracy, as a speculative venture. He also granted a large tract in Ulster County to his friend, Lewis Morris and others, in 1715,[78] for speculative purposes. Of all the New York governors, Hunter, though known as the most able, probably did most to perpetuate the land problem. The confirmatory grant with representation in the assembly to Robert Livingston for his over-large manor has already been described.

Hunter, however, was a party to a unique naturalization act, which naturalized the dead! The ulterior purpose of the New York Act of 1715 was to confirm the possession of large tracts of land to certain holders, whose titles might have been challenged as illegal. When the colony had been taken over finally by the English in 1674, the articles of surrender stipulated that all the people in the colony at the time should continue free denizens and enjoy their lands and houses and dispose of them as they pleased. An act of the assembly of

[76] *C. C. 1700*, 678.

[77] *N. Y. Col. Docs.*, V, 480.

[78] N. Y. S. L., Frey Collection, MS. of the Grant, February 10, 1715.

New York in 1683 naturalized all those of foreign nations then in the colony and professing Christianity. To further encourage the immigration of foreigners, it was also provided that any foreigners professing Christianity might any time after their arrival be naturalized by an act of the assembly, if they took the oaths of allegiance required.[79]

Now, there were at least two possible difficulties for the land proprietors of New York. The articles of surrender might not be fully carried out, and those who held lands based on patents issued before the surrender might find their title challenged; or, the proprietors might have acquired land from aliens who had neglected to be naturalized by act of the assembly as required by the law of 1683. Such aliens could not sell or devise land legally and consequently such titles might be assailed. That there was a disposition on the part of the British authorities to challenge the legality of large grants has been mentioned earlier. The 1708 confirmation by the London Authorities[80] of the "Act for Vacating, Breaking and Annulling the several Extravagant Grants" made by Governor Benjamin Fletcher, passed in New York in 1699, appears to have alarmed the New York proprietors. The adoption of a new land policy by the Crown of restricting New York grants to 2,000 acres to any one person for a quit-rent of 2 shillings, 6 pence for every hundred acres and requiring the cultivation of at least three acres for every fifty acres held, within three years of receiving the grant,[81] also hinted at trouble.

When Hunter arrived in the colony with the Palatines and instructions to have them naturalized immediately by act of the assembly "without fee or reward," the assembly was

[79] N. Y. Col. Docs., V, 496.

[80] N. Y. Col. Docs., V, 25, 48. Indeed, on March 15, 1716, the Board of Trade suggested to Hunter that the New York assembly might be induced to vacate other extravagant grants of land. C. C. 1716–1717, 49.

[81] Eccles. Rec., III, 1709.

apathetic.[82] Years passed and nothing was done. In fact, the governor's salary was not paid and even the ordinary expenses of the government were not provided for, so that an act of Parliament was considered in London to establish a revenue for the New York government. These developments have been referred to in Chapter VII. Hunter grew tired of waiting for succor from England, and finding his credit so seriously impaired by the attitude of the assembly and the lack of financial support from London for the Palatine project to manufacture naval stores, he became more amenable to the suggestions of the New York proprietors in the assembly.

The naturalization act, passed July 5, 1715,[83] was part of a working agreement arranged between the governor and the assembly. The governor was to approve the naturalization act and was to receive in reward "an honourable support of the Government and not a scanty one" for five years, and the payment of the debt owed to the governor by the province.[84] This compromise was a culmination of a long struggle in the colony between the prerogative and the landowning class.[85] The prerogative gave way for a temporary gain and lost the more permanent threat it had held of revising the land grants possessed by the New York aristocracy. Hunter apologized to the British colonial authorities for his approval of the law.[86] In spite of Attorney-General Northey's opinion that it was contrary to the act of navigation,[87] the naturalization law of 1715 was not disallowed for some time largely because of Hunter's desires that such action be delayed so that his difficulties in New York might be eased.[88]

[82] Charles Z. Lincoln, *Messages from the New York Governors 1683–1906* (Albany, 1909), I, 146, 147.

[83] *Colonial Laws of New York* (Albany, 1894), I, 858.

[84] *Jour. of the New York Legislative Council*, 386; *N. Y. Col. Docs.*, V, 416; *C. C. 1714–1715*, 308; Osgood, *op. cit.*, II, 113; C. W. Spencer, *Phases of Royal Government in New York 1691–1719* (Columbus, Ohio, 1905), 146, 149, 155.

[85] Greene, *op. cit.*, 184.

[86] *N. Y. Col. Docs.*, V, 403, 416.   [87] *Ibid.*, 497.

[88] *C. C. 1716–1717*, 182; *1717–1718*, 360.

Ostensibly, the naturalization act was suggested by Hunter pursuant to his instructions to secure the naturalization of the Palatines. This suggestion took the form of a general naturalization act.[89] It was seized by the anxious landed gentry in the assembly as a foil for the protection of their ill-gotten possessions, for it provided that all persons of foreign birth alive in New York in 1683, possessing land, were naturalized by the act and their grants made good; all persons of foreign birth who had come and inhabited New York since 1689 and secured lands, or died in possession of them, were deemed to be naturalized; and all persons of foreign birth inhabitants of New York in 1715 and Protestants were naturalized, provided they took the oath of Allegiance and Supremacy and subscribed to the Test and the Abjuration Oath. But if the latter class died without taking the oaths within the nine months grace allowed, they were naturalized.[90] It should be clear that by this act all weakness of land titles, secured before the English took possession of New York or acquired from aliens since then, was legally removed. The Attorney-General of England, in recommending the disallowance of this act, suggested that instead of encouraging foreigners to settle in the colonies without naturalization, it would be better to confirm the titles of the subjects of New York even though they claimed from persons not naturalized.[91] His suggestion does not appear to have been accepted, however.[92] A large number of Palatines availed themselves of their opportunity for naturalization under the act.[93]

Turning for a last glance at the Newburgh settlement made by Kocherthal and his party in 1709, we find that they

---

[89] *Jour. of New York Legislative Council,* 305.

[90] *Col. Laws of New York,* I, 858.

[91] *N. Y. Col. Docs.,* V, 497.

[92] Carpenter, *loc. cit.,* 302.

[93] Munsell, *op. cit.,* VII, 40-52 *passim.*

had not prospered. It was a poor commentary on either the Palatines or New York that all of the people had sold or disposed of their rights and moved away by 1751, except a Margaret Ward. The latter was willing to conform to the Church of England and so the Lutheran Glebe was turned over to the Anglican Church.[94] Few Palatines were settling in New York. The stream of German immigration was flowing heavily into Pennsylvania and we may next seek reasons for this phenomenon.

That Pennsylvania was the beneficiary of a large amount of publicity has been noted. The effects of the advertising were felt throughout the eighteenth century. In 1717 an agent of George I, then King of England, offered lands to Germans beyond the Allegheny Mountains west of Pennsylvania.[95] A group of German immigrants in Pennsylvania in 1734 wrote that they had "heard when in our native Country the great Blessings of Peace and Liberty enjoy'd by the People of Pennsilvania under a good and Pious Proprietor."[96] Christopher Sauer, who came to Pennsylvania in 1725, remarked, "I wrote largely to my friends and acquaintances of the civil and religious liberties. . . . My letters were printed and reprinted, whereby thousands were provoked to come to the province, and they desired their friends to come."[97] The land agents (or Neülanders) often repressed unfavorable news from the colonies.[98] In fact, advertising materials in various forms

[94] Doc. Hist., III, 598–606.

[95] J. D. de Hoop Scheffer, "Mennonite Emigration to Pennsylvania," in Pennsylvania Magazine of History (1878, no. 2), II, 119.

[96] H. S. P., Misc. Papers, Streper, Bucks County 1682–1772.

[97] I. D. Rupp, History of Northumberland . . . Co. (Lancaster, Pennsylvania, 1845), 55. How the friends in the Fatherland must have envied the New Jersey pioneer who wrote to them, "jeder hat 50 Morgen Land, hält 12 Küh und 8 pferde, gibt jährig einen Reichs thaler schatzund." Goebel, "Briefe," in op. cit., 188.

[98] Mittelberger, op. cit., 42; Hallesche Nachrichten, II, 412.

were issued throughout the greater part of the century.[99] An important consideration for those Germans contemplating settlement in British America was "that more German colonies have established themselves there [in Pennsylvania] than in any other single part of the English plantations in America, a thing which those people should note, who perhaps might be expecting some help and assistance upon their first arrival."[100] This became increasingly important as the arrival of religious sects began to swell the immigrant numbers.[101]

That the advertising received by Pennsylvania had great influence in causing the flow of migration thence, was admitted by Clarke, President of the New York council, and later Lieutenant-Governor. On May 26, 1736, he informed the Board of Trade that what New York needed was publicity of its land terms and opportunities.[102] A number of New York proposals were actually sent to Amsterdam, to be translated into "high Dutch," and disseminated.[103] Although New York had occasional German immigration, as the small group under Reverend John James Ehlig in 1722[104] who settled at Canajoharie among the other Palatine settlers in the Mohawk Valley, it never was so well known and appreciated in the Germanies as was Pennsylvania.

It appears that writers have lost sight of the fact which explains the phenomenon of German immigration to Pennsylvania. Pennsylvania was the most widely advertised of the British colonies in America. The liberal terms offered, the promised religious toleration, the known settlements of Germans already there, were more important factors than

[99] Geiser, *op. cit.*, 14.

[100] *Das verlangte nicht erlangte Canaan*, 4.

[101] H. S. P., Misc. Penn and Baltimore MSS., 1725–1739, 28.

[102] *Eccles. Rec.*, IV, 2671.

[103] *Ibid.*, 2680.

[104] *Ibid.*, III, 2195; L. C., S. P. G. MSS., A-26, 68. This immigration also used Nutten Island (now Governor's Island) as an immigration station. *Doc. Hist.*, III, 715.

the resentment of the sixty families who moved to Pennsylvania from Schoharie. For to be truly effective, such letters, as Kalm mentioned condemning settlement in New York, must necessarily have been widely published in Germany. In 1750 a Reverend Peter Brunnholtz in Germantown, Pennsylvania, thought that the real difficulties in America should be reported in newspapers in Germany, but reconsidering asked, "Still what good would it do? The farmers don't get to read the papers, and many indeed would not believe it as they moreover have a mind to come."[105] The German readers too would have had to accept the statements at their full value rather than as German governmental propaganda to keep them in the Rhineland. Such an improbable sequence was unlikely and indeed unnecessary for New York was not widely known in the Palatinate and its neighboring districts. Pennsylvania was the "promised land." The Palatine immigrations of 1708 and 1709 were diverted to New York by the British government for its own purposes. New York was a royal province and it was thought that the manufacture of naval stores could be promoted there. It was also considered quite important to strengthen the New York frontier,[106] and we may next consider how the Palatines fared in their relations with the French and Indians.

The relations between the Indians and the Palatines of the Schoharie Valley were usually quite friendly and satisfactory as has been pointed out earlier. Perhaps the chief reason was the influence with the natives held by Conrad Weiser, who it will be remembered was taken when a young man by the Indian chief Quaynant to live with him. Weiser lived with the Indians for several years, often hiding in fear of his

---

[105] *Hallesche Nachrichten* (Oswald trans.), II, 413.

[106] The December 5, 1709 representation of the Board of Trade on the New York experiment in the production of naval stores emphasized first of all the importance of strengthening the New York frontier, the "most advanced" of all the colonies and necessary "to the security of all the rest." *N. Y. Col. Docs.*, V, 117.

life from the drunken braves, but he learned their language
and later served as interpreter and peacemaker between the
settlers and their savage friends.[107] Indeed, the danger from
drunken Indians was no small matter, as Reverend Frederick
Haeger found on one occasion in October, 1717, while driving
down from Schenectady to the Livingston Manor settlement.
A party of Indians on a spree gave chase after the wagon.
The driver whipped up the horses to such a speed that the
pastor feared they would be dashed to pieces instead of being
scalped.[108]

When the settling of Palatines in New York was first
considered by the Board of Trade on August 30, 1709, the
Board had hopes that they would not only serve as a frontier
barrier to the French but that "in process of time by marrying
with the neighboring Indians (as the French do) they may be
capable of rendering great service to Her Majesty's subjects
there."[109] While the frontier was pushed westward into the
Schoharie and Mohawk Valleys by these Palatine pioneers,
it does not appear that they intermarried with Indians as the
Board of Trade's matchmaking desires anticipated.

The participation of 300 Palatines in the failure of the
joint English and colonial expedition against Canada in 1711
has been mentioned in Chapter VII. The Palatines had gone
quite willingly, expecting to make the frontier safe for their
eventual settlement there[110] and the failure was a grievous
disappointment to them. When the French and Indian War
broke out, the Palatines in the Mohawk Valley were concerned for their safety, although they had five blockhouses,
and a fort was situated several miles away. They made over-
tures to the French Indians, complaining of the treatment
accorded them by the English, and proposed an alliance for

[107] Weiser Diary, 17, 19, 25, in *loc. cit.*, VIII, 798.

[108] L. C., S. P. G. MSS., A-12, 341; N. Y. H. S., Hawks Trans., I, 532.

[109] *N. Y. Col. Docs.*, V, 88.

[110] L. C., S. P. G. MSS., A-7, 223.

joint defense against the English. The Indians reported the proposal to the Marquis de Vaudreuil, the Governor of Canada, in a conference on December 24, 1756.[111] De Vaudreuil advised the Indians to inform the Palatines that if they were sincere, he would sustain them as soon as they joined the Indians, and "If it [the Palatine nation] will retire close to me, I shall receive it and furnish it with lands." But he warned that in case the proposal of the Palatines was offered only to guarantee their settlements against the French and their Indians, the trick would not avail them.

The French Governor's threat was not idle language, for in November of 1757 a strong force of 300 marine troops, Canadians and Indian braves descended upon the Mohawk Valley Palatines. On November 12th, they attacked with such vigor and blood-curdling war-whoops that the Mayor of the village of Palatine, Johan Jost Petrie, threw open one blockhouse and asked for quarter. After plundering for forty-eight hours and standing off meanwhile an English attack from the neighboring fort, the French and Indians retired with nearly 150 men, women, and children as prisoners. They had great booty and lost not a single man, so they reported with glee.[112] The Germans remained in Canada until they were exchanged for other prisoners of the English in September of 1758.[113]

Our classic historian of the frontier, the late Frederick Jackson Turner, pointed out the non-English character of the frontiersmen of New York and Pennsylvania and the consequent typical "American" character of that part of the "Old West," with respect to tolerance and an easygoing cosmopolitanism.[114] Turner likewise appreciated that the difficulty New York had to surmount, because of the Indian barrier

[111] N. Y. Col. Docs., X, 513, 514.
[112] Ibid., X, 673.
[113] Ibid., X, 881.
[114] Turner, The Frontier in American History (New York, 1920), 22, 28.

presented by the Six Nations, was the sparseness of the European population, which may be said to have lacked effective expansive power for that reason.[115] He also regarded the land system of the colony as a serious obstacle, not only because of the large grants of land to the Lords of Manors but also because of their insistence on leases or shares often, as opposed to outright sale. In this connection, he mentioned the experience of the Palatines at Schoharie, feeling that had their their experience been more successful, "the tide of German settlement which finally sought Pennsylvania and the up-country of the South might have flowed into New York."[116] This view supposes that Pennsylvania was settled by the Germans, because the bad land system of New York was well-known in Germany. That such was not the case has been indicated in this study, and it therefore seems that the appeal of Pennsylvania in the Rhineland lay rather in the effectiveness of the publicity put over by William Penn. On the other hand it is quite possible that had New York embarked on an advertising campaign similar to the pamphlet barrage of Pennsylvania and publicized the German settlements in New York, the Germans would have chosen the latter place for their destination.

Professor Turner's emphasis on the frontier as productive of individualism has served a useful purpose in calling the attention of American historians to an indigenous influence not fully appreciated before. In view of this study of the Palatine immigration, a small modification of the frontier's influence should be considered. In the first place the frontier did not only force modification on mankind by the need of conforming to natural environments, as described by Turner, but it also attracted only certain types of mankind to its area. These types were the unruly, the rash, the non-conformformists who often refused to accept the regulations and

[115] *Ibid.*, 80.
[116] *Ibid.*, 82.

obligations of more organized communities. The timid, faint-hearted conformist usually favored the comparative safety of the established settlements. This was largely true of the Palatine immigration under discussion. Only one-fourth of the Palatines on Livingston Manor moved to the unprotected Schoharie frontier, and these were largely the trouble-makers, so Governor Hunter and other officials often stated.[117] Regardless of the handicaps they suffered, three-fourths of the Palatines remained on lands, in the possession of which the Indians need not be challenged or the French incursions feared. Is it not possible that the individualism produced by the frontier was largely due to the type of men it attracted? Was not the frontier influence a selective process as well as a creative power?

Furthermore, if we are to consider the Palatines in the Schoharie and the Mohawk Valleys as typical examples of the "Old West" frontier,[118] we should note that their individualism was tempered by much community co-operation. The very necessities of the hard frontier life produced a co-operation often lacking among the individuals of an older community. The joint purchase of a horse, the borrowing of harness, plows and other scarce articles and the combined effort to clear the land and win sustenance, to omit the requirements of joint defense against the savages, were examples of this co-operation. Individualism there certainly was on the frontier, but was it due to the frontier conditions or the calibre of the men, or to both? Is it not true that the frontier conditions called for a type of co-operation different from that required in more civilized communities, but even more essential for survival?

In passing it may be noted that the first limitations on the power of the Crown as it reposed in the governor was made in eighteenth century New York by the colonial proprietors,

[117] C. C. 1712–1714, 71; N. Y. Col. Docs., V, 552; C. C. 1722–1723, 318.
[118] Turner, op. cit., 28.

who in their selfish desire to be free from direct control and taxes, were refighting the English constitutional battles of the seventeenth century, by controlling the purse-strings, and laying down the conditions of political co-operation.[119] The coastal settlements and the great proprietors could hardly be considered as influenced by the frontier. But when the dominance of the hinterland by the coastal settlers became a political issue with the frontiersmen, Turner's thesis of democratic influence resulting from proximity to the frontier seems well established. Even then however, it may be considered as a continuation of the struggle of the underprivileged for rights corresponding to the political theories of the day. The occurrence of these phenomena is not peculiar to America, but it may assuredly have been stimulated here and hence developed earlier than in Europe because of the nature of the settlers, repelled by European oppression and attracted by the free conditions of the New World. The environment of the frontier, it seems to me, must share honors with the dissatisfied temperaments and the new-deal desires of the pioneers.

In summarizing the rôle played by the Palatine immigration in the history of the "Old West," it may be pointed out that the Palatines pushed westward the New York frontier into the Mohawk Valley, and the Pennsylvania frontier into the Great Appalachian Valley. They gave valiant service against the French and their Indians, while their friendly relations with the Indians of the Six Nations allied with the English was in sharp contrast to the general hostility of the Scotch-Irish settlers, who invariably had trouble with the Indians. In their efforts to settle the frontier lands, the Palatines had many obstacles to overcome in addition to the hardships of pioneer life. The difficulties occasioned by the short-sighted opposition of colonial authorities and the self-

[119] N. Y. Col. Docs., V, 552, C. C. 1711–1712, 228; P. R. O., C. O. 324/11, 177, 214.

ish exploitation by colonial land speculators were courage-
ously, one might even say obstinately, fought by the Palatine
settlers. The eighteenth century immigrant was the same fair
game for exploitation by selfish interests as today. It should
not be surprising then that immigrants often turned resentful
and difficult to assimilate.

CONCLUSION

INFLUENCED BY a robust mercantilism, full fifty years before the age of laissez-faire, the British government attempted an experiment in public operation of an industry in competition with private business. This experiment was neither scientifically planned nor deliberately undertaken. The British government had obligated itself by implication to support German immigrants. It had transported them and given them relief at public expense, thus establishing a precedent for state aided and controlled migration. The authorities simply sought under the spur of the drain on the treasury some way of recouping the unexpectedly heavy expenditures. How they tried to "kill two birds with one stone" by solving their naval stores problem as well, has been pointed out. From a rational point of view, the venture had everything to recommend it. It gave promise of providing England with a highly valued staple commodity from the northern continental colonies, comparable to the tobacco from Virginia and the sugar from the West Indies. The weakest part of the colonial frontier was also to be strengthened by the settlement. Of all these promises, only the last was actually realized, and that, indeed, over the opposition of the governor in charge of operations.

It remains to point out why this forgotten attempt at public operation of an industry failed, even before the days of prejudice against government operation of industry. The very haste with which the venture was decided upon and prepared were obstacles. Proper instruction by experts, definitely assigned to the work and given responsibility for it, was not insisted upon. Nevertheless, the venture might have muddled through to success, had financial support from England not ceased before it was well under way. The decisive influence of the Ministerial Revolution in England in 1711 and the subsequent search for campaign material to win the next election has been emphasized. It would seem that such political considerations must be ruled out, if public operation of any industry is to succeed.

The naval stores project, however, was not a sheer failure. The British attempts to build up a naval stores industry in their colonies in America were effective in maintaining low prices for Swedish tar. Without the possibility of colonial competition the Swedish tar would have been obtainable only on most disadvantageous terms. Therefore, the British Navy Board played into the hands of the Swedish Company when it opposed the encouragement of colonial naval stores on the grounds that they were much more expensive than the products of the Baltic countries. Considering only the practical side of securing moderately priced naval stores, the colonial project would seem to have been reasonably successful.

The failure of the naval stores settlement spelled opportunity to the Palatines and indeed this too must be considered in explaining the lack of success with tar manufacturing. The Palatines were individualists, as most farmers are, and sought fertile lands for themselves and their posterity. The virgin lands of the frontier beckoned to these Old World farmers. They pushed the frontier before them as they moved into the Mohawk and Susquehanna Valleys. They prospered and many of their descendants still own the lands taken up by their ancestors in the eighteenth century. The dreams of these early pioneers have been realized.

More importance should be attached to the effect these migrations of 1708 and 1709 had in the Germanies. The reports of the good treatment received from the British government, which really was most benevolent under the stress of a war period, encouraged a steady stream of emigration. Kocherthal's pamphlet with its appendix, describing the aid extended to the immigrants, was one of the most influential of these works, encouraging emigration. To this group must be added Simmendinger's little pamphlet, with its appendix of many pages of Palatine families happily settled in the "Land of Promise." Shortly after the latter publication appeared, about 1717, a steady stream of German redemptioners began to flow into Pennsylvania.

It has seemed advisable to point out that our colonial histories have overstressed Peter Kalm's casual explanation in accounting for the absence of German immigration to the colony of New York, while Pennsylvania felt itself so flooded by these people that it considered restricting the immigration to preserve the English character of the settlement. The real problem has been to explain why Germans settled in New York rather than why they continued to immigrate to Pennsylvania. Pennsylvania of all the English colonies was the most publicized in Germany in the early eighteenth century. The Palatine immigrations of 1709 and 1710 to New York were diversions from the normal course of German immigration, made by the British government for its own purposes, as this study has shown. No other English province was able to overcome the magnetic attraction of Pennsylvania for the Germans in the eighteenth century.

This study further suggests that Frederick Jackson Turner's thesis of the frontier's influence on the European settlers should be understood not only as a creative but also as a selective process, for the frontier attracted only the independent, freedom-loving types of men. It also appears necessary to appreciate that there was much co-operation required in frontier life. Only the trappers and the rabid frontiersmen were as anti-social as Professor Turner described the pioneers. While his theory of the influence of the frontier on the rise of democracy in this country appears to be sound, it should be realized that in the colonial period it was the wealthy merchants and the landed proprietors who laid the basis for the American Revolution by limiting the power of the Crown's representatives, the colonial governors. The frontier had little influence upon those privileged classes.

BIBLIOGRAPHY

Bibliographical Guides

Allison, William Henry, *Inventory of Unpublished Materials for American Religious History in Protestant Church Archives and other Repositories* (Washington, 1910).

Andrews, Charles M., *Guide to the Materials for American History to 1783 in the Public Record Office of Great Britain*, 2 vols. (Washington, 1912–1914).

Andrews, Charles M. and Davenport, F. G., *Guide to Manuscript Materials for the History of the United States to 1783 in the British Museum* (Washington, 1908).

Davies, Godfrey, *Bibliography of British History; Stuart Period, 1603–1714* (Oxford, 1928).

Faust, Albert B., *Guide to the Materials for American History in Swiss and Austrian Archives* (Washington, 1916).

Flagg, C. A. and Jennings, J. T., *Bibliography of New York Colonial History* (Albany, 1902).

Greene, E. B. and Morris, R. B., *Guide to the Principal Sources for Early American History (1600–1800) in the City of New York* (New York, 1929).

Learned, Marion Dexter, *Guide to the Manuscript Materials Relating to American History in the German State Archives* (Washington, 1912).

Morgan, William Thomas, *Bibliography of British History 1700–1715* (Bloomington, Indiana, 1934–), only Volume I has appeared so far.

Primary Sources

UNPUBLISHED

British Museum, London. This depository contains many valuable manuscript materials, especially the Strafford Papers in the Additional Manuscripts Collection.

Historical Society of Pennsylvania Library contains colonial correspondence, and transcripts of Dutch Archives made for J. F. Sachse. It also contains a splendid collection of transcripts of the British Colonial Office Records, including the Board of Trade Journal 1675–1782 (93 large folio volumes), Plantations General 1689–1780 (31 large folio volumes), and the Proprieties 1697–1776 (24 large folio volumes).

Huntington Library, San Marino, California, possesses many contemporary manuscripts of great value secured from English sources. Letters of William Penn and Robert Hunter are included.

Kingsley Manuscripts in the possession of the Kingsley family, The Rocks, Schoharie, New York, are made up principally of an old recommendation and a Family Bible brought from Germany.

Library of Congress, Washington, D. C., has transcripts and photostats of British documents, especially of the Colonial Office. It also possesses the Archdale Manuscripts valuable for the activities of the Carolina proprietors. It has recently acquired transcripts and photostats of the Records of the Society for the Propagation of the Gospel from London. These are letters from the ministers in the colonies and extremely valuable, as they sometimes contain vital statistics.

Livingston Family Manuscripts in the possession of the Johnston Livingston Redmont Estate, New York City. This valuable collection contains many items on Indian Affairs, the first lord of the Manor having been commissioner of Indian Affairs in the early eighteenth century.

Moravian Archives (Moravian Seminary), Bethlehem, Pennsylvania, contains the first records of the early church at Tulpehocken, entitled "Kirchen Buch von die Evangelisch Lutherisch Gemein in Tulpehocken, 1733." This is the manuscript account of the so-called "Tulpehocken Confusion," attested to by Conrad Weiser, and later published. The early records of the Schäffer, Walborn, Rieth, Lösh, and Zerbe families are in this script book.

New York Historical Society Library contains a manuscript of an Indian Treaty with regard to Schoharie, New York and the Palatines. It also possesses several colonial manuscripts on the subject as well as a transcript of a Harleian Manuscript in the British Museum. The Hawks Transcripts of the Records of the Society for the Propagation of the Gospel, London, were transferred here from the Church Mission House, New York. Many of the latter are only extracts.

New York Public Library preserves manuscript notes of Abraham Yates on early colonial history of New York, and the Chalmers Collection of New York colonial documents. It also contains rare volumes, particularly Simmendinger's Pamphlet.

New York State Archives at Albany, New York are rich in colonial manuscripts on the subject. The few volumes on this period lost in the 1911 fire contained only two documents on the Palatines, as indicated by the *Calendar*. It also has valuable manuscript materials for the 1711 expedition against Canada.

Old Stone Fort of Schoharie County Historical Society, Schoharie, New York, contains many items of great value dealing with the early Palatine settlers. The collection is particularly rich in historical relics, showing the life of pioneer days.

Pennsylvania State Archives at Harrisburg, Pennsylvania are comparatively poor in materials on this particular migration. Correspondence of the Penn family and Conrad Weiser are the chief items. The archives are sadly in need of a subject index as the present name index is adequate for genealogical purposes only.

Public Record Office, London. A large proportion of the official records concerning the governmental project are preserved here. Reclassification in progress accounts for variations in the method of citation in some footnotes.

Schwenkfelder Library at Pennsburg, Pennsylvania, has purchased many items formerly in Judge Pennypacker's collection of pamphlets on Pennsylvania German immigration.

Widener Library, Harvard University, possesses several rare contemporary pamphlets as well as the only known copy of Robert Hunter's "*Androborus*" (August, 1714), a biographical farce indicating his friends and enemies in the province of New York.

Other libraries consulted include Yale University Library at New Haven, Connecticut; Lebanon County Historical Society, Lebanon, Pennsylvania; Historical Society of Berks County, Reading, Pennsylvania; the Public Library of Boston, Massachusetts; the Morgan Library, New York City; and the Holland Society Library, New York City.

PUBLISHED—OFFICIAL

Acts of the Privy Council, Colonial, 1680–1720 (1910), also volume of *Unbound Papers* (published in 1912).

Calendar of Council Minutes of New York 1668–1683 (Albany, 1902).

Calendar of State Papers, Colonial, America and the West Indies, 1689–1693 (1921) *to 1722–1723* (1934).

Calendar of Treasury Papers 1556–1696 (1868) *to 1714–1719* (1883).

Calendar of New York Colonial Manuscripts indorsed Land Papers 1643–1803 (Albany, 1864).

Calendar of New York Historical Manuscripts, edited by E. B. O'Callaghan, 2 vols. (Albany, 1865–6).

Colonial Laws of New York from 1664–1776, 5 vols. (Albany, 1896).

Colonial Records of North Carolina, 1662–1790 (Raleigh, North Carolina, 1886–1903).

Documentary History of the State of New York, edited by E. B. O'Callaghan, Vol. III (Albany, 1850).

Documents Relative to the Colonial History of New York by John Romeyn Brodhead, edited by E. B. O'Callaghan, 11 vols. (Albany, 1851–61).

Ecclesiastical Records of the State of New York, edited by Hugh Hastings, *et al.*, 8 vols. (Albany, 1901–1916).

Historical Manuscript Commission Reports, Great Britain.

Journal of the Commissioners of Trade and Plantations, 1704–1708 (1920) *to 1718–1722* (1925).

Journal of the House of Commons, especially Vol. XVI.

Journal of the Legislative Council of the Colony of New York 1691–1743, Vol. I (Albany, 1861).

Journal of the Votes and Proceedings of the General Assembly of New York 1691–1743, Vol. I (New York, 1764).

Messages from the New York Governors to the Legislatures 1683–1906 . . ., edited by C. Z. Lincoln (Albany, 1909).

Minutes of the Common Council of the City of New York, Vol. II (New York, 1905).

Minutes of the Provincial Assembly of Pennsylvania, Vol. III (Philadelphia, 1852).

Parliamentary History of England, by William Cobbett (London, 1806–1820), the antecedent of the *Parliamentary Debates*.

Pennsylvania Archives 1664–1698, 1st series, 12 vols.; 2nd series, 12 vols.; 3rd series, 30 vols. (Harrisburg, 1852–99).

Proceedings and Debates of the British Parliaments respecting North America 1542–1727, edited by L. F. Stock, 3 vols. (Washington, 1924–1930).

Statutes-at-Large, Reign of Queen Anne.

Statutes of the Realm, 1235–1713, Vol. XI (London, 1824).

PUBLISHED—UNOFFICIAL

[Anonymous] *History of the Life and Reign of Queen Anne* (London, 1740).

Burnet, Bishop Gilbert, *History of His Own Times*, 6 vols. (Oxford, 1833).

Boyer, Abel, *History of the Reign of Queen Anne, digested into Annals 1709* (London, 1710).

Boyer, Abel, *Political State of Great Britain*, Vol. I (London, 1711).

Brown, J. M., *Brief Sketch of the First Settlement of the County of Schoharie by the Germans* (Schoharie, New York, 1823).

Chamberlen, Paul, *An Impartial History of the Life and Reign of our late Sovereign Queen Anne* . . . (London, 1738).

Child, Sir Josiah, *New Discourse of Trade* (London, 1693, first edition 1692).

Correspondence between William Penn and James Logan, secretary of the province of Pennsylvania and others 1700–1750, 2 vols. (Philadelphia, The Historical Society of Pennsylvania, 1870–1872).

Falckner, Daniel, *Curieuse Nachricht von Pennsylvania* (translated and published by J. F. Sachse, printed privately in Philadelphia, 1905).

Gibson, *Memoirs of Queen Anne* (London, 1729).

Goebel, Julius, Sr., editor, "Briefe Deutscher Auswanderer aus dem Jahre 1709," in *Jahrbuch der Deutsch=amerikanischen Historischen Gesellschaft von Illinois* (Chicago, 1912).

Goebel, Julius, Sr., editor, "Neue Dokumente zur Geschichte der Massenaus=wanderung im Jahre 1709" in *Jahrbuch der Deutsch=amerikanischen His=torischen Gesellschaft von Illinois* (Chicago, 1913).

Hallesche Nachrichten, *Nachrichten von den vereinigten deutschen evangelisch=lutherischen Gemeinen in Nord=America, absonderlich in Pensylvanien;* first published in 2 vols. Halle, 1782, edited by W. J. Mann, B. M. Schmucher and W. Germann (1st vol. Allentown, Pennsylvania, 1886) (2nd vol. Philadelphia, 1895). Vol. I, translated by C. W. Schaffer, Reading, Pennsylvania, 1882; Vols. I and II, translated by Jonathan Oswald, Philadelphia, 1880 and 1881.

[Hare, Francis], *Canary Birds Naturaliz'd in Utopia* (London, 1709).

[Hare, Francis], *The Reception of the Palatines Vindicated in a Fifth Letter to a Tory Member* (London, 1711).

Höen, Moritz W., editor, *Das verlangte nicht erlangte Canaan bey den Lust=Gräbern; oder Ausführliche Beschreibung von der Unglücklichen Reise derer jüngsthin aus Teutschland nach dem Engelländischen in America gelegnen Carolina und Pensylvanien wallenden Pilgrim absonderlich dem einseitigen übelgegrundeten Kochenthalersichen Bericht wohlbedächtig entgegen gesetzt* (Franckfurt, Leipzig, 1711).

Kalm, Peter, *Travels into North America*, 3 vols. (Warrington, England, 1770), translated by John Reinhold Forster.

Kocherthal, Josua, *Ausführlich, und umständ=licher Bericht von der berühmten Landschafft Carolina, in dem engelländischen America gelegen* (Franckfurt=am= Mäyn, 1709). A copy of the second edition is in the Historical Society of Pennsylvania Library; one of the fourth edition is in the Library of Congress.

"Kocherthal Records," early vital statistics of St. Paul's Evangelical Lutheran Church of West Camp, New York, kept by Reverend Josua Kocherthal and others. Translated by Christian Krahmer in *Olde Ulster*, Vols. III, IV (Kingston, New York, 1907 and 1908). Also a new translation by Mr. Krahmer in *Lutheran Quarterly*, Vol. LVII (Gettysburg, Pennsylvania, 1927).

Luttrell, Narcissus, *A Brief Historical Relation of State Affairs, 1678–1714*, 6 vols. (Oxford, 1857).

Maitland, William, *History and Survey of London*, 2 vols. (London, 1756).

Mittelberger, Gottlieb, *Journey to Pennsylvania in 1750 and Return to Germany 1754*. . . . (Philadelphia, 1898).

Monthly Mercury, Vol. XX (London, 1709).

Penn, William, *Information and Direction to such persons as are inclined to America more especially those related to the Province of Pennsylvania* (London, 1684).

Private Correspondence of Sarah, Duchess of Marlborough, 2 vols. (London, 1838, 2nd edition).

Proud, Robert, *History of Pennsylvania from the Original Settlement under William Penn in 1681 till after 1742 . . .*, 2 vols. (Philadelphia, 1797–98).

Simmendinger, Ulrich, *Warhaffte und glaubwürdige Verzeichnüss jeniger Personen; welche sich Anno 1709 unter des Herren wunderbarer Führung aus Teutschland in Americam oder Neue Welt begeben . . .* (Reuttlingen, ca. 1717).

Smith, Samuel, *The History of the Colony of Nova-Caesaria, or New Jersey, to the year 1721. With particulars since, and a short view of its present state . . .* (Burlington, New Jersey, 1765, 2nd edition, 1877).

Smith, William, *History of the Late Province of New York*, 2 vols. (New York, 1829–32, also London, 1857).

Somerville, Thomas, *The History of Great Britain during the Reign of Queen Anne* (London, 1798).

Stanhope, P. H., *History of England comprising the Reign of Queen Anne, 1701–1713*, 2 vols. (London, 1872, 4th edition).

Stow, John, *Survey of the Cities of London and Westminister . . .*, 2 vols. (London, 1720).

The State of the Palatines for Fifty Years Past to This Present Time (London, 1709).

The Piety and Bounty of the Queen of Great Britain, with the charitable benevolences of her living Subjects toward the Support and Settlement of the Distressed Protestant Palatines (London, 1709).

Tindal, Nicholas, *Continuation of Mr. Rapin's History of England; from the Revolution to the Present Times* (London, 1756–63).

Todd, Vincent H., and Julius Goebel, Sr., *Christoph von Graffenried's Account of the Founding of New Bern, edited with a historical introduction and an English translation* (Raleigh, North Carolina, 1920).

Toland, John, *Declaration Lately Published by the Elector Palatine in Favor of his Protestant Subjects* (London, 1714).

Weiser, Conrad, "Diary" in *Americana* (New York, September, 1913), Vol. VIII; Also in *Olde Ulster* (Kingston, New York, 1906), Vol. II. And in *Der deutsche Pionier* (Cincinnati, Ohio, 1870), Vol. II. The manuscript has recently been acquired by the Library of Congress.

Wesley, John, *Works of*, 1st American edition from 5th edition of London (New York, 1831).

Secondary Sources

general works

Adams, J. T., *Provincial Society 1690–1763* (New York, 1928).

Anderson, Adam, *Historical and Chronological Origin of Commerce*, 2 vols. (London, 1764).

Beer, G. L., *The Old Colonial System*, 2 vols. (New York, 1912).

Bolton, H. E. and Marshall, T. M., *The Colonization of North America 1492–1783* (New York, 1920).

Burke, Edmund, *An Account of the European Settlements in America*, 2 vols. (London, 1770, 5th edition).

Cambridge History of the British Empire, edited by J. H. Rose, A. P. Newton and E. A. Benians (New York, 1929).

Channing, Edward, *History of United States*, Vol. II (New York, 1908).

Chitwood, O. P., *A History of Colonial America* (New York, 1931).

Cunningham, William, *Growth of English Industry and Commerce*, 3 vols. (Cambridge, England, 1910–12, 5th edition).

Dickerson, O. M., *American Colonial Government 1696–1763* (Cleveland, Ohio, 1912).

Douglass, William *The British Settlements in North America*, 2 vols. (Boston, 1749–53).

Doyle, J. A., *English Colonies in America*, 5 vols. (New York, 1882–1907).

Egerton, H. E., *A Short History of British Colonial Policy* (London, 1897).

Flick, A. C., editor, *History of the State of New York, under Duke and King*, Vol. II (New York, 1933).

Garis, R. L., *Immigration Restriction* (New York, 1928).

Greene, E. B., *Provincial America 1690–1740* (New York, 1905).

Heckscher, E. F., *Mercantilism*, 2 vols. (London, 1935).

Hill, D. J., *A History of Diplomacy in the International Development of Europe*, 3 vols. (New York, 1905–14).

Jernegan, M. W., *The American Colonies* (New York, 1929).

Lipson, E., *The Economic History of England*, 3 vols. (London, 1920–1931).

Macpherson, David, *Annals of Commerce*, 4 vols. (London, 1805).

Mahan, Admiral A. T., *The Influence of Sea Power upon History* (Boston, 1894).

Morris, H. C., *The History of Colonization*, 2 vols. (New York, 1908).

Osgood, H. L., *American Colonies in the Eighteenth Century*, Vols. I and II (New York, 1924).

Raynal, Abbé, *Philosophical and Political History of the British Settlements and Trade in North America*, 2 vols. (Edinburgh, 1776).

Stanhope, P. H., *History of England 1702–1713* (London, 1870).

Turner, Frederick Jackson, *The Frontier in American History* (New York, 1920).

Van Noorden, Carl, *Europäesche Geschichte im achtzehnten Jahrhundert* (Düsseldorf, 1870–72).

SPECIAL WORKS

Albion, R. G., *Forests and Sea Power* (Cambridge, Massachusetts, 1926).

Barber, J. W., and Howe, Henry, *Historical Collections of the State of New Jersey* (Newark, New Jersey, 1857).

Beer, G. L., *Commercial Policy of England toward the American Colonies* (New York, 1893).

Beidelman, William, *Story of the Pennsylvania Germans* (Easton, Pennsylvania, 1898).

Benton, N. S., *History of Herkimer County including the Upper Mohawk Valley* (Albany, 1856).

Bernheim, G. D., *History of the German Settlements and of the Lutheran Church in North and South Carolina* . . . (Philadelphia, 1872).

Bittinger, L. F., *The Germans in Colonial Times* (Philadelphia and London, 1901).

Bond, W. B., *The Quit-Rent System in the American Colonies* (New Haven, Connecticut, 1919).

Brink, B. M., *Early History of Saugerties 1660–1825* (Kingston, New York, 1902).

Burns, J. F., *Controversies between Royal Governors and their Assemblies in the Northern American Colonies* (Villanova, Pennsylvania, 1923).

Chambers, T. F., *Early Germans of New Jersey* (Dover, New Jersey, 1895).

Charlevoix, P. F. X., *History and General Description of New France*, 6 vols. (London, 1902).

Cobb, S. H., *The Story of the Palatines* (New York, 1897).

Correll, E. H., *Das Schweizerische Täufermennonitentum* (Tübingen, 1925).

Croll, P. C., *Annals of Womelsdorf, Pennsylvania and the Tulpehocken Community* (1923).

Crook, William, *The Palatines in Ireland* (London, 1866).

Cunningham, William, *Alien Immigrants to England* (London, 1897).

De Long, I. H., *The Lineage of Malcolm Metzger Parker* (Lancaster, Pennsylvania, 1926).

Diefendorf, M. R., *The Historic Mohawk* (New York, 1910).

Eberlein, H. D., *The Manors and Historic Homes of the Hudson Valley* (Philadelphia and London, 1924).

Egle, W. H., editor, *Names of Foreigners who took the Oath of Allegiance to the Province and State of Pennsylvania 1727–1775 and 1786–1808* (Harrisburg, Pennsylvania, 1892).

Eickhoff, Anton, *In der neuen Heimath; geschichtliche Mittheilungen über die deutschen Einwanderer in allen Theilen der Union*, 2 vols. (New York, 1884).

Eshleman, H. F., *Historic Background and Annals of the Swiss and German Pioneer Settlers of Southeastern Pennsylvania* (Lancaster, Pennsylvania, 1917).

Faust, A. B., *German Element in the United States*, 2 vols. (New York, 1909), new edition, 2 vols. in one, 1927.

Fischer, P. D., *Die Anfänge der deutschen Auswanderung nach Amerika* (Berlin, 1870).

Fox, Dixon Ryan, *Caleb Heathcote, Gentleman Colonist* (New York, 1926).

Gamble, Thomas, editor, *Naval Stores; History, Production, Distribution and Consumption* (Savannah, Georgia, 1921).

Geiser, K. R., *Redemptioners and Indentured Servants in the Colony and Commonwealth of Pennsylvania* (New Haven, Connecticut, 1901).

Goebel, Julius, Sr., *Das Deutschtum in den Vereinigten Staaten von Nord= Amerika* (München, 1904).

Gordon, T. F., *History of Pennsylvania from its Discovery to 1776* (Philadelphia, 1829).

Gümbel, T., *Die Geschichte der Protest. Kirche der Pfalz* (Kaiserslautern, 1885).

Guttridge, G. H., *The Colonial Policy of William III in America and the West Indies* (Cambridge, Massachusetts, 1922).

Häberle, Daniel, *Auswanderung und Koloniegründungen der Pfälzer im 18. Jahrhundert* (Kaiserlautern, 1909).

Halsey, F. W., *Old New York Frontier* (New York, 1901).

Hasbrouck, Frank, *The History of Dutchess County, New York* (Poughkeepsie, New York, 1909).

Häusser, Ludwig, *Geschichte der Rheinischen Pfalz . . .*, Vol. II (Heidelberg, 1845).

Herrick, C. A., *White Servitude in Pennsylvania* (Philadelphia, 1926).

Heuser, Emil, *Pennsylvanien im 17. Jahrhundred und die ausgewanderten Pfälzer in England* (Neustadt, 1910).

Higgins, R. L., *Expansion in New York in the Eighteenth Century* (Columbus, Ohio, 1931).

Hulbert, A. B., *Soil; Its Influence on the History of the United States . . .* (New Haven, Connecticut and London, 1930).

Hunt, Thomas, *A Historical Sketch of the Town of Clermont* (Hudson, New York, 1928).

Janney, S. M., *The Life of William Penn* (Philadelphia, 1852).

Jernegan, M. W., *Laboring and Dependent Classes in Colonial America 1607–1783* (Chicago, 1932).

Kapp, Friedrich, *Die Deutschen im Staate New York während des 18. Jahrhunderts*

(New York, 1884); Vol. I of *Geschichtsblätter, Bilder und Mittheilungen aus dem Leben der Deutschen in Amerika*, edited by C. von Schurz.

Kapp, Friedrich, *Geschichte der Deutschen Einwanderung in Amerika* (Leipzig, 1868), Vol. I of *Geschichte der deutschen Einwanderung in Amerika*.

Kohl, Johann G., *Travels in Ireland* (London, 1844).

Kuhns, Oscar, *The German and Swiss Settlements of Colonial Pennsylvania* (New York, 1901).

Löher, Franz von, *Geschichte und Zustände der Deutschen in Amerika* (Cincinnati, Ohio, 1847).

Lohr, Otto, *The First Germans in North America and the German Element of New Netherland* (New York, 1912).

Lord, E. L., *Industrial Experiments in the British Colonies of North America* (Baltimore, 1898).

Mann, W. J., *Life and Times of Henry Melchior Mühlenberg* (Philadelphia, 1887).

Martin, R. M., *Ireland Before and After the Union with Great Britain* (London, 1848, 3rd edition).

Mayer, Frederick [Reinhard, A. W.,] *Fifty Years in the Wilderness* (Los Angeles, California, 1931). A work of fiction so realistic and so close to the facts that the casual reader may take it for what it purports to be, a translation of a contemporary diary of Palatine life in Schoharie Valley.

Mellick, A. D., *The Story of an Old Farm in New Jersey in the Eighteenth Century* (Somerville, New Jersey, 1889).

Mershon, S. L., *The Power of the Crown in the Valley of the Hudson* (Brattleboro, Vermont, 1925).

Michaux, F. A., *The North American Sylva, a description of the forest trees of United States, Canada and Nova Scotia . . .*, 2 vols. (Paris, 1819 edition).

Montgomery, M. L., *History of Berks County in Pennsylvania* (Philadelphia, 1886).

Morgan, William Thomas, *English Political Parties and Leaders in the Reign of Queen Anne, 1702–1710* (New Haven, Connecticut, 1920).

Munsell, J., *Annals of Albany*, 10 vols. (Albany, 1850–1859).

Myers, A. C., *Immigration of the Irish Quakers into Pennsylvania 1682–1750* (Swarthmore, Pennsylvania, 1902).

Nettels, C. P., *The Money Supply of the American Colonies before 1720* (Madison, Wisconsin, 1934).

Pascoe, C. F., *Two Hundred Years of the Society for the Propagation of the Gospel 1701–1900 . . .*, 2 vols. (London, 1901).

Pennypacker, S. W., *Historical and Biographical Sketches* (Philadelphia, 1883).

Pletcher, N. M., *Some Chapters from the History of the Rhine Country* (New York, 1907).

Poole, R. L., *A History of the Huguenots of the Dispersion at the Recall of the Edict of Nantes* (London, 1880).

Proper, E. E., *Colonial Immigration Laws . . .* (New York, 1900).

Proud, Robert, *History of Pennsylvania, 1681–1742 . . .*, 2 vols. (Philadelphia, 1797–8).

Reid, W. M., *The Mohawk Valley, its Legends and its History* (New York, 1907).

Richards, G. W., *The German Pioneers in Pennsylvania* (Philadelphia, 1905).
Riehl, W. H., *Die Pfälzer; ein rheinisches volksbild* (Stuttgart, 1858).
Rivers, W. J., *A Sketch of the History of South Carolina to the close of the Proprietary Government by the Revolution of 1719* (Charleston, South Carolina, 1856).
Roberts, E. H., *New York; the Planting and the Growth of the Empire State*, 2 vols. (Boston, 1904).
Roscoe, W. E., *History of Schoharie County, New York* (Syracuse, New York, 1882).
Rupp, I. D., *History of Northampton, Berks, Monroe, Carbon and Schuylkill Counties* (Lancaster, Pennsylvania, 1845).
Rupp, I. D., *Thirty Thousand Names of German, Swiss, French and others in Pennsylvania 1727-1776* (Philadelphia, 1898). Also published in Leipzig (1931) with an index to the names listed.
Sachse, J. F., *Benjamin Furly, "an English merchant at Rotterdam," who promoted the first German emigration to America* (Philadelphia, 1895).
Sachse, J. F., *The German Pietists of Provincial Pennsylvania* (Philadelphia, 1895).
Sachse, J. F., *The German Sectarians of Pennsylvania 1708-1800*, 2 vols. (Philadelphia, 1899-1900).
Scharf, J. T., *History of Maryland . . .*, 3 vols. (Baltimore, 1879).
Schuyler, G. W., *Colonial New York*, 2 vols. (New York, 1885).
Scott, W. R., *Constitutions and Finances of English, Scottish and Irish Joint-stock Companies to 1720*, 3 vols. (Cambridge, England, 1910-1912).
Seidensticker, Oswald, *Die Erste Deutsche Einwanderung in Amerika, 1683* (Philadelphia, 1883).
Simms, J. R., *History of Schoharie County . . .* (Albany, 1845).
Simms, J. R., *The Frontiersmen of New York*, 2 vols. (Albany, 1882-1883).
Smith, P. H., *General History of Dutchess County, New York, 1609-1876* (Pawling, New York, 1877).
Smith, William, *History of the Province of New York . . .*, 2 vols. (London, 1776).
Spencer, C. W., *Phases of Royal Government in New York, 1691-1719* (Columbus, Ohio, 1905).
Stokes, I. N. Phelps, *The Iconography of Manhattan Island*, 2 vols. (New York, 1914-1916).
Strassburger, R. B., *Pennsylvania German Pioneers, a Publication of the Original Lists of Arrivals in the Port of Philadelphia from 1727 to 1808*, edited by W. J. Hinke, 3 vols. (Norristown, Pennsylvania, 1934).
Struve, B. G., *Ausführlicher Bericht von der pfältzischen Kirchen=historie . . .* (Franckfurt, 1721).
Walton, J. S., *Conrad Weiser and the Indian Policy of Colonial Pennsylvania* (Philadelphia, [1900]).
Watson, J. F., *Annals of Philadelphia, and Pennsylvania, in the Olden Time*, 2 vols. (Philadelphia, 1857).
Weiser, C. Z., *The Life of Conrad Weiser* (Reading, Pennsylvania, 1899).
Wenner, G. U., *The Lutherans of New York, their Story and their Problems* (New York, 1918).

Williamson, Hugh, *History of North Carolina*, 2 vols. (Philadelphia, 1812).
Yates, J. V. N., *History of the State of New York* . . . (New York, 1824).
Young, Arthur, *Tour in Ireland*, 2 vols. (Dublin, 1780).

PERIODICAL AND LEARNED SOCIETY CONTRIBUTIONS

Ames, Herman V., "The Peopling of the English Colonies in America" in *University of Pennsylvania Lectures* (Philadelphia, 1915).
Beyer, R. L., "Relations of New York and Pennsylvania 1710–1719," in *New York Historical Society Quarterly Bulletin*, Vol. XIV (New York, April, 1930).
Brink, B. M., "Naval Stores Project," in *Olde Ulster*, Vol. III (Kingston, New York, 1907).
Brink, B. M., "The Palatine Settlements," in *New York State Historical Association Proceedings*, Vol. XI (Albany, 1912).
Carpenter, A. H., "Naturalization in England and the American Colonies," in *American Historical Review*, Vol. IX (New York, January, 1904).
Chichester, H. M., "Robert Hunter," in *Dictionary of National Biography*, Vol. LXIII (New York, 1891)*.
Clark, M. P., "The Board of Trade at Work," in *American Historical Review*, Vol. XVII (1911–12).
Cobb, S. H., "The Palatine, or German, Immigration to New York and Pennsylvania," in *Wyoming Historical and Genealogical Society Proceedings*, Vol. VII (Wilkes-Barre, Pennsylvania, 1897).
Colden "Letters on Smith's History of New York," in *New York Historical Society Collections*, Vol. I (New York, 1869).
Diffenderffer, F. R., "German Immigration into Pennsylvania through the Port of Philadelphia (1700–1775)." Part II, "The Redemptioners," in *Pennsylvania- German Society Proceedings*, Vol. X (Lancaster, Pennsylvania, 1900).
Diffenderffer, F. R., "The German Exodus to England in 1709," in *Pennsylvania=German Society Proceedings*, Vol. VII (Lancaster, Pennsylvania, 1897).
Earl, Robert, "Mohawk Valley and the Palatines," in *Herkimer Historical Society Papers* (1898).
Earl, Samuel, "The Palatines and their Settlement in the Valley of the Mohawk," in *Oneida Historical Society Transactions*, Vol. I (Utica, New York, 1881).
Edgett, Mrs. H. R., "The Palatines," in *Fort Orange Monthly* (Albany, 1886).
Ellsworth, Reverend W. W., "The Palatines in the Mohawk Valley," in *New York Historical Association Proceedings*, Vol. XIV (1915).
Fernsemer, O. F. W., "Daniel Defoe and the Palatine Emigration of 1709.

*A supplementary study of Robert Hunter is the work of Richard Laurence Beyer' "Robert Hunter, Royal Governor of New York; a study in Colonial Administration," a manuscript dissertation for the doctorate at the University of Iowa (1929). Professor Beyer deals especially with the political background of the colony and the New York frontier.

A New View of the Origin of Robinson Crusoe," in *Journal of English and Germanic Philology*, Vol. XIX (Urbana, Illinois, 1920).

Hill, C. F., "The Palatines of 1723," in *Wyoming Historical Society Proceedings*, Vol. V (Wilkes-Barre, Pennsylvania, 1895).

Hinke, W. J., "The First German Reformed Colony in Virginia 1714-1750," in *Journal of the Presbyterian Historical Society*, Vol. II (Philadelphia, 1903).

Holmes, H. A., "The Palatine Emigration to England in 1709," in *Albany Institute Transactions*, Vol. VII (1872).

Honeyman, A. van Doven, "Early Palatine Immigration," in *Proceedings of New Jersey Historical Society*, New Series, Vol. X (1925).

Honeyman, A. van Doven, "The Lutheran Church of Raritan in the Hills," in *Somerset County Historical Quarterly*, Vol. II (Somerville, New Jersey, 1913).

Jacobs, H. E., "The German Emigration to America, 1709-1740," in *Pennsylvania=German Society Proceedings*, Vol. VIII (Lancaster, Pennsylvania, 1898).

Katscher, Leopold, "German Life in London," in *Nineteenth Century Magazine*, Vol. XXI (London, May, 1887).

Learned, M. D., "Life of Francis Daniel Pastorius the Founder of Germantown" in *German-American Annals*, Vols. IX and X (Philadelphia, 1908-9).

Matthews, Albert, "The Word 'Palatine' in America," in *The Nation*, Vol. LXXIV (Cambridge, Massachusetts, 1904).

Mays, George, "Palatine and Scotch-Irish Settlers of Lebanon," in *Lebanon County Historical Society*, Vol. I (1902).

Mellick, A. D., Jr., "German Emigration to the American Colonies," in *Pennsylvania Magazine of History and Biography*, Vol. X (1886).

Morgan, William Thomas, "Some Attempts at Imperial Co-operation during the Reign of Queen Anne," in *Transcripts of Royal Historical Society*, 4th series, Vol. X (London, 1927).

Morgan, William Thomas, "The Five Nations and Queen Anne," in *Mississippi Valley Historical Review*, Vol. XIII (1926).

Morgan, William Thomas, "The Ministerial Revolution of 1710 in England," in *Poltical Science Quarterly*, Vol. XXXVI, number 2 (June, 1921).

Pennypacker, S. W., "The Settlement of Germantown," in *Pennsylvania= German Society Proceedings*, Vol. IX (Lancaster, Pennsylvania, 1899).

Richards, H. M. M., "German Emigration from New York Province into Pennsylvania," in *Pennsylvania=German Society Proceedings*, Vol. IX (Lancaster, Pennsylvania, 1899).

Richards, H. M. M., "The Weiser Family," in *Pennsylvania=German Society Proceedings*, Vol. XXXII (Lancaster, Pennsylvania, 1924).

R. J. G., "The Palatines in New York and Pennsylvania," in *German-American Annals*, Vol. X (Philadelphia, 1908).

Sachse, J. F., "The Fatherland 1450-1700," in *Pennsylvania=German Society Proceedings*, Vol. VII (Philadelphia, 1897).

Sauer, Christopher, "An Early Description of Pennsylvania," written (in

1724), translated by R. W. Kelsey in *Pennsylvania Magazine of History and Biography*, Vol. XLV (Philadelphia, 1921).

Scheffer, J. G. de Hoop, "Mennonite Emigration to Pennsylvania," in *Pennsylvania Magazine of History and Biography*, Vol. II (1878, number 2).

Seidensticker, Oswald, "William Penn's Travels in Holland and Germany in 1677," in *Pennsylvania Magazine of History and Biography*, Vol. II (Philadelphia, 1878).

Smith, C. H., "The Mennonite Immigration to Pennsylvania in the 18th Century," in *Pennsylvania=German Society Proceedings*, Vol. XXXV (Norristown, Pennsylvania, 1929).

Spencer, C. W., "The Cornbury Legend," in *New York Historical Association Proceedings*, Vol. XIII (1916).

Spencer, C. W., "The Land System of Colonial New York," in *New York State Historical Association Proceedings*, Vol. XVI (1917).

Todd, C. B., "Robert Hunter and the Settlement of the Palatines 1710–1719," in Wilson, J. G., *Memorial History of New York*, Vol. II (New York, 1892).

Todd, C. B., "Robert Hunter and the Settlement of the Palatines," in *The National Magazine*, Vol. XVII (February, 1893).

Todd, C. B., "The Story of the Palatines," in *The Lippincott Magazine*, Vol. XXXI (March, 1883).

Trinity College Historical Society, "De Graffenried and the Swiss and Palatine Settlement of New Bern, North Carolina," in *Trinity College Historical Society Papers*, 4th series (1900).

Wilson, J. G., "Lovelace and the Second Canadian Campaign," in *American Historical Association Annual Reports for 1891* (Washington, D. C., 1892).

INTRODUCTION TO APPENDICES

THE PALATINE IMMIGRATION was so involved financially with the British government that many lists of these immigrants were drawn up. Most of these lists, heretofore unpublished, were turned up in the course of this research. They constitute a most valuable addition to genealogical information, since the most difficult problem confronting the genealogists is that part of the link which establishes just when the colonial ancestor arrived. Heretofore, the largest list of these emigrants published contained only 6,000 people. The lists given here double that total.

For convenience in referring to the lists, they have been arranged in this order under these headings.

A. The Kocherthal Party—the 1708 Emigration.
B. The First Board of Trade List of Palatines in London (May 6, 1709).
C. The Embarkation Lists from Holland.
D. The Roman Catholic Palatines Returned to Holland.
E. The New York Subsistence List.
F. The Simmendinger Register.
G. The Pennsylvania Palatine Lists.
H. The Petition List of Palatines in North Carolina.
I. The Irish Palatine List.

Each list has been briefly described under its heading and the source of the information given. All information in the lists has been included, except where otherwise stated as in Appendix B. No attempt has been made to reconcile the spellings between any two of the lists as it was felt that each record had best stand upon its own merits. There is a great deal of variation in the spelling of the names among the various lists, which may be accounted for by the eighteenth century habit of spelling a word the way it was pronounced, a habit now lost but of some merit, and by the difficulties of list-makers writing names in a language often strange to them. The latter difficulty is not so valid with the Palatine list-makers, who were in most instances German or Dutch, the latter not unrelated to German. Perhaps the worst difficulty was the illiteracy of a number of the Palatines, who may be presumed to have been able to pronounce but not spell their names. The use of the feminine ending "in" at the end of the women's family names should not be confusing to the casual reader of the lists; it simply denotes that the female in question was unhampered by any present male attachment, she being either an unmarried girl or a widow

A. THE KOCHERTHAL PARTY—THE 1708 IMMIGRATION TO NEW YORK

REVEREND KOCHERTHAL was the leader of a band of forty-one persons from the Palatinate, who came to London in 1708 and were sent to New York with Governor Lovelace as described in Chapter II. They first settled at Newburgh on the Hudson River. The data given in the list below was compiled from the following sources: P. R. O., C. O. 5, 67 ii; N. Y. Col. Docs., V, 52; Doc. Hist., III, 543; C. C. 1706-1708, 722. "w." indicates wife in the family notations.

Family	No. of Persons
Fiscar (Fischer), John; w. Maria Barbara.	2
Gülch (Hilg or Gilles), Melchior; w. Anne Catherine and ch., Magdalena 12 and Heinrich 10.	4
Kocherdal (Kocherthal), Joshua de; w. Sibylle Charlotte and ch. Benigna Sibylle 10, Christian Joshua 7 and Susanna Sibylle 3.	5
Plettell (Pletel), John Jacob; w. Anne Elisabeth and ch. Margaretha 10, Anna Sara 7 and Catharine 7.	5
Rennau, Henry; w. Johanna and 2 sisters Sussanna Liboscha 15, and Maria Johanna Liboscha 10; ch. Lorenz 2 and Heinrich 2 mo.	6

Schwiser (Schwisser), Lorentz; w. Anne Catherine and ch.
    Johanna 6 mo.   3
Turk (Türck), Isaac (a bachelor).   1
Volck, Andrew; w. Anna Catherine, 3 ch. Maria Barbara 5,
    Heironemus 4 and Anne Gertrude 1.   5
Weber, Jacob; w. Anna Elisabethe, and 2 daughters, Eva
    Maria 4 and Eva Elisabethe 1.   4
Wigand (Weigand), Michael; w. Anne Catherine and ch.
    Anna Maria 13, Tobias 7 and Georg 5. Also a cousin 22.   6

To the forty-one persons of Kocherthal's original party
were added fourteen Germans who came to London a little
later as described in Chapter II. The list of them given below
is taken from P. R. O., C. O. 1049/57, 139 and *C. C. 1706-
1708*, 738.

Feber, Isaac; w. Catharine, ch. Abraham 2.   3
Fiere, Daniel; w. Anna Maria, ch. Andreas 7 and Johannes 6. 4
Hübertsen, Peter (widower); son Jacob 15.   2
Rose, Peter; w. Johanna.   2
Schüneman, Herman (a bachelor).   1
Wemarin, Maria (Peter's widow), and daughter Catha-
    rina 2.   2

B. THE BOARD OF TRADE LIST OF FIRST PARTY OF PALATINES IN LONDON, MAY 3, 1709

THIS LIST is the first of four lists of Palatines compiled up
to June 16, 1709 by Reverend John Tribbeko and Reverend
George Andrew Ruperti. The four lists include only the first
6,000 of the Germans to arrive in that year. The lists, which
contain information on the age and occupation of the head
of the family, numbers and age of the members of the family
and religion, may be found in the Public Record Office, C. O.
388/76, 56 ii, 64, and 68-70. They have been published without change in the *New York Genealogical and Biographical
Records* (New York, 1909 and 1910), XL, 49-54, 93-100, 160-
167, 241-248; XLI, 10-19. They are also published in L. D.

MacWethy, *The Book of Names especially Relating to the Early Palatines and the First Settlers in the Mohawk Valley* (St. Johnsville, New York, 1933) in an alphabetical order and an abridged form. In the latter version there are errors, which are excusable because of the nature of the material but the bad alphabetising of the names is not to be regarded so lightly.

Only the first of the four Board of Trade Lists (that of May 6, 1709) is included here because that group of 825 persons is unmentioned in the Embarkation Lists from Holland, which are here given in Appendix C. They were sent, as related in Chapter III, before the arrangement, by which the British government financed their passage to London, was well worked out. This first Board of Trade List given below has been carefully alphabetised, but the information given as to occupation, religion and age has not been included here for a number of reasons: 1) it is accessible elsewhere, 2) it would crowd an already lengthy Appendix, 3) it would not conform to the Embarkation Lists which it is intended to supplement here. The abbreviation w. denotes the presence of the wife.

Adeler, Henry—w. 1 son
Albenz, Christoph
Albrecht, James—w.
Andrew, Benedict—w. 1 son
Anke, Joseph

Bahr, John—w. 3 sons
Bauer, Christian—w. 2 sons, 3 daus
Bauer, Christina
Bauer, George
Baumann, Michael—w. 1 dau
Becker, Gerhard—w. 1 son, 1 dau
Bekell, Philip—w. 1 son, 5 daus
Beller, Jacob—w. 1 son
Berg, Frederick—w. 1 son, 1 dau
Bergleuchter, Anton
Berstler, Adam—w. 2 sons, 1 dau
Bettinger, Anna Christina
Bien, John
Blesinger, Daniel—w. 2 daus
Bohm, Johannes
Bolker, Charles—w.

Bollon, Christoff—w. 1 son, 2 daus
Boos, John Henry—w.
Bretschi, Lorentz
Bruchly, John Henry—w. 2 sons
Buehler, John—w. 3 daus
Buff, George—w. 1 dau

Cathrina—servant maid
Clemens, Gerhard—w. 2 sons
Closterbeker, John—w. 1 son, 2 daus

Daninger, Jacob—w. 2 sons, 2 daus
Daun, George—w. 1 dau
Degen, Felix
Denias, Philip
deRocheford, Peter—w. 2 sons, 2 daus
Dieterich, John—w. 1 son
Dixion, David—w. 1 son
Drechsler, John Peter—w. 1 dau
DuBois, Abraham—w. 3 sons, 1 dau
Durbecker, John Adam—w. 2 daus
Durk, John Adam—w. 1 son, 2 daus

Ebert, Hartman—w.
Emichen, Ernst—w. 4 sons
Ende, John Philip am—w. 1 son, 1 dau
Ends, Matthew—w. 1 son
Engelsbruecher, Nicol—w. 1 dau
Erkel, Bernard—w.
Eschelmanns, Anna—1 son
Escherich, John
Eyeach, John Valentine

Faubell, John—w. 1 dau
Fodder, John—w. 2 sons, 1 dau
Frey, Conrad—w. 2 sons, 2 daus
Friede, Cathrina
Fuhrman, Jacob—2 daus

Galathe, Jacob
Galathe, John Jacob—w. 1 son, 1 dau
Garrinot, Peter—w.
Geisell, George—w. 2 sons
Gerhard, John George—w. 2 sons, 4 daus
Gessienger, Henry—w. 1 dau
Glaents, John—w. 1 son
Gnaedi, Benedict—w. 1 son, 1 dau
Goebell, Paul—w. 1 son, 1 dau
Gothzeit, William—w. 1 son, 1 dau
Graeff, Jacob—his parents live in Pennsylvania
Gring, Jacob—w. 1 dau
Gruendner, Matthew
Guth, Henry

Haas, John—w. 2 sons, 2 daus
Hagder, John
Hagenbeck, Frederick—w. 2 sons
Hahrlaender, Conrad—w. 2 sons
Hakl, John George—w. 1 son, 3 daus
Hartman, John George—w. 1 son
Hassmer, John
Haun, Andrew—w. 5 sons, 2 daus
Hebenstreit, John Jas.—w.
Heffen, Bartin
Heidman, Peter—w. 3 dau
Helffert, Peter—w.
Henrich, Lorentz—w. 1 son, 1 dau
Herman, Daniel—w. 1 son, 1 dau
Herman, Jacob
Herman, Niclas
Herman, Peter—w. 2 sons, 1 dau
Herman, Valentine—w. 1 son
Hermann, Niclas
Hesse, John—w. 2 daus
Heyde, Peter—w. 1 son
Hirtzbach, Anton—w. 3 sons, 1 dau
Hirzeach, Martin—w. 2 sons, 2 daus
Hobler, Abraham—w. 1 son, 1 dau
Hocky, Andrew

Hocky, Peter
Hoffart, John Adam—w.
Hoffstaetter, Philip
Hohenstein, Christian—w. 2 sons, 1 dau
Hoherluth, George Adam—w. 2 sons, 2 daus
Hornigh, John George—w. 2 sons, 2 daus
Hubscher, Andrew—w. 1 son, 4 daus
Hubmacher, Niclas—w. 1 son, 2 daus
Huebner, Anton—w. 2 sons, 1 dau

Jacobi, John Thomas—w. 2 sons, 1 dau
Jalathe, John William—w. 2 sons, 1 dau

Kaff, Bazar—w. 3 sons
Kaldauer, Valentine—w. 2 sons, 3 daus
Keyser, George Frederick—w. 2 daus
Kinfeller, Frederick—w. 1 son, 1 dau
Kirchofen, Francis Ludwig
Klaemer, Ludwig—w. 1 son, 2 daus
Klein, John Jacob—w. 1 son
Klein, John—w. 2 sons
Klein, Michael, sister-in-law of
Klein, Michael—w. 2 daus
Klein, Peter—w. 1 son, 1 dau
Klug, George—w. 1 son
Klug, George, his sister and son, a boy of 15 years
Koenig, John Adam
Kolb, Arnold
Kolb, Henry—w. 3 daus
Kueffer, John—w. 2 daus
Kuhlwein, Philip
Kuhner, Jacob—w. 3 sons, 1 dau

laForge, John Wm.—w.
Lang, Johan—4 in family
Lang, Philip—w. 1 son, 1 dau
Lauber, Jacob—w. 3 daus
Le Dee, John—2 daus
Le Fevre, Abram—w. 1 son, 1 dau
Leibengut, John Wendell—1 son
Leucht, Lewis—w. 1 son
Lichtnegger, Gottlob August
Lucas, Francis—w. 2 sons, 5 daus
Lup, Henry—w. 3 sons, 1 dau

Machtig, Jacob—w. 2 sons, 2 daus
Martins, Gertrud—1 son
Mason, Niclas
Mendon, Jacob
Meningen, John—w. 2 sons
Messer, Sylvester—w. 2 sons, 2 daus
Mey, David—w.
Meyer, Hartman—w. 1 son, 2 daus
Meyer, Henry—w. 2 daus
Meyer, Henry—sister of

Moor, Austin
Moor, John
Moor, John William
Mueller, John Jacob—w 6 sons, 1 dau
Mueller, Valentine
Muller, Daniel

Nagel, John—w. 1 dau
Neidhofer, John Quirinus—w. 1 son,
   1 dau
Notzel, Rudolf—w. 3 daus

Obender, Samuel—w. 1 dau
Oberholtzer, Mark—w. 3 sons, 2 daus

Pelle, Peter
Penning, Daniel
Pens, Benedict—4 in family
Pfeiffer, John Jacob—w. 1 son, 1 dau
Presler, Valentine—w. 3 sons, 2 daus

Rath (Bath), John—w. 1 son, 1 dau
Raths, Jane
Rausch, George
Rebell, Jacob
Reiser, John Peter—w. 5 sons
Reuling, Jacob—w. 1 dau
Rheine, John am—w.
Rider, Niclas—w.
Riedel, George—mother-in-law of
Riedell, John George—w. 1 son, 1 dau
Rohrbach, Christian—w. 1 dau
Rose, Anna—1 son, 2 daus
Rose, Catherine—1 dau
Rudolff, John

Schaeffer, John—w. 1 son
Schaeffer, John—w. 4 sons, 2 daus
Schaeffer, John Conrad
Schaeffer, Joseph—w. 2 sons, 4 daus
Schletzer, Jeremy—w. 2 sons, 3 daus
Schlingluff, John—w. 3 sons
Schlottenhofer, Christof—w. 2 sons
Schmitzer, John Martin—w. 1 son
Schneider, Philip—w. 2 sons, 1 dau
Schneider, John Michael—w. 1 son,
   1 dau
Schoen, Maria Cathrina—3 sons, 1 dau
Schrager, Andrew—w. 2 daus
Schuetz, John—w. 4 daus
Schwaegerin, Apollonia
Schwengel, John—w. 1 son, 3 daus

Seibert, Conrad—w. 1 son, 1 dau
Seibert, Martin—w. 1 son, 1 dau
Sheuer, John Adam—w. 2 sons, 1 dau
Shonweiss, John—w. 1 son, 2 daus
Shwab, Peter—w. 1 son, 1 dau
Shwartz, Matthias—w. 2 sons, 1 dau
Shwartze, John—w. 1 son, 1 dau
Smith, Henry—w. 4 sons, 1 dau
Smith, Jacob—w. 2 sons, 1 dau
Smith, John—w. 4 sons, 6 daus
Spuehler, Jacob—w. 1 son
Staehler, Peter
Stutz, Eberhard—5 in family
Stutz, John Eberhard—w. 2 sons, 1 dau

Turch, Caspar
Tanner, Cathrina—1 dau
Thevoux, Daniel—w. 1 son, 1 dau
Thomas, John George—w. 2 sons, 1 dau
Thor, Conrad am—w. 1 dau
Trombauer, Niclas—w. 1 son, 2 daus
Truat, John—w. 2 sons
Trumph, John Michael—1 son

Vogt, Abraham—w. 1 son, 3 daus
Vogt, John—w. 1 son
Volweider, Jacob—w.

Wagner, John—w. 2 sons, 3 daus
Wagner, Mary Elizabeth
Walter, John George—w. 3 sons, 2 daus
Warambour, Mary—4 sons, 1 dau
Wayner, Henry—w. 2 sons, 1 dau
Weber, John Engel—w. 5 daus
Weber, John Jacob—w.
Weinrich, Balzar—w. 3 sons, 1 dau
Weitzell, John—w. 2 sons
Wenig, Peter—w. 1 dau
Wentzen, Peter
Werner, Christoff—w. 1 dau
Willich, Peter—w. 2 daus
Winter, Maria Cathrina—1 dau
Wismar, Jacob—w. 1 son, 1 dau

Zeber, John—w. 2 sons, 2 daus
Zeisler, Lorentz—w. 2 sons, 1 dau
Zeitz, John Peter
Ziegler, Michael
Zimmerman, John Wolff—w. 2 sons,
   4 daus
Zinkhan, Conrad—w. 1 son, 2 daus
Zitel, Jacob—w.

C. THE EMBARKATION LISTS FROM HOLLAND

THESE LISTS comprise the enumeration of five separate sailings of Palatines from Holland, as sent by the Rotterdam Commissioners, van Toren and van Gent, to Minister Dayrolle, who forwarded them to England. The lists were found in the Public Record Office, T 1/119, 6-10, 19-26, 68-72, 58-65, 79-82. They comprise notations of about 11,000 persons, by far the largest list of all the lists relating to this immigration, although even the Embarkation Lists are not complete. They lack the enumeration of the first party to sail in 1709, the 825 persons given in Appendix B. They do not include those Palatines who paid their own way to London or were sent by private charity in August and October, 1709 as related in Chapter III.

So far as possible the enumerations have been retained in exactly the form in which the Dutchmen made them. This was considered most desirable for genealogists, who will use them to greatest advantage. For the ordinary reader, it may be necessary to explain further that "vrouw" means wife; "weduw^e," widow; "moeder," mother; "swister," sister; "swager," brother-in-law; "swagerin," sister-in-law; and "knegt," servant. Of course, each sailing list has been alphabetised to facilitate their use. When names are indented, they are the names of children which happen to be mentioned, and they are not included in the additional number of children ending the line.

SECOND PARTY SAILING MAY 23, 1709

Aldemos, Philip
Altúm, Hans & vrouw, 2 ch.
Aman, Johannes
Amand, Johannes & vrouw
Arm, David & vrouw
  Johan Arm, Izaak, Kristina,
  David, & 2 ch.
Atam, Hans & vrouw, 1 ch.

Back, Joh^s & vrouw
  Anna Margreta, Ane Marÿa,
  & 1 ch.

Balbar, Krÿn & vrouw, 2 ch.
Bampert, Johans & vrouw
  Anna Krita, Gÿsbert, Frans
  Adam, & 2 ch.
Barban, Hans Wolf & vrouw
  Anna & 2 ch.
Bastiaen, Andries
Batyn, Nicolaas & vrouw, 2 ch.
Baur, Elias
Beck, Johannes
Beck, Thobias & vrouw, 5 ch.
Bergs, Hans

Berkman & vrouw
   Anna Elisabet Betha, Anna
   Margreta, Anna Barbera,
   Johannes Berkma [sic], & 1 ch.
Berthram, Pr
Besser, Johan Peter
Better, Johan Peter & vrouw, 1 ch.
Bickman, Jacob & vrouw
   Andries Vredrig, Justina
   Madeleena, Anna Christina,
   Abraham, Maria Dorta, & 2 ch.
Bilar, Johan & vrouw, 3 ch.
Binder, Johannes & vrouw, 3 ch.
Binder, Valentÿn & vrouw, 1 ch.
Bischop, Lodewÿk
Blaum, Herman & vrouw
   Gerrard, Anna Cartel, & 1 ch.
Bolla, Jacob
Bols, Johan
Bols, Jorig & vrouw
   Júrig Bols & 2 ch.
Bornman, Hans Peter & vrouw, 2 ch.
Bortran, Pieter
Bos, Kasper & vrouw, 1 ch.
Bos, Philip & vrouw
   Hans Bos, Mighiel Bos, & 3 ch.
Boúwer, Elias
Boúwer, Kristiaan & vrouw
   Elisa Margreta & 1 ch.
Brensard, Johan Júrrey & vrouw, 3ch.
Breslÿ, Johan & vrouw, 3 ch.
Brúg, Johannes
Búckjo, Abraham
Búckjo, Izaak
Búckjo, Jacob & vrouw, 3 ch.
Búckjo, Johan Jorge
Burdin, Johan
   Nog een vrouws persoon
Bús, Daniel & vrouw
   Margriet [child]

Cartuir, Peter & vrouw
   Johannes & 2 ch.
Caúer, Jacob Mittell & vrouw, 3 ch.
Clös, Henrig & vrouw
   Maria Dore, Maria Clös, & 4 ch.
Codevina, Steṁa
Coúis, Magdeleena
Coúis, Maria
Cous, Hans & vrouw
   Johannes & 2 ch.
Crisser, Hans Músil & vrouw
   Hans Músil, Katrina, & 2 ch.
Cúits, Johan Kristoffel

Darsel, Philip & vrouw
   Abram Dars, Maria Susanna, & 3 ch.

Daslúm, Lampare & vrouw
   Maria Lÿsa
de Waal, Antony & vrouw, 3 ch.
Diderig, & vrouw, 2 ch. [sic.]
Diderig, Hans & vrouw, 6 ch.
Diderig, John Peter & vrouw, 3 ch.
Dilbern, Johan & vrouw, 1 ch.
Dinant, Hans Pieter & vrouw
   Súsanna, Hans Philip, & 4 ch.
Dinges, Paulus & vrouw, 3 ch.
Dirll, Bernhard & vrouw
   Anna Elisa, Magdaleena, Maria Cröda,
   Hans Fildin, Jörg Henry, & 3 ch.
Divin, Anna
Dobÿs, Jorig & vrouw
Dopper, Leborges & vrouw
   Johan Peter, Angeniet, & 2 ch.
Dor, Peter & vrouw, 3 ch.
Doúb-dÿsul, Peter
Dúister, Johannes & vrouw, 4 ch.
Duits, Pieter

Ebrosard, Johannes & vrouw
   Jacob, Sirnner, Hanrich, & 1 ch.
Eemig, Johan Nicolaes
Eger, Daniel
Einbag, Hans Júrig & vrouw, 2 ch.
Elenberger, Júrig & vrouw
   Júrig
Ewold, Koenraet & vrouw, 4 ch.

Faleé, Hans & vrouw, 3 ch.
Falthum, Peter & vrouw
   Henrig, & 1 ch.
Feske, Jacob & vrouw
   Daniel, Jacob
Fischbac, Johannes & vrouw
   Johannes & 2 ch.
Fraús, Peter & vrouw, 9 ch.
Freeder, Johan & vrouw, 5 ch.
Frei, Jo Hendrik & vrouw, 2 ch.
Frenger, Michel
Fridl, Jacob & vrouw
Froes, Hans Jacob & vrouw
Froth, Fredig & vrouw, 3 ch.
Froúg, Júrig & vrouw, 2 ch.
Fúsror, Henrig & vrouw, 4 ch.

Gewte [blotted] Jacob & vrouw, 5 ch.
Gocú [?], Ulia
Godvried, Ester Sosannah
   Katrina, Rosemonda, Nicolaas, & 2 ch.
Gramli, Soloma
Greef, Andreg
Griet, Hans Júrig & vrouw
   Maria Bern, Hans Lenart, Johan Júrig,
   Hans Miggel, Hans Peter, & 3 ch.

Groos, Philippús & vrouw
  Geertrúy, Anna Madeleena
Groots, Philipp[s], 2 ch.

Haber, Barthel & vrouw
  Susanna & 3 ch.
Haen, Marthin & vrouw
Haiser, Johannes & vrouw, 3 ch.
Haldeman, Ulrig & vrouw
  Hans Henrig & 3 ch.
Halig, Koenraet & vrouw
  Johan Diderig, Johan Phillippus, &
  Anna Katrina
Hannal, Camúrs & vrouw, 2 ch.
Hardwick, Mattÿs & vrouw
Harman, Bastiaan
Harnas, Johannes & vrouw, 1 ch.
Hart, Simon & vrouw, 3 ch.
Hartman, Hans Júrig & vrouw, 1 ch.
Hartogin, Anna Elisabet
Hartong, Kasper
Hartwig, Kasper & vrouw, 3 ch.
Heller, Hans Atam & vrouw
  Johannes
Heller, Jacob & vrouw, 1 ch.
Helm, p[r] & vrouw
  Simon, Leenhart, & 5 ch.
Helwig, Hendrik & vrouw, 1 ch.
Hendrig, Wendel & vrouw, 4 ch.
Henkel, Hans Júrig & vrouw
Henrig, Johan & vrouw, 2 ch.
Hepman, Williger & vrouw
  Haningel, Maria Geertúit, & 1 ch.
Herber, John Jacob
Hermickel, Hendrig & vrouw
  Maria Beck & 2 ch.
Heve, Johannes & vrouw, 1 ch.
Hivang, Henrig & vrouw, 2 ch.
Hobbersin, Johan Júrig
Hoest, Jacob & vrouw
  Michel, Johannes
Hofer, Simon & vrouw
Hofman, Gabriel
Hofman, Johan Kasper
Holzir, Hans & vrouw, 1 ch.
Húreuter, Willem & vrouw, 3 ch.

Imig, Paulús & vrouw

Jaeger, Daniel & vrouw
Jacob, Hans & vrouw, 1 ch.
Jacob, Hans & vrouw
  Anna & 1 ch.
Jacob, Kristiaan & vrouw, 3 ch.
Jong, Elisabeth
  Pieter Jong, Katrina, Maria Katharina,
  Hendr. Pieter

Jonge, Jacob
Joost, Johan & vrouw, 2 ch.
Jorden, Koenraed
Jörgen, Hans
Jorter, Andries & vrouw, 3 ch.
Joseph, Júrig
Joúrg, Hans & vrouw, 2 ch.
Júdik, Maria, 1 ch.
Júng, John & vrouw
Júrig, Abraham

Kaeiman & vrouw, 2 ch. [sic]
Karty, Johan
Kast, Balter & vrouw
  Marita, Anna Marÿ, & 2 ch.
Katrina [sic]
Keizer, Mattheús & vrouw
  Anna Elisabet
Kelger, Peter
Keller, Joh[s] & vrouw, 1 ch.
Keller, Nicolaas & vrouw
Kernar, Wolf & vrouw, 2 ch.
Kernerin, Anna Maria
Kernreiter, Johannes & vrouw, 3 ch.
Kerry, Falentÿn & vrouw, 5 ch.
Keulen, Koenraet
Keyzer, Henrig & vrouw, 3 ch.
Kilberin, Barbera
Klein, Jacob
Kleus, Johannes & vrouw
  Harler, Margriet
Klinger, Nicolaes & vrouw, 4 ch.
Kliuwe, Joh[s]
Kloútt, Henrig & vrouw, 2 ch.
Koen, Koenraet & vrouw
  Hans Veldekoen, Hans Deterkoen,
  Hans Júrgekeon, & 1 ch.
Koen, Mattheús & vrouw, 1 ch.
Koenraed, Johan
Koenraet, Martÿn & vrouw
  Anna Katrina, John Joris, & 2 ch.
Kont, Nicolaas & vrouw
Kop, Henrig, & vrouw
  Hans Peter, Ursela, & 2 ch.
Korin, Johannes & vrouw, 2 ch.
Krems, Johannes & vrouw
  Anna Kristina & 1 ch.
Kreps, Pieter & vrouw
  Salme, Johannes Rudolf, & 2 ch.
Kriget, Arnold & vrouw, 2 ch.
Kris, Henrig & vrouw, 3 ch.
Kristaan & vrouw, 4 ch. [sic]
Kristoffel, Johan & vrouw
  Andreas, Hans Sellim, Johan Henrig,
  & 3 ch.

Kroevenag, Penetik & vrouw
  Marÿ Sebille, Júliaèn, Anna Eva,
  & 3 ch.
Krol, Hans Júrig & vrouw, 1 ch.
Kroohart, Michel
Kúiber, Daniel
Kúrby, Michel & vrouw, 2 ch.

Lang, Jacob & vrouw, 2 ch.
Lang, Johannes & vrouw
  Barbera, Peter, Catharina, & 2 ch.
Langbrin, Kristoffel
Laúrens, Peter & vrouw
  Anna Margreta, Maria Margreta,
  Anna Rosina, & 1 ch.
Leiser, Castiaen & vrouw
  Johan Jacob, Anna Margraet, Anna Lys,
  Anna Castiaens, Hans Júrig, & 5 ch.
Lenhart, Hans & vrouw, 1 ch.
Listaboris, Lúcas & vrouw
Litig, Hans Jagol
Litig, Hans Koenraet
Litig, Jacob
Litig, Kristoffel
Lodwig, Antony
Loedolf, Johannes & vrouw, 4 ch.
Loedolf, Koenrad
Loet, Hans Peter & vrouw
  Balthazer Loet & 2 ch.
Lott, Johs & vrouw, 9 ch.
Loúrens, Johannes & vrouw
  Anna Lÿs, Anna Margriet, Magdelena,
  & 3 other children
Lúsa, Maria
Lútig, Johan
Lúts, Hans Adam
Lúts, Jan Júrig & vrouw, 4 ch.
Lúttig, Kristiaan
Lúúr, Johan & vrouw
  Kornelūs & 2 ch.

Maartsen, Hans Júrig & vrouw
  Marÿ, Magdeleena, Anna Katrina,
  Hans Júrig, & 2 ch.
Maerten, Matthÿs & vrouw
  Maria, Katharina, Barbera, & 1 ch.
Marines & vrouw [sic]
Martÿn, Thoms
Mathell, Willem & vrouw, 1 ch.
Meder, Johan & vrouw
Meier, Johannes & vrouw
  Johan Koenraad, Johannes, Anna
  Devoda, Maria Lisaba
Melck, Mighel & vrouw, 1 ch.
Melries, Johannes & vrouw, 2 ch.
Messer, Pieter,
  Jacobus & 1 ch.

Michel, Johan & vrouw, 1 ch.
Milbert, John Martin & vrouw
Miller, Falentyn & vrouw, 1 ch.
Miller, Hans Jacob, 2 ch.
Miller, Johannes
Miller, Johannes & vrouw
  Jacob Miller & 4 ch.
Miller, Peter & vrouw
  vroús swister & 2 ch.
Miller, Smich & vrouw
  Johan Nickel, Willem, Johannes,
  Katrina, & 1 ch.
Miller, Steve & vrouw
  Philips
Minkeler, Kelioen & vrouw
  Anna Margreta
Misselman, Daniel & vrouw
  Swagers Moeder & 3 ch.
Miÿn, Joseph & vrouw, 1 ch.
Mockel, Ulrig & vrouw, 2 ch.
Montria, Paulus, & vrouw, 4 ch.
Moon, Klemen & vrouw, 4 ch.
Morrer, Jacob & vrouw
  Anna Appel, Susan, & 2 ch.
Morrits, Mattheus
Mossel, Jacob & vrouw
  Hans Develt, Anna Maria, Johannes
  Mossel, & 1 ch. [The last two are
  probably sister and brother of Jacob
  Mossel, since their names are given
  after those of the children in the
  family.]
Múding, Pieter & vrouw
  Maria & 1 ch.
Múldering, Maria Katharin over
Mulnier, Johannes & vrouw, 2 ch.
Muver[?], Hans Júrig & vrouw, 1 ch.

Naeboúr, Andries & vrouw, 3 ch.
Nicolaes & vrouw [sic]

Ode, Johannes & vrouw, 5 ch.
Omstad, Veldin
Ooster, Arent & vrouw

Pallaúeborg, Koenraed & vrouw, 1 ch.
Pelmúg, John & vrouw, 3 ch.
Peter, Johan & vrouw, 1 ch.
Peter, Johan & vrouw, 2 ch.
Peters, Frans Henrig
Petri, Johan Henrig
Phat, Henrig & vrouw, 4 ch.
Phat, Masel & vrouw
Philips, Johan & vrouw
  Kristina, Anna Dors
Pogeman, Jacob & vrouw, 2 ch.

Ponis, Július & vrouw
  Johannes & 2 ch.
Poort, Pieter
Porst, Joris, & vrouw, 2 ch.
Pÿn, Marten & vrouw

Reiner, Hans Júrig & vrouw
  Johan Peter Reiner, Barbera,
  Elisabet, & 3 ch.
Reitwel, Jacob
Reÿnart, Hans, & vrouw
  Katrina Reÿnart, Michel, Margreta,
  & 3 ch.
Reÿnart, Pieter & vrouw, 4 ch.
Riesin, Mathÿs & vrouw, 3 ch.
Ritwell, Fredrig & vrouw, 1 ch.
Rohter, Hans Pet & vrouw, 1 ch.
Roost, Johan & vrouw
  Anna Maria
Rop, Johannes
Roth, Hans Peter & vrouw, 2 ch.
Roúg, Kasper
Rústiw, Andries & vrouw, 4 ch.
Ruth & vrouw, 5 ch. [sic]
Ruth, Kristiaan, & vrouw, 1 ch.

Scheever, Hendrig & vrouw, 2 ch.
Scherp, Jacob & vrouw, 2 ch.
Schipper, Júrig
Schneider, Bernhard & vrouw
  Ariaan, Anna Bara, & 1 ch.
Scholtes, Johannes & vrouw, 1 ch.
Schoolmeester, Súurlotte
Schreets, Mighiel
Schrúner, Isaak & vrouw
Siake, Súsan
Sigmúnd, Johannes
Simbluv, Johannes & vrouw, 1 ch.
Sleephaan, Johannes
Slúÿber, Sacharias & vrouw, 3 ch.
Smies, Theodorus & vrouw, 1 ch.
Smith, John Willem & vrouw
  Margreta & 3 ch.
Smith, Kasper
  Magdeleena, Maria Barbera, Nicolaus,
  Peter, & 4 ch.
Smith, Sigmúd
Snel, Mathÿs
Snitzer, Jacob & vrouw, 2 ch.
Soerl, Michal & vrouw, 2 ch.
Soets, Diderig & vrouw
  Hans Pieter & 2 ch.
Soús, Hans Pieter
Soús, Johannes & vrouw
  Hans Pr Soús, Maria, Magdaleena,
  Maria Lúcina

Spanemer, Júrig & vrouw
  Maria Rosina, Anna Maria, & 2 ch.
Spinler, Kasper, & vrouw
  Liliana, Dorethea, Zimon, & 1 ch.
Sprosser, Anthony & vrouw
Spÿkerman, Sebastiaen
Spÿs, John Peter
Staan, Johannes & vrouw
Stambag, Jacob & vrouw
Steenbergen, Hans Jacob & vrouw
  Johan Adam, Anna Katrina, & 2 ch.
Stevvel, Frans & vrouw, 3 ch.
Stoffer, Andries, 2 ch.
Stol, Johannes
Stoppelbeen, Pieter & vrouw, 2 ch.
Súller, Hans Jorig & vrouw
  Anna & 1 ch.
Swarts, Kristiaan
Swik, Mathÿs & vrouw
  Anna Margriet, Hans Júrig, & 2 ch.

Tebalt, Júrig
Terber, Johan Adolf, 4 ch.
Toup, Michel & vrouw

Ulrig, Kristoffel & vrouw
  Daniel, Anna Maria, Elisabet,
  Katharina, & 3 ch.
Urzel, Hans Migel & vrouw, 1 ch.

van Kunter, Klaas, & vrouw, 5 ch.
Vereter, Hans Júrig & vrouw
  Anna Lotsia & 2 ch.
Ving, Andreas, & vrouw, 1 ch.
Vinis, Hans Jacob & vrouw
  Johannes, Elizabet, Nicolaes, & 2 ch.
Vink, Hendrik Lodwig
Vink, Johan Cristof
Vink, Johan Godvÿd
Voerman, Hans Michel & vrouw
  Magdleena & 2 ch.
Voes, Andries & vrouw
  Anna Lÿs & 3 ch.
Voes, Johannes & vrouw, 3 ch.
Vogel, Spavger Jochem
Volhand, Engelhart & vrouw
Vrick, Hendrik & vrouw
Vriesig, [Wiesig?], Kasper & vrouw
  2 ch.
Vuer, Jacob

Wagenaar, Andries & vrouw, 2 ch.
Walrenis, Peter & vrouw, 3 ch.
Wanbag, Nicolaes & vrouw
  Hans Peter & 4 ch.
Webel, Hans Jacob & vrouw
  Orzel & 4 ch.

Weier, Johan Jorig & vrouw, 2 ch.
Weistemar, Velten
  Johan Philip, Anna Barber, & 2 ch.
Wentel, John Júrig
Werner, Mighel & vrouw
  Anna Geertruýt
Wever [blotted], Philip
Wihart, Jacob & vrouw
  John Hendrig & 3 ch.
Wilhelm, Johan & vrouw, 2 ch.
Willem, Hans
Willi, Johan Hanrús & vrouw
  Johan Gristia & 2 ch.
Wilsing, Maria
Winbold, Búrg
Windel, Johan
Wittel, Geertrúy, 3 ch.

Wolf, Michel
Woltman, Leenhard & vrouw, 3 ch.
Wonderlig, Kristiaan
Wortman, Johannes & vrouw
  Anna Margreth, Hendr. Wortman
  & 2 ch.
Wústúm, Peter
Wÿneberger, Jacob & vrouw
  Johannes & 3 ch.
Wyterman, Ulrig & vrouw
  Koenraet, Frans Seler

Zegeler, Henrig & vrouw
  Andries, Kasper, & 1 ch.
Zsimet, Joost & vrouw, 2 ch.

Anonymous 4

THIRD PARTY—EMBARKED JUNE 5 TO JUNE 10, 1709

Abal, Michel & vrouw, 2 ch.
Abelman, Jacob
Abelt, Hans Jacob
Aberrs (Aberse), Ulrig
Achber, (Nachber?), Falenteyn & vrouw,
  2 ch.
Adam, Johan's soujúger
Aeier, Hans Jacob
Aelbert, Jacob
Aelbert, Johan
Albersmit, Wilhelm
Alleman, Simon
Alsemúsch, Philippús & vrouw, 4 ch.
Altfatter, Felten & vrouw
Althenser, Mattÿs
Altlind, Arnold & vrouw, 6 ch.
Andries, Hans Mighel & vrouw, 1 ch.
Andries, Peter, & vrouw, 3 ch.
Anweillersz, Johan & vrouw, 1 ch.
Aochn, Johan & vrouw, 8 ch.
Appel, Johan Hoog & vrouw, 5 ch.
Arbonús, Kasper, & vrouw, 1 ch.
Assenbier, Frans Willem & vrouw
Atzperger, Anna Maria

Balniger, Frans & vrouw, 3 ch.
Barbara, Maria & child
Barkman, Joost & vrouw, 2 ch.
Barrabam, Andries & vrouw
Bast, Michel & vrouw, 6 ch.
Baúer, Anna Margreet
Beckman, Michel & vrouw, 4 ch.
Beisch, Johan & vrouw, 3 ch.
Bek, Johannes & vrouw
Bekker, Michel
Bekker, Mighel & vrouw, 2 ch.
Bekker, Johan Peter

Bekker, Simon & vrouw, 8 ch.
Bekker, Antonÿ & vrouw, 2 ch.
Belts, Leenart
Bender, Henrig & vrouw, 3 ch.
Berger, Kornelis Reusner, & vrouw, 3 ch.
Bergman, Andreas & vrouw, 2 ch.
Bes, Johan & vrouw
Beschop, Berhard
Beschop, Henrig, & vrouw, 2 ch.
Beÿscher, Johan & vrouw, 4 ch.
Bieler, Henrig
Biettelman, Hans Michel & vrouw, 3 ch.
Birber, Sacharias & vrouw
Blasch, Koenraet & vrouw, 5 ch.
Bles, Penetek & vrouw, 3 ch.
Bloms, Kristiaen & vrouw
Blosch, Jacob
Boeÿ, Wendel & vrouw, 5 ch.
Bol, Gerarde, & vrouw
Bom, Frans, & vrouw, 6 ch.
Bonderskel, Johan & vrouw, 5 ch.
Bonn, Frans & vrouw, 3 ch.
Borits, Johannes & vrouw, 3 ch.
Borniger, Kasper & vrouw, 3 ch.
Borsing, Rudolph
Bos, Hans Janz
Botermer, Joseph & vrouw, 2 ch.
Bouwer, Johan
Bouwer, Tomas & vrouw, 9 ch.
Braem, Bastiaen & vrouw, 3 ch.
Brand, Koenraet
Brandlÿn, Kasper & vrouw, 2 ch.
Braum, Andries & vrouw, 4 ch.
Brekedir, Barent & vrouw, 4 ch.
Brekhamer, Throk & vrouw, 4 ch.
Brill, Johannes & vrouw, 3 ch.
Brom, Johannes Joost & vrouw, 7 ch.

Brosch, Frederig, & vrouw, 2 ch.
Brouwer, Diderick
Brummer, Johannes & vrouw, 2 ch.
Brúnk, Johan Michel
Buisch, Johan Rain & vrouw, 1 ch.
Buks, Johan Bernhart & vrouw, 5 ch.
Búmer, Simon
Bún, Johannes & vrouw, 3 ch.
Bungert, Hans Willem & vrouw, 2 ch.
Bungert, Jacob & vrouw, 2 ch.
Bungert, Mattÿs & vrouw, 2 ch.
Búrger, Frÿt, & vrouw, 2 ch.
Búsch, Herman & vrouw, 6 ch.

Ceúbel, Hans Dienes & vrouw
Chiernte (?), Mischael & vrouw, 2 ch.
Chreiter, Kristoffel
Chrisfilips, Domink & vrouw, 5 ch.
Chrisfilips, Hans Wilhem & vrouw, 4 ch.
Chrisfilips, Jeúrg & vrouw, 1 ch.
Ci———— [blotted], Johan & vrouw, 1 ch.
Cirbb, Philippús Jacob & vrouw, 5 ch.
Citider, Martin & vrouw, 5 ch.
Cloos, Peter & vrouw, 5 ch.
Copal, Barnhart (minister) & vrouw, 1 ch.
Crieg, Johan Júst & vrouw, 4 ch.

Danner, Urban & vrouw, 4 ch.
Daull, Mattÿs
Daúmer, Johan
Deis, Peter & vrouw, 1 ch.
Deúr, Koenraet
Deútger, Paúlús & vrouw, 2 ch.
Dich, Martin & vrouw, 5 ch.
Diderick, Jacob & vrouw, 7 ch.
Diderick, Johan & vrouw, 1 ch.
Didert, Andries & vrouw, 1 ch.
Diel, Johan & vrouw
Dieleman, Hans & vrouw
Dies, Johan & vrouw
Diredúrf, Henrig
Ditir, Hans Bernhart
Dog, Frans Henrig & vrouw, 3 ch.
Dolmet, Johan & vrouw, 5 ch.
Domnis, Mattÿs & vrouw, 5 ch.
Dorff, Reÿs, & vrouw, 2 ch.
Dulies, Koenraet & vrouw, 5 ch.
Durding, Koenraet

Ebregt, Johan & vrouw, 2 ch.
Eding, Bastiaen & vrouw, 1 ch.
Eeger, Dirk & moeder
Eker, Jacob & vrouw
Emmell, Johannes & vrouw, 2 ch.
Emrig, Peter & vrouw, 1 ch.
Engel, Adam & vrouw, 3 ch.
Engel, Martin & vrouw, 4 ch.

Engel, Robbt. & vrouw, 5 ch.
Eperhart, Johan Mighel & vrouw, 4 ch.
Eralter, Hans Jacob
Erbs, Hans Henrig & vrouw, 3 ch.
Evathi, Barbara, 2 ch.
Eweling, Johan & vrouw, 4 ch.

Falig, Arholt, & vrouw, 2 ch.
Filips, Paulús & vrouw, 5 ch.
Flehr, Johan & vrouw, 2 ch.
Flies, Nicolaes
Floer, Johan & vrouw, 3 ch.
Flohr, Johan Peter
Folleg, Peter & vrouw, 5 ch.
Forer, Hans & vrouw, 1 ch.
Frank, Johan Marten
Frank, Michal
Frantz, Johan Koenraet
Fredrig, Gerard
Fredrig, Johan Nicolaes & vrouw, 4 ch.
Fremmen, Johan Júrg & vrouw, 5 ch.
Fres, Tomas & vrouw, 1 ch.
Freÿsen, Johan Rikes & vrouw, 5 ch.
Frib, Hans Peter & vrouw, 1 ch.
Fuhrman, Mattÿs & vrouw
Fuÿken, Orghel & vrouw, 2 ch.

Ganner, Jacob nog twe gebroeders
Gants, Johan Nicolaes
Geiser, Johan Paltzer
Genedig, Johan & vrouw, 3 ch.
Genir, Jacob & vrouw, 7 ch.
Gerard, Hans Peter & vrouw
Gerhart, Valenteÿn & vrouw, 5 ch.
Get, Peter
Gilig, Andreas & vrouw, 1 ch.
Gitz, Frederigh, & vrouw, 3 ch.
Glaser, Hans Jurg & vrouw, 2 ch.
Gloos, Valenteÿn—Anna Maria
Gneÿzer, David & vrouw, 4 ch.
Goestamt, Johan Philip
Gorg, Hans & vrouw, 3 ch.
Gottel, Jacob & vrouw, 7 ch.
Graef, Hans Jacob Mark & vrouw, 4 ch.
Groúsch, Han Miggel & vrouw, 2 ch.
Grejster, Johannes & vrouw, 3 ch.
Greÿloff, Urbÿ & vrouw, 2 ch.
Grieschman, Johan Heinrig
Grosch, Falenteÿn & vrouw
Grosch, Joggen & vrouw
Grosch, Philips Leinhart & vrouw, 5 ch.
Grosch, Wilhem & vrouw, 2 ch.
Groschman, Johan & vrouw, 3 ch.
Gross (?), Bendrick & vrouw
Gross, Johan & vrouw
Gross, Johan Jorg & vrouw, 2 ch.
Grÿsman, Henrig

Gúint, Anders, 1 ch.
Gulk, Johannes & vrouw, 3 ch.

Hack, Johan Koenraed & vrouw, 2 ch.
Hairtinam Koenraet & vrouw, 1 ch.
Haister, Martin & vrouw, 6 ch.
Halles, Johan Willem & vrouw, 4 ch.
Hamer, Johan Peter
Hansz, Schrenhart & vrouw, 4 ch.
Harna, Jacob & vrouw, 2 ch.
Hart, Johannes
Hasch, Anna Elisabeth
Hasch, Nicolaes & vrouw, 4 ch.
Hasen, (Hafen?), Willem
Haúbt, Kristoffel
Haüs, Johan Adam
Hebús, Johan & vrouw, 3 ch.
Heck, Sebastiaen & vrouw, 3 ch.
Hegt, Kasper & vrouw, 7 ch.
Heimsein, Paúl & vrouw, 1 ch.
Heister, Johan Jacob & vrouw, 6 ch.
Heistrebach, Nicolaes & vrouw, 4 ch.
Helscher, Kristoffel & vrouw
Herbener, Henrig & vrouw, 4 ch.
Herber, Johan Kasper
Herman, Philippus & vrouw, 1 ch.
Hernan, Frederig & vrouw, 2 ch.
Herst, Jacob & vrouw, 2 ch.
Hertman, Koenraet & vrouw, 3 ch.
Hes, Fredrig & vrouw, 3 ch.
Hes, Andries
Hetin, Anna Maria
Heÿg, Alexander
Heÿll, Balser & vrouw, 5 ch.
Heÿll, Mattheÿs Jurg & vrouw
Heÿm, Johs & vrouw, 5 ch.
Heÿmerleÿ, Johan Jacob & vrouw, 4 ch.
Heÿster, Herman & vrouw, 4 ch.
Hiebis, Henrig & vrouw
Hiel, Rudolf & vrouw
Hielman, Johan
Hirt, Stoffel & vrouw, 4 ch.
Hisirber, Johannes & vrouw, 4 ch.
Hobst, Tomas & vrouw
Hoentz, Nicolaes & vrouw
Hoeper, Jacob & vrouw, 3 ch.
Hofen, Wilhem & vrouw, 2 ch.
Hoffenbraut, Johan & vrouw, 2 ch.
Hoffner, Jeulÿ Maÿer
Hofman, Henrig & vrouw, 3 ch.
Hofmenin, Katarina
Höigt, Wirchart & vrouw, 2 ch.
Hol, Migel
Holgaerden, Hans Peter
Hollander, Johan Melchior(?)
Hollerin, Anna Katrina
Holwaserz, Antonÿ, 1 ch.

Homberg, Krÿn
Hoppf, Hans Júrg & vrouw
Horents, Michel & vrouw, 4 ch.
Horling, Johan Koenraet
Horts, Walter & vrouw, 3 ch.
Hortz, Hans Fletter & vrouw, 2 ch.
Hosserlwegh, & vrouw, 4 ch.
Húberin, Margreta
Hŭn, Matÿs
Huns, Koenraet & vrouw, 2 ch.
Husman, Johannes & vrouw, 5 ch.

Isler, Nicolaes & vrouw, 5 ch.

Jacob, Hans
Jacob, Hans & vrouw, 10 ch.
Jacob, Johan & vrouw, 3 ch.
Jacobi, Johan Adam & vrouw, 8 ch.
Johan Henrig & vrouw, 4 ch.
Jsbraut, Hans Wolf
Junik, Hans Ari
Júnik, Johan
Júrg, Hans & vrouw
Júrg, Johan
Júrig, Johan & vrouw, 2 ch.

Kaisser, Johs & vrouw, 6 ch.
Kak, Peter, & vrouw, 4 ch.
Karb, Johan Philip & vrouw, 5 ch.
Kaúlil, Frederig, & vrouw, 2 ch.
Keichel, Johan
Keiger, Johan
Keil, Henrig, & vrouw, 2 ch.
Keler, Peter & vrouw, 1 ch.
Kelil, Johan
Keller, Jacob & vrouw, 6 ch.
Kerger, Johan & vrouw, 1 ch.
Kersner, Philip & vrouw, 3 ch.
Keúler, Hans Peter
Keyserin, Anna Maria
Kien, Hendrig & vrouw, 2 ch.
Kirches, Paúlús
Kisleback, Johan & vrouw, 3 ch.
Kister, Fredrig & vrouw, 2 ch.
Kister, Palters & vrouw, 3 ch.
Klaas, Peter
Klaser, Ditter & vrouw, 3 ch.
Kletters, Johan & vrouw, 2 ch.
Kleÿn, Hans Willem & vrouw, 3 ch.
Kleÿn, Koenraet
Kleÿn, Lodewÿk
Kleÿn, Ludwig
Kleÿn, Michael & vrouw, 5 ch.
Kleÿter, Hans Júrg & vrouw, 1 ch.
Klippingen, Johan Peter
Klos, Willem & vrouw, 5 ch.
Kloter, Johan Paúl & vrouw, 4 ch.

Kloter, Paúlus & vrouw, 5 ch.
Klún, Jacob & vrouw, 1 ch.
Klÿn, Johan Palser & vrouw, 4 ch.
Knaús, Hans Kristoffel & vrouw, 2 ch.
Knegt, Miggel & vrouw, 4 ch.
Knÿkers, Johan & vrouw
Kock, Martin
Koeman, Bastiaen & vrouw, 1 ch.
Koenraet, Koenraet & vrouw, 2 ch.
Koenraet, Kristoffel
Koenraet, Mattÿs
Koenraet, Mattÿs
Koenraet, Nicolaes
Kohler, [Jacob?] & vrouw, 9 ch.
Koll, Frans & vrouw, 3 ch.
Koller, Martin
Koller, Simon & vrouw, 3 ch.
Konig, Johan Joost & vrouw, 2 ch.
Korier, Karel Henrig & vrouw
Koris, Johannes & vrouw, 4 ch.
Kormer, Nicolaes & vrouw, 4 ch.
Kost, Johan Júrg & vrouw, 4 ch.
Koúnt, Philippus
Kraft, Valenteÿn & vrouw, 5 ch.
Kramer, Johan & vrouw, 1 ch.
Kramer, Philippus & vrouw
Kraud, Johan
Kraút, Peter & vrouw, 4 ch.
Kreegelman, Leenhart, & vrouw, 3 ch.
Krestoffel, Mattÿs & vrouw, 4 ch.
Kreÿser, Lodewÿk
Krimp, Frederik
———, Kristiaen (no other name given)
   & vrouw, 1 ch.
Kristina, Anna
Kroon, Hans Júrg & vrouw, 1 ch.
Kroúwel, Loret & vrouw, 1 ch.
Krüel, Herman
Krÿmaiser, Jacob & vrouw, 3 ch.
Kúseteler, Hendrig & vrouw, 2 ch.
Kulk, Johan Peter
Kúmel, Peter & vrouw, 6 ch.
Kuminer, Hans Peter & vrouw, 2 ch.
Kummer, Hans Peter & vrouw
Kunen, Nicolaes & vrouw, 2 ch.
Kúntelman, Kasper & 2 ch.
Kurger, Henrig—Elisabeth

Laam, Frans & vrouw, 3 ch.
Lambreg, Hans Júrg & vrouw, 5 ch.
Lamoth, Johan Daniel & vrouw, 2 ch.
Land, Andanig & vrouw, 5 ch.
Lang, Eles
Lang, Kristiaen & vrouw, 4 ch.
Lang, Peter & vrouw, 2 ch.
Lank, Hans Philip
Lant, Philippus & vrouw, 3 ch.

Laúrens, Mattÿs
Laúrmen, Eva
Layper, Johan & vrouw, 3 ch.
Lecobs, (or Lecolis), Peter & vrouw, 2 ch.
Leenhart, Hans Peter & vrouw, 1 ch.
Leinweber, Johan & vrouw, 2 ch.
Lenard (no family name given) & vrouw,
   2 ch.
Lepús, Mattÿs
Lersas, Hans Philips & vrouw, 1 ch.
Lesch, Johan Henrig & vrouw, 3 ch.
Leschemis, Jeremias & vrouw, 3 ch.
Lesorin, Magdalena
Lesser, Kristoffel & vrouw, 4 ch.
Libern, Ludwig & vrouw, 1 ch.
Liespel, Maria
Lippert, Johan Walter
Los, Johan Adam
Lots, Johan & vrouw, 2 ch.
Lou, Johan Michel & vrouw, 2 ch.
Lourens, (only name given) & vrouw,
   7 ch.
Lout, Henrig, & vrouw, 3 ch.
Luth, Hans Jacob & vrouw, 2 ch.
Lútz, Jeorg & vrouw, 1 ch.
Lutz, Peter & vrouw, 3 ch.
Lútz, Peter & vrouw, 4 ch.
Lÿbok, Reinhart & vrouw, 3 ch.

Madelaer, Michel & vrouw, 4 ch.
Maes, Johan Philip & vrouw, 5 ch.
Maeÿer, Just Tomas & vrouw, 2 ch.
Mager, Nicolaes & vrouw, 3 ch.
Maier, Andries
Maller, Bastiaen & vrouw
Maltsberger, Philippús & vrouw, 1 ch.
Marea, Eva & 1 ch.
Margriet, Anna
Maria, Anna
Marks, Joseph & vrouw
Marman, Hans Joost & vrouw
Marstall, Kristoffel
Marsteller, Henrig & vrouw, 5 ch.
Marstil, Kristoffel
Märten, Adam & vrouw, 3 ch.
Marten, Stoffel & vrouw, 4 ch.
Martin, Nicolaas & child
Matheÿs, Hendrig & vrouw, 6 ch.
Mattÿs, Johannes & vrouw, 3 ch.
Mattÿs, Peter's (Wed^e.), 3 ch.
Mattÿskolk, Johan & vrouw, 6 ch.
Maÿ, Peter & vrouw, 4 ch.
Maÿër, Kristoffel & vrouw, 1 ch.
Meeis, Matÿs & vrouw, 1 ch.
Meier, Paúlús & vrouw, 5 ch.
Meinhober, Philippús & vrouw
Meis, Henrig & vrouw, 3 ch.

Meliger, Frans & vrouw, 2 ch.
Menges, Hans & vrouw
Menias, Johan & vrouw, 4 ch.
Mensch, Antonÿ & vrouw, 2 ch.
Mensch, Johan Jurg
Mentzeberges, Diderig & vrouw, 7 ch.
Merks, Peter
Merschel, Peter & vrouw, 2 ch.
Mese, David & vrouw, 2 ch.
Messer, Koenraet & vrouw
Metor, Dangel & vrouw, 4 ch.
Mets, Andreas & vrouw, 4 ch.
Metsler, Philippus & vrouw, 6 ch.
Meyer, Johan & vrouw, 3 ch.
Meÿer, Hans Jacob
Meÿer, Henrig & vrouw, 2 ch.
Meÿer, Johannes & vrouw, 5 ch.
Michel, Otto Henrig & vrouw, 1 ch.
Miesch, Paúl & vrouw
Migel, Hans & vrouw, 2 ch.
Migel, Otto Henrig & vrouw, 1 ch.
Milcr, Hans Júrig
Millerin, Súsanna
Ming, Kristoffel & vrouw, 2 ch.
Mink, Hans Hendrig & vrouw, 5 ch.
Mink, Hendrig & vrouw, 4 ch.
Mites, Hans Bartel & vrouw
Mitteler, Engel Bertus
Mitteler, Juliaen & vrouw
Moelleremt, Kasper & vrouw, 2 ch.
Mohr, Jonas & vrouw, 1 ch.
Moht (Mohr), Kristoffel & vrouw
Monboúwer, Hans Adam
Monik, Jacob & vrouw, 3 ch.
Mosch, Emgen & vrouw
Moúl, Hans Henrig & vrouw, 5 ch.
Muillensz, Georg Philip & vrouw, 5 ch.
Mukket, Johannes & vrouw, 1 ch.
Mullendÿk, Herman & vrouw, 2 ch.
Múller, Johan Adam & vrouw, 3 ch.
Mûller, Johan Philips
Múllerin, Margreta
Múncanas, Joseph & vrouw
Múse, Johan Jacob & vrouw, 6 ch.
Múster, Lambaert & vrouw, 2 ch.

Nagel, Hans Jacob
Nagtegael, Koenraet & vrouw, 2 ch.
Nasar, Hans Migel, & vrouw, 4 ch.
Nau, Peter Hans & vrouw, 3 ch.
Naúthil, Sacharianen & vrouw, 4 ch.
Neeÿ, Hans Michel & vrouw, 6 ch.
Nepeler, Johan
Neuman, Lodewÿk & vrouw, 5 ch.
Neúmeiyer, Frans & vrouw, 2 ch.
Neúsch, Andreas
Neÿmeÿer, Ats & vrouw, 4 ch.

Nidermeÿer, Andries & vrouw, 4 ch.
Noll, Johan Danyell
Nols, Bernhart & vrouw

Olthanier, Hans Jurg & vrouw, 6 ch.
Olthanier, Hans Jurg's moeder
Ordenier, Nicolaes & vrouw, 4 ch.
Ott, Johan & vrouw

Pachman, Johan & vrouw, 2 ch.
Pack, Jacob & vrouw, 1 ch.
Palerwaltman, Johan
Paul, Johan Daniell, 4 ch.
Peckert, Koenraet & vrouw, 3 ch.
Pergen, Jorig & vrouw, 5 ch.
Peschart, Koenraet & vrouw, 3 ch.
Peter, Johan Adam
Petreÿ, Hans Jacob & vrouw, 6 ch.
Petri, Jacob & vrouw, 6 ch.
Petri, Nicolaes & vrouw, 3 ch.
Petrÿ, Henrÿ & vrouw, 5 ch.
Petteren, Johannes & vrouw, 3 ch.
Pettig, Johan Dederig & vrouw, 1 ch.
Pfeffer, Hans Peter & vrouw, 2 ch.
Philips, Hans Jacob
Philÿps, Hans
Pinter, Johan Foost
Pirk, Johan
Pith, (sic) Jacob & vrouw
Pits, Joseph & vrouw, 2 ch.
Pittig, Henrig & vrouw, 5 ch.
Plak, Kristiaen
Pliemelin, Krestman & vrouw, 4 ch.
Poller, Philippús & vrouw, 5 ch.
Prang, Herman
Praúw, Arnold & vrouw, 1 ch.
Praúx, Felten & vrouw, 3 ch.
Preg, Michel & vrouw, 1 ch.
Preker, Paulús & vrouw, 3 ch.
Pscheere (no other name given)
Púdúm, Lúcus & vrouw, 2 ch.
Puths, Wilhem
Pútsch, Johannes & vrouw, 1 ch.

Rab, Killiaen & vrouw, 3 ch.
Ram, Nicolaes & vrouw, 4 ch.
Reiger, Henrig
Rein, Antonÿ & vrouw, 2 ch.
Reÿgert, Kaspert & vrouw, 2 ch.
    Kaspert Reÿgerts vrouws moeder, 4 ch.
Reÿnard, Johan & vrouw, 2 ch.
Reynhart, Hendrig & vrouw, 1 ch.
Reÿser, Michel
Ribel, Johan Nicolaes & vrouw, 6 ch.
Rickert, Koenraet & vrouw, 3 ch.
Rieckker, Johan Tiell
Rief, Hans Pieter

Rigel, Jacob & vrouw, 5 ch.
Rigell, Kasper & vrouw, 1 ch.
Ritter, Philip & vrouw, 5 ch.
Rob, Hans Júrg
Roe, Hans Jacob & vrouw, 2 ch.
Ros, Frederig & vrouw
Rot, Philÿppus & vrouw, 4 ch.
Roth, Johan Joost & vrouw, 3 ch.
Rúchsal, Jacob & vrouw, 3 ch.
Rupert, Rudolph
Russer, Johan Peter

Sainmoft, Sailalt & vrouw, 7 ch.
Samúel, Jonas
Sarborger, Frans & vrouw, 4 ch.
Sarborger, Hans David & vrouw, 2 ch.
Sardis, Isaek & vrouw
Sauffert, Felten & vrouw, 1 ch.
Schafer, Philip & vrouw, 2 ch.
Schaffer, Bernhard & vrouw, 3 ch.
Schaffer, Johan & vrouw, 3 ch.
Scham, Hans Júrg & vrouw
Schammel, Peter & vrouw
Schant, Johan & vrouw, 2 ch.
Schar, Peter
Schbút, Ellrúg & vrouw, 3 ch.
Schefer, Loúrens
Scheffer, Hans Adam & vrouw, 6 ch.
Scheffer, Hans Peter & vrouw
Scheffier, Matteÿs & vrouw, 2 ch.
Schellenperge, Koenraet & vrouw, 2 ch.
Schellenperger, Hans Jeorg & vrouw, 1 ch.
Schenkelberger, Hans Jacob & vrouw, 5 ch.
Scherhinger, Johs, & vrouw, 3 ch.
Scherman, Valentÿn
Schermig, Andries & vrouw, 2 ch.
Scherver, Joost & vrouw, 4 ch.
Schesting, Johannes & vrouw, 2 ch.
Schetmak, Johan
Scheúreder, Handerig & vrouw, 1 ch.
Scheÿt, Mander & vrouw, 1 ch.
Schier, Hans Ulrig, 2 ch.
Schiloser, Johan & vrouw, 2 ch.
Schimell, Johan Nicolaes
Schimtin, Eva Maria
Schlegt, Johan & vrouw, 1 ch.
Schlepusch, Hans Peter
Schleÿer, Johan & vrouw, 3 ch.
Schlúg, Johan & Paulús
Schlúk, Martin & vrouw
Schmick, Nicolaes & vrouw, 6 ch.
Schmiet, Nicolaes & vrouw, 3 ch.
Schminch, Johan
Schmit, Hans Jacob & vrouw, 1 ch.
Schmit, Esmist
Schmit, Johan Adam

Schmit, Hans Migel & vrouw, 5 ch.
Schmit, Hans Peter & vrouw, 5 ch.
Schmit, Mattÿs & vrouw, 2 ch.
Schmit, Nicolaes & vrouw, 3 ch.
Schmit, Philippus & vrouw, 4 ch.
Schmit, Johan & vrouw, 3 ch.
Schmit, Kasper & vrouw, 4 ch.
Schneide, Johan & vrouw, 2 ch.
Schneide, Johan & vrouw, 3 ch.
Schneider, Koenraet & vrouw, 2 ch.
Schnel, Mattÿs & vrouw, 5 ch.
Schneÿer, Hans Georg & vrouw, 2 ch.
Schober, Kristiaen & vrouw, 2 ch.
Schoeck, Nicolaes & vrouw, 2 ch.
Schoenmager, Henrig & vrouw, 1 ch.
Schreiner, Hans Jacob & vrouw, 4 ch.
Schriber, Albertús
Schwan, Johan
Schúl, Martin & vrouw, 4 ch.
Schwarts, Júrg & vrouw, 8 ch.
Schwartz, Jacob & vrouw
Schwartz, Jacob en knegt & groohm
Schwel, Roedolf & vrouw, 3 ch.
Schwin, Johs & vrouw
Seipert, Johan Henrig & vrouw, 4 ch.
Seldvaû, Mattÿs & vrouw, 5 ch.
Serberger, Hansatt & vrouw, 2 ch.
Sermis, Johan & vrouw, 2 ch.
Sescher, Johan & vrouw, 1 ch.
Sigeler, Kristiaen & vrouw, 2 ch.
Sikert, Basser & vrouw, 2 ch. Johannes 1
Silbús, Hans
Sildere, Johan
Sillo, Klaúd & vrouw
Simen, Johan Adam & vrouw, 3 ch.
Simmerman, Johan Júrg & vrouw, 3 ch.
Simon, Philippús & vrouw, 1 ch.
Sinder, Henrig Johan, 5 ch.
Singraaf, Henrig & vrouw, 4 ch.
Smeÿer, Johannes & vrouw, 4 ch.
Smit, Andries & vrouw, 5 ch.
Smit, Daniel & vrouw, 2 ch.
Smit, Hendrig & vrouw, 5 ch.
Smit, Johannes & vrouw, 4 ch.
Smit, Kasper & vrouw, 1 ch.
Smit, Michel & vrouw, 5 ch.
Snegel, (Fregel?) Johan Nicolaes & vrouw, 3 ch.
Snÿder, Koenraet & vrouw, 2 ch.
Soúwerman, Samuel
Spath, Mattheÿs & vrouw, 2 ch.
Spengeler, Fredrig & vrouw, 2 ch.
Spengeler, Johan Frans & vrouw
Spies, Werner & vrouw, 6 ch.
Spolgt, Johan & vrouw, 3 ch.
Spropssel, Jeorg & vrouw, 2 ch.
Staenhaúwer, Kristian & vrouw, 6 ch.

Staes, Hans Bernhard & vrouw, 2 ch.
Staúck, Johan & vrouw, 1 ch.
Steinbekker, Hans Philip & vrouw, 1 ch.
Stek, Herman, & vrouw, 2 ch.
Steÿner, Migel & vrouw, 4 ch.
Sticker, Johan
Stikker, Michel
Stil, Willem & vrouw, 4 ch.
Stoffel, Johan & vrouw, 5 ch.
Stog, Hans Ledendig & vrouw
Stok, Johan Henrig & vrouw
Stork, Hans Henrig & vrouw, 5 ch.
Strab, Loúrens & vrouw, 6 ch.
Straetbarger, Baltzar & vrouw, 1 ch.
Straúp, Johan & vrouw, 1 ch.
Straÿsmil, Jacob & vrouw, 5 ch.
Streÿt, Ludwig & vrouw, 4 ch.
Strib, Hans Peter & vrouw, 3 ch.
Stúrpert, Kasper
Stúrÿ, Alexander
Stúts, Johan & vrouw, 4 ch.
Súchs, Johan Tilbs, & vrouw, 5 ch.
Súkors, Johan
Suller, Mattÿs & vrouw, 4 ch.

Tainck, Kasper & vrouw, 2 ch.
Tamis, Arÿ & vrouw, 5 ch.
Teister, Daniel & vrouw, 2 ch.
Tes, Johan Wilhem & vrouw, 1 ch.
Tharsch, Henrig & vrouw, 2 ch.
Thomar, Gerhart
Tibere, Peter
Tibre, Jean & vrouw, 2 ch.
Timmerman, Matÿs & vrouw, 2 ch.
Titemer, Hans Martin & vrouw
Torer, Hans & vrouw, 2 ch.
Treatteman, Martin
Trift, Matteús & vrouw, 2 ch.
Trip, Mattÿs & vrouw
    Katarina Margreet, 2 ch.
Tsmallenberger, Zill & vrouw, 1 ch.

Ubel, Kristiaen & vrouw, 3 ch.
Ullerig, Hans Jeorg & vrouw, 3 ch.
Ullersz, Henrig & vrouw, 2 ch.
Unis, Johan & vrouw, 2 ch.

Van Staek, Peter
Vapaneiker, Nicolaes & vrouw
Vasch, Godevrig & vrouw, 2 ch.
Vaugh, Johannes
Velinger, Hans Ulrig & vrouw
Veller, Johan & vrouw, 4 ch.
Vendel, Johan Nicolaes & vrouw, 3 ch.
Vetgen, Henrig Peter & vrouw, 2 ch.
Vevel, Daniel
Vhoris, Johannes

Voerman, Nicolaes
Vogt, Daniel & vrouw, 3 ch.
Vogt, Joh. & vrouw, 3 ch.
Volkenburg, Johan Felden & vrouw, 2 ch.
Volpertin, Anna Margreta, 3 ch.
Vondermúl, Philippus & vrouw, 9 ch.
Von Reÿn, Kristiaen & vrouw, 1 ch.
Vootenfloor, Joh: & vrouw, 4 ch.
Vossina, Antonÿ & vrouw
Vôsseyen, Goyert & vrouw, 5 ch.
Vrisal, Fredrik & vrouw, 1 ch.

Wagenaer, Berhart & vrouw, 2 ch.
Wagenaer, Koenraet & vrouw, 6 ch.
Wagenaer, Lodewig & vrouw, 6 ch.
Wagenaer, Velden & vrouw, 3 ch.
Wagenaer, Windel & vrouw, 4 ch.
Walkker, Johan Henrig & vrouw
Walpnet, Jacob & vrouw, 3 ch.
Walter, Hans Jacob & vrouw, 2 ch.
Waschpaelt, Johan & vrouw, 7 ch.
Wasser, Rudolf & vrouw, 2 ch.
Weber, Martin & vrouw, 2 ch.
Weber, Mighiel & vrouw, 2 ch.
Weber, Philip & vrouw, 1 ch.
Weber, Nicolaes & vrouw, 2 ch.
Weber, Valenteÿn & vrouw, 1 ch.
Wedz, Anna Maria, 2 ch.
Weer, Frederig & vrouw
Wegman, Matÿs & vrouw, 7 ch.
Wehr, Kristiaen & vrouw, 2 ch.
Weickel, Velden & vrouw, 5 ch.
Weiller, Andries & vrouw, 3 ch.
Weiller, Johan & vrouw
Weiner, Simon & vrouw, 5 ch.
Weitseerges, Magdelena
Wekiter, Philip & vrouw, 2 ch.
Wekkert, Johan Melgert
Weller, Kasper & vrouw, 2 ch.
Wendel, Peter & vrouw, 2 ch.
Wens, Johan
Wensch, Johannes & vrouw, 3 ch.
Wensell, Loúrens & vrouw, 6 ch.
Wensz, Balzer
Weṕer, Henrig & vrouw, 4 ch.
Werner, Hendrig
Wesbak, Wendel & vrouw, 4 ch.
Westheser, Johan Jacob, 1 ch.
Wetteg, Barht. & vrouw, 2 ch.
Wever, Henrig & vrouw, 6 ch.
Weÿngert, Johan Melchier
Wiekel, Johan & vrouw
Wilbert, Hans Marten & vrouw, 5 ch.
Wilhelm, Henrig & vrouw
Wilhelm, Johan Simon & vrouw, 2 ch.
Winter, Melger, & vrouw, 1 ch.
Wintter, Henrig & vrouw, 5 ch.

Wissenmiker, Kasper
Wollten, Philip & vrouw, 3 ch.
Wolf, Johan Júrg & vrouw, 4 ch.
Wolf, Johan
Wolf, Petrús
Wolf, Koenraet & vrouw, 1 ch.
Wolffler, Peter & vrouw
Wolfskël, Hans Júrg & vrouw
Wolleben, (John) & vrouw, 5 ch.
Woller, Philip & vrouw, 3 ch.
Wollfslager, Melchior
Wolter, Adam & vrouw, 8 ch.
Woú, Hans Frederig

Wupf, Hans Jacob & vrouw, 1 ch.
Wÿngert, Koenraet & vrouw, 3 ch.
Wÿnman, Andries & vrouw, 3 ch.

Zebersz, Joseph
Zeÿps, Balter & vrouw, 4 ch.
Zingeler, Nicolaes & vrouw, 4 ch.
Zink, Rúdolf & vrouw, 4 ch.
Zolzeber, Albertús & vrouw, 5 ch.
Zútinger, Georg Peter & vrouw, 3 ch.
Zÿck, Koenraet

Anonymous (6)

FOURTH PARTY—EMBARKED JUNE 10 TO JUNE 19, SAILED JUNE 21, 1709

Adam, Jacob & vrouw
Adler, Paúlús & vrouw, 5 ch.
Albiger, Wilhelm & vrouw
——, Anna Maria (no other name given)
Arnolt, Philippús & vrouw, 2 ch.
Ätter, Johan & vrouw, 4 ch.

Backer, Ferdinant & vrouw, 2 ch.
Baltzer, Hans Jacob & vrouw, 3 ch.
Bambra, Johan
Barbara, Anna & 3 ch.
Barkman, Izaac & vrouw, 3 ch.
Bart, Henrik & vrouw, 5 ch.
Bartel, Henrik & vrouw, 5 ch.
Basseler, Frants & vrouw, 3 ch.
Baúg, Fredrig & vrouw, 4 ch.
Baúg, Johan & vrouw, 6 ch.
Baúm, Abram & vrouw, 5 ch.
Baúr, Johan Mikel
Baúr, Kristoffel
Bechtel, Jacob & vrouw
Becker, Johan & vrouw, 1 ch.
Becker, Johan & vrouw
Becker, Johan & vrouw, 2 ch.
Beehr, Nicolaas & vrouw, 1 ch.
Beller, Hans Jacob & vrouw, 2 ch.
Bensch, Jacob & vrouw, 2 ch.
Berdolff, Jacob & vrouw, 4 ch.
Bergen, Hans & vrouw, 2 ch.
Besser, Júrg & vrouw, 4 ch.
Besser, Kasper & vrouw, 3 ch.
Beÿer, Tomas & vrouw, 3 ch.
Birck, Henrig & vrouw, 3 ch.
Birk, Lÿs
Birk, Mattÿs & vrouw, 6 ch.
Bleezen, Kristiaan & vrouw
Böhr, Mattÿs & vrouw, 2 ch.
Bornwaster, Herman & vrouw, 1 ch.
Bots, Fredrig & vrouw, 3 ch.
Boúmain, Anna Maria
Brandeaú, Johan Weÿant & vrouw

Brando, John Willem & vrouw, 1 ch.
Braun, Johan Júrg & vrouw, 5 ch.
Braún, Johan Niklaas & vrouw, 6 ch.
Bresch, Klaas
Briti, Jacob & vrouw, 2 ch.
Bröhen, Nicolas & vrouw, 1 ch.
Brotheder, Joost & vrouw, 5 ch.
Brúll, Joost & vrouw
Búchler, Michel & vrouw, 6 ch.
Búderman, Johan & vrouw, 7 ch.
Búenner, Jeúrg Baltazev
Búg, Henrig & vrouw, 3 ch.
Búger, Kasper
Búgspúl, Aúgústÿn & vrouw, 7 ch.
Bulffer, Wendel & vrouw, 2 ch.
Búmer, Júrg Baltzaser
Búmmery, Bongratsgi & vrouw, 3 ch.
Búrger, Johan & vrouw, 2 ch.
Burobesch, Herman & vrouw, 1 ch.
Búsch, Daniel & vrouw
Búsekart, Daniel & vrouw, 8 ch.
Bústz, Joost
Bútting, Eberhard

Camerd, Johan & vrouw, 4 ch.
Coblentzer, Johan & vrouw, 2 ch.
Creitzin, Elizabeth & 6 ch.

Dames, Mattÿs
Daniel, Antony & vrouw, 7 ch.
Daúck, Johan Júrg & vrouw, 3 ch.
Decker, Johan & vrouw, 1 ch.
Dedler, Johan Jacob
de Witz, Frantz
Dieer, Philippús
Diel, Henrig
Dimer, Johan & vrouw, 5 ch.
Dimkel, Andries & vrouw, 4 ch.
Doñi, Johan Martin & vrouw, 2 ch.
Drisel, Johan & vrouw, 1 ch.
Drissell, Willem, & vrouw

Eberhart, Michel & vrouw, 4 ch.
Egh, Hans Jacob & vrouw, 1 ch.
Egh, Hans Júrg & vrouw
Eigman, Henrig & vrouw, 1 ch.
Eiller, Johan Henrig & vrouw, 3 ch.
Einel, Stoffel & vrouw, 1 ch.
Engel, Jacob & vrouw
Engel, Johan & vrouw, 3 ch.
Engel, Johan Willem & vrouw
Engeler, Peter & vrouw, 2 ch.
Erberg, Ary Mag Ronolt & vrouw, 4 ch.
Ermitter, Frants & vrouw, 3 ch.
Eschweiler, Jacob & vrouw, 3 ch.
Eschweiler, Tomas & vrouw, 2 ch.
Eulembag, Hans Júrg & vrouw, 5 ch.
————, Ewertrÿ (no other name)

Faver, Adam
Felt, Gerhart & vrouw, 6 ch.
Feúhert, Emig & vrouw, 2 ch.
Focks, Johan Peter & vrouw, 2 ch.
Fogelsberger, Peter & vrouw, 1 ch.
Folhart, Johan & vrouw, 5 ch.
Forbet (Sorbet?), Hans Júrg & vrouw, 1 ch.
Formen, Kristoffel & vrouw, 1 ch.
Forster, Johan Mikel
Freÿhaúsch, Joseph & vrouw, 1 ch.
Frisch, Johan & vrouw, 4 ch.
Frits, Niklaas & vrouw, 7 ch.
Frobús, Jorúg & vrouw, 5 ch.
Fúkendem, Bernhart & vrouw, 4 ch.
Fúx, Johan Jorig & vrouw, 6 ch.

Gablen, Johan
Gebell, Henrig & vrouw, 4 ch.
Gebell, Johan Andries & vrouw, 1 ch.
Geerlach, Johan Koenraet & vrouw, 4 ch.
Geisch, Johan
Gesel, Johan Philippús & vrouw, 6 ch.
Gessner, Koenraet & vrouw, 2 ch.
Gib, Michel & vrouw
Ginter, Kristiaan & vrouw, 4 ch.
Gottman, Kasper & vrouw, 8 ch.
Graúsch, Katrina & 2 ch.
Gritnig, Hans & vrouw, 2 ch.
Grosch, Diderig & vrouw
Grosch, Willem & vrouw, 3 ch.
Grÿbel, Johan Bernhart & vrouw, 4 ch.
Gútir, Johan Philip & vrouw, 2 ch.
Gysbert, Johan Joost & vrouw, 4 ch.

Haas, Michel
Hag, Johan Henrik & vrouw, 5 ch.
Hagedoren, Peter & vrouw, 5 ch.
Hanheimer, Paúlus & vrouw, 3 ch.
Haúb, Leickert & vrouw, 2 ch.

Heer, Johan & vrouw, 3 ch.
Heitwig, Frants
Helfrig, Henrig & vrouw, 2 ch.
Heller, Wolff
Henrig, Andreas
Hensch, Hans Adam & vrouw, 2 ch.
Hensell, Jacob & vrouw, 1 ch.
Herdel, Adam & vrouw, 1 ch.
Herman, Bastiaan & vrouw
Herman, Johan Joost & vrouw, 2 ch.
Hermans, Jan
Herschbag, Diederig & vrouw, 2 ch.
Hetirm, Koenraet & vrouw, 1 ch.
Heúd, Jacob & vrouw, 1 ch.
Heus, Johan Mikel
    Katrina
Hodel, Izaak & vrouw, 1 ch.
Hodrigzedel, Laúrents
Hoffman, Johan Philippus & vrouw, 1 ch.
Hoffman, Koenraet & vrouw, 3 ch.
Hofman, Jacob & vrouw, 1 ch.
Holts, Andreas
Holts, Hans Peter
Hong, Lúcas & vrouw, 9 ch.
Hontsz, Koenraet & vrouw, 2 ch.
Hoofdman, Sofia
Hornúng, Gerhart & vrouw, 2 ch.
Húbig, Lisa Margreta & 3 ch.
Huerig, Joost & vrouw, 6 ch.
Húpter, David & vrouw, 2 ch.

Jacobs, Barth
Jeger, Karolus & vrouw, 2 ch.
Jeorg, Hans & vrouw, 1 ch.
Jeug, Johan Mikel
Jöhn, Johan Elia
Jöhn, Johan Philips
————, Júd (no other name given)
Julig, Johan Henrig

Kalboúr, Johan Kasper
Kargard, Peter & vrouw, 1 ch.
————, Katrina (no other name given)
Kauts, Andreas
Kers, Adam & vrouw, 3 ch.
Keseler, Kasper & 2 ch.
Kessler, Frans Niklaas & vrouw, 2 ch.
Keusel, Hans Jacob & vrouw, 5 ch.
Klaas, Johan & vrouw, 2 ch.
Klein, Johan Willem & vrouw, 3 ch.
Klein, Philip & vrouw, 3 ch.
Kleman, Pieter
Klepper, Koenraet & vrouw, 3 ch.
Kloosch, Simon & vrouw, 1 ch.
Knaúer, Sacharias
Koenraet, Johan
Kog, Johan Mattÿs & vrouw, 5 ch.

Kog, Johan Philips & vrouw, 2 ch.
Kokkin, Anna Lÿs
Koog, Johan & vrouw, 1 ch.
Korlús, Lucas & vrouw, 3 ch.
Krants, Koenraet & vrouw, 1 ch.
Kraúwer, Hans Jacob
Kreúber, Mattÿs & vrouw, 5 ch.
Krisman, Hans & vrouw, 4 ch.
Kro, Johan Jeorg & vrouw, 3 ch.
Kruitsch, Johan & vrouw, 5 ch.
Küfaber, Johan Adam & vrouw, 4 ch.
Kúlen, Peter
Kún, Herman & vrouw, 3 ch.
Kúrts, Hans Júrg & vrouw, 1 ch.

Landolt, Samuel & vrouw, 3 ch.
Lang, Hans Wolf & vrouw, 3 ch.
Lang, Morits & vrouw, 5 ch.
Laúrens, Diderig & vrouw, 3 ch.
Laúv, Johan & vrouw, 3 ch.
LaVore, Johan & vrouw, 1 ch.
Leenhart, Johan & vrouw, 5 ch.
Leib, Johan & vrouw, 4 ch.
Leig, Simon & vrouw, 3 ch.
Lenarker, Peter & vrouw, 8 ch.
Lenenbaig, Stoffel & vrouw, 2 ch.
Lerner, Mattÿs & vrouw, 5 ch.
Lesch, Búrchent & vrouw
Leschner, Michel & vrouw, 2 ch.
Liesen, Anna Eva & 3 ch.
Linck, Martin & vrouw, 5 ch.
Linenbaúg, Peter & vrouw, 2 ch.
————, Lodewig (no other name
   given)
Lodewÿk, Antonÿ & vrouw, 3 ch.
Lúdt, Castman & vrouw, 2 ch.
Lúdwig, Johan Henrig & vrouw, 2 ch.
Lúts, Johan & vrouw, 6 ch.
Lútz, Hans & vrouw
Lúwÿ, Hans Nickel & vrouw, 4 ch.
Lÿs, Mattÿs & vrouw, 7 ch.

Mag, Johan Júrg
Maier, Hans Adam & vrouw
Mansbeil, Kasper & vrouw, 1 ch.
————, Maria Barbara (no other name)
————, Maria Magdleena & 2 swisters
   (no other name)
Martin, Peter & vrouw, 3 ch.
————, Mary Barbara (no other name)
Matterm, Abram
Mattheús, Martin & vrouw, 4 ch.
Mattÿs, Laúrents & 1 ch.
Maúr, Johan & vrouw, 5 ch.
Maús, Michel
Maÿbag, Dirk & vrouw, 3 ch.
Megel, Hans Wendel & vrouw, 2 ch.

Meister, Koenraet
Menimeier, Frants
Mest, Abram & vrouw, 2 ch.
Mets, Simon & vrouw, 3 ch.
Metseger, Johan & vrouw, 1 ch.
Meúrin, Margreta
Meÿer, Arent
Meÿer, Bartel & vrouw, 4 ch.
Meÿer, Henrig & vrouw, 2 ch.
Meyer, Henrig & vrouw, 3 ch.
Meÿer, Paúlús & vrouw, 1 ch.
Michel, Henrig & vrouw, 3 ch.
Michel, Niklas & vrouw
Miller, Antony & vrouw
Miller, Jacob & vrouw, 3 ch.
Miller, Johan Jacob & vrouw, 1 ch.
Miller, Johan Willem
Miller, Peter & vrouw, 5 ch
Miller, Samuel
Mitelig, Herman & vrouw, 2 ch
Mohr, Augustÿn & vrouw, 4 ch.
Moll, Kasper & vrouw, 1 ch.
Morheisser, Niklaas & vrouw, 3 ch.
Motji, Johan & vrouw, 4 ch.
Moze, David
Múller, Gerlag & vrouw, 1 ch.
Múller, Hans Martin & vrouw, 4 ch.
Múller, Henrig & vrouw, 3 ch.
Múller, Jacob & vrouw, 2 ch.
Múller, Michael & vrouw, 2 ch.
Múller, Peter & vrouw, 3 ch.
Mummenthal, Jacob & vrouw
Múnster, Johan Peter & vrouw, 5 ch.
Múts, Diderig & vrouw, 3 ch.
Mútsch, Fredrig & vrouw

Nadoor, Johan
Nobel, Jacob & vrouw, 3 ch.
Noú, Wendel
Núdig, Hans & vrouw, 5 ch.
Núsch, Lodwÿk & vrouw, 3 ch.
Nutzberger, Mattÿs & vrouw, 4 ch.

Oberhúbel, Jacob & vrouw, 3 ch.
Odilioswal, ———— & vrouw [sic]
Öhll, Peter & vrouw, 7 ch.
Ostwalt, Johan & vrouw, 4 ch.

Paf, Johan Andries & vrouw, 5 ch.
Paltzer, Henrig & vrouw, 3 ch.
Paúl, Henrig & vrouw, 7 ch.
Pellesheim, Johan Peter & vrouw, 1 ch.
Peter, Jacob & vrouw
Peter, Klaas & vrouw, 6 ch.
Peter, Klaas & vrouw, 7 ch.
Peter, Philip & vrouw, 1 ch.
Piccisch, Adam & vrouw, 2 ch.

Ping, Melger
Pinheimer, Barth & vrouw, 4 ch.
Ponts, Niklaas & vrouw, 3 ch.
Pribl, Michel
Propper, Johan Júst & vrouw, 3 ch.
Púll, Johan Peter & vrouw, 5 ch.

Raads, Pieter
Red, Johan & vrouw, 5 ch.
Redel, Johan Henrig & vrouw, 3 ch.
Reiter, Henrig & vrouw, 2 ch.
Reiter, Johan Lodewÿk & vrouw
Reútter, Nicolas
Reÿer, Henrig & vrouw, 3 ch.
Richart, François & vrouw, 1 ch.
Rieter, Hans & vrouw, 3 ch.
Rigel, Kristiaan
Rŏmer, Johan & vrouw, 3 ch.
Roos, Kristoffel
Rosenboom, Pieter & vrouw, 4 ch.
Rosor, Martinus Fredrik & vrouw, 2 ch.
Rostbach, Peter & vrouw, 2 ch.
Rot, Peter & vrouw, 5 ch.
Rúbel, Johan & vrouw, 1 ch.
Rúch, Nicolas & vrouw, 5 ch.
Rússing, Mattÿs

Saar, Johan & vrouw, 7 ch.
Salbach, Johan & vrouw, 2 ch.
Salbach, Johan Emend & vrouw
Sanse, Peter
Saúns, Johan Peter
Schalosch, Peter & vrouw, 3 ch.
Scheffer, Andries & vrouw, 4 ch.
Schein, Michel Meing
Schellenberger, Koenraet
Scheller, Johan & vrouw
Schelling, Johan & vrouw
Schesbli, Joost Koenraet
Schesselnin, Henrig & vrouw, 1 ch.
Schester, Serbús & vrouw, 1 ch.
Schilt, Johan Henrig & vrouw
Schithel, Jacob & vrouw
Schits, Marten & vrouw, 1 ch.
Schling, Henrik & vrouw
Schmit, Adam & vrouw, 3 ch.
Schmit, Henrig & vrouw, 7 ch.
Schmit, Jeorg Mikel & vrouw
Schmit, Johan & vrouw, 3 ch.
Schmit, Johan Peter
Schmit, Johan Peter & vrouw, 5 ch.
Schmit, Niklaas & vrouw, 1 ch.
Schmit, Peter & vrouw, 5 ch.
Schneiter, Ulrig & vrouw, 2 ch.
Schnitzerling, Johan & vrouw, 3 ch.
Schnoenmaker, Barth & 5 ch.

Scholler, Peter & vrouw, 5 ch.
Schommer, Johan
Schŏnwolff, Johan
Schöpfer, Hans Jacob & vrouw
Schoútner, Diebelt & vrouw, 4 ch.
Schreits, Mattÿs & vrouw, 6 ch.
Schreling, Peter & vrouw, 6 ch.
Schreÿer, Johan & vrouw, 1 ch.
Schreÿts, Johan & vrouw, 3 ch.
Schúmacher, Johan
Schúmes, Ebrehart
Schwarts, Hans Jacob
Schwed, Jacob & vrouw, 7 ch.
Seimer, Simon & vrouw, 5 ch.
Sibel, Falenteÿn
Siles, Mickel & vrouw, 4 ch.
Silesÿ, Katrina & 1 ch.
Siller, Johan & vrouw
Sipler, Kristiaan
Sitig, Herman & vrouw, 5 ch.
Sleiger, Johan Júrg & vrouw, 4 ch.
Sleiger, Johan Michel & vrouw, 5 ch.
Smit, Georg Volpert & vrouw, 7 ch.
Smit, Hans Miggel & vrouw
Smit, Johan & vrouw
Smit, Johan Adam & vrouw, 3 ch.
Smit, Karel & vrouw, 6 ch.
Smit, Kasper & vrouw, 1 ch.
Sneÿder, Frants
Snor, Johan Nickel & vrouw, 3 ch.
Soffer, Niklaas & vrouw, 3 ch.
Sondtag, Frants & vrouw, 4 ch.
Sorg, Mattÿs & vrouw, 3 ch.
Speiherman, Johan Henrig & vrouw, 2 ch.
Staal, Johan Diderig & vrouw, 1 ch.
Steem, Johan & vrouw, 5 ch.
Steeren, Mattÿs
Steffen, Johan & vrouw, 4 ch.
Steiner, Michel & vrouw
Steún, Johan & vrouw, 3 ch.
Stoúts, ——— [illegible] & vrouw
Ströser, Daniel & vrouw, 1 ch.
Suner, Johan Michel & vrouw, 6 ch.
Sweeber, Bastiaan
Sweeber, Hendrik
Sÿpel, Hans Júrg

Talheimer, Henrig & vrouw, 2 ch.
Telers, Johan
Thenster, Sibmasers
Thirffenbach, Hans Koenraet & vrouw, 3 ch.
Thirffenbachrin, Anna
Tiell, Ananias & vrouw, 2 ch.
Tiell, Herman & vrouw, 1 ch.
Tiell, Johan & vrouw, 2 ch.
Tielman, ——— (no other name)

Tilman, Hans Koenraet & vrouw, 4 ch.
Túbenbeeker, Johan

Ulrig, Johan Elias & vrouw, 3 ch.

Valendin, Velden & vrouw, 7 ch.
Veesch, Johan Adam & vrouw, 5 ch.
Veldents, Henrig
Vinschbag, Kristiaan & vrouw
Visser, Pieter & vrouw, 2 ch.
Vogt, Henrig & vrouw, 1 ch.
Volks, Arnold & vrouw, 4 ch.
Vorster, Jurg & vrouw, 4 ch.

Wadenpoll, Jacob & vrouw, 2 ch.
Walter, Johan & vrouw, 2 ch.
Walter, Kasper & vrouw, 10 ch.
Weber, Diderig & vrouw, 2 ch.
Weins, Bastiaan & vrouw, 3 ch.
Weiroúg, Peter & vrouw, 4 ch.
Weÿant, Johan Martin & vrouw
Weÿant's Swager & 1 ch.

Weÿsgerber, Johan & vrouw, 2 ch.
Wiggert, Hans & vrouw, 5 ch.
Wighalm, Mattÿs & vrouw, 3 ch.
Wilhelm, Jan & vrouw
William, Johanna
William, Paúl
Wilmer, Anton & vrouw, 1 ch.
Wind, Henrig & vrouw, 3 ch.
Wind, Peter & vrouw, 5 ch.
Windt, Henrig & vrouw, 4 ch.
Winkel, Henrig
Wisser, Jacob & vrouw, 1 ch.
Wob, Philippús
Woger, Nicolas & vrouw, 2 ch.
Wúlgraaf, Múller

Zeb, Leonart & vrouw, 4 ch.
Zeerbisch, Johan Peter & vrouw, 9 ch.
Zerber, Johan Martin & vrouw, 4 ch.
Zerber, Philip
Zeÿt, Mattÿs & vrouw, 1 ch.
Zigler, Andries & vrouw, 4 ch.

FIFTH PARTY—EMBARKED JULY 3 TO JULY 10, SAILED JULY 15, 1709

Adolf, Peter & vrouw, 1 ch.
Albert, Lodewÿk & vrouw, 2 ch.
Andries, Koenraet & vrouw, 7 ch.
Andries, Peter & vrouw, 1 ch.
Anna Katrina, 2 ch.
Anna Magdleena (Wed^e.), 1 ch.
Anna Mary, 2 ch. (no other name)
Appel, Andreas
Appelman, Hans Peter & vrouw, 3 ch.
Arnolt, Hans Görg & vrouw, 6 ch.
Arnolt, Johan & vrouw, 5 ch.
Atorf, Tÿs & vrouw, 4 ch.
Aúst, Johan Philips
Aútfetter, Felten & vrouw, 1 ch.

Baar, Johan
Baptist, Johan
Barbera, Anna
Barbera, Anna, 1 ch.
Batelman, Mattias & vrouw, 2 ch.
Baúr, Kasper & vrouw, 3 ch.
Baúwer, Peeter & vrouw, 3 ch.
Becker, Johan & vrouw, 3 ch.
Becker, Zoden & vrouw, 6 ch.
Beesch, Ludwig & vrouw, 1 ch.
Bender, Henrig & vrouw, 3 ch.
Bender, Johan Bernhart & vrouw, 4 ch.
Bender, Koenraet & vrouw, 2 ch.
Benedik, Peter
Benter, Baltes & vrouw, 5 ch.
Bentram, Geerlof
Ber, Andries & vrouw

Ber, Hans Peter & vrouw
Berderúm, Philips
Berg, Kasper
Berlag, Koenraet & vrouw, 4 ch.
Berman, Johan & vrouw
Berner, Mattÿs & vrouw, 2 ch.
Bernhart, Peeter & vrouw, 3 ch.
Bert, Johan & vrouw, 3 ch.
Bert, Johan & vrouw, 4 ch.
Bert, Willem
Besser, Niklaas & vrouw, 3 ch.
Beús, Ferdinant & vrouw, 1 ch.
Bëvit, Johan & vrouw, 4 ch.
Beÿer, Hans Peter & vrouw, 2 ch.
Bëyer, Henrig & vrouw, 5 ch.
Bickel, Hans Michel & vrouw, 2 ch.
Bienlein, Hans
Biettel, Willem
Biltstein, Hans Jacob & vrouw, 4 ch.
Bintslin, Anna Kornelia
Birck, Johan & vrouw, 4 ch.
Bitz, Hans Görg & vrouw, 4 ch.
Blank, Niklaas & vrouw, 2 ch.
Blittersdorf, Koenraet & vrouw, 3 ch.
Blomreeder, Willem & vrouw, 3 ch.
Bok, Joseph
Bol, Gerland & vrouw, 8 ch.
Boller, Philips & vrouw, 5 ch.
Born, Görg & vrouw, 5 ch.
Born, Hans & vrouw, 1 ch.
Borninger, Kasper & vrouw, 3 ch.
Boúman, Jacob & vrouw

Boúman, Joost & 2 ch.
Boúwerman, Miggel & vrouw, 3 ch.
Braedvis, Godvried
Branck, Emanuel
Brandeúrf, Joost & vrouw, 4 ch.
Braun, Bastiaan & vrouw, 3 ch.
Braún, Ulrig & vrouw, 4 ch.
Bretta, Mary
Breÿn, Johan Belzar
Brick ,Maria Elizabeth
Broúnet, Hans Philips & vrouw, 3 ch.
Broúve, Hans Jacob & vrouw, 4 ch.
Brown, Johan & vrouw, 1 ch.
Brown, Johan Peter & vrouw, 4 ch.
Brúckin, Katrina, 5 ch.
Brúg, Carla
Buch, Fredrig & vrouw, 4 ch.
Buch, Hans Görg & vrouw, 5 ch.
Búk, Dúnges & vrouw, 1 ch.
Búrckert, Mattÿs & vrouw, 2 ch.
Búrger, Hans Jacob & vrouw, 3 ch.
Búrket, Kasper & vrouw, 2 ch.
Búster, Henrig & vrouw, 6 ch.

Cebi, Kristiaan
Cloos, Peeter & vrouw, 5 ch.
Collet, Michel & vrouw, 7 ch.
Copiak, Mattÿs

Dal, Andreas & vrouw, 1 ch.
Daüb, Michel & vrouw, 1 ch.
Debesman, David
Decker, Hans Schiedt & vrouw, 1 ch.
Dederin, Maria
Deis, Johan & vrouw, 3 ch.
Deis, Marcús & vrouw, 3 ch.
Deisinger, Hans Jörg
Deisinger, Peter
Dem, Joost & vrouw, 4 ch.
Denemarker, Kristoffel & vrouw, 3 ch.
Dennerey, Jacob & vrouw
Derner, Hans Jacob & vrouw, 2 ch.
Diel, Kristiaan & vrouw
Dielsneyder, Johan & vrouw, 4 ch.
Dierig, Neeltje
Dieschell, Hans Görg
Diets, Johan Jorg & vrouw, 6 ch.
Dikert, Henrig & vrouw, 4 ch.
Dilshinit, Johan
Dorst, Robbert & vrouw
Doúp, Diderig
Drom, Andries & vrouw, 5 ch.
Droús, Kristiaan
Dúboús, Michel
Duffing, Willem & vrouw, 4 ch.

Ecktwalt, Kasper & vrouw, 2 ch.

Egeler, Johan & vrouw
Egred, Louwis
Elhart, Johan & vrouw
Elizabeth, Anna
Elkener, Hans Adam & vrouw, 4 ch.
Elroot, Johan Dider & vrouw, 1 ch.
Emmell, Johan & vrouw, 2 ch.
Engel, ——— & vrouw (no other name)
Engel, Johan
Engel, Margreta (Wede:), 2 ch.
Engel, Philip & vrouw, 4 ch.
Erbs, Hans Henrig & vrouw, 3 ch.
Escher, Jacob & vrouw, 2 ch.
Eva, Anna

Faech, Johan & vrouw, 4 ch.
Feel, Jacob & vrouw, 3 ch.
Fink, Johan Willem & vrouw, 6 ch.
Fink, Kasper & vrouw, 2 ch.
Finkin (Wede.), 2 ch.
Finsinger, Philips & vrouw, 1 ch.
Fisel, Adam & vrouw, 3 ch.
Flip, Jörg & vrouw, 3 ch.
Foght, Hans Peter
Frans, Johan & vrouw, 5 ch.
Fransnus, Johan Paúl & vrouw
Fredrig, Cartes & vrouw, 5 ch.
Fredrig, Hans Adam & vrouw, 1 ch.
Fredrik, Koenraet & vrouw, 2 ch.
Freÿmeier, Michel & vrouw, 5 ch.
Freonet, Philip & vrouw,
Frölúg, Valentÿn & vrouw, 2 ch.
Frowberg, Mattÿs
Fúriger, Fredrig & vrouw, 2 ch.

Gardner, Peeter & vrouw, 5 ch.
Geerlof, ——— & vrouw, 3 ch. (no
    other name)
Geerlof, Johan Krist & vrouw, 3 ch.
Geerlof, Peeter & vrouw, 4 ch.
Geertrúg, Anna
———, Geertrúy (Wede.), 3 ch. (no
    other name)
Gees, Júrg & vrouw, 1 ch.
Geis, Niklass & vrouw, 4 ch.
Gems, Jorg Adam & vrouw
Gerber, Jacob
Geres, Júrg & vrouw, 5 ch.
Gerhart, Falentÿn & vrouw, 5 ch.
Gerhart, Johan & vrouw
Gerheim, Johan & vrouw, 3 ch.
Gerlin, Johan
Gertner, Jacob, 1 ch.
Giseling, Johan Hendrig
Goettel, Daniel & vrouw, 7 ch.
Goftig (Gostig), Korn, & vrouw, 4 ch.
Gonan, Johan Hendrik

Gopalt, Kasper
Graúsch, Jacob's (Wed^e:), 3 ch.
Grausch, Johan Peeter & vrouw, 4 ch.
Grefter, Simon & vrouw, 5 ch.
Grúg, Hans Görg & vrouw, 5 ch.
Grúnnig, Bendik & vrouw, 4 ch.
Gúdtud, Peter & vrouw

Haas, Hend·:
Haas, Paúlús, & vrouw, 2 ch.
Haber, Ditmút & vrouw, 6 ch.
Hag, Kristiaan & vrouw, 4 ch.
Ham, Mattÿs & vrouw, 2 ch.
Haman, Andries & vrouw
Hannes, Willem & vrouw, 2 ch.
Hans (Haus), Glein & vrouw
Harbag, Andreas & vrouw, 2 ch.
Hardwig, Johan Jacob & vrouw, 2 ch.
Haring, Godvrÿd
Härman, Johan
Hatenkrowst, Philip
Hattler, Ulrig & vrouw, 9 ch.
Haúsman, Ludwig & vrouw
Heipt, Philippús & vrouw, 3 ch.
Helmet, Philips & vrouw, 6 ch.
Helsch, Maarten & vrouw, 3 ch.
Hemberg, Johan
Henrig, Andreas & vrouw, 3 ch.
Herschner, Steve & vrouw
Hertzeel, Jacob & vrouw, 1 ch.
Hes, Johan
Hes, Koenraet & vrouw, 3 ch.
Hes, Tomas & vrouw, 3 ch.
Hes, Ulrig & vrouw, 2 ch.
Het, Koenraet & vrouw, 3 ch.
Heu, Fredrig & vrouw, 3 ch.
Heu, Kasper & vrouw, 3 ch.
Heúl, Mattÿs Görg & vrouw
Heÿt, Joost & vrouw, 1 ch.
Hiebesch, Johan
Hilsch, Kristoffel & vrouw
Hober, Krist
Hoch, Michel & vrouw, 2 ch.
Hoepert, Hans & vrouw
Hoffman, Albert & vrouw, 6 ch.
Hoffman, Henrig & vrouw, 1 ch.
Hoffman, Mattÿs & vrouw, 2 ch.
Hoffman, Michel
Hoffrin, Katrina
Hoof, Hans Peter & vrouw, 5 ch.
Hoofman, Joost & vrouw
Hoost, Johan Felten & vrouw, 4 ch.
Horlakker, Hans Júrg
Horn, Kasper & vrouw, 3 ch.
Hörsch, Peter & vrouw, 1 ch.
Hoúser, Hans & vrouw, 3 ch.
Hoútrúg, Jörg & vrouw, 3 ch.

Húniaben, Willem

Illes, Róypert & vrouw, 4 ch.

Jacob, Johan
Jacob, Johan
Jáger, Baltes & vrouw, 1 ch.
Janse, Willem
Jeger, Kristiaan & vrouw, 1 ch.
Jemal (Wed^e), 5 ch.
Joggem, Johan & vrouw, 1 ch.
Joosten, Johan & vrouw, 6 ch.
Jörg, Hans
Josep, Anna
Júng, Johan
Jung, Johan & vrouw
Jung, Johan Peter
Júng, Klaus & vrouw, 3 ch.
Jungst, Johan Henrig & vrouw, 3 ch.
Júrg, Johan & vrouw, 2 ch.

K——— [blotted], Johan Jacob.& vrouw,
    4 ch.
Kamd (Kame?), Görg & vrouw, 5 ch.
Kämp, Koenraet & vrouw, 3 ch.
Kanhorner, Margreeta, 1 ch.
Karn, Michel & vrouw, 2 ch.
Karol, Jacob & vrouw, 5 ch.
Kas, Andries Laúrens & vrouw, 1 ch.
Kasner, Andreas & vrouw, 5 ch.
Katrina, Anna
Katrina, Maria
Katrina (Wed^e:), 1 ch.
Kaÿg, Anna Katrina, 3 ch.
Kebels, Andries & vrouw, 1 ch.
Keelman, Michel & vrouw, 3 ch.
Kees, Johan Peter & vrouw, 3 ch.
Kel, Peeter & vrouw, 3 ch.
Kell, Niklaas & vrouw
Keneman, Júrg Karel
Kenmer, Hans Nikel
Kerbel, Kasper & vrouw, 7 ch.
Kerbel, Peter & vrouw, 1 ch.
Kerger, Johan & vrouw, 1 ch.
Kermerroot, Johan & vrouw, 6 ch.
Kerver, Niklaas & vrouw, 2 ch.
Kessen, Hoúpvig & vrouw
Kever, Hans Philip & vrouw, 7 ch.
Kever, Philip & vrouw, 1 ch.
Kieselbag, Johan & vrouw, 3 ch.
Kigel, Henrig & vrouw, 1 ch.
Kindr, Bendik & vrouw, 3 ch.
Kittert, Mattÿs
Klaar, Anna
Klaas, Bartel & vrouw, 2 ch.
Klam, Daniel & vrouw, 3 ch.

Klapper, Johan Willem & vrouw, 3 ch.
Klaus, Bernhart & vrouw, 4 ch.
Klein, Jeronimús & vrouw, 3 ch.
Klein, Mattÿs & vrouw, 1 ch.
Klein, Peeter & vrouw
Klein, Peter & vrouw
Kleinkor, Korn̄ & vrouw, 1 ch.
Kletters, Johan & vrouw, 2 ch.
Kloe, Barlin & vrouw, 2 ch.
Klop, Johan Nikel & vrouw, 4 ch.
Klopper, Johan Willem & vrouw, 3 ch.
Knap, Hans Nikel & vrouw, 3 ch.
Kneskern, Johan Peter & vrouw
Knevel, Andries, 2 ch.
Knever, Paúlús & vrouw, 6 ch.
Koen, Dinges
Koenraet, Hans
Koert, Michel & vrouw, 8 ch.
Kog, Niklaas & vrouw, 2 ch.
Kollet, Gerhart & vrouw, 2 ch.
König, Johan Joost & vrouw, 2 ch.
Kop, Jacob & vrouw, 4 ch.
Kreber, Peeter & vrouw
Kreffúlm, Jacob
Kreider, Bernhardt
Kremer, Peter
Kreps, Joost
Krilion, Johan & vrouw, 1 ch.
Krist, Johan & vrouw, 3 ch.
Kroutner, Mattÿs
Krow, Koenraet & vrouw
Krúis, Jacob & vrouw, 2 ch.
Krúm, Johan Herman
Krÿs, Mattÿs & vrouw, 3 ch.
Kúmenstein, Johan Nikel & vrouw, 4 ch.
Kún, Philippus & vrouw, 6 ch.
Kuntz, Koenraet & vrouw, 3 ch.

Lab, Gëorg & vrouw, 2 ch.
Labag, Adam & vrouw, 5 ch.
Labag, Adam & vrouw, 5 ch.
Lang, Ab^m. & vrouw, 3 ch.
Lang, Johan & vrouw
Langevelt, Hend‹.
Lank, Peter & vrouw
Lankr (?), Felten & vrouw, 4 ch.
Leber, Willem & vrouw, 2 ch.
Lei, Hans Henrig & vrouw
Leidecker, Henderick & vrouw
Leitner, Johan Adam & vrouw, 2 ch.
Lenken, Jan Willem & vrouw
Lepper, Philippus Herman & vrouw, 5 ch.
Lergerseiler, Johan Willem & vrouw, 1 ch.
Lesering, Antonÿ
Leúven, Marÿ Katrÿn

Level, Johan Koenraet & vrouw, 3 ch.
Licks, Willem Bernhart & vrouw
Lieger, Johan Adam
Lingelbach, Baltes & vrouw, 3 ch.
Lingoret, Bernhart & vrouw, 1 ch.
Lochrúgs, Ulrig & vrouw, 1 ch.
Locks, Hans Nikel & vrouw, 3 ch.
Lodewÿk, Hendrik & vrouw, 4 ch.
Logrúgs, Mattÿs & vrouw, 3 ch.
Losch, Mattÿs & vrouw, 3 ch.
Loúck, Hans Michel & vrouw, 1 ch.
Loúck, Johan
Lúber, Gabriel & vrouw, 3 ch.
Ludwig, Andreas
Ludwig, Johan & vrouw, 6 ch.
Lúdwig, Mattÿs & vrouw, 4 ch.
Lúkas, Hans Görg & vrouw, 7 ch.
Lútz, Peter & vrouw, 4 ch.
Lÿs, Katrÿn
Lÿsbet, Anna

Maester, Paúlús & vrouw, 1 ch.
Magdleena (wed^e.), 5 ch.
Man, Herman & vrouw, 3 ch.
Mandenagt, Willem
Mangel, Johan Jurg
Margreet, Anna
Margreet, Anna
Maria, Anna
Maria, Anna (Wed^e:), 1 ch.
Maria (Wed^e.) (no other name)
Maria (Wed^e.), 1 ch. (no other name)
Martman, Lúdwig
Mary, Anna
Masge, Niklaas & vrouw, 7 ch.
Matser, Johan & vrouw, 3 ch.
Mattÿs, ―― & vrouw, 2 ch. (no other name)
Mattÿs, Peter & vrouw, 5 ch.
Mattÿs, Webbers
Mäy, Johan Peter & vrouw, 2 ch.
Meesterin, Margreeta, 2 ch.
Meier, Koenraet & vrouw
Meinhober, Philippús & vrouw
Meinsinger, Koenraet & vrouw, 1 ch.
Melbreg, Adam & vrouw
Melbreg, Johan
Melsers, Stoffel & vrouw, 2 ch.
Meltsberger, Philips & vrouw, 2 ch.
Mengel, Hans Jörg & vrouw, 5 ch.
Mengje, Fredrig & vrouw, 8 ch.
Menin, Johan
Menst, Peter & vrouw, 2 ch.
Mese, Mattÿs & vrouw, 5 ch.
Mets, Andreas & vrouw, 4 ch.
Metsgennen, Doretta
Meÿ, Johan Dinges (Wed^e.), 1 ch.

Meÿer, Bastiaan
Meÿer, Henrig & vrouw, 2 ch.
Mikkeler, Johan & vrouw, 1 ch.
Mikle, Henrig & vrouw, 3 ch.
Miller, Johan
Miller, Niklaas
Minsinger, Bastiaan & vrouw, 3 ch.
Mitler, Joost
Miyn, Johan & vrouw, 7 ch.
Mönd, Ferdinand & vrouw, 4 ch.
Moor, Andreas & vrouw, 7 ch.
Moor, Johan Koenraet & vrouw, 1 ch.
Moor, Johan Krist & vrouw, 6 ch.
Moor, Philip Willem & vrouw, 2 ch.
Morial, Hendr'k.
Morees, Frans
Mous, Miggel & vrouw
Múleri, Ula
Múller, Anna Mary
Múller, Hans Georg & vrouw, 1 ch.
Múller, Jacob & vrouw, 5 ch.
Müller, Johan & vrouw, 4 ch.
Múller, Johan Benedik & vrouw, 3 ch.
Múller, Johan Henrig & vrouw, 4 ch.
Múller, Johan Jacob & vrouw
Múller, Johan Joost & vrouw, 6 ch.
Múller, Johan Mikel & vrouw, 1 ch.
Múller, Johan Sebastiaan & vrouw
Múller, Johan Tÿs & vrouw, 2 ch.
Múller, Johan Tÿs & vrouw, 2 ch.
Múller, Michel & vrouw, 6 ch.
Múller, Niklaas & vrouw, 5 ch.
Múller, Peter
Múller, Peter & vrouw, 3 ch.
Múller, Philip & vrouw, 2 ch.
Múller, Philippús & vrouw, 8 ch.
Mullerÿn, Anna Mary
Múseler, Jacob & vrouw, 4 ch.

Negs, Jacob & vrouw, 7 ch.
Niesch, Görg Willem & vrouw, 2 ch.
Niklaas, Júties & vrouw, 7 ch.
Niklaas, Peeter & vrouw, 2 ch.
Nol, Herbert & vrouw
Nonius, Johan Peter

Obel, Johan & vrouw, 1 ch.
Obreschur (?), Johan Hendrig & vrouw,
    7 ch.
Octer, Kristoffel
Odilja (Wed^e.), 3 ch.
Ogs, Hans Mikel & vrouw, 2 ch.
Oosterman, Johan & vrouw, 5 ch.
Openheizer, Philip

Patturf, Peter & vrouw, 5 ch.
Paúlús, Johan Henrig & vrouw, 1 ch.

Paúlús, Michel
Peerelman, Johan & vrouw, 3 ch.
Peerschoor, Hans Jacob & vrouw, 6 ch.
Peeter, Andreas
Peeter, Johan
Peeter, Mattÿs
Peffer, Miggel & vrouw, 2 ch.
Pender, Jacob
Penenstehl, Niklaas & vrouw, 2 ch.
Perriger, Jacob & vrouw
Peter, Ludwig
Petoriús, Gerhart & vrouw, 7 ch.
Pettemer, Fredrig & vrouw, 4 ch.
Pheÿffer, Júriaan & vrouw, 5 ch.
Pieleman, Pieter & vrouw, 1 ch.
Plein, Jacob & vrouw, 5 ch.
Poel, Mikel & vrouw, 2 ch.
Poel, Nikel & vrouw, 2 ch.
Prak, Hans Michel & vrouw, 1 ch.
Prettert, Jeúnes & vrouw, 2 ch.
Printz, Daniel & vrouw, 3 ch.
Prouk, Peter & vrouw, 3 ch.
Prúnck, Peter

Rageútzwey, Húybert & vrouw, 3 ch.
Ram, Niklaas & vrouw, 4 ch.
Range, Martin & vrouw
Ras, Michel & vrouw, 1 ch.
Raú, Johan Jacob & vrouw, 2 ch.
Rechten, Túnes & vrouw, 1 ch.
Reder, Laúrents
Regebag, Johan & vrouw, 8 ch.
Reinbalt, Mattÿs & vrouw, 2 ch.
Reinhart, Kasper & vrouw, 3 ch.
Reinhart, Koenraet & vrouw, 3 ch.
Reiter, Mattÿs & vrouw, 2 ch.
Reiter, Samuel, 3 ch.
Remmer, Johan Willem & vrouw, 5 ch.
Rensten, Henrig
Riger, Johan Philips & vrouw, 4 ch.
Ringer, Jacob & vrouw, 1 ch.
Risch, Hans Jörg & vrouw, 5 ch.
Rodenberger, Johan
Rodenmeÿer, Tobias
Roel, Maria Katrina
Roel, Niklaas & vrouw, 2 ch.
Roer, Laúrens & vrouw, 3 ch.
Roeterscheg, Johan Júrg & vrouw, 3 ch.
Roll, Jörg Willem & vrouw, 3 ch.
Roschkop, Martin & vrouw, 3 ch.
Rover, Hans Jacob & vrouw, 1 ch.
Rúbert, Arnold
Rúff, Johan & vrouw, 3 ch.
Rúntz, Matteús & vrouw, 6 ch.

Sacks, Bastiaan & vrouw, 4 ch.
Sairbúrger, Hans Júrg & vrouw, 1 ch.

Sairbúrger, Hans Michel
Saly, Dominic & vrouw, 6 ch.
Schaff, Bartel & vrouw, 1 ch.
Schaft, Bartel & vrouw, 1 ch.
Schaft, Johan & vrouw, 3 ch.
Schart, Johan Daniel
Scheefer, Geerard & vrouw, 2 ch.
Scheefer, Niklaas & vrouw
Scheenberger, Johan
Scheever, Johan Hendrig & vrouw
Scheffener, Reinart & vrouw, 2 ch.
Scheffer, Jacob & vrouw, 2 ch.
Schehart, Michel & vrouw, 2 ch.
Schel, Jacob & vrouw, 3 ch.
Schelter, Kasper & vrouw, 4 ch.
Schenk, Hans Koenraet & vrouw, 2 ch.
Schenk, Hans Nikel & vrouw
Scherdel, Koenraet & vrouw, 4 ch.
Scherver, Philippus
Scheser (Schever?), Hans Hendrik
Schester, Philip & vrouw, 5 ch.
Scheúcher, Michel & vrouw, 5 ch.
Scheúe, Gilles & vrouw, 3 ch.
Scheúgh, Mattÿs & vrouw, 4 ch.
Scheÿ, Hans Peter & vrouw, 3 ch.
Schilderin, Margreet, 3 ch.
Schilling, —— & vrouw, 3 ch. [Sic]
Schimberger, Henrig
Schinberger, Bartel
Schinberger, Súsan
Schmit, Michel
Schmitz, Johan & vrouw, 2 ch.
Schneider, Peter & vrouw, 2 ch.
Schner, Johan & vrouw
Schniter, Peter & vrouw
Schnitspan, Korn & vrouw, 5 ch.
Schnüg, Johan Adam
Schnúg, Willem
Schober, Peter
Schoek, Niklaas & vrouw, 2 ch.
Schoenmager, Jörg Willem & vrouw, 4 ch.
Schoenmager, Mattÿs
Schöffer, Jacob & vrouw, 8 ch.
Schog, Johan Hendrig & vrouw, 1 ch.
Schog, Kristiaan & vrouw, 6 ch.
Schoof, Johan
Schoteis, Johan Júrg & vrouw, 2 ch.
Schover, Kristiaan
Schram, Pieter & vrouw, 3 ch.
Schreeder, Onelgert & vrouw, 7 ch.
Schreider, Philip & vrouw, 5 ch.
Schriber, Jacob & vrouw, 7 ch.
Schroút, Levi
Schúdelbag, Martin & vrouw
Schúg, Miklaas & vrouw, 8 ch.
Schulerd, Koenraet & vrouw, 3 ch.

Schuller, Hans Jacob & vrouw, 1 ch.
Schúltheisch, Johan
Schúmager, Daniel & vrouw, 3 ch.
Schupman, Herman & vrouw, 7 ch.
Schús, Johan & vrouw, 4 ch.
Schúts, Philips & vrouw, 4 ch.
Schwarts, Júrg & vrouw, 4 ch.
Schwer, Adam & vrouw, 1 ch.
Seder, Johan & vrouw, 1 ch.
Sies, Hans Peter & vrouw, 6 ch.
Sikart, Mattÿs & vrouw, 4 ch.
Simon, Benedik & vrouw, 4 ch.
Simon, Laurents
Simon, Peter
Simon, Sagarias & vrouw, 3 ch.
Sitig, Krist & vrouw, 1 ch.
Slesser, Hendrik & vrouw, 5 ch.
Sligt, Hans
Slosher, Andreas, 2 ch.
Smit, Hans Peter
Smit, Johan Andreas & vrouw, 4 ch.
Smit, Joost
Smit, Niklaas & vrouw, 4 ch.
Smit, Thomas
Sneider, Arnold & vrouw, 3 ch.
Sneider, Jacob
Sneider, Johan & vrouw, 3 ch.
Sneiter, Henrig & vrouw, 3 ch.
Sneÿder, Johan & vrouw
Sneÿder, Johan Willem & vrouw, 1 ch.
Sneyder, Kasper & vrouw, 6 ch.
Sneÿder, Kristiaan & vrouw, 3 ch.
Sneÿder, Miggel & vrouw, 4 ch.
Sneÿter, Juriaan & vrouw, 1 ch.
Snÿder, Johan & vrouw, 3 ch.
Soelst, Johan Jürg & vrouw, 1 ch.
Sommer, Hans Jacob & vrouw, 1 ch.
Sool, Johan & vrouw, 5 ch.
Sool, Kristiaan & vrouw, 6 ch.
Spengeler, Johan Frans & vrouw
Sporin, Anna Katrina
Stal, Martin & vrouw, 1 ch.
Stall, Henrig & vrouw, 4 ch.
Stamber, Melger & vrouw, 1 ch.
Staúber, Jacob & vrouw, 1 ch.
Steen, Elias & vrouw, 3 ch.
Steever, Mattÿs & vrouw, 2 ch.
Steier, Johan Mikel
Stein, Martin
Stein, Michel & vrouw, 3 ch.
Steiner, Jorg & vrouw
Stekle, Benedik & vrouw, 5 ch.
Sterm, Kristiaan & vrouw, 1 ch.
Stern, Jacob & vrouw, 2 ch.
Stern, Philip & vrouw, 1 ch.
Stik, Mattÿs & vrouw, 3 ch.
Stor, Miggel & vrouw, 4 ch.

Straes, Andreas & vrouw, 2 ch.
Straetsborger, Baltes & vrouw, 1 ch.
Stree, Herman
Streit, Kristiaan & vrouw, 5 ch.
Strook, Kristiaan & vrouw, 2 ch.
Stúb, Maarten, 3 ch.
Stúbinger, Hans
Swal, Johan Geerard & vrouw, 1 ch.
Swart, Hans Adam & vrouw
Swartbag, Hartel & vrouw, 7 ch.
Switseler, Henrig & vrouw, 4 ch.

Tamboer, Henrig & vrouw, 3 ch.
Tewisman, Emrig & vrouw, 2 ch.
t'Foos, Serris & vrouw, 5 ch. [sic]
Theis, Johan
Theis, Thomas
Thomas, Peeter & vrouw, 2 ch.
Tietrúy, Hans Willem & vrouw, 5 ch.
Timmerman, M. & vrouw, 1 ch.
Timmerman, Willem, 2 ch.
Tipenhove, Hans Júrg & vrouw, 3 ch.
Tomas, Hans Willem & vrouw, 2 ch.
Tomas, Johan & vrouw, 6 ch.
Tomas, Mattÿs
Triespeisser (?), Johan
Tÿs, Mattÿs & vrouw, 5 ch.
Tzoll, Hans Jacob

Ulrig, Albregt & vrouw, 1 ch.
Ulrig, Hans
Umdrucht, Jacob & vrouw, 5 ch.
Urban, Michel & vrouw, 4 ch.

Vaar, Daniel & vrouw
van Bergen, Hans Peter & vrouw, 2 ch.
Vasbender, Bertram & vrouw, 3 ch.
Vegt, Simon & vrouw
Vesser, Hans Júrg & vrouw, 2 ch.
Visser, Garrard & vrouw, 3 ch.
Visser, Hans & vrouw, 2 ch.
Visser, Hendk & vrouw
Visser, Johan & vrouw, 1 ch.
Vos, Johan
Vúlman, Laúrens
Vúlman, Mattÿs & vrouw, 4 ch.

Waal, Kristoffel & vrouw, 6 ch.
Wagenaar, Johan Hendrik
Wagenaar, Niklaas & vrouw, 3 ch.
Wagman, Abᵐ: & vrouw, 2 ch.
Wagnaar, Willem
Wagner, Johan & vrouw, 1 ch.
Wagner, Niklaas & vrouw, 4 ch.
Wagner, Philippús & vrouw, 2 ch.
Walen, Johan
Walter, Johan Henrig & vrouw, 4 ch.

Wannemager, Peter & vrouw
Weber, Baltes
Weber, Hans Jacob & vrouw, 4 ch.
Weber, Jacob & vrouw, 1 ch.
Weber, Johan Henrig & vrouw, 1 ch.
Weber, Johan Koenraet & vrouw, 5 ch.
Weber, Mattÿs
Weber, Niklaas & vrouw
Weber, Philip
Weber, Simon & vrouw, 2 ch.
Wechel, Hans Michel & vrouw, 2 ch.
Wedebag, Peter
Weilant, Peeter & vrouw, 2 ch.
Weiller, Johan & vrouw, 1 ch.
Weinberg, Koenraet & vrouw
Welsaker, Stoffel & vrouw, 1 ch.
Welter, Matteús
Wendesheimer, Stoffel & vrouw, 5 ch.
Weÿsch, Matteús & vrouw, 5 ch.
Weyspaart, Júrg & vrouw, 3 ch.
Wiesener, Johan & vrouw, 6 ch.
Wilhellem, Henrig & vrouw, 5 ch.
Willem, Jörg & vrouw
Willem, Mikel & vrouw, 2 ch.
Wilmy, Jacob & vrouw, 4 ch.
Winsman, Henrig & vrouw, 3 ch.
Wintik, Johan Jacob
Wisner, Johan & vrouw, 6 ch.
Wistenroot, Anneke
Wolfskël, Hans Görg & vrouw
Wolft, Bertram & vrouw, 4 ch.
Wolkin, Anna Barber, 2 ch.
Wolleben, Hans Felten & vrouw, 3 ch.
Wolleben, Hans Miggel & vrouw, 1 ch.
Wolleben, Johan
Worms, Kristiaan & vrouw, 4 ch.
Wormster, Bastiaan & vrouw, 2 ch.
Woúst, Felix
Wúgin, Lizabet, 1 ch.
Wyngaertenaer, Peter & vrouw, 3 ch.
Wÿs, Johan Hendrig & vrouw, 4 ch.
Wÿskerver, Johan Hendrig, & vrouw,
    4 ch.
Wÿst, Koenraet & vrouw, 3 ch.

Yslant, David & vrouw, 1 ch.

Zamer, Maarten & vrouw, 5 ch.
Zeiger, Júrg & vrouw, 2 ch.
Zeiter, Andries & vrouw, 3 ch.
Zeiter, Hans & vrouw
Zekel, Willem & vrouw
Zetgen, Henrig Peter & vrouw, 2 ch.
Ziel, Marcus & vrouw, 1 ch.
Zigler, Koenraet & vrouw, 1 ch.
Zosin, ———— & vrouw, 4 ch. [sic.]
Zouwe, Mattÿs & vrouw, 5 ch.

SIXTH PARTY—EMBARKED JULY 27, SAILED JULY 28, 1709

Ache, Johan
Achenbag, Johan
Agenbag, Anna Margreta
Aggenbag, Johan Jacob & vrouw & 4 ch.
Allebag, Andrass & vrouw
Allebag, Elizabet
Antonin, Anna Margreta & 1 ch.
Appel, Johan
Ar, Johan Willem & vrouw & 6 ch.
Arendorff, Johan Henrig & vrouw & 1 ch.
Arnold, Johan & vrouw
Arommenúil, Geerhart
Aterbag, Jurg & vrouw

Bang, Kristiaan & vrouw & 3 ch.
Bast, Joost Hendrig & vrouw & 5 ch.
Baúerin, Anna Maria
Baúme, Frants Heller & vrouw & 4 ch.
Beck, Simon & vrouw & 8 ch.
Becker, Albert & vrouw & 1 ch.
Becker, Hans Henrig
Becker, Johan & vrouw & 3 ch.
Bele, Johan Jacob
Belger, Johan & vrouw & 1 ch.
Belts, Johan
Berdram, Johan & vrouw
Berg, Johan Henrig
Berks, Martin & vrouw
Berlee, Frans & vrouw & 2 ch.
Berner, Johan & vrouw & 3 ch.
Bernhard, Jozep & vrouw
Bernhart, Johan
Bernhart, Johan & vrouw & 2 ch.
Bernhart, Johan & vrouw & 2 ch.
Bescher, Henrig & vrouw & 3 ch.
Besme, Henrig & vrouw & 3 ch.
Best, Johan Hirg & vrouw & 1 ch.
Beÿer, Mikel & swister
Beÿer, Sagond & swister
Blasch, Johan & vrouw & 2 ch.
Botser, Anna Maria
Bötser, Johan Herman, & vrouw & 8 ch.
Bremer, Jacob & vrouw & 4 ch.
Bron, Mattys & vrouw & 2 ch.
Brúch, Hans Henrig & vrouw & 4 ch.
Brúsel, Johan Nikel & vrouw & 4 ch.
Brústel, Johan Gorg & vrouw & 4 ch.

Daústel, Johan Melgior & vrouw & 3 ch.
de Hed, Kristoffel & vrouw & 4 ch.
Deiritsbacher, Michel
Deisch, Andreas & vrouw & 4 ch.
Deiwig, Simon & vrouw & 3 ch.
den Decker, Peter Jansz & vrouw & 5 ch.
Detweider, Jacob & vrouw & 2 ch.
de Wolf, Godvried & vrouw & 3 ch.

Dickl, Johan & vrouw & 4 ch.
Diel, Johan Júrg & vrouw & 1 ch.
Diepel, Johan Peter & vrouw & 3 ch.
Dilcher, Herman & vrouw & 3 ch.
Dilser, Koenraet's (Wed^e.) & 1 ch.
Diltey, Hans Jacob & vrouw & 5 ch.
Dinges, Hans Jacob & vrouw & 4 ch.
Doll, Hans Adam & vrouw, & 2 ch.
Domels, Barber & 2 ch.
Dorman, Johannes & 2 ch.
Dorreman, Geertrúy
Draks, Johan Jacob & vrouw & 4 ch.
Drechel, Johan Jurg & vrouw
Drefhaúser, Willem & vrouw & 3 ch.

Eberhartin, Anna Barber
Ebers, Daniel & vrouw & 3 ch.
Eberts, Johan Peter & vrouw & 2 ch.
Eeisenberg, Antoniús
Ekman, Daniel & vrouw & 1 ch.
Emaus, Bonefaciús & vrouw & 5 ch.
Engelsman, Júrg & vrouw & 3 ch.
Erlang, Johan & vrouw & 4 ch.

Feigsfint, Mattÿs
Feschler, Johan Wendel & vrouw & 3 ch.
Feÿsters, Herman & vrouw & 2 ch.
Fiedel, Fredrik & vrouw & 3 ch.
Fischbag, Diderig
Fischbag, Johan Bast & vrouw & 2 ch.
Fischbag, Joost
Fisser, Andries & vrouw & 7 ch.
Fleuter, David
Folant, Johan Willem & vrouw & 3 ch.
Fosch, Martin's (Wed^e.) & 3 ch.
Frants, Anna & 2 ch.
Frants, Henrig & vrouw & 7 ch.
Frants, Paúlús
Fredrig, Hans Felten & vrouw & 5 ch.
Frits, Júrg Willem & vrouw & 3 ch.
Fúnck, Anna Katrina
Fúnck, Peter & vrouw & 4 ch.
Fúrster, Michel & vrouw & 3 ch.
Fÿk, Anna Katrina

Geiseler, Andreas & vrouw & 2 ch.
Gerdener, Hans Júrg & vrouw & 1 ch.
Gerserin, Geertrúg
Getter, Henrig & vrouw & 2 ch.
Giseler, Johan Henrig & vrouw & 1 ch.
Gleich, Sovia
Gnalder, Andries
Godwig, Antoniús & vrouw
Goltman, Koenraet & vrouw & 5 ch.
Greff, Philips Jacob & vrouw & 2 ch.
Greidter, Joggem

Grein, Anna Katrina
Grosch, Johannes & vrouw & 5 ch.
Grúwer, Hans & vrouw & 3 ch.
Gúth, Johan

Haan, Johan Júrg & vrouw & 7 ch.
Haberstig, Henrig & vrouw
Halte, Hans Felten & vrouw & 2 ch.
Hamon, Johan Willem & vrouw & 4 ch.
Harger, Sondag
Hartman, Fredrig & vrouw & 2 ch.
Hartwig, Hans Gorg & 2 ch.
Haús, Johan's (Wed^e.) & 3 ch.
Heck, Henrig & vrouw & 3 ch.
Heger, Johan Fredrik
Heidelberger, Hirchel & vrouw & 2 ch.
Heil, Hans Jacob
Held, Henrig & vrouw & 3 ch.
Hell, Johan & vrouw & 4 ch.
Helman, Adam
Henrig, Johan & vrouw & 3 ch.
Herberts, Jacob & vrouw & 2 ch.
Herling, Henrig
Hesche, Niklas & vrouw & 1 ch.
Heydee, Peeter & vrouw & 1 ch.
Heyer, Johan Júrg & vrouw
Hindterschit, Michel & vrouw & 3 ch.
Hitserin, Kristiaan
Hock, Johan & vrouw & 3 ch.
Hoff, Johan Melgior & vrouw & 6 ch.
Hoffman, Henrig & vrouw & 2 ch.
Hoffsteittler, Kristiaan & vrouw & 5 ch.
Hoperhempt, Fredrik & vrouw & 2 ch.
Húmmel, Herman & vrouw & 1 ch.
Húppers, Henrig & vrouw & 8 ch.

Ingold, Hans & vrouw & 5 ch.

Jacob, Johan
Jacob, Johan
Jacob, Johan & vrouw & 2 ch.
Jacobi, Philip & vrouw
Jacobsz, Roel
Joggem, Mattys
Joost, Kristoffel & vrouw & 1 ch.
Jorg, Antoný & vrouw & 6 ch.
Josten, Margreta & 1 ch.
Júng, Johan Eberhard & vrouw & 1 ch.
Júnge, Johannes' (Wed^e.) & 5 ch.
Júrg, Johan

Kartneer, Johan & 3 ch.
Kastner, Johan & 7 ch.
Keil, Johann & vrouw & 2 ch.
Keiming, Johan Markús & vrouw & 3 ch.
Keiseham, Johan Joost's (Wed^e.) & 1 ch.
Keldereich, Abram & vrouw & 3 ch.

Kell, Júrg, Andries, & vrouw & 1 ch.
Keys, Johan Philip & vrouw & 1 ch.
Kirch, Johan Deisch
Klein, Johan & vrouw & 2 ch.
Kleisch, Kristoffel & vrouw
Klengs, Johan & vrouw
Klengs, Johan Gorg & vrouw & 3 ch.
Klengs, Johan Henrig & vrouw & 4 ch.
Knuppelberg, Paúl
Koch, Johan & vrouw
Koenraed, Johan Anders & vrouw & 5 ch.
Koenraed, Salmon & 2 ch.
Kog, Hans Henrig & vrouw & 5 ch.
Kogh, Júrg & vrouw & 4 ch.
Kolb, Jacob & 2 ch.
Kolbin, Maria Tÿs
Kölle, Hans Jacob
Koltman, Koenraet & vrouw & 5 ch.
Koog, Johan Antony
Koog, Johan Willem & vrouw & 1 ch.
Köselich, David
Kramerin, Súsanne
Kristhaús, Johan & vrouw & 6 ch.
Krooschler, Johan Koenraet
Kúm, Hans Jacob & vrouw & 5 ch.
Kúmpff, Johan Peeter & 5 ch.
Kúrts, Johan Kristoffel & vrouw & 2 ch.

Lamain, Frants & vrouw & 4 ch.
Laue, Johan Peter & vrouw & 4 ch.
Lents, Henrig
Lents, Willem & vrouw & 5 ch.
Leúben, Peter & vrouw & 2 ch.
Leÿger, Koenraet & vrouw & 2 ch.
Leÿn, Eberhart Hieronimús & vrouw &
    4 ch.
Lind, Gerhard
Loost, Andires & vrouw & 3 ch.
Lúck, Anoniús

Margreet, Anna
Mattern, Marcús
Matthÿs, Hans
Maúl, Fredrig & vrouw & 2 ch.
Maúl, Hendk. & vrouw
Maúl, Johan & vrouw & 7 ch.
Meisser, Johan Júrg & vrouw & 4 ch.
Melsch, Johan & vrouw
Merlee, Willem & vrouw
Mescherling, Benedik
Mets, Johan & vrouw & 2 ch.
Metsch, Maria Tÿs
Meÿer, Antony & vrouw & 3 ch.
Meÿer, Johan Jacob & vrouw & 6 ch.
Meÿer, Kristiaan
Mëyer, Leendert & vrouw & 1 ch.
Meyer, Simon & 2 ch.

Meÿer, Weÿand & swister
Michel, Johan & vrouw & 2 ch.
Michel, Kasper & vrouw & 3 ch.
Miller, Hans Görg & vrouw & 1 ch.
Moll, Johan Wiand
Mons, Paúlús & vrouw & 2 ch.
Mouts, Kleman & vrouw
Múller, Hans Merde
Múller, Jozep
Múller, Thÿs & vrouw & 1 ch.
Músche, Maria Tÿs

Nagel, Herman
Nef, Júrg, Fredrig & 1 ch.
Nier, Johan Godvried & vrouw & 2 ch.
Niesch, Anna
Niesch, Anna Margreta
Niesch, Hans Henrig & vrouw & 5 ch.
Niesch, Jacob
Niesch, Thomas & 1 ch.
Noigt, Johan Philip & vrouw & 1 ch.

Obber, Valentÿn & vrouw & 2 ch.
Obers, Peter & vrouw & 1 ch.
Örder (?), Johan Adam & vrouw & 2 ch.
Ort, Hans Jacob & vrouw

Peeter, Johan & 2 ch.
Peeter, Johan Koenraet & vrouw & 1 ch.
Peifer, Johan Willem
Petri, Johan Jacob
Petrin, Elizabet & 1 ch.
Petrosines, Remediús & vrouw
Petrÿ, Arent & vrouw & 1 ch.
Petrÿ, Kristiaan & vrouw & 1 ch.
Philip, Johan & vrouw & 3 ch.
Philips, Johan Fredrig & vrouw & 2 ch.
Pinel, Antony & vrouw & 3 ch.
Plenter, Frants
Poller, Kristiaan
Poppelsdorff, Kasper & vrouw & 3 ch.
Prints, Johan & vrouw & 4 ch.
Provo, Hans Peter & vrouw & 3 ch.

Raminger, Daniel & vrouw & 1 ch.
Raúbel, Jacob
Rauch, Johan Kasper & vrouw & 3 ch.
Reck, Samuel
Reinhart, Jozep & vrouw & 6 ch.
Reinhelt, Júrg & vrouw
Repscher, Johan Peter
Repscher, Philip & vrouw & 3 ch.
Restein, Johan & vrouw & 1 ch.
Retschhuff, Johan Paúl
Ritsel, Johan & vrouw & 6 ch.
Ritter, Johan Michel
Rogge, Hans

Rönche, Thÿs & vrouw & 1 ch.
Rosenberger, Johan Philip
Roth, Johan Engelbert
Roth, Joost & vrouw & 3 ch.
Rutsel, Kasper & vrouw & 1 ch.

Salbag, Anna Margreta
Sampt, Johan Sudor & vrouw
Sargúsch, Philip & vrouw & 5 ch.
Sattler, Johan Jacob & vrouw & 1 ch.
Schalt, Johan Peter & vrouw & 6 ch.
Schantsman, Koenraet & vrouw & 3 ch.
Scheefer, Hans Jacob & vrouw & 4 ch.
Scheefer, Johan Andries & vrouw & 2 ch.
Schefer, Johan Mikel & vrouw & 6 ch.
Scheff, Johan Willem & vrouw
Scheffer, Johan Görg
Scheffing, Johanna
Scheifer, Gerhardús
Scheifer, Hans & vrouw & 3 ch.
Schenkelberger, Herman & vrouw & 4 ch.
Schepp, Antonÿ
Schesdons, Kristoffel & vrouw & 3 ch.
Schet, Johan Henrig & 1 ch.
Schilfer, Ludwig & vrouw & 2 ch.
Schitsin, Anna & 7 ch.
Schneider, Gorg
Schneider, Henrig & vrouw & 1 ch.
Schneider, Johan Jacob
Schneiter, Johan Henrig
Schnider, Valentÿn & vrouw & 6 ch.
Schniter, Johan Diderig & vrouw & 6 ch.
Schnüt, Anna Geertrúyt
Schog, Johan Henrig
Schonholts, Ulrig & vrouw & 3 ch.
Schönwolf, Johan Bernhardús
Schredt, Johan & vrouw
Schreiner, Jacob & vrouw & 3 ch.
Schriber, Tieleman
Schú, Johan & vrouw & 4 ch.
Schwab, Hans Otta & vrouw & 1 ch.
Schwachin, Maria Dúrt & 1 ch.
Schwarts, Antony & vrouw & 3 ch.
Sedel, Johan
Seel, Koenraet & vrouw & 2 ch.
Seger, Johan Henrig & vrouw & 1 ch.
Sehn, Johan & vrouw & 4 ch.
Seiner, Gorg
Selter, Kristoffel & vrouw & 3 ch.
Sempt, Peter Adam & vrouw & 6 ch.
Siegman, Hans Peter & vrouw
Smit, Bernhart & vrouw
Smit, Hans Martin & vrouw & 2 ch.
Smit, Johan & vrouw
Smit, Johan Elias
Smit, Johan Joost & vrouw & 4 ch.
Sneider, Hans Willem & vrouw & 6 ch.

Sneiter, Johan Wilhellem
Soeg, Henrik & vrouw & 3 ch.
Solinger, Peter
Spanjert, Johan & vrouw & 4 ch.
Stang, Hans Jacob & vrouw & 3 ch.
Steibing, Johan Peter & vrouw & 2 ch.
Steinebag, Kristoffel & vrouw & 2 ch.
Steinbag, Willem & vrouw & 4 ch.
Steir, Joost & vrouw & 3 ch.
Stelzer, Kasper & vrouw & 5 ch.
Steyg, Miggel
Stier, Peter Adolph & vrouw & 3 ch.
Straúp, Mattÿs
Stúl, Johan Henrig
Stumpf, Hans Görg & vrouw & 2 ch.
Stúner, Johan Michel & vrouw & 2 ch.
Sweever, Margreeta & 3 ch.

Tiedberger, Hans & vrouw & 3 ch.
Teilhauzer, Jacob & vrouw & 7 ch.
Tilenz, Johan Martin
Timmerman, Johan Peter
Timmerman, Koenraet

Ulrig, Fredrig Hartman & vrouw & 2 ch.
Ulrig, Johan & vrouw

Vater, Henrig Michel & vrouw & 3 ch.
Vierstein, Hans & vrouw & 3 ch.
Visbag, Joost
Vischbag, Johan Jacob & vrouw & 7 ch.
Vischer, Sebastiaan & vrouw & 2 ch.
Volk, Johan & vrouw & 1 ch.

Wabel, Hans Jacob & vrouw & 5 ch.
Wabel, Miklas & vrouw & 3 ch.
Walje, Jacob

Wanmager, Koenraet & vrouw & 8 ch.
Wanniger, Johan & vrouw
Wanpag, Herman & vrouw & 4 ch.
Weber, Michel
Weil, Hans Jacob & vrouw & 3 ch.
Weischgerterin, Maria Katrina
Weiser, Johan Koenraet & vrouw & 8 ch.
Wendel, Johan Jacob & vrouw & 1 ch.
Wendel, Peter & vrouw & 3 ch.
Wepel, Valentÿn & vrouw
Werner, Hans & vrouw & 2 ch.
Weÿants, Benedik & vrouw & 1 ch.
Widt, Johan Joost & vrouw & 1 ch.
Wiesner, Görg & vrouw & 2 ch.
Wilhellem, Andreas' (Wed^e.) & 4 ch.
Wilhellem, Johan Joost & vrouw & 3 ch.
Willem, Antonÿ & vrouw & 2 ch.
Willem, Johan & vrouw & 3 ch.
Willemse, Adriaan & vrouw & 4 ch.
Winter, Thomas & vrouw & 4 ch.
Witsch, Niklaas & vrouw & 2 ch.
Witse, Johan Ulrig & vrouw & 2 ch.
Wolff, Hans
Wolff, Johan Richard
Wolfin, Anna & 2 ch.
Wolfin, Eva
Wúst, Leenhart & vrouw & 1 ch.

Yúng, Johan Mikel & vrouw

Zambag, Mathys & vrouw & 5 ch.
Zelts, Adam & vrouw & 1 ch.
Zimmerman, Jacob & vrouw & 3 ch.
Zoot, Fredrig & vrouw & 4 ch.
Zuber, Ulrig & vrouw
Zufungs, Görg & vrouw & 3 ch.

D. ROMAN CATHOLIC PALATINES RETURNED TO HOLLAND

THE TWO lists presented below were found in the Public Record Office, T 1/119, 136-153; T 1/132, 167-170. The first list comprises 2,257 Palatines sent back in 1709, the second includes those 618 returned early in 1711. Because of the difference in the time of their sailing to Holland, it has been considered desirable that the lists be given here separately. Indeed, from the correspondence it appears that another list of about 900 Catholic Palatines should be found in the Treasury Papers in the Public Record Office. Such a list has not turned up and it may be that the 900 mentioned as sailing in 1710 were simply part of the 2,257 Palatines returned in 1709. The lists are not labelled carefully. As to their value generally, the disappointed Palatines may have found their own way eventually to the English colonies, particularly to Pennsylvania, as the large movement to that colony was to swell about 1717 and these people certainly had shown a desire to emigrate.

RETURNED TO HOLLAND IN 1709

Abel, Michel—w. & 2 ch.
Acht, Velden—w. & 2 ch.
Anweÿler, John—w. & 1 ch.
Appel, John Jacob
Arnoldi, Philippus—w. & 1 ch.
Arnolr, John—w. & 5 ch.
Assenbreuer, Wolff

Bachteler, Michel—w. & 4 ch.
Backer, Henry—w. & 8 ch.
Bakkus, Ferdinand—w. & 1 ch.
Balinger, Frantz—w. & 1 ch.
Baseler, Frans—w. & 2 ch.
Bauer, Andreas—w. & 6 ch.
Baum, Feirig—w. & 4 ch.
Baur, Peter—w. & 3 ch.
Baur, Thomas—w. & 8 ch.
Becker, Anthony—w.
Beckman, Michel—w. & 1 ch.
Bekker, John—w.
Bekker, John—w. & 1 ch.
Bellesheim, Peter—w. & 1 ch.
Benedictus, Peter
Bergman, Nicolas—w. & 1 ch.
Bernet, Matthias—w. & 2 ch.
Berrier, John—w. & 2 ch.
Bidsi, Adam—w. & 2 ch.
Bidtiss, John Riedrich—w. & 1 ch.
Biedliss, Henry—w. & 5 ch.
Bietz John's,—widow & 3 ch.
Bigerin, Elisabeth & 1 ch.
Bigerin, Magdalena & 5 ch.
Bilstein, Jacob—w. & 4 ch.
Binder, John—w. & 3 ch.
Birgh, Henry & 3 ch.
Blaese, Christian—w.
Blase, Mary
Boepeleriter, Christian—w. & 3 ch.
Borber, Philips
Bortholm, Matthias—w. & 2 ch.
Braun, Ulrich—w. & 4 ch.

Braune, Andries—w. & 2 ch.
Brick, John—w. & 2 ch.
Brieck, Matthias
Bruiner, John—w.
Brune, Philip—w. & 4 ch.
Bucks, John Bernard—w. & 4 ch.
Bug, Henry—w. & 2 ch.
Bug, John—w.
Bumri, Pancras—w. & 3 ch.
Bundersgell, John—w. & 4 ch.

Calas, Lucas—w. & 3 ch.
Catharina, Anna
Claes, Peter
Claes, Simon—w.
Claesen, John Dietrich—w. & 3 ch.
Cobwasser, Anton—w. & 1 ch.
Coenrad, Matthias
Collet, Michel—w. & 6 ch.
Comas, Peter—w. & 4 ch.
Conrads, Conrad—w. & 1 ch.
Cosch, John Dam—w. & 4 ch.
Crist, John—w. & 2 ch.

Daniel, Anthony—w. & 5 ch.
Dekker, John—w. & 1 ch.
Delman, John—w.
Diere, Hans Martin—w. & 2 ch.
Dietrich, Claes—w. & 7 ch.
Dievedal, Hans Jürg
Dipo, Abraham—w. & 3 ch.
Diwid, Frans—w.
Dohsban, Michael—w. & 4 ch.
Dol, John
Domas, Frans—w. & 1 ch.
Domin, Anna—& 3 ch.

Eberhard, John—w. & 4 ch.
Edian, Bastian—w. & 1 ch.
Eeter, John—w. & 4 ch.
Ehrhard, Michel—w. & 1 ch.

Eiep, Conrad
Eigenman, John—w.
Einhorn, Caspar—w. & 3 ch.
Ellenbergerin, Eva
Engel, John Wᵐ.—w. & 1 ch.
Engel, Martin—w. & 2 ch.
Engel, Peter—w. & 2 ch.
Engel, Robert—w. & 4 ch.
Eninghover, Philip—w.
Erwein, John—w.
Eteler, Paulus—w. & 3 ch.
Euller, Jacob—w.
Eweling, John—w. & 3 ch.
Eÿg, Martin—w. & 4 ch.
Eÿler, Henry—w. & 2 ch.

Feld, Hans Gerard—w. & 6 ch.
Fing, Adam—w. & 1 ch.
Fingin, Orsel—w. & 1 ch.
Finken, Elisabeth
Fischer, Gerhard—w. & 3 ch.
Fischer, Henry—w.
Fischer, John—w. & 1 ch.
Fischerin, Marg
Flohr, John—w. & 4 ch.
Flohr, Peter
Foog, Henry—w. & 1 ch.
Forer, John—w. & 2 ch.
Franck, Michel
Friderick, Charles—w. & 4 ch.
Frisch, Nicolas—w. & 3 ch.
Friss, John—w. & 2 ch.
Funck, Caspar—w. & 1 ch.

Gali, Andreas
Gali, Jacob
Gallobers, Gobeck—w. & 3 ch.
Garino, Peter—w.
Gavas, Thomas—w. & 3 ch.
Gebel, Anth.—w. & 6 ch.
Gebell, Henry—w. & 2 ch.
Gerber, Jacob
Geres, John—w. & 2 ch.
Gerhard, Hans Peter—w.
Gieng, Elisabeth
Glasser, Bartholomeus—w. & 2 ch.
Gräber, Peter—w.
Gress, Georg—w. & 5 ch.
Gress, Georg, jun.—w. & 1 ch.
Grosman, John—w. & 3 ch.
Gru, David—w.
Gudt, John—w. & 2 ch.
Guttien, Nicolas—w. & 6 ch.

Haen, Michael—w.
Hag, Christian—w. & 3 ch.
Hageboech, Dietrich—w. & 2 ch.

Hain, Friedrich—w. & 2 ch.
Hains, John Valentin—w. & 2 ch.
Hamer, John Wilhelm—w. & 4 ch.
Han, Caspar—w. & 1 ch.
Han, Matthias—w. & 2 ch.
Hans, Michel
Hansen, Bernard—w. & 3 ch.
Hansin, Anna Maria & 5 ch.
Hansin, Eva
Hardman, John Conrad—w. & 2 ch.
Hardt, John
Hartman, Hans Jurg—w. & 1 ch.
Hartwig, Matth.—w.
Hauff, Peter—w.
Havig, Jost—w. & 6 ch.
Heber, Joseph
Heins, Nicolas—w. & 1 ch.
Heiser, Jacob—w. & 4 ch.
Heiserin, Cristina
Hell, Balth.—w. & 5 ch.
Helmschrodt, John—w.
Hemerstorff, Haubert
Herbst, Hans Georg—w. & 3 ch.
Herfener, John Steffen
Hergaet, Peter—w. & 1 ch.
Herland, Conrad—w. & 3 ch.
Herman, Wikket—w. & 2 ch.
Herr, John—w. & 3 ch.
Hersin, Margareta & 3 ch.
Heyneman, John Henry—w. & 2 ch.
Hill, John—w. & 2 ch.
Hoff, Peter—w. & 5 ch.
Hoffer, Christian
Hoffman, Jost—w. & 2 ch.
Hogenberger, John Nicolas—w. & 4 ch.
Holtzlender, Albertus—w. & 5 ch.
Huberin, Marg
Hulgas, Conrad—w. & 4 ch.

Jacks, Peter—w. & 3 ch.
Jägerin, Mary
Jener, Jörg—w. & 1 ch.
Jkkert, Paltis—w. & 2 ch.
Jndepan, Stoffel—w. & 1 ch.
Jockim, John—w. & 1 ch.
Jong, John—w. & 1 ch.
Joon, Henry—w. & 5 ch.
Jörgo, Anthony—w. & 5 ch.
Joseph, Cornelis—w. & 3 ch.
Josten, Johannes—w. & 5 ch.
Jrwitter, Francis—w. & 2 ch.
Justina, Margareta & 1 ch.

Kaltdauer, Michel—w.
Kaltdauer, Velten—w. & 5 ch.
Keers, Adam—w. & 1 ch.
Keiseler, Hans Jurg—w. & 1 ch.

Keisser, Philippus—w. & 1 ch.
Kerger, John—w. & 1 ch.
Kern, Frederic—w. & 1 ch.
Kern, Michel—w. & 2 ch.
Kerpen, Nicolaes—w. & 1 ch.
Kert, Anthonius—w. & 1 ch.
Kesserling, Henry—w. & 1 ch.
Keÿer, John
Kien, Herman—w. & 1 ch.
Kien, John—w. & 1 ch.
Kies, John Jost—w. & 3 ch.
Kiffer, Philip—w. & 7 ch.
Kimmel, Hans Peter—w. & 5 ch.
Klaes, William—w. & 1 ch.
Klé, Charles & 2 ch.
Kleemans, Felte—w. & 1 ch.
Klees, John—w.
Klein, Matth.—w. & 1 ch.
Klein, William—w. & 3 ch.
Kleiss, Jorg—w.
Klapper, Conrad—w. & 3 ch.
Kleÿn, Michel—w. & 5 ch.
Klitter, Georg—w.
Knauber, Paulus—w. & 6 ch.
Knedig, Jonas—w. & 1 ch.
Knees, Michael—w. & 4 ch.
Knepel, Andreas—w. & 3 ch.
Knittelmeÿer, Caspar
Köchin, Cath. & 3 ch.
Kolb, Frans—w. & 2 ch.
Koll, Conrad
Koll, Peter
Kollet, Gerhard—w. & 2 ch.
Konig, Jacob—w. & 8 ch.
Kontenskein, Andreas—w. & 3 ch.
Koping, Cristoph
Korn, Michel—w. & 8 ch.
Kosserer, John—w. & 4 ch.
Krafft, Matthias—w. & 3 ch.
Krass, Philip—w. & 4 ch.
Krebs, Jost
Krehmer, Philip—w.
Krielion, John—w. & 1 ch.
Kries, John—w. & 5 ch.
Krissilles, Dominick—w. & 1 ch.
Krissilles, Wm.—w. & 4 ch.
Kristilles, Jurg—w.
Kroebard, Matth.—w. & 4 ch.
Krumbs, Jacob—w. & 1 ch.
Krÿss, Matth.—w. & 6 ch.
Krÿts, John—w. & 2 ch.
Kÿrsteen, Martin
Kun, Mattheus—w. & 1 ch.
Kurtz, John—w. & 2 ch.

Laan, Philip—w. & 2 ch.

Land, Anthon—w.
Land, Philip—w.
Lang, Christian—w. & 4 ch.
Lang, Peter—w. & 2 ch.
Langin, Lea
Lans, Moritz—w. & 4 ch.
Laras, John—w. & 6 ch.
Lasara, Anna & her sister
Lassarig, John—w.
Lauer, Hans Nicolas—w. & 1 ch.
Lauer, John—w. & 3 ch.
Lauer, John—w. & 4 ch.
Laurens, Michel—w. & 4 ch.
Lautwein, Henry—w. & 4 ch.
Leberd, Hans Jacob—w. & 3 ch.
Leborn, Matthias
Ledig, Hans Nickel—w. & 1 ch.
Leephaen, John & 1 ch.
Leijdecker, Henry—w.
Lenaker, Peter—w. & 4 ch.
Lens, Henry—w. & 3 ch.
Leonhard, Peter—w. & 1 ch.
Leonora, Barbara
Leora, Anna
Lerny, Matth.—w. & 3 ch.
Less, John Adam—w. & 3 ch.
Levin, Maria
Levin, Wm.—w. & 1 ch.
Liber, John
Lindeboom, Peter—w. & 1 ch.
Linderin, Anna Maria
Littermeÿer, Andreas—w. & 3 ch.
Loos, John—w. & 2 ch.
Loriss, Matthew—w. & 3 ch.
Loriss, Ulrich—w. & 1 ch.
Louka, Maria & 4 ch.
Ludwig, Andreas
Ludwig, Anthony—w.
Lut, Ulrich—w. & 3 ch.
Luts, John—w. & 2 ch.
Lutser, John—w. & 2 ch.
Lutz, John—w. & 4 ch.
Lux, Adam

Malena, Maria & 1 ch.
Malleberger, Till—w.
Mallefyn, John Peter—w. & 1 ch.
Mallerswed, Bastiaen
Mandernock, Wm.
Marcks, Matth.—w.
Marg:, Anna
Maria, a widow, 2 ch.
Martin, Matth.—w. & 3 ch.
Martin, Peter—w.
Massia, Nicolas—w. & 6 ch.
Massin, Cath.

Matthew, Peter—w. & 4 ch.
Matthias, John—w. & 3 ch.
Matzer, Paulus—w.
Maur, Hans—w. & 5 ch.
Maurer, John Jacob—w. & 1 ch.
Meenen, John
Meens, Anthony—w. & 2 ch.
Meerman, Jost—w.
Megler, John Mattheus
Melchior, Frantz—w.
Mellerd, John Nikel—w. & 1 ch.
Mengel, Hans Georg—w. & 4 ch.
Mets, Simon—w. & 3 ch.
Metshouer, John—w. & 1 ch.
Mey, Peter—w. & 2 ch.
Meÿer, Hirg—w.
Meÿer, John Adam—w. & 1 ch.
Meyer, Paulus—w. & 1 ch.
Mieler, Caspar—w. & 2 ch.
Miller, Anna Marg
Miller, Peter—w. & 2 ch.
Miller, Peter—w. & 2 ch.
Min, John—w. & 6 ch.
Minck, Peter—w. & 2 ch.
Mini, Jör—w. & 4 ch.
Mitwig, Hermanus—w. & 2 ch.
Mondriaen, Salus—w. & 3 ch.
Moor, Gerhard—w. & 4 ch.
Morheister, Nicolas—w. & 2 ch.
Moriz, Dietrich—w. & 3 ch.
Mosi, Matthias—w. & 5 ch.
Mostert, Lambert—w. & 3 ch.
Mots, Frederick—w.
Muller, Ehrhard—w. & 1 ch.
Muller, Hans Hurge—w.
Muller, Henry—w. & 4 ch.
Muller, John—w. & 1 ch.
Muller, Kilian—w.
Muller, Nicholaus—w. & 4 ch.
Muller, Philip—w. & 3 ch.
Mullerin, Barbara
Mullerin, Maria
Mullerin, Maria & 6 ch.
Mulseberg, Dietrich—w. & 6 ch.
Musseler, Jacob—w. & 1 ch.

Negener, Michel—w. & 1 ch.
Neles, Michel—widow & 2 ch.
Nelles, John Jacob—w. & 3 ch.
Nettel, Laurens Hagen
Neumenin, Maria
Neumeÿer, Wentz—w. & 2 ch.
Neuss, Andreas
Nicola, Peter—w. & 3 ch.
Nilgen, Maria
Noll, Herbert
Notterman, John—w. & 4 ch.

Null, Herbert

Obel, John—w. & 1 ch.
Obernheimer, Henry—w. & 1 ch.
Oberreidter, Hans Georg—w. & 3 ch.
Oberscheiner, Peter—w. & 2 ch.
Obert, Martin—w. & 1 ch.
Oostwaltin, Otelia & 1 ch.
Opperdubbel, John Jacob—w. & 2 ch.
Ortering, Nicolas—w. & 4 ch.
Otsbergerin, Anna Cath.
Otsenberger, John—w. & 1 ch.
Otterman, John—w. & 4 ch.

Palser, Jacob—w. & 3 ch.
Paner, Jacob—w. & 1 ch.
Paulus, Michel
Paulusin, Agnes & 2 ch.
Peer, Frederic—w.
Peltemer, John—w. & 2 ch.
Pens, Jacob—w. & 2 ch.
Perkin, Elisabeth
Petri, Adam—w.
Petri, Andreas—w. & 3 ch.
Petruzin, Remetius—w.
Petter, Jacob—w.
Pieck, Conrad
Pinheimer, Bartholome—w. & 3 ch.
Pleij, John—w. & 3 ch.
Pletseler, Georg—w. & 2 ch.
Plinling, Cristian—w. & 4 ch.
Poeck, Joseph
Polser, Henry—w. & 2 ch.
Pon, Hans William—w.
Pons, Nicolas—w. & 3 ch.
Pooser, Nicolaes—w. & 3 ch.
Portman, Jost—w. & 1 ch.
Poself, John
Poster, Arend—w.
Pouer, Matthew—w. & 2 ch.
Pras, Andreas—w. & 2 ch.
Preiss, John
Premer, Jacob—w. & 4 ch.
Pretser, Ulrich—w. & 3 ch.
Prietzgis, Friederic—w. & 1 ch.
Pritz, John—w. & 3 ch.
Prol, Jost—w.
Pross, Hans Peter—w. & 3 ch.
Pull, Nicolas

Quint, Anthony—w. & 1 ch.

Rauch, Matthias—& 4 ch.
Reggert, John Henry
Rehrer, Hans Jacob—w. & 1 ch.
Reicherd, Dietrich
Reidinger, Adam—w.

Reinhart, Caspar—w. & 1 ch.
Reise, John Henry—w. & 4 ch.
Reisenberg, Lorens—w.
Reiter, Matth.—w. & 1 ch.
Remer, John—w. & 2 ch.
Rick, Jacob—w. & 2 ch.
Riel, Jacob—w. & 5 ch.
Ries, Matthew
Riesen, Anna Catharina—& 1 ch.
Ring, Anthony—w. & 1 ch.
Ringer, Jacob—w. & 1 ch.
Ritterstein, Georg—w. & 3 ch.
Ritz, John
Ritz, Jörg—w.
Ritzkorn, Hans Michel & 1 ch.
Robbenicker, Nicolaes—w.
Rodenfluger, John—w. & 1 ch.
Rose, Laurentz—w. & 2 ch.
Rosmarien, Catharina
Rosskops, Martin—w. & 3 ch.
Roth, Jacob—w. & 2 ch.
Rupen, Arnold
Rupix, Matth.
Ryes, Hans Georg—w. & 2 ch.

Sachs, Bastian—w. & ch.
Sarton, Henry—w. & 3 ch.
Schadt, John Peter—w. & 5 ch.
Schaff, Bartholomeus—w. & 1 ch.
Schaffern, Marg: & 3 ch.
Schamerin, Catharina & 4 ch.
Scharning, Andreas—w. & 2 ch.
Scheefer, Gerhard—w. & 2 ch.
Scheeser, Philip—w. & 1 ch.
Scheffer, John—w. & 4 ch.
Scheffer, Laurens
Scheffer, Reinhard—w. & 2 ch.
Scheffer, Servas—w. & 1 ch.
Scheffle, Henry—w. & 1 ch.
Scherner, Michaël—w. & 5 ch.
Scheul, Flg.—w. & 2 ch.
Schiffer, Nicholaus—w.
Schilder, John—w.
Schinkel, Hans Jacob—w. & 3 ch.
Schleÿer, John—w. & 1 ch.
Schlitz, Martinitz—w. & 1 ch.
Schmidt, Hans Michel—w.
Schmidt, Matthias—w.
Schmidt, Nicolas—w. & 4 ch.
Schmidt, Peter
Schneider, Arnold—w. & 2 ch.
Schneider, Casper—w. & 5 ch.
Schneider, Hans Michel—w. & 2 ch.
Schneider, John—w. & 2 ch.
Schneider, Nicolas—w. & 3 ch.
Schneider, Peter—w. & 2 ch.
Schneider, Philip—w. & 3 ch.

Schneider, Philip—w. & 4 ch.
Schnell, Mattheus
Schöfferin, Catharina
Scholt, John—w. & 1 ch.
Scholter, Tebalt—w. & 4 ch.
Schönberger, Bartholomeus—w. & 1 ch.
Schorin, Anna Cristina
Schreiner, Jacob—w. & 1 ch.
Schreiner, John Martin
Schrÿver, Jacob—w. & 6 ch.
Schuch, Nicolas—w. & 7 ch.
Schüler, Matthias—w. & 4 ch.
Schüler, Peter—w. & 5 ch.
Seiger, John—w.
Serbing, John—w. & 1 ch.
Sernart, John, Jr.—w.
Seyberger—w. & 4 ch.
Sider, John—w. & 1 ch.
Sieffer, Bastian—w.
Sirin, Jurg Peter—w. & 1 ch.
Siss, Peter—w. & 6 ch.
Sissig, Herman—w. & 3 ch.
Sivin, John—w. & 1 ch.
Sleiss, Matth.—w. & 7 ch.
Slick, Martin—w.
Smit, Hans Peter—w. & 2 ch.
Smit, Jaspar—& 8 ch.
Smit, John—w. & 1 ch.
Smit, Michel—w. & 1 ch.
Smit, Nicolas—w. & 3 ch.
Smith, Nicolas—w. & 1 ch.
Smonck, Joseph—w.
Soeck, Peter—w. & 2 ch.
Soller, Dominicus—w. & 6 ch.
Sommer, Jacob—w. & 1 ch.
Sondag, Francis—w. & 2 ch.
Sorg, Matthias—w. & 3 ch.
Spadt, Ludwig
Specht, John—w. & 2 ch.
Speiss, Ferdinandus—w. & 1 ch.
Spierck, Martin—w. & 6 ch.
Spinler, Caspar—w. & 4 ch.
Spoor, Matth.—w. & 1 ch.
Stahl, Dietrich—w. & 1 ch.
Stahl, Hans Georg—w. & 3 ch.
Stahl, Martin—w. & 1 ch.
Steenhouer, Christian—w. & 4 ch.
Steffing, Catharina
Stein, Hans Michel—w. & 3 ch.
Ster, Cristian—w. & 1 ch.
Steyn, John—w.
Steÿner, Michel—w.
Stick, Herman—w. & 2 ch.
Sticker, Michel—[sic]
Stress, Michel
Stucker, John—[sic]
Sturtüe, Caspar

Stutz, John—w. & 4 ch.
Swaebs, Philip
Swertel, Conrad—w. & 4 ch.
Syman, Simon—w. & 4 ch.

Taelem, Lambert—w. & 1 ch.
Taes, John—w. & 3 ch.
Tamper, Henry—w. & 3 ch.
Taub, Michel—w. & 1 ch.
Teiss, Thomas—w. & 1 ch.
Thibelhoffen, Jörg—w. & 3 ch.
Thilschneider, John—w. & 2 ch.
Thinkel, Andreas—w. & 2 ch.
Thomas, Johannes—w. & 5 ch.
Thomas, John
Thomas, Matth:
Thomas, Matth.
Thomasin, Barbara & 2 ch.
Tielman's widow & 3 ch. (no other name)
Tielsbergen, Georg—w. & 1 ch.
Ties, Hans Peter
Tirstin (sic)—w. & 4 ch.
Tirt, Hans Adam—w. & 2 ch.
Tragseil, Jacob—w. & 5 ch.
Trap, Laurens—w. & 4 ch.
Treeser, John—w. & 2 ch.
Tres, John—w.
Trip, Matth:—w.
Tusch, John—w. & 4 ch.

Uder, Michel—w. & 5 ch.

Vagner, Nicolas—w. & 1 ch.
Valadin, John—w. & 4 ch.
Veigert, John Valentin
Veilandt, Peter—w. & 1 ch.
Viber, John Matth.
Visering, Anna Marie
Vogelsberger, Peter—w.
Vogt, Daniel—w. & 2 ch.
Volck, John—w. & 1 ch.
Voltraut, John Matthias—w. & 5 ch.
von Bergen, Hans Peter—w. & 1 ch.
Voos, Serves—w. & 5 ch.
Vorbeck, Hane Georg—w. & 2 ch.
Vot, Hans Peter—w. & 2 ch.
Vuchs, Arnold—w. & 3 ch.

Wagener, Cath:
Wagener, Felte—w. & 3 ch.
Wagener, John—w. & 1 ch.
Wagener, John Eberhard—w. & 2 ch.
Wagener, Nicolas—w. & 4 ch.
Wald, Caspar Rickte—w. & 2 ch.
Waller, John—w.
Walter, Adam—w. & 3 ch.
Wälter, Matth.—w. & 4 ch.
Wanemacher, Henry—w. & 1 ch.
Warner, Andreas—w. & 2 ch.
Weber, Auinstin—w.
Weber, Dietrich—w. & 2 ch.
Weber, Jacob—w. & 3 ch.
Weber, Matth.—w.
Weber, Michel—w. & 2 ch.
Weber, Philip
Weillmacher, Matthias—w. & 3 ch.
Weinberg, Conrad—w.
Weisgerber, John—w. & 2 ch.
Wels, Jacob
Wenmer, John—w.
Widi, Bernard—w. & 4 ch.
Widschlägem, Magdalena
Wikketeÿ, Philip—w.
Wilbert, Hans Martin—w. & 4 ch.
Wilhelmi, John—w. & 3 ch.
Wilhelmse, Adrian—w. & 2 ch.
Will, John
Willer, Philips—w. & 3 ch.
Wimer, Simon
Wind, Peter—w. & 3 ch.
Wintenseimer, Christoph—w. & 5 ch.
Winter, Thomas—w. & 3 ch.
Wintzenheimer, Peter
Witer, Martin—w. & 4 ch.
Witner, Michel—w. & 3 ch.
Wolff, Caspar
Wolff, Henry—w.
Wolff, Jörg—w. & 4 ch.
Wölffle, Peter—w.
Wolschlager, Michel
Wÿckel, Felte—w. & 5 ch.

Ysel, Anthony—w. & 1 ch.

Zirvas, Peter—w. & 6 ch.

RETURNED TO HOLLAND IN 1711
Additional persons are signified by pr. or prs.

Albrecht, Jacob
Altvader, Faltin & 2 prs.
Alwiger, Hans Wilhelm
Apple, Christian & 5 prs.
Ascher, Jacob & 4 prs.

Baeker, Andreas & 3 prs.

Bahr, Andreas & 1 pr.
Bath, George & 1 pr.
Bauman, Joost & 2 prs.
Bauwer, Christiaen & 2 prs.
Becker, Frederick & 2 prs.
Bher, Peter & 1 pr.
Beihard, Eliz.

Bihm, Martin & 1 pr.
Braun, Dewald & 2 prs.
Brener, George & 1 pr.

Casner, Andreas & 5 prs.
Casnerin, Mar: Eliz: widow
Cleman, Bestian & 4 prs.
Cleman, Peter & 1 pr.
Cramer, Ludwick & 2 prs.
Craemer, Pieter
Creitzin, Eliz., wid. & 4 prs.

Dauhn, George & 2 prs.
Dhiel, Christiaan & 1 pr.
Diehl, Herman & 3 prs.
Ditner, David & 2 prs.
Dohrbach, Johan Jost
Donnerel, Jacob & 1 pr.

Eberech, Johannes & 3 prs.
Eberhartin, Fronick & 3 prs.
Ecker, Jacob & 2 prs.
Elberger, Hans George & 2 prs.
Emmel, Anthony & 4 prs.

Faller, Johannes & 5 prs.
Farey, Henrich & 4 prs.
Fatheyer, George & 4 prs.
Fatheyer, Martzele & 1 pr.
Feyersteen, Leonard & 5 prs.
Fucs, Andreas & 4 prs.
Fuhrman, Mathias & 1 pr.
Frebes, Joh. Nicolaes & 7 prs.

Gerbie, Michael & 2 prs.
Gess, Godfried & 3 prs.
Getell, Joh. Peter & 1 pr.
Geyer, David & 4 prs.
Gross, Frederick & 2 prs.
Gruberin, Marg.

Hahn, Mathias & 1 pr.
Harnisch, Johannes & 2 prs.
Hatt, Conrad & 2 prs.
Hawel, Andreas & 2 prs.
Hecht, Caspar & 7 prs.
Heck, Conrad & 3 prs.
Heck, Henrick & 3 prs.
Hein, Daniels
Herbert, Jacob & 3 prs.
Herman, Bastian & 1 pr.
Hern, Hans Henrich & 4 prs.
Hertzheimer, Henrik Thiel & 1 pr.
Hes, Jeremias & 3 prs.
Heym, Paul & 2 prs.
Heymaker, Johan Jacob & 1 pr.
Hillard, Marg.
Hiram, Christina & 1 pr.

Jacob, Christian & 3 prs.
Jacobs, Barth. & 2 prs.
Jager, Balthazer & 2 prs.
Jost, Christopher & 2 prs.

Kehl, Adam & 1 pr.
Kehl, Peter & 3 prs.
Khyn, Hendrick & 3 prs.
Kiefer, Daniel & 2 prs.
Klogner, Adam & 5 prs.
Klop, Nicolaes & 5 prs.
Klotter, Johan & 1 pr.
Koller, Jacob & 7 prs.
Kornman, Peter & 2 prs.
Kuts, George & 3 prs.
Kyhn, Peter & 2 prs.
Kytter, Diedrick & 5 prs.

Labegeyer, Godfried & 1 pr.
Lang, Johannes & 5 prs.
Leiterman, Christopher & 1 pr.
Lingelbach, Barbara, widow & 3 prs.
Loch, Henrich & 4 prs.

Messer, Sylvester & 4 prs.
Meyer, Henrick & 3 prs.
Meyer, Leonard & 2 prs.
Mick, Johannes & 2 prs.
Mickel, Caspas & 4 prs.
Miller, Jacob & 2 prs.
Mitterbauer, Jacob & 3 prs.
Muller, Peter & 7 prs.
Muller, Valentin & 1 pr.
Musher, Jacob & 1 pr.

Netzel, Rudolph & 3 prs.
Neyman, Ludwick & 3 prs.
Nonius, Johan Peter & 2 prs.

Ohness, Henrich & 2 prs.

duPré, Johan & 2 prs.
Reisser, Michael & 2 prs.
Reitzer, Johannes & 1 pr.
Reuter, Wilhelm & 2 prs.
Rinck, Melchior & 4 prs.
Ritte, Nicolaes
Roerbach, Christian & 2 prs.
Rohn, Johan & 7 prs.
Roop, Johannis & 1 pr.
Roth, Johannes & 3 prs.
Roth, Johannes Jost & 3 prs.
Rottelin, Maria, widow & 6 prs.

Schaffer, Adam & 3 prs.
Schaffer, Conrad

Schelberger, Conrad & 2 prs.
Schenk, Nicolaes & 1 pr.
Schenkin, Anna Maria & 1 pr.
Schick, Mathys & 2 prs.
Schickedanee, Christopher & 3 prs.
Schildebuck, Martin & 1 pr.
Schildt, Henrich & 2 prs.
Schuck, Nicolaes & 5 prs.
Seydelmeyer, Mich. & 1 pr.
Shaffer, Johan & 2 prs.
Shaffer, Nicolaes & 4 prs.
Shaller, Jacob & 1 pr.
Sharr, Daniel & 2 prs.
Shober, Christiaen & 3 prs.
Sieb, Michael & 2 prs.
Simon, Zacharias & 4 prs.
Sinkhaen, Conrad & 2 prs.
Sletzer, Jeremias & 5 prs.
Slingloff, Johannes & 4 prs.
Slisser, Andreas & 3 prs.
Smith, Casper & 3 prs.
Smitzer, Martin & 2 prs.
Sneider, Peter & 2 prs.
Spengler, Frans & 1 pr.
Spengler, Fredr. & 4 prs.
Steyer, George & 4 prs.
Swartz, Christiaen & 1 pr.
Swartz, Johannes & 3 prs.

Theyse, Peter & 2 prs.
Thiel, George & 4 prs.
Thiel, Johannes & 2 prs.
Tickert, Andires & 3 prs.

Umbach, Johan Georg & 3 prs.
Unverricht, Jacob & 5 prs.

van der Myl, Philip & 8 prs.
Voight, Abraham & 5 prs.

Wabbel, Jacob & 5 prs.
Walter, Philip & 2 prs.
Waltman, Leonard & 3 prs.
Weber, Casper
Weber, Henrich & 5 prs.
Weisman, Henrick & 4 prs.
Weisner, Elisabeth, widow & 2 prs.
Weissin, Elisabeth & 1 pr.
Weyler, Andris & 4 prs.
Wickel, Jonas & 1 pr.
Windt, Henrich & 5 prs.
Wipff, Jacob & 1 pr.

Zents, Mathias & 1 pr.
Zieger, George & 3 prs.
Ziegler, Nicolaes & 4 prs.
Zinck, Rudolph & 4 prs.
Zittel, Jacob & 3 prs.
Zwartz, Jacob & 7 prs.

E. THE NEW YORK SUBSISTENCE LIST

THIS LIST was compiled from the "journal" of Palatine debtors to the British government for subsistence given either in New York City or in the Hudson River settlements, from their landing in 1710 to September, 1712. The list was found in the Public Record Office, C. O. 5/1230 and was corrected from the accompanying "ledger," C. O. 5/1231. As it seemed advisable to include some indication of the number in each family and since limitations of space forbade the inclusion of the six notations at various times given in the journal, only two notations have been given here, that is, the first in 1710 usually and the last in 1712 normally. Thus, with "Abelman, Johann Peter 2-1, 2-0," the size of the family signified is two adults and one child under ten years of age; by 1712 the child had died for we have noted only two adults. All children over ten years of age were given the full allowance for adults and were therefore not distinguished from more mature members of the family. Where only one notation of family size appears, the presumption is of death, or in the case of women, of marriage.

Abelman, Johann Peter 2–1, 2–0
Anspach, Johann Balthaser 2–0, 2–0
Anthes, Conrad's (widow) Margretha
   3–1, 2–1
Arnold, Jacob (Arnoldi, Johannes) 4–0,
   5–0
Arthopoeus, Johann Adolph 3–0, 3–0
Asmer, Philipp 2–0, 2–0

Baches, Agnes 1–0
Bähr, Johannes 2–2, 6–2
Bähr, Jacob's (widow) 2–2, 2–0
Ballin, Anna Catharina 3–1, 3–1
Barthel, Henrich 4–1, 4–1
Barthelin, Anna Dorothe 1–0
Barthin, Anna 3–1
Bason, Nicolas 1–2, 2–2
Bäst, Johann Henrich 2–2, 2–3
Bäst, Jacob 2–0, 2–0
Bäst, George 1–1, 2–0
Battorffin, Anna 3–0, 1–0
Batzin, Anna Catharina 1–1, 1–1
Bauch, Christian 2–2, 4–1
Baum, Mathias 3–0, 1–0
Baumann, Adam 4–2, 3–2
Baumannin, Anna Margretha 1–0, 3–0
Baumarsin, Anna Maria 1–0, 1–0
Bayerin, Anna Margretha 2–0, 2–0
Beck, Andreas Friderich 1–2, 2–2
Becker, Peter 2–0, 2–1
Becker, Johann Friderich 0–1, 4–1
Beckerin, Maria 1–0, 1–0
Beckerin, Senr, Elizabeth 1–0
Beckerin, Junr, Elizabeth 1–0, 1–0
Beckerin, Anna Catharina 2–2, 1–2
   (married Johann Christian Haus)
Beckerin, Anna Dorothe 1–0, 1–0
Beckerin, Magdalena 2–2, 2–2
Bellin, Elizabetha 2–0, 4–1
Bellinger, Henrich 2–0, 2–1
Bellinger, Johannes 4–0, 5–0
Bellinger, Marcus 4–0, 4–1
Bellinger, Nicolaus 6–0, 3–0
Bellingin, Elizabeth 2–0, 2–0
Bender, Georg 2–1, 3–1
Bender, Valentin 2–1, 2–0
Bender, Peter's (widow) 3–1, 3–1
Benderin, Anna Maria 3–2, 1–1
Berck, Christian 1–0
Berg, Johannes 2–1, 3–0

Berg, Abraham 2–0, 2–1
Bergman, Andreas 3–0, 1–0
Beringer, Conrad 1–0, 2–2
Berlemann, Johannes 1–0, 2–1
Berner, Georg Ludwig 1–3, 2–1
Bernhardt, Johann Jost 2–0, 2–1
Bernhardt, Johannes 2–2, 3–3
Bernhardt, Ulrich 2–0, 2–0
Berter, Gerhard & Anna Bertin 1–0, 1–0
Bertram, Jacob 3–0, 2–0
Betzer, Hermann 5–2, 5–1
Beyer, Johann Jacob 1–1, 1–1
Beyerin (dicta Beurin), Susanna 1–1, 1–1
Bierman, Johannes 1–2, 3–1
Blass, Johannes 2–1, 3–2
Böhler, Johann Henrich 1–0, 3–3
Böhm, Henrich 2–0, 3–0
Bollin, Sophia 1–0, 1–0
Bonn, Frantz (Le Febvre dictum Bonn)
   2–0, 1–0
Bonenstiel, Niclaus 2–0, 3–1
Bonroth, Johannes 1–0, 4–0
Born, Jacob and his sister 2–0, 2–0
Börsch, Ludwig 2–1, 3–2
Börsch, Jonas 3–2
Borst, Jacob 2–0, 2–2
Böshaar, Jacob 6–2, 5–2
Böshaar, Johann Jacob 2–0, 3–0
Bousche, Daniel 2–0, 2–0
Brachin, Anna Catharina 1–0
Brack, Johann Michael 2–0, 2–0
Brandaw, Wilhelm 2–1, 2–2
Brandorff, Jost 3–1
Braun, Johann Jost 3–5, 5–3
Braun, Johann Paul 2–0, 2–0
Brendel, Caspar 2–2, 1–1
Bresseler, Valentin 4–2, 5–2
Bretter, Anthoni 1–0, 2–0
Briegel, Georg 2–0, 2–0
Brillin, Anna Margretha 2–1, 3–1
Brillemännin, Helena 3–0, 1–0
Bromwasser, Anna Gertrud 1–0, 1–0
Brong (Bronck), Matheus 3–0, 4–0
Bruchle, Henrich 1–0, 2–0
Bruyere, Susanne 2–0, 2–0
Bruyere, Jeanne 2–1, 2–1
Buff, Johann Georg 2–0
Buok (Buk), Martin 2–2, 2–2
Burckardt, Ulrich (dicta Brucker) 3–0, 3–1
Burckhardt, Johannes 4–1, 1–0

Bouche, Daniel 2–0, 1–0
Busch, Senr, Daniel 2–2, 3–0

Caputscher, Johann Jacob 4–1, 4–1
Cast, Johannes 1–0, 1–0
Castner, Johann Conrad 5–0, 1–0
Castner, Johann Peter 2–0, 3–2
Champanois, Daniel 2–2, 2–2
Christmann, Hanns 3–3, 5–3
Christmännin, Elizabeth 1–2, 3–0
Clevenius, Bernhard 2–3, 4–0
Conrad, Henrich 2–0, 2–1
Conradin, Anna 2–1, 2–1
Coring, Ludolph 6–1, 3–1

Dachstätter, Georg 2–1, 2–2
Dahles, Johann Wilhelm 2–0, 2–1
Danler, Ulrich 1–0, 2–1
Dannemarcker, Christoph 3–1, 3–1
Darrey, Conrad 1–0, 1–0
Däther, Lorentz 3–0, 3–0
Datt, Johann Bernhard 2–2, 3–1
Dausweber, Melchior 5–0, 4–1
Deffu, Daniel 2–2, 3–1
Demuth, Jacob 4–2, 5–0
Demuthin, Anna Catharina & son George
    4–0, 4–0
Demuthin, Anna Maria 1–0
Demuthin, Agnes 2–0
Deubig, Johann Paul 1–1, 1–0
Dietrich, Christian 3–2, 4–0
Dietrich, Johann Jacob 6–2, 5–2
Dietrich, Johann Wilhelm 4–0, 4–1
Dietrichin, Anna Elizabeth 3–1, 3–0
Dievenbach, Conrad & mother Anna 3–1,
    1–0
Diewel, Johannes 2–1, 3–2
Diewel, Johann Peter 2–0, 2–1
Diewehert (Deuchert), Werner 5–2, 6–3
Dill, Annanias (alias Thiel) 2–2, 1–2
Dill, Wilhelm 1–2, 1–0
Dillin, Anna Clara 1–0, 1–0
Dillebachin, Barbara & son Martin 2–0,
    2–1
Dilteyin, Catharina 5–1, 6–0
Dinant, Peter 2–2, 2–1
Dings, Jacob 4–0, 5–0
Dorn, Lazarus (alias Trum) 2–4, 2–3
Dörner, Johannes 2–1, 2–0
Dörner, Jacob 3–0, 3–0
Dornheiser, Jacob 1–0
Dontzbachin, Anna Elizabeth 3–0
Dontzbach, Frantz 4–0, 2–1
Dopff, Johann Peter 5–0, 5–0
Drauth, Ludwig's (widow) 1–0, 1–0
Drechsler, Peter 2–1, 2–2
Dreuthin, Catharina 4–1, 1–0

Dreuthin, Elizabeth 1–0
Drumm, Andreas 3–1, 3–1
Drumbaur, Niclaus 2–3, 3–3
Duntzer (Duntier), Paulus 2–1, 3–0

Eberhard, Johannes 1–0, 2–0
Eckardt, Niclaus 2–0, 1–0
Eckardtin, Gertrud 2–1, 3–0
Eckhardt, Adam 2–1, 3–0
Eckling, Johann Georg 2–3, 4–3
Ehemann, Thomas 1–1, 3–0
Ehlig (Ehelig), Andreas 2–1, 2–2
Eigenbrod, Elizabeth 2–0
Eigler, Christian 2–0, 2–1
Elsass, Paul 2–0, 1–1
Emichen (Emigen), Johann Ernest 2–2,
    4–0
Emich, Johann Niclaus 2–0, 2–1
Emmerich, Johannes 3–0, 2–1
Emmerich, Johann Michael 2–0, 2–0
Emrichin, Anna Maria 1–1, 1–1
Engel, Johannes 2–2, 2–2
Engelin, Maria Elizabetha 1–0, 1–0
Engelbert, Johan Peter 3–0, 3–0
Engelsbrucher, Niclaus 3–0, 3–0
Engstenburger, Tilleman 1–0
Enners, Bertram 3–0, 3–0
Erbin, Catharina 1–1, 1–1
Erckel, Bernhard 1–0, 2–0
Erhardt, Simon 1–3, 3–2
Eschenreuter, Henrich 2–0, 2–0
Eschoffin, Catharina 1–0, 1–0
Eschwein, Thomas' (widow) 2–0, 2–0
Ess, Jacob 2–0, 2–0
Eswein, Jacob 3–3, 2–3
Eygner, Peter's (widow) 1–0, 2–0
Eygner, Peter 2–0, 2–1
Eygnerin, Jeremia 1–0

Faeg, Peter 2–3, 3–2
Faeg, Johannes 7–0, 7–1
Fähling, Henrich 2–1, 2–1
Falck, Arnold 2–1, 2–0
Falckenburg, Johann Wilhelm 1–1, 2–1
Fasius, Johannes 0–1, 1–0
Fasius, Valentin 1–0, 1–0
Feller, Niclaus 2–2, 4–2
Fewersbach, Dietrich 1–0, 1–0
Fidler, Gottfrid 2–0, 2–0
Fils (Fills), Wilhelm Philipp 1–0, 1–0
Fills, Philipp 2–0
Finck, Johann Wilhelm 2–2
Finck, Frantz 2–0, 1–0
Finck, Andreas 3–0, 3–1
Finckin, Magdalena 2–2, 1–1
Filtz, Melchior 2–0, 2–1
Finckel, Johann Philipp 2–2, 2–1

Fischer, Peter 1–0
Fischer, Sebastian 2–1, 2–1
Flugler, Zacharias 1–1, 3–0
Förster, Johan Georg 3–1, 3–2
Franck, Johannes 1–0, 3–2
Fred, Johann Georg 2–0, 2–0
Freil, Christoph 1–0
Frey, Henrich 2–1, 2–0
Freyin, Barbara 1–1, 2–0
    (married Paulus Duntzer)
Freymeyer, Michael 3–2, 3–4
Friderich, Conrad 4–0, 4–0
Friderich, Hanns Adam 1–0, 2–0
Frillin, Maria Elizabeth 1–0, 1–0
Fritz, John Wilhelm (Johann Wilhelm)
    3–0, 3–0
Frölich, Stephan 2–3, 3–1
Frölich, Valentin 2–2, 2–2
Fuchs, Johann Christoph 2–0, 3–0
Fuchs, Johann Philipp 8–0, 7–0
Fuchs, Johann Peter 2–1, 3–0
Fuhrer (Fühler), Johannes 3–1, 4–1
Funck, Peter 2–4, 4–2
Fuhrman, Jacob (Fuhrmann) 3–1, 4–0

Galadeh, Anna Maria & brother 2–1, 1–0
Gantz, Johannes 3–0, 2–2
Gebelin, Anna Margretha 2–1, 1–2
    (married Philipp Wolleben)
Georg, Johann Anthoni 2–0, 1–0
    (Johann Anthony)
Georg, Johann Wilhelm 2–0, 2–1
Georgin, Anna Elizabeth 1–0, 1–0
Gerlach, Johann Christ 3–2, 5–1
Gerlach, Peter 3–0, 3–0
Gerlachin, Ottilia 1–2, 1–2
Germann, Jacob 2–1, 2–1
Gerner, Georg
Gesinger, Henrich 3–0, 2–1
Getel, Daniel's (widow) 6–2, 3–0
Gettmännin, Barbara 2–0
Gettmännin, Maria Barbara 2–0
Gieserin, Sibilla (Sybilla) 1–0
    (married John Eberhardt)
Giesler, Peter 3–1, 2–2
Glock, Henrich 1–3, 3–2
Glump, Philipp 2–0, 2–1
Goldmann, Conrad 2–3, 4–1
Gondermann, Johann Friderich 3–2, 6–0
Grad, Johannes 3–2, 3–3
Grauberger, Philipp Peter 2–0, 3–1
Graw, Gerlach's (widow) 4–3, 2–0
    (Ledger adds Catharina Grawin)
Grawsin, Anna Maria 1–2, 1–2
Greisler, Johann Philipp 2–2, 4–0
Gresserin, Maria Elizabeth 3–1, 3–1
Griffon, Marie 1–1, 1–1

Griot, Jean 1–0, 1–0
Grucko, Arnold 1–2, 1–2
Grucko, Johann Peter 1–0

Haas, Simon 2–1, 3–2
Haas, Niclaus 3–3, 4–3
Haber, Christian 3–0, 1–0
    (Ledger adds Elizabeth Haberin)
Hagedorn, Peter 7–0, 6–0
Hagedorn, Johann Peter 1–0, 1–0
Häger, Johann Friderich 1–0, 1–0
Hägerin, Maria 1–1, 2–0
    (married a Joh. Muller)
Hähn, Johann Georg 2–1, 3–1
Haintz, Urbanus 3–0, 3–1
Hambuch, Johann Wilhelm 2–0, 2–0
Hämer, Johann Henrich 4–0, 4–1
Hamm, Conrad 2–0, 2–1
Hamm, Peter 2–1, 2–2
Hammin, Gertrude 1–0
    (married Zacharias Flugler)
Härter, Johan Michael 3–3, 4–2
Härter, Johann Niclaus 3–2, 3–2
Hartman, Johann Herman 2–0, 2–1
Hartmann, Peter 2–1, 2–1
Hartmännin, Anna Maria 1–0, 1–0
Hartwig, Caspar 2–3, 3–2
Harttwell (Härttel), Adam 3–0, 3–1
Häsel, Wilhelm 1–0, 1–0
Häselin, Johann Henrich 1–0, 1–0
Hassmann, Dietrich 2–0, 2–1
Häupt (Haupt), Philipp 3–0, 2–1
Hassman (see Hussmann), Herman
Haug, Lucas' (widow) (Margretha) 4–2,
    6–1
Haug, Plaichard 2–1, 2–2
Haus, Johann Christian 4–3, 5–4
Hayd, Niclaus 2–0, 2–1
Hayd, Johann Jost 2–0, 2–1
Hayd, Peter 2–2, 2–1
Haÿdin, Maria Cunigunda 1–1, 1–0
Häyer, Henrich 2–1, 2–1
Hebmann, Michael 4–2, 6–0
Heel, Jacob 2–1, 2–0
Heitersbach (Heyterbach), Niclaus 1–2,
    1–2
Helmer, Philipp 5–3, 7–1
Helmer, Peter 2–2, 2–2
Hemmerle, Anna Barbara 1–1, 1–1
Henneschiedt, Michael 2–3, 3–2
Henrich, Lorentz 1–1, 2–4
Herman, Jost 3–1, 3–1
Herner, Ludwig Ernest 4–1, 3–1
Hertzel, Jacob 3–1, 3–0
Hertzog, Henrich's (widow) 1–0, 1–0
Hess, Johannes 1–0, 2–0
Hess, Niclaus 2–3, 2–3

Hetterich, Johannes 2–1, 2–0
Hettich, Johannes Conrad 2–0, 2–1
Heuser, Johann Peter 3–0, 2–2
Heydelberg, Georg Jacob 2–3, 2–3
Heydin, Anna Maria 1–1, 1–0
Heydorn, Henrich 3–1, 4–1
Heyner, Johannes 1–0, 2–1
Hildebrand (Hildebrandtin) Anna Catharina 1–0
Hirchemer, Georg 2–1, 4–0
Hoff, Johann Adam 3–0, 3–0
Hoff, Andreas 2–0, 2–0
Hoffertin, Anna Maria 1–0, 1–0
Hoffin, Margretha 3–0
Hoffmann, Conrad 3–3, 4–3
Hoffmann, Gabriel 2–0, 2–2
Hoffmann, Herman 2–1, 2–0
Hoffmann, Jacob 2–0, 2–1
Hoffmann, Henrich 1–2, 5–1
Hoffmännin, Anna Eva 1–0, 1–0
Hoffmännin, Anna Catharina 1–0
Homburger, Thomas 2–0, 1–0
Höniger, Michael 2–0, 2–0
Horne, John 2–0, 3–0
Horne, Caspar 2–0
Hornich, Niclaus 2–0, 1–0
Horning, Gerhard 2–0, 2–0
Hothenrothin, Veronica 2–0
Huckin, Barbara 1–0, 1–0
Huls, (Hülls), Christoph 4–1, 4–2
Hummel, Georg 3–0, 3–0
Hummel, Herman 3–0, 2–0
Huner, Benedict 2–2, 2–2
Huppert, David 3–1, 4–0
Hussmaun, Johann Adam 1–0
Hussmann, Hermann 3–5, 6–2

Jacobi, Ulrich 2–0, 2–0
Jäger, Wendel 3–1, 3–0
Jäger, Christian 1–0, 2–1
Jamm, Peter 1–1, 1–1
Jifflandt, Johann David 2–1, 2–3
Jngold, Ulrich 2–0, 2–0
Jttich, Johann Michael 1–2, 3–2
Jung, Henrich 2–0, 2–1
Jung, Johann Eberhard 2–1, 1–1
Jung, Johannes 2–0, 2–0
Jung, Peter 2–0
Jung, Theobald 1–0, 1–0
Jungin, Anna Elizabeth 3–1, 4–0
Jungin, Juliana 1–0, 1–0
Jungin, Maria 3–0, 3–0
Jungens, Niclaus 2–0, 2–0

Kabsin, Anna Sibilla (Anna Sybilla) 1–0, 1–0
Kähl, Johann Wilhelm 2–1, 2–1

Kämer, Johann Wilhelm 3–2, 3–1
Kämg, Johann Peter 3–0, 3–0
Käschelin, Anna Margretha 1–0, 1–0
Kasselmann, Christian 2–0, 2–1
Kasselmann, Dietrich 4–1, 4–1
Kasr, Johann Georg 2–3, 3–3
Kaÿsser, Johann Wilhelm 3–1, 4–1
Kayser, Johann Matheus 1–0, 1–0
Kayserin, Maria 3–0, 1–0
Käsin, Eva Catharina 1–0, 0–1
Keller, Frantz 2–0, 2–1
Keller, Christian's (widow) 5–1, 4–1
Kercherin, Anna Maria 3–1, 2–0
Kessler, Johannes 2–0, 2–0
Kisslerin, Anna Maria 1–0, 1–0
Ketter, Henrich 2–2, 2–2
Kieffer, Johann Wilhelm 4–2, 5–0
Kiesler, David 1–0, 2–0
Kirtzenberg, Elizabetha 1–0
Klapperin, Anna Agatha 1–1, 1–0
Klein, Adam 1–0, 1–0
Klein, Henrich 1–0, 1–0
Klein, Hyeronimus 2–2, 4–1
Klein, Johann Herman 1–0, 2–0
Klein, Johann Jacob 2–1, 3–1
Klein, Johannes 2–0, 2–0
Klein, Peter's (widow) 1–1, 1–1
    (married John Blass)
Kleinin, Helena 1–1, 1–1
Klopp, Peter 1–0, 1–0
Klotterin, Susanna & son Caspar 2–4, 1–0
Klotter, Henrich 2–2
Klug, Johann Georg 2–1, 2–1
Knab, Ludwig 1–1, 1–1
Kneibin, Helena Sophia 1–0, 1–0
Kneskern, Johann Peter 2–0, 3–0
    (Hans Peter)
Kobel, Jacob 1–0, 2–1
Koch, George Ludwig 2–0, 2–1
Kocherthal, Josua 1–0, 4–2
Kohlmeyerin, Catharina 1–0, 1–0
Kölsch, Anna Eva 1–0
Kölsch, Johann Henrich 1–0, 1–0
König, Marcus 4–0, 3–1
Kopff, Jacob 1–0, 6–0
Korn, Johann Henrich 1–0, 2–1
Körner, Niclaus 2–4, 4–1
Kornmann, Peter Jacob 3–0, 4–0
Krafftin, Ann Ursula 1–0
Krämer, Anthoni 1–1, 3–0
Krämer, Johannes 2–1, 1–2
Krämerin, Anna Maria & Michael Krämer 4–3, 2–3
Krantz, Johann Henrich 1–2, 4–0
Krantz, Conrad 2–1, 1–0
Krembs, Johannes 2–0, 2–2
Kugel, Johannes 2–0, 2–0

Kuhlmer, Johannes 3–3, 4–2
Kuhlmann, Georg 2–3, 6–2
Kuhn, Conrad & son Valentin 2–1, 2–0
Kuhn, Johann Jacob 3–0, 3–0
Kuhn, Samuel 6–1, 4–2
Kuhn, Valentin (son of Conrad) 1–0, 2–1
Kuhner, Benedict 2–2, 2–2
Kundy, (Gundy) Matheus' (widow) 2–0, 2–0
Kuntz, Mathias 5–1, 3–2
Kuntz, Matheus 3–0
Kuntz, 1st, Jacob 2–0, 2–0
Kuntz, 2nd, Jacob 2–0
Kuntz, Johannes 1–1, 4–1
Kurtz, Johann Christoph 2–2, 2–2

Labach, Johannes 2–0
Laib, Johann Caspar 1–1, 1–1
Lahmeyer, Johannes 1–0, 1–0
Lambertin, Elizabeth 3–1, 2–0
Lamet, Johannes 2–0, 2–0
Lampmann, Peter 3–2, 3–1
Läncker, Johannes 2–0
Landgraff, Georg 4–0, 4–0
Langer [alias Lelong], Abraham 2–1, 5–0
Langin, Magdalena 1–2
Lantin, Anna Catharina 3–1, 5–0
Lappin, Agnes 2–0, 3–0
Lauck, Abraham 2–1, 4–1
Lauck, Johann Jacob's (widow Elizabeth) 2–0, 1–0
Laucks, Johann Niclaus 2–0, 2–1
Laux, Georg 6–0, 5–0
Laux, Johann Dietrich 2–1, 2–0
Laux, Johann Jost 2–0, 3–0
Laux, Johann Philipp 3–0, 2–2
Laux, Johannes 2–0, 2–0
Laux, Philipp 1–0, 2–3
Lawer, Peter 3–1, 3–1
Lehemann, Wilhelm 2–1
Lehr, Johannes 3–2, 5–1
Leicht, Henrich 2–0, 3–0
Leicht, Ludwig 2–0, 2–0
Leick, Johannes 2–0, 3–0
Lein, Conrad 4–3, 5–1
Lenckin, Maria Catharina (& son) 2–0, 2–0
Lepper, Philipp Hermann's (widow) 1–0, 2–0
Lesch, Balthasar's (widow) (Susanna) 2–3, 3–1
Lescherin, Magdalena 3–2, 1–1
Leyer, Johannes 4–0, 2–1
Lickard, Bernard 2–0, 2–0
Lincken, Johann Wilhelm 2–0, 2–2
Linsin, Appolonia 3–1, 3–1

Lorentz, Johannes 5–1, 5–1
Löscher, Jacob 2–2, 2–3
Löscher, Sebastian 5–4, 5–3
Lottin, Anna Catharina 2–2, 2–2
Lucas, Georg 2–1, 6–1
Lucas, François 3–3, 4–3
Ludwig, Johann Henrich 2–0, 3–1
Lutzin, Anna Barbara 2–0, 2–0
Lutzin, Magdalena 2–0, 2–0

Madebachin, Eleonora 1–0
Maisinger, Conrad 2–0, 3–3
Maisinger, Sebastian & son Nicholas 1–1, 2–0
Manck, Jacob 3–2, 6–0
Mann, Henrich 2–0, 2–1
Marterstock, Albrecht Dietrich 1–0, 2–1
Martin, Johann Conrad 1–1, 4–0
Marxin, Maria Magdalena 1–0
Mathesin, Anna 2–0, 3–0
Matheus, Andreas 1–0, 1–0
Matheus, (Matthias) Georg 2–0, 2–0
Matheus, Johann Martin 1–0, 2–0
Mathias, (Matheus) Henrich 4–3, 4–3
Mauer, Georg 3–0, 3–0
Maul, Christoph 2–0, 2–0
Maul, Johann Friderich 2–2, 4–2
Maul, Johannes' (widow) 2–4, 4–1
Maurer, Johann Georg 2–0, 3–0
Maurer, Peter 3–0, 3–0
Mauser, Johann Georg 2–2, 2–1
Mausin, Eva 1–0, 1–0
May, Christoph's (widow) 1–0
May, Peter 2–3, 2–2
Mayin, Ottilia 1–0
Mengelin, Anna Maria (Wengel Mengel's widow) 1–1, 1–3
Menges, Johannes 3–2, 3–0
Mentgen, Ferdinand 4–1, 4–0
Merckel, Friderich 3–2, 6–1
Mertzin, Anna Catharina 1–3, 2–2
Mess, Henrich 2–0, 2–0
Messerin, Anna Margretha 2–1, 2–1
Meyer, Christian 2–0, 2–0
Meyer, Friderich 3–1, 4–0
Meyer, Henrich 1–0, 1–0
Meyer, Henrich (another) 1–0, 2–1
Meyerin, Elizabeth 1–2, 2–0
Meyin, Barbara 1–0
Meyin, Maria 1–1, 1–0
Meysenheim, Anna Gertrud 0–1
Michael, Hans Henrich (& Sydonia Michel) 1–0, 3–3
Michael, Johann Georg's (widow) 2–2. 2–1
Micheal, Niclaus 2–0, 2–1
Milch, Johann Eberhard 1–0, 1–0

Milges, Johann Wilhelm 4–1, 2–1
Minckler, Kilian 4–1, 3–1
Mittler, Johannes 1–0, 3–0
Monin, Maria 2–1, 1–1
Moor, Henrich 2–0, 2–1
Moor, Johann Christ 3–1, 3–1
Moor, Philipp Wilhelm 1–1, 2–0
Morellin, Anna Eva 3–1, 2–0
Motsch, Johannes 2–0, 2–0
Muller, Adam 3–1, 0–1
Muller, Adam 2–1, 4–0
Muller, Johann Christoph 1–0, 1–0
Muller, Johann Conrad 2–1, 2–1
Muller, Johann Georg 2–0, 2–2
Muller, Johann Henrich 1–2, 1–0
Muller, Johann Wilhelm 2–0
Muller, Johann Wilhelm 2–0, 1–0
Muller, 1st, Johannes 2–0, 2–1
Muller, 2nd, Johannes 2–0, 2–0
Muller, Johannes' (widow) (Elizabeth)
    4–2, 2–2
Muller, 1st, Philipp 5–3, 6–0
Muller, 2nd, Philipp 2–1, 4–0
Muller, 2nd, Philipp's (widow) (Maria)
    1–1
Muller, Samuel 2–0, 3–1
Mullerin, Anna Margretha 1–1
Mullerin, Anna Margretha 3–0, 2–0
Mullerin, Anna Maria 1–0, 1–0
Mullerin, Catharina 1–0
Mullerin, Christina 1–0, 1–0
Musig, Johann Jost 1–0
Musig, Veit 2–1, 2–1
Musinger, Jacob 3–0, 5–0

Neff, Georg Friderich 2–1, 1–1
Neher, Carl (Carol) 1–3, 3–2
Neis, Abraham's (widow) 3–1, 3–1
Nelles, Johannes Wilhelm 3–1, 3–1
Nellesin, Maria Elizabeth 3–1, 3–1
Nerbel, Johann Georg 1–1
Ness, Georg Wilhelm's (widow) (An:
    Cath.) 4–0, 2–0
Netzbackes, Johann Martin 2–0, 2–0
Newkirch, Johann Henrich 3–2, 4–1
Neythäber, Quirinus 4–0, 4–0
Noll, Bernhard 2–0, 2–0
Nollin, Anna Margreth 1–0
Nollin, Elizabeth 1–0, 1–0

Oberbach, Georg 4–0, 5–0
Oberbach, Johann Peter 2–0, 2–1
Oberbach, Peter 2–0, 2–1
Oberer, Johann Jacob's (widow) 2–0, 2–2
Oberin, Anna 1–0, 1–0
Off, Jacob, 2–3, 2–3
Ohrendorff, Henrich 2–0, 2–1

Pasch, Daniel's (widow) (Veronica) 3–0,
    2–0
Peter, Philipp 3–0, 3–0
Peterin, Anna Gertrude 1–0, 1–0
Petri, Gertrude 2–1, 2–1
Petri, Johann Jost 2–0, 2–0
Pfeffer, Michael's (widow) Catharine &
    son Michael 2–0, 2–1
Pfeiffer, Henrich's (widow Catharina)
    2–1, 2–0
Pfeiffer, Severin's child 0–1
Pfuhl, Johann Peter 3–1, 3–1
Philips, Peter 3–1, 5–0
Planck, Johannes 3–1, 3–2
Plies, Emerich 2–0, 2–1
Pottner, Johann Paul 2–0, 3–0
Proppert, Johann Jost 3–2, 3–2
Prunet, Paul 1–1, 2–0
Pulver, Johann Wilhelm 2–2, 3–3

Räbel, Daniel 1–0, 1–0
Rainault, Peter 1–0, 1–0
Rainault, Pierre 1–0, 5–0
Rauch, Niclaus 3–0, 4–1
Raudenbusch, Johann's (widow) 1–0, 1–1
Rausch, Caspar 3–2, 3–3
Rauscher, Martin 2–0, 2–0
Raw, Niclaus (orphan) 0–1, 1–0
Rawin, Anna & Joh. Georg Raw 3–1, 3–1
Reich, Balthasar 3–1, 2–1
Reichardt, Joseph, his wife A. M.
    Träberin 4–0, 3–0
Reiffenberg, Johann Georg 4–0, 3–1
Reinboldt, Matheus 4–0, 4–0
Reisdorff, Johannes 1–0, 2–1
Reitschuff, Johann Paul 1–0, 2–1
Reitzbackes, Johannes 2–2, 3–2
Reuther, Henrich 2–0, 2–2
Richter, Andreas 3–2, 3–0
Rickardt, Conrad 2–3, 3–2
Riclausin, Christina 1–0, 1–0
Riedt, Johann Leonhardt 5–2, 2–1
Riedtin, Anna Catharina 6–1, 4–1
Riegel, Christoph 1–0
Riehl, Gottfrid 1–0, 2–0
Rietich, Johann Peter 4–0
Rietichin, Amalia 1–0, 1–0
Risch (Reisch), Jacob 3–2, 3–3
Ritzwig, Johannes 1–0
Rohrbach, Johannes 4–2, 4–2
Rohrbachin, Anna Elizabeth 1–1, 1–1
Römer, Georg 1–1, 2–1
Römsch, Christian 3–0
Roos, Andreas 3–1, 1–0
Roschmann, Johannes 2–1, 2–2
Rosenbaum, Bernhard 4–1, 3–1
Rosenzweig, Agnes Gertrude 1–0, 1–1

Rothin, Anna Catharina 1–0
Rouch, Friderich 3–2, 3–2
Rues, Ludwig 3–3, 1–1
  (Ledger includes Cunigunda Rusin)
Ruffner, Thomas 2–0, 2–0
Ruger, Johann Philipp 3–0, 4–1
Ruhl, Niclaus 2–2, 3–1

Salbach, Johann Egmund 2–0, 2–0
Salbach, Johannes 3–0, 2–0
Saxin, Anna Gertrude 4–0, 4–0
Saxin, Anna Maria 1–0, 1–0
Schäff, Wilhelm 3–0, 7–0
Schäffer, Friderich 2–0, 2–1
Schäffer, Georg 2–0, 1–1
Schäffer, Gerhard 3–1, 4–1
Schäffer, Jacob 2–1, 1–1
Schäffer, Johann Niclaus 4–4, 8–3
Schäffer, Johann Werner 2–0, 2–0
Schäffer, Johannes 5–2, 5–1
Schäffer, Joseph 3–4, 2–2
Schäffer, Jost Henrich 2–1, 3–0
Schäffer, Reinhard 2–0, 2–1
Schäfferin, Elizabetha 1–0, 1–0
Schäfferin, Maria Elizabeth 4–2, 5–3
Schäfferin, Maria Margretha 1–0
  (married Henrich Glock)
Schaib, Hyeronimus 2–0, 3–1
Schaidt, Anthoni 2–0, 2–0
Schantz, David 2–0, 1–0
Schawerin, Magdelena 2–2, 2–2
Schawermann, Conrad 2–1, 2–1
Schellin, Anna Gertrud 1–0
Schellin, Anna Margretha 1–0, 1–0
Schenckel, Jonas 3–2, 4–1
Schenckelberg, Christina 1–0, 1–0
Scherb, Jacob 2–1, 2–2
Scherer, Johann Theobald 2–0, 3–3
Scherer, Ulrich's (widow) 2–0, 1–0
Schermann, Henrich 3–0, 4–0
Schieffer, Philipp 4–1, 4–1
Schienck, Michael 1–0, 1–0
Schleumer, Mathias 3–0, 3–1
Schley, Johann Peter 3–0, 3–0
Schlicherin, Anna Margretha 2–1, 1–1
Schmidin, Anna Barbara 2–0
Schmidin, Elizabeth 1–1, 1–1
Schmidin, Gertrude (Gertrud) 1–1, 1–0
Schmidin, Margretha or Adam Michael
  Schmïd. 1–1, 1–1. Five payments were
  made: the first 4 to Margretha Schmidin
  and the last to Adam Michael Schmid.
Schmidt, Adam's (widow, Anna Barbara)
  3–2, 1–1
Schmidt, Bernhardt 2–0, 2–1
Schmidt, Georg Adam 1–0, 2–0

Schmidt, George Volbert & son Adam
  4–1, 3–1
Schmidt, Henrich, Senr. 3–0, 4–1
Schmidt, Henrich, Junr. 2–1, 2–0
Schmidt, Johann Adam 1–0
Schmidt, Johann Georg 2–1, 2–2
Schmidt, Johann Henrich 2–3, 6–0
Schmidt, Johann Wilhelm 1–0, 1–0
Schmidt, Ludwig 2–0, 2–0
Schmidt, Martin 1–0
Schmidt, Nicolaus 6–1, 5–2
Schmidt, Peter 1–0, 2–1
Schmidt, Ulrich 4–0, 3–2
Schmidt, Valentin 6–1
Schneider, Henrich 2–1, 2–2
Schneider, Jacob 2–1, 2–1
Schneider, Jacob 2–1
Schneider, Johann Dietrich 4–2, 4–2
Schneider, Johann Wilhelm 1–0, 2–0
Schneider, Johann Wilhelm, Senr. 5–0, 5–1
Schneider, Johann Wilhelm, Junr. 1–0, 1–0
Schneider, 1st, Johannes 2–3, 3–2
Schneider, 2nd, Johannes 3–0, 3–0
Schneiderin, Catherina & son Peter 1–0,
  1–0
Schnell, Jacob 4–2, 4–2
Schottin, Anna Maria 1–0
Schramn, Henrich 4–1, 5–0
Schreiber, Albertus 2–0, 2–1
Schremle, Henrich 1–2, 1–1
Schuch, Johann Wilhelm 2–1, 1–1
Schuch, Johannes 4–0, 5–1
Schucherin, Anna Catharina, 1–1, 1–1
Schultheis, Johann Georg 6–2, 6–1
Schultheis, Johannes 1–0, 2–0
Schultheisin, Anna Barbara 1–0
Schultzin, Anna Elizabetha 1–0
Schumacher, Daniel 2–2, 2–2
Schumacher, Jacob 3–0, 3–1
Schumacher, Thomas 2–1, 1–0
Schumacherin, Anna Eva 1–3, 1–1
Schunemann, Herman 1–1, 2–1
Schuppmaun, Herman 6–2, 4–2
Schurtz, Michael & his son Andreas 6–1,
  5–1
Schutz, Conrad 5–0, 4–0
Schutz, Johan Adam 3–1, 3–0
Schutz, 1st, Philipp 4–0, 2–1
Schutz, 2nd, Philipp's (widow, Catha-
  rine) 3–1, 3–1
Schwalb, Johannes 2–0, 2–0
Schwedin, Anna Elizabeth 3–1, 2–0
Schwitzler, Henrich 4–0, 3–1
Segendorff, Johann Adam's (widow) 3–0,
  3–0
Seib, Henrich's (widow) 2–1, 1–1
Sein, Johann Peter 1–0, 2–0

Selner, (Sellner), Johann Adam 1–1, 4–0
Seubert, Johann Martin 2–2, 2–2
Sex, Henrich's (widow) 3–0, 1–0
Sibelin, Anna Getha 3–1, 4–0
Signer, Johannes' (widow) 1–3, 1–1
Simendinger, Ulrich 1–0, 2–0
Simon, Philipp's (widow) 1–0, 1–0
Simon, Wilhelm 1–1, 2–2
Simonin, Anna Margretha 1–0
Simonin, Maria Magdalena 1–0
Sitternich, Christian 3–1, 3–1
Spanheimer, Johann Georg 4–1, 4–1
Speder, Johannes 2–0, 3–1
Speichermann, Sebastian 1–0, 2–1
Spickerman, Johann Herman 1–0, 5–1
Spies, Peter 1–0, 1–0
Spoon (alias Muller), Henrich. 2–1, 2–1
    In the Ledger this is entered
    "Heinrich Muller, natus Spon"
Spuler, Jacob 2–0, 1–0
Stahl, Henrich 3–1, 2–0
Stahl, Johannes 3–0, 3–1
Stähl, Joseph 2–0, 1–0
Stähl, Rudolph 3–1, 2–2
Stambuchin, Anna Margretha 1–0, 1–0
Staringer, Niclaus 3–0, 4–2
Stayger, Nicolaus 3–2, 4–1
Stayger, Stephan 2–0, 2–0
Stein, Martin 1–0, 3–1
Sterenberger (Sternberger), Jacob 2–0, 4–2
Stier, Jost 3–0, 2–0
Stöckelin, Anna Maria 2–1, 2–1
Stoppelbein, Peter 2–1, 2–1
Storr, Michael 2–1, 3–1
Straub, Johannes 2–0, 2–1
Streith, Christian 4–3, 4–2
Streithin, Magdalena 1–4, 1–3
Strichhäuser, Balthasar 3–2, 4–1
Stubenrauch, Georg Henrich 2–0, 2–1
Stuber, Henrich Balthasar 1–0, 2–0
Stuber, Jacob 3–1, 3–1
Stuckradt, Johann Wilhelm 2–3, 3–2
Stumpff, Johann Georg 2–1, 4–0
Stupp, Martin 4–0, 4–0
Sutz, Johann Dietrich 3–1, 3–0

Täschem, Hubert 2–0, 1–0
Theis, Johann Philipp 2–0, 3–0
Thiel, Adolph 2–1, 2–1
Thomas, Andreas 1–1, 4–0
Thomas, Henrich 5–1, 6–0
Thomas, Henrich Peter 2–2, 2–2
Thomas, Johann Georg 2–1, 2–0
Träberin, (erroneously Täberin in Sum-
    mary) Anna Maria (married to Jos.
    Reichard) 2–1, 2–1
Trillheuser, Johannes 2–0, 1–0

Uhl, Carol 4–1, 3–1
Uhl, Henrich 2–0, 2–1
Ulrich, Johann Elias 2–0
Umbertro, Valentin 1–0, 1–0

Vandeberg, Cornelius 2–1
Velten, Johann Wilhelm 3–1, 4–0
Vogt, Simon 2–0, 2–0
Volbert, Jacob's (widow) 2–2, 2–1
    (Ledger adds Catharina Volbertin)
Vollandin, Anna Regina 1–2, 1–2

Wagner, Johann Christ 1–0
Wagner, Peter 2–1, 2–1
Walborn, Johann Adam 4–3, 5–2
Wallrath (Walrath), Henrich Conrad
    2–0, 2–1
Walrath (Walraht), Gerhardt 2–2, 3–0
Wannemacher, Dietrich 2–0, 3–0
Wannemacher, Peter 1–0, 1–0
Wanner, Ludwig 2–1, 2–2
Warembourg, Maria 5–0, 5–0
Warno, Jacob 2–0, 1–0
Weber, Henrich 2–1, 2–1
Weber, Jacob 2–1, 2–0
Weber, Niclaus 2–0, 2–1
Weber, Valentin 2–0, 2–0
Weber, Wigand 1–0, 0–1
Weberin, Ottilia 2–0, 2–0
Wegele (Wegle), Michael 1–2, 2–1
Weidschopff, Johann Peter 1–0
Weillin, Catharina 2–0, 2–0
Weis, Mathias 1–0, 1–0
Weis, Stephan 2–0, 2–0
Weisborn, Georg 3–1
Weiser, Johann Conrad 5–2, 6–1
Weisin, Susanna 1–1, 1–1
Weller, Hyeronimus 2–0, 2–1
Wendelin, Anna Juliana 1–0, 1–0
Wennerich, Balthasar 3–2, 5–1
Wennerich, Benedict 2–2, 2–2
Werner, Christoph 2–1, 2–2
Werner, Michael 3–0, 2–0
Weydin, Gertrude 2–2, 2–1
Weydknecht (Weidknicht), Andreas 3–1,
    3–0
Wickhausen, Peter 2–0, 2–1
Widerwachs, Henrich 3–1, 3–2
Wies, Melchior 4–1, 5–1
Wilhelm, Anthoni's (widow) 2–0, 1–0
Wilhelm, Niclaus' (widow) 3–1, 2–0
Wilhelm, Paul 2–0, 2–0
Windecker, Harttman 1–2, 3–2
Winninger, Ulrich 2–1, 2–0
Winther, Henrich 5–0, 5–0
Wisener (Wiesener), Johannes 3–1, 5–0
Wittmann, Johann Martin 1–0, 3–1

Wittmuchin (Wittmachin), Maria Catharina 1–0, 1–0
Wohleben, Anna Catharina 5–0, 2–0
Wohleben, Christoph 2–0, 2–0
Wohleben, Michael 1–0, 1–0
Wohleben, Philipp 1–0, 3–0
Wohleben, Valentin 2–1, 2–0
Wolbach, Engelbert 1–0, 1–0
Wolbert, Niclaus 1–1, 1–1
Wolffin, Anna Gertrud 3–1, 2–1
Wolffin, Maria Catharina 1–0
Wolffin, Maria Clara 0–1, 0–1
Wolleben, Peter 2–2, 2–0
Wormbs, Christian 5–1, 6–0
Woschel, Augustin 4–2, 4–0

Woschel, Peter Anthoni 2–0, 1–1
Wulffen, Gottfrid 4–0, 4–0
Wurmserin, Anna 1–1
Wüst, Conrad 2–2, 3–2

Zangerin, Johanna 2–3, 1–2
Zehe, Johannes 3–0, 3–1
Zeller, Johann Henrich 2–0, 3–1
Zeller, Johannes 4–0, 5–0
Zerbe, Martin 3–4, 3–3
Zerbe, Philipp 2–0, 2–1
Zimmermann, Johann Jacob 3–1, 2–0
Zipperle, Bernhard 3–2, 3–2
Zufeld, Johann Georg 2–3, 3–2
Zwickin, Veronica 3–2, 2–2

F. THE SIMMENDINGER REGISTER

THIS LIST contains the Appendix of Ulrich Simmendinger's pamphlet, *Warhoffte und glaubwürdige Verzeichnüss jeniger Personen; welche sich anno 1709 aus Teutschland in Americam oder neue welt begeben.* . . . (Reuttlingen, ca. 1717). A copy is in the rare book room of the New York Public Library. Another copy is in the possession of Dr. Gustav Anjou, West New Brighton, Staten Island, New York. Simmendinger, who was one of the immigrants himself, returned to Germany in 1717 and there published this brief account of the emigration and the names of those Palatine families still living in New York. The family names were given by Simmendinger under fourteen locations. These lists have been brought together into one alphabetised list, but the locations are preserved by including after the family head's name the letter of the alphabet, denoting the location according to the following key.

Quüinsberg	= (a)	Neu = Quüinsberg	= (h)
Wormsdorff	= (b)	Neu = Heidelberg	= (i)
Hunderston	= (c)	Neu = Heessberg	= (j)
Heessberg	= (d)	Neu = Ansberg	= (k)
Becksmansland	= (e)	Diese Menschen wohnen auf	
		dem Rarendantz	= (l)
Neu = Stuttgardt	= (f)	In Neu = Yorck	= (m)
Neu = Cassel	= (g)	Hackensack	= (n)

The first four villages comprised East Camp on the land purchased from Robert Livingston on the east side of the Hudson River. These villages have been identified as Queensbury, Annsbury, Hunterstown, and Haysbury respectively, as they are named in the New York Colonial MMS., LV, 100. Beckmansland, judged by the identification of certain individuals in the list, comprised the three villages on the west side (West Camp), given in *loc. cit.* as Elizabeth Town, George Town, and New Town. However, it is possible that the families identified may have moved to the east side of the river south of Livingston Manor, and the location of Beckmansland may be the Rhinebeck area. The objection to this surmise is that it leaves us without any notation of families living in West Camp. The villages marked (f) to (l) are apparently German names for the seven Schoharie Valley settlements, probably used only in the pamphlet to impress the people in the Fatherland for whom the lists were prepared. Tentatively, by the identification of a few family names known to reside in the several villages, they appear to be as follows:

Neu = Stuttgardt (f)	——	Weiserdorf
Neu = Cassel (g)	——	Gerlachsdorf
Neu = Quünsberg (h)	——	Hartmansdorf
Neu = Heidelberg (i)	——	Brunnendorf
Neu = Heesberg (j)	——	Fuchsendorf
Neu = Ansberg (k)	——	Schmidsdorf
Auf dem Rarendantz	——	Kniskerndorf

It is interesting to note in passing that neither John Conrad Kneskern nor Hartman Windecker lived in the villages named after them, as has been assumed by students of these settlements. Neu = Yorck of course is New York City. Hackensack is the present town of Hackensack, New Jersey. The entire Simmendinger pamphlet has been translated by Reverend Herman Vesper of Canajoharie, New York and published by Mr. L. D. MacWethy of St. Johnsville, New York in 1934.

SIMMENDINGER LIST

Anspach, Balthasar, (c) w. & ch.
Arnold, Jacob, (e) w. Elisabeth

Badtorffin, Anna, (k) widow & 2 ch.
Bär, Johannes, (l) w. & 4 ch.
Bartel, Heinrich, (c) w. Anna Catharine & 2 ch.
Bassan, Nicolaus, (l) w. Maria & 4 ch.
Bast, Jacob, (d) w. Anna Catharine & 1 ch.
Bauch, Christian, (f) w. Anna Dorothea & 5 ch.
Baumann, Adam, (h) w. Maria Margaretha & 5 ch.
Becker, Conrad, (f)
Becker, Friederich, (n) sister Anna Elisabeth Becker
Becker, Jacob, (b) w. & ch.
Becker, Johann Jacob, (g) w. Maria Elisabeth
Becker, Peter, (e) w. Elisabeth
Bell, Johann Friederich, (h) w. Anna Maria & 4 ch.
Bellinger, Heinrich, (k) w. Anna Maria & 2 ch.
Bellinger, Johann Friederich, (j) w. Anna Elisabeth & 3 ch.
Bellinger, Johannes, (h) w. Anna Maria Margaretha & 2 ch.
Bellinger, Marx, (k) Anna & 5 ch.
Bellinger, Nicolaus, (k) widower & 1 ch.
Bender, Georg, (i) w. Maria Dorothea & 2 ch.
Benderin, Anna Maria, (m) widow & 5 ch.
Berg, Abraham, (i) w. Anna Catharine & 3 ch.
Bergner, Conrad, (c) w. Anna Elisabeth & 5 ch.
Bernhard, Johann, (b) w. Anna Eulalia & 5 ch.
Bernhard, Just, (m) w. Elisabeth & 1 ch.
Bernhard, Ulrich, (c) w. Elisabeth
Betzer, Hermann, (b) w. Elsen Maria & 3 ch.
Betzerin, Anna Maria, (b)
Biefrim, Peter, (n)
Biefrim, William, (n)
Biermann, Johann, (k) w. & 3 ch.
Binder, Valentin, (e) w. Anna Maria Margreta & 1 ch.
Blanck, Johanes, (e) w. Maria Margretha & 3 ch.
Blass, Johannes, (a) w. & 4 ch.
Bliss, Enoch, (c) w. & ch.

Bodler, Adam (l) ⎫
Bodler, Christina, (l) ⎬ Brothers and sister, all single
Bodler, Paulus (l) ⎭
Böhm, Heinrich, (e) w. & ch.
Bohnenstiel, Nicolaus, (c) w. Margaretha & 2 ch.
Borst, Jacob, (g) w. Anna Maria & 3 ch.
Bösshoren, Johann Jacob, (j) w. Anna Catharine & 2 ch.
Bost, Just Heinrich, (l) w. & 5 ch.
Brack, Michael, (c) w. Anna Maria & 3 ch.
Braun, Paulus, (l) w.
Branthau, Joh. Wilhelm, (e) w. Margaretha Elisabeth & 3 ch.
Breder, Antoni, (l) w.
Brenger, Georg, (f) w. Anna Barbara & 4 ch.
Brobert, Just, (c) w. & ch.
Brugel, Johann Georg, (d) w. & ch.
Brugler, Heinrich, (a) w. Magdalena & 1 ch.
Buch, Martin, (a) Nicolaus Hamen's widow & 2 ch.
Buchdrucher, Marcus König, (m) w. & 2 ch.
Buff, Georg, (l) w. & 2 ch.
Burckhardt, Elisabetha, (e) widow & 2 ch.
Burckhardt, Ulrich, (k) w. Anna Maria & 2 ch.
Buss, Jacob, (m) w. Magdalena Loescher & 5 ch.

Cabbutzer, Jacob, (b) w. & ch.
Casselmann, Dietrich, (f) w. Anna & 2 ch.
Casser, Conrad, (l) ⎫
Casser, Georg, (l) ⎬ 3 brothers
Casser, Johannes, (l) ⎭
Christmann, Hanss, (k) w. Anna Gertraud & 6 ch.
Colmer, Georg, (d) w. & ch.
Conrad, Johann Heinrich, (b) w. Gertraud & 2 ch.
Conrad, Johannes, (k) w. Gertraud & 3 ch.
Conreckert, (no Christian name given), (k) w. Sara Catharine & 4 ch.
Cuntermann, Friederich, (d) w. Maria Barbara & 3 ch.
Cuntz, Jacob, (c) w. Susanna & 1 ch.
Cuntz, Johannes, (k) w. Maria Catharine & 4 ch.
Cuntz, Mätthaus, (a) w. Anna Margaretha & 5 ch.

Dachstätter, Georg, (h) w. Anna Elisabeth & 4 ch.
Dalles, Wilhelm, (d) w. & ch.
Dantler, Ulrich, (k) w. Maria Margaretha & 1 ch.
Deickert, Peter, (j) w. Anna Elisabeth
Deickert, Werner, (h) w. Anna Catharine & 6 ch.
Demuth, Georg, (d) w. & ch.
Demuth, Jacob, (e) w. Anna Elisabetha & 3 ch.
Demuth, Jacob, (n) w. & 3 ch.
Demuth, Peter, (n)
Deuss, Johannes, (n) w. & 2 ch.
Dhöns, Jacob, (d) w. & ch.
Dhorn, Lazarus, (c) w. Anna Catharine & 4 ch.
Diebel, Peter, (e) w. & 3 ch.
Diebel, Peter, (n) w. Anna Catharine & 3 ch.
Dieffenbach, Conrad, (k) w. Maria Barbara & 5 ch.
Diefuh, Daniel, (e) w. Maria Barbara & 2 ch.
Dielenbach, Martin, (g) w. Elisabeth & 2 ch.
Diell, Wilhelm, (m) w. & 1 ch.
Dieterich, Johann, (g) w. Maria Catharine & 2 ch.
Dietrich, Christian, (d) w. Anna Maria & 1 ch.
Dietrich, Jacob's (a) widow & 4 ch.
Dietrich, Johann Wilhelm, (e) w. Anna Margaretha & 3 ch.
Dildein, Hermann, (n) Dildein, Franz & his sister
Dilldein, Georg, (n) w. & 1 ch.
Dipel, Georg, (l) bachelor
Dob, Peter, (d) w. & 3 ch.
Dörner, Jacob, (e) w. & 2 ch.

Eberhard, Johann, (e) w. & 2 ch.
Ecker, Adam, (e) second w. & ch.
Eiber, Johannes, (n) w. & 2 ch.
Ehlich, Andreas, (e) w. Sophia & 3 ch.
Ehmann, Thomas, (f) w. Anna Elisabeth & 1 ch.
Emgen, Johann Ernst, (j) w. Anna Christana & 2 ch.
Emrich, Johann Michael, (k) w. Elisabeth & 2 ch.
Enrich, Johannes, (e) w. Anna Margretha & 2 ch.
Endes, Bartholomäus, (i) w. Maria Christina & 3 ch.
Engelsprecher, Michael, (a) w. Anna Catharine & 1 ch.

Erckelt, Bernhard, (n) w.
Erhardt, Simon, (j) w. Anna Margaretha & 5 ch.
Eschrodter's (a) widow, Maria Margaretha
Eschwein, Jacob, (c) w. & ch.
Ess, Jacob, (k) w. Anna Catharine
Eygner, Peter, (e) w. Anna Margaretha & 2 ch.

Falck, Arnold, (e) w. Anna Elisabeth & 1 ch.
Falckenburg, Valentin, (e) w. Elisabeth & 2 ch.
Fallinger, Heinrich, (k) w. & 3 ch.
Falmert, Nicolaus, (n) w. Anna Maria & 3 ch.
Feck, Joh., (f) w. Anna Maria Margaretha & 5 ch.
Feck, Leonhard, (f) w. Catharine
Feck, Peter, (f) w. Anna Maria & 4 ch.
Feller, Nicolaus, (h) w. Elisabeth & 6 ch.
Felten, Johann Valentin, (e) w. Apollonia & 3 ch.
Finck, Andreas, (k) w. Anna Marie & 2 ch.
Finck, Frantz, (n) w. Anna Elizabeth & 1 ch.
Finckin, Anna Margaretha, (a)
Finckin, Maria, (a)
Finckel, Philipp, (b) w. Anna Catharine & 3 ch.
Fischer, Sebastian, (g) w. Susanna & 3 ch.
Fliegler, Zacharias, (d) w. Anna Elisabeth & 2 ch.
Focht, Simon, (l) w. & 3 ch.
Folbertin, Catharina, (m) widow & 3 ch.
Foltz, Melchior, (j) w. Margaretha & 3 ch.
Forster, Georg, (a) w. Maria Margaretha & 3 ch.
Forster, Peter, (n)
Frantz, Johannes, (d) w. Magdalena & 2 ch.
Frey, Heinrich, (h) w. Maria Margaretha & 1 ch.
Freyin, Anna Barbara, (j) widow & 2 ch.
Freymäyer, Michael, (f) w. Anna Elisabeth & 6 ch.
Friederich, Conrad, (n) w. Anna Maria & 2 ch.
Friedrich, Johann Adam, (e) w. Regina Maria
Fritz, Georg Wilhelm, (c) w. & ch.
Frölich, Stephen, (e) w. Anna Elisabeth & 2 ch.

Fuchs, Philipp, (j) w. Anna Eva & 4 ch.
Fuhrmann, Jacob, (b) w. & ch.
Funck, Peter, (c) w. & 4 ch.

Gantz, Johannes, (c) w. & ch.
Geller, Frantz, (d) w. Barbara & 3 ch.
Georg, Wilhelm, (f) w. Anna Marie & 3 ch.
Gerlach, Johann Christian, (g) w. Anna Maria Margaretha & 3 ch.
Gerlach, Peter, (n) w. & 1 ch.
German, Jacob, (a) w. Maria Catharine & 1 ch.
Gissener, Heinrich, (m) w. & 1 ch.
Gitter, Bernhard, (l) w. Elisabeth
Gletch, Hans Georg, (n) w. & 2 ch.
Glump, Philipp, (d) w. & ch.
Goldmann, Conrad's (k) widow & 3 ch.
Groberger, Peter, (n) w. Barbara & 2 ch.

Hagendorn, Cristoph, (a) w. Anna Barbara & 1 ch.
Hagendorn, Peter, (a) w. Elisabeth Catharine & 4 ch.
Hambuch, Thomas, (i)
Hanbuch, Wilhelm, (d) widower
Hamen, Caspar, (a) as yet single
Hamen, Conrad, (a) w. Rachel & 3 ch.
Hamen, Peter, (a) w. Anna Maria Christina Sibylla & 3 ch.
Hannamann, (d) (no christian name given) w. & ch.
Härter, Michael's (a) widow & 4 ch.
Hartmann, Hanss Hermann, (e) w. Anna & 1 ch.
Hartwig, Caspar, (l) w. & 3 ch.
Hass, (Haas), Simon, (b) w. & ch.
Hassin, Maria Sophia, (e) widow & 5 ch.
Haug, Michael, (a) w. Magdalena & 2 ch.
Hauss, Christian, (j) w. Maria Catharine & 8 ch.
Heding, Conrad's surviving widow, (n) & Meisingerin (no chr. name)
Heinrich, Lorentz, (d) w. Regina & 5 ch.
Heintz, Urban, (n) son
Helm, Johann Michael, (m)
Helm, Peter, (m)
Helm, Simon, (m)
Helmer, Philipp, (g) w. Elisabeth & 5 ch.
Hermannes-Hanss Wilhelm Schneider's son-in-law with sons and daughter lived with Schneider
Hertel, Adam, (e) w. Gertraud & 3 ch.
Hess, Joseph, (j) w. Catharine & 1 ch.
Hess, Wilhelm, (n) w.

Heudohrn, Heinrich, (c) w. Elisabeth & 2 ch.
Heupt, Philipp, (a) w. Gertrud & 3 ch.
Heusser, Peter, (c) w. Anna Elisabeth & 5 ch.
Heyd, Peter, (e) w. Maria Elisabeth & 1 ch.
Heyd, Nicolaus, (l) w. & 2 ch.
Himel, Jacob, (m) & sister Anna Barbara
Hinterschied, Michael, (l) w. Anna Catharine & 4 ch.
Hirchmer, Georg, (i) w. Magdalena & 1 ch.
Hoff, Andreas, (d) w. Catharine Margret & 2 ch.
Hoff, Jacob, (f) w. Susanna & 4 ch.
Hoff, Johann Adam, (d) w. Anna Catharina
Hoffin, Anna Margaretha, (d) widow & 1 ch.
Hofmann, Conrad, (c) w. Anna Maria Margaretha & 5 ch.
Hofmann, Gabriel, (f) w. Anna Catharine & 2 ch.
Hofmann, Heinrich, (a) w. & 3 ch.
Hönner, Johannes, (a) w. & ch.
Hornig, Johann Rudolph, (j) w.
Hornig, Nicolaus, (i) w. Anna Maria & 4 ch.
Hossmann (Hoffmann), Hermann, (d) w. Anna Maria & 6 ch.
Hubert, David, (c) w. & ch.
Hüitz or Hültz, Christoph, (i) w. Eva Catharine & 5 ch.
Huss, Hanss Reinhard, (n) w. Anna Elisabeth & 1 ch.

Jäger, Wendel, (a) w. Christina Elisabetha & 2 ch.
Jung, Dewalt, (j) w. Maria Catharine
Jung, Eberhard, (d) w. & ch.
Jungin, Elisabetha, (e)
Jung, Heinrich, (j) w. Anna Margaretha & 4 ch.

Kasselmann, Christian, (e) w. Maria Judith & 2 ch.
Kassner, Peter, (l) w. Magdalena & 3 ch.
Käyser, Johannes, (j) w. Margaretha & 2 ch.
Kayser, Martin, (l)
Kell, Georg Wilhelm, (e) w. Anna Gertraud & 2 ch.
Keller, Conrad, (c) mother & her ch.
Kern, Hanss Jurg, (g) w. Veronica & 5 ch.
Kessler, Johannes, (h) w. Maria Margaretha & 3 ch.

Keiffer, Wilhelm, (e) w. Catherine & 3 ch.
Kiner, Benedict, (l) w. & 2 ch.
Kinget, Anna, (n) & 3 ch.
Kistlich, David, (c) & w. Catharine
Klein, Adam, (i) w. Catharine & 2 ch.
Klein, Johann Hermann, (k) w. Anna Magdalena & 3 ch.
Klein, Hieronymus, (e) w. Maria Margareta & 2 ch.
Klob, Peter, (k) w. Magdalena & 2 ch.
Klock, Heinrich, (h) w. Maria Margaretha & 4 ch.
Klug, Georg, (n) w. Susanna & 2 ch.
Knesskern, Johann Peter, (i) w. Elisabetha Barbara & 3 ch.
Kobel, Jacob, (i) w. Anna Maria & 2 ch.
Kochin, Anna Maria, (c) widow & 3 ch.
Kolmann, Johannes, (a) w. Juliana & 3 ch.
Kollmer, Leonhard, (g) w. Elisabeth & 2 ch.
Körner, Nicolaus, (e) w. Magdalena & 4 ch.
Krämer, Antonius, (d) w. Gertraud & 1 ch.
Krämer, Johann Wilhelm, (k) w. Anna Maria & 1 ch.
Kramer, Johannes, (i) w. Anna Margaretha & 3 ch.
Krämerin, Anna Maria, (m) widow & 7 ch.
Krantz, Heinrich, (d) w. Anna Catharine & 4 ch.
Krembs, Johannes, (h) w. Apolonia & 1 ch.
Kreussler, Joh. Philipp, (e) Anna Catharine & 3 ch.
Kreussler, Peter, (e) w. Anna Lucia & 3 ch.
Kroin, Catharina, (n) widow & 3 ch.
Kroth, Johannes, (b) w. Walburgis & 5 ch.
Kuhn, Conrad, (k) w. Anna Margaretha & 2 ch.
Kuhn, Jacob, (d) w. & ch.
Kuhn, Valentin, (k) w. Anna Catharine & 3 ch.
Kun, Samuel, (b) w. Elisabeth & 5 ch.
Kurtzin, Maria Elisabetha, (n)

Lampmann, Peter, (b) w. Catharine & 2 ch.
Lämert, Johannes, (e) w. & ch.
Landgraff, Georg, (i) w. Elisabeth Catharine & 1 ch.
Lang, Abraham, (d) w. Anna Maria & 4 ch.

Langmann, Just, (n) w.
Last, Johann Georg, (f) w. Anna & 7 ch.
Lauck, Abraham, (d) w. & ch.
Lauer, Peter, (c) w. Anna Catharina & 2 ch.
Launert, Johann Georg, (d) w. & ch.
Laux, Johann Just, (j) w. Maria
Laux, Johannes, (l) w. Anna Elisabeth
Laux, Heinrich, (j) Anna Margretha & 2 ch.
Laux, Michael, (d) w. Anna Elisabeth & 3 ch.
Laux, Philipp, (e) w. & ch.
Lauxin, Eva, (d) Mother-in-law of Johann Georg Launert, lived with that family
Lehr, Johann, (g) w. Sibylla Catharine & 5 ch.
Leick, Hanss, (d) w. & ch.
Lein, Conrad, (n) w. Margaretha & 6 ch.
Lescher, Sebastian, (b) w. Elisabeth & 6 ch.
Leyck, Johannes, (b) w. Anna Barbara & 3 ch.
Leyer, Johannes, (f) w. Elisabeth & 2 ch.
Lieckhart, Bernhard, (e) w. Justina & 1 ch.
Lieffland, Johann David, (h) w. Anna Maria & 4 ch.
Linck, Johannes, (b) w. & 3 ch.
Linsin, Apolonia, (m) widow & 3 ch.
Lorenz, Johannes, (l) w. Anna Margaretha & 6 ch.
Löscher, Jacob's (d) widow & 4 ch.
Lucas, Frantz, (l) widower & 5 ch.
Ludwig, Heinrich, (c) w. & ch.
Lutin, Anna Catharina, (d) widow & 3 ch.

Magdalena [no family name given], (f) widow & 2 ch.
Magdalena, Maria [no family name], (f) widow & 4 ch.
Mängen, Ferdinand, (b) w. Anna Clara & 2 ch.
Manck, Jacob, (e) w. Anna Margaretha
Mann, Heinrich, (g) w. Elisabetha Margretha & 2 ch.
Mannlin, Elisabetha, (m) widow & 4 ch.
Märterstock, Albrecht, (d) w. Elisabeth
Mathus, Andreas, (b)
Matthäus, Heinrich, (f) w. Catharine & 4 ch.
Mattheus, Georg, (h) w. Catharine & 1 ch.
Mattheus, Martin's widow, (h) is 110 yrs.

Mauer, Georg, (c) w. Apolonia & 1 ch.

Maul, Christoph, (d) w. & ch.

Maul, Friederich, (e) w. Anna Ursula & 4 ch.

Maurer, Georg, (l)

Maurer, Peter, (e) w. Catharine & 2 ch.

Meisingerin (?)—[see under Heding, Conrad]

Mengefin, Anna Maria, (m) widow & 3 ch.

Meraet (?), Frederick, (e) w. Anna Barbara & 6 ch.

Merckel, Johann's (k) widow & 2 ch.

Merten, Conrad, (e) w. Anna Maria & 3 ch.

Mess, Heinrich, (l) w. Magdalena & 2 ch.

Metzger, Hanss, (n) is Just Langmann's step-son

Meusinger, Conrad, (n) w. Anna Margaretha & 5 ch.

Meusinger, Nicolaus, (n) w. Anna Maria & 2 ch.

Meyen, Peter's (c) [widow & 3 ch.]

Meyer, Abel, (l) w. & 3 ch.

Meyer, Christian, (e) w. Anna Gertraud & 2 ch.

Meyer, Heinrich, (h) w. Kunigunda & 3 ch.

Michael, Johann Heinrich, (c) w. Rosina & 4 ch.

Michlin, Anna Sibylla, (n) widow & 2 ch.

Milig, the late Johann Wilhelm's 2 surviving sons (b)

Mohr, Johannes, (f) w. Elisabeth & 1 ch.

Mohr, Heinrich, (e) w. Anna Margretha & 3 ch.

Mohrin, Anna Kunigunda, (f) widow & 1 ch.

Moohr, Johann Cornelius, (n) ⎫ brothers
Moohr, Michael, (n)   ⎬ & sister
Moohrin, Margretha, (n) ⎭

Moret, Jacob's widow (l) & 3 ch.

Mühl, Johannes, (k)

Muhler, Georg, (i) w. Anna Maria & 1 ch.

Muhler, Johann Christian, (b) w.

Muhler, Johannes, (j) w. Maria & 4 ch.

Muhler, Philipp, (e) w. Anna Margaretha & 2 ch.

Muhler, Samuel, (c) w. Anna Margreta & 3 ch.

Müller, Adam, (n) w. & 2 ch.

Müller, Wilhelm, (l) w. Margaretha & 1 ch.

Müllerin, Elisabetha, (l) widow & 4 ch.

Müssig, Veit, (c) w. Maria Catharina & 3 ch.

Mutsch, Johannes, (n) w. Elisabeth

Mutzier, Jacob, (a) w. & 3 ch.

Neukircher, Joh. Heinrich, (e) w. Anna Maria & 2 ch.

Noll, Christoph, (n) & Maria Elisabetha Nollin

Oberbach, Georg, (e) w. Justina Catharine & 5 ch.

Oberbach, Johann Peter, (e) w. Margaretha Christina & 3 ch.

Oberbach, Peter, (e) w. Elisabeth & 3 ch.

Ohrendorff, Heinrich, (k) w. Anna Margaretha & 3 ch.

Petri, Just, (k) w. Anna Catharine & 3 ch.

Pfeffer, Michael, (m) w. Anna Maria & 3 ch.

Pfeifferin, Catharina, (h) widow & 1 ch.

Pflug, Peter, (l) w. & 5 ch.

Philipp, Peter, (a) w. Magdalena & 5 ch.

Polffer, Wendel, (c) w. & ch.

Querinus, Johannes, (m) w. & 3 ch.

Rauch, Friederich, (a) w. Maria Catharine & 3 ch.

Rauh, Nicolaus, (d) w. & ch.

Rausch, Casper, (d) w. & ch.

Redtschäffin, Anna Maria, (j) widow & 2 ch.

Reger, Christian, (n) w. & 2 ch.

Reibel, Johannes, (m) & his sister

Reichert, Joseph, (e) w. Anna Maria & 2 ch.

Reiffenberger, Georg, (d) w. & ch.

Reinbold, Mattheus, (i) w. & 1 ch.

Reissdorff, Johannes, (d) w. & ch.

Reuter, Heinrich, (e) w. Anna Juliana & 2 ch.

Richter, Andreas, (e) w. Elisabeth & 1 ch.

Ried, Leonhard, (m) 5 brothers & mother

Riegel, Gottfried, (l) w. Anna Elisabeth & 2 ch.

Rieth, Leonhard, (f) w. Elisabeth Catharine & 2 ch.

Riethin, Catharina, (f) widow & 4 ch.

Risch, Jacob, (l) w. & 3 ch.

Römer, Georg, (l) w. Elisabeth & 3 ch.

Roschel, Augustinus, (e) w. Catharine & 2 ch.

Roschel, Peter, (e) w. Anna Maria
Rosenbaum, Bernhard, (l) w. Catharine & 3 ch.
Ross, Andreas, (l) w. & 2 ch.
Rossman, Johannes, (c) w. & ch.
Ruhl, Nicolaus, (k) w. Anna Dorothea & 4 ch.

Sayn, Peter, (e) w. & ch.
Schäffer, Georg, (a) w. Anna Maria & 1 ch.
Schäffer, Hanss Werner, (a) w. Maria Margaretha
Schäffer, Heinrich, (h) w. Rosina & 1 ch.
Schäffer, Jacob, (a) Dorothea & 1 ch.
Schäffer, Johann Heinrich, (e) w. Agnes & 1 ch.
Schäffer, Johann Wilhelm, (j) w. Anna Catharine & 5 ch.
Schäffer, Johannes, (k) w. Anna Maria
Schäffer, Joseph, (b) w.
Schäffer, Nicolaus, (f) w. Maria Catharine & 4 ch.
Schäffer, Reinhard, (i) w. Maria & 2 ch.
Schäfferin, Doroteha, [sic] widow & 1 ch. (e)
Schäfferin, Elisabetha, widow (a) & 3 ch.
Schambidy, (n) [a Frenchman] w.
Schantz, David, (d) w. Anna Barbara & 3 ch.
Schärmann, Heinrich, (e) w. Anna Catharine & 2 ch.
Schenckel, Jonas, (c) Sibylla & 3 ch.
Scherb, Jacob, (a) w. Anna Maria & 2 ch.
Scherer, Dewalt, (d) w. & ch.
Schib, Hieronymus, (e) w. Anna Catharine & 1 ch.
Schiffer, Philipp, (b) w. Magdalena & 4 ch.
Schlömer, Matthäus, (e) w. Anna Veronica & 2 ch.
Schmid, Adam, (h) w. Anna Dorothea & 2 ch.
Schmid, Bernhard, (a) w. Anna Margaretha & 2 ch.
Schmid, Georg Adam, (c) w. & ch.
Schmid, Heinrich, (n) w. & 2 ch.
Schmid, Ulrich's, (c) widow & 4 ch.
Schmidt, Hanss Georg, (k) w. Anna Elisabeth & 3 ch.
Schmidt, Johann Peter, (c) w. Elizabeth & 3 ch.
Schmidt, Ludwig, (l) w.
Schneider, Hanss Wilhelm, (e) w. Cecilia [together with Hermannes, his son-in-law with sons and daughters]

Schneider, Heinrich, (c) w. Anna & 2 ch.
Schneider, Jacob, (k) w. Anna Barbara & 3 ch.
Schneider, Johann Dietrich, (d) w. & ch.
Schneiderin, Maria Catharina, (m)
Schnell, Jacob, (h) w. Elisabeth & 4 ch.
Schnell, Just, (h) w. Catharine
Schönermann, Conrad, (c) w. & ch.
Schram, Heinrich, (e) w. Anna Margaretha & 5 ch.
Schrämling, Heinrich, (i) w. Maria Elisabeth & 5 ch.
Schreiber, Albertus, (d) w. & ch.
Schuh, Johannes, (b) w. & 3 ch.
Schuh, Wilhelm, (b) w. Gertrud & 3 ch.
Schuhmacher, Daniel, (l) w. Anna Maria & 5 ch.
Schuhmacher, Thomas, (k) w. Ann Dorothea & 1 ch.
Schumacher, Jacob, (a) Anna Barbara & 1 ch.
Schuldtes, Johann Georg, (j) w. Anna Kunigunda & 2 ch.
Schultes, Johannes, (i) w. Anna Barbara & 2 ch.
Schurtz, Andreas, (e) his mother & her 4 ch.
Schütz, Conrad, (j) w. Anna Maria Margaretha
Schütz, Hanss Adam, (k) w. Anna Catharine & 1 ch.
Schützin, Catharina, (e)
Schwalb, Johannes, (l) w. Philippina Rosina & 3 ch.
Schwed, Arnold, (l) & sister Anna
Schwitzler, Heinrich, (d) w. & ch.
Sech, Heinrich, (k) w. Christina & 1 ch.
Segendorff, Hermann, (d) w. & ch.
Seibert, Johann Martin, (j) w. Anna Marie & 3 ch.
Semerin, Elisabetha Catharina, (d)
Semerin, Maria Christina, (d)
Sicknerin, Apolonia, (n) widow & 1 ch.
Simon, Wilhelm, (c) w. & ch.
Später, Johannes, (l) w. Dorothea & 5 ch.
Speichermann, Johann Herman, (d) w. Anna Catharina & 3 ch.
Spiess, Peter, (j) w. Anna Elisabeth
Spon, Heinrich, (h) w. Maria Catharine & 3 ch.
Sponheimer, Georg, (e) Anna Maria & 3 ch.
Sponheimer, Georg, (l) w. Magdalena & 3 ch.
Stahrenbergerin, Christina, (g) widow & 4 ch.

Stahring, Adam, (g) w. Anna Maria & 3 ch.
Stall, Johannes, (e) w. Anna Ursula & 1 ch.
Steiger, Nicolaus, (b) w. & ch.
Steiger, Stephan, (b) w. & ch.
Stoffelbein, Peter, (a) w. & 3 ch.
Stein, Martin, (l) w. & 3 ch.
Stell, Rudolph, (i) w. Maria Dorothea & 4 ch.
Stickermann, Sebastian, (c) w. & ch.
Stieber, Balthasar, (b) w. & 1 ch.
Stig, Michael, (k) w. & 4 ch.
Stnich, Christian, (k) w. Anna Margretha & 2 ch.
Stor, Michael, (n) w. Elisabeth & 3 ch.
Streit, Christian, (n) w. & 8 ch.
Stub, Martin, (k) w. Anna Catharine & 1 ch.
Stuber, Jacob, (c) w. & ch.
Stuberauch, Georg Henrich, (i) w. Anna Catharine & 2 ch.
Stumpff, Johann Georg, (j) w. Anna Margaretha & 3 ch.
Sutz, Dieterich, (e) w. Magdalena & 2 ch.
Sutz, Peter, (l) w. & 1 ch.

Thomas, Andreas, (d) w. Anna Eva & 3 ch.
Thomas, Georg, (h) w. Anna & 2 ch.
Thomas, Peter, (i) w. Anna Maria & 2 ch.
Trum, Andreas, (c) w. Margaretha Magdalena & 5 ch.
Trumbohr, Nicolaus, (e) w. Magdalena & 4 ch.

Uhl, Carolus, (e) w. & 3 ch.
Uhl, Heinrich, (a) w. Anna Maria von Totert & 2 ch.

Vesi, Valentin; William Vesi; Anna Vesin, (n)
Viedler, Gottfrid, (i) w. Anna Elisabetha & 2 ch.

Wagner, Peter, (g) w. Anna Maria & 2 ch.
Wahner, Ludwig, (i) w. Anna Barbara & 3 ch.
Wallborn, Hanss Adam, (k) w. Anna Elisabeth & 6 ch.
Wallerrath, Gerhard, (h) w. Maria & 3 ch.
Wallerrath, Heinrich, (h) w. Christina & 2 ch.
Wannemacher, Dieterich, (n) w.

Wannemacher, Peter, (n) w. & 1 ch.
Warno, Jacob, (i) w. Sibylla & 1 ch.
Weber, Jacob, (h) w. Elisabeth Maria
Weber, Heinrich, (l) w. Christina & 3 ch.
Weber, Nicolaus, (h) w. Barbara & 2 ch.
Weber, Valentin, (l) w. Charlotte & 2 ch.
Weidknechtin, Margretha, (l) widow & 2 ch.
Weilin, Anna Catharina, (m) widow & 1 ch.
Weisser, Conrad, (f) w. Maria Margaretha & 8 ch.
Weissin, Stephan's (l) widow & 2 ch.
Weitin, Gertraud, (e) widow & 2 ch.
Weller, Hieronymus, (e) w. Anna Juliana & 2 ch.
Wenrig, Balthasar, (b) w. & ch.
Werner, Christoph, (f) w. Magdalena & 3 ch.
Werner, Michael, (c) w. Catharine
Widerwax, Heinrich, (a) w. Anna Sibylla & 5 ch.
Wilcherwist, Melchior, (k) w. Anna Maria Margretha & 4 ch.
Wilhelm, Johann Nicolaus, (n) w. Anna Elisabeth & 1 ch.
Windecker, Hartmann, (k) w. Barbara & 5 ch.
Winiger, Ulrich, (d) w. Anna & 2 ch.
Winter, Heinrich, (b) w. Anna Maria & 4 ch.
Wiss, Johannes, (k) w. Anna Margaretha & 1 ch.
Wissbohren, Georg, (b) [has left a daughter]
Wixheusser, Peter, (e) w. Elisabeth Maria & 1 ch.
Wolleber, Peter, (e) w. Anna Rosina & 5 ch.
Wolleber, Philipp, (e)
Wolleber, Valentin, (e) w. Susanna
Wolleberin, Catharina, (h) widow & 2 ch.
Wust, Conrad, (b) w. Maria Abel & 5 ch.

Zeh, Johannes, (f) w. Magdalena & 4 ch.
Zerben, Jacob, (b) w. Maria Catharine
Zerben, Martin, (b) w. Maria Catherine & 4 ch.
Ziebleore, Leonhard, (b) w. Anna Maria & 3 ch.
Zimmermann, Jacob, (j) w. Anna Margareth & 1 ch.
Zöller, Hanss Henrich, (k) w. & 3 ch.
Zöller, Johannes, (k) w. Anna Catharina & 2 ch.
Zufelten, Georg, (b) w. & ch.

G. PALATINES WHO MOVED TO THE TULPEHOCKEN VALLEY IN PENNSYLVANIA

THE FIRST list given below (I) is a compilation of two documents. The fifteen names followed by asterisks are the first settlers who arrived in that region before May 13, 1723. These names are signed to a petition given in *Colonial Records of Pennsylvania*, III, 323. The other names in the list are taken from a petition for a road from Olney to Tulpehocken presented to the Court of Quarter Sessions at Philadelphia in September, 1727. Professor William T. Hinke of Auburn Seminary, Auburn, New York, deserves credit for his fine work in identifying these names.

The second list (II) was compiled by Mr. C. Lindemuth, now deceased, from land deeds and land patents and published in *The Pennsylvania German* (Lebanon, Pennsylvania, 1904), V, 191. Although the map drawn up by Mr. Lindemuth, locating the patents, was dated by him "1723," it obviously should be of some later date, certainly after 1728.

COLONIAL RECORDS OF PENNSYLVANIA LIST (I)

Aemrich, Michgel

Barben, Martin
Batdorff, Martin
Braun, Pfilbes

Christ, Jocham Michael*
Christman, Johannes

Diffenbach, Conrad

Enterfelt, Johan

Feg, Lenhart
Fidler, Godfrey*
Fischer, Sebastian*

Herner, Michael Ernst

Klob, Peter
Kobff, Jacob
Korbell, Jacob

Lantz, Johannes*
Lauk, Abraham
Lesch, Adam
Lesch, Georg

Nefs, Niclas
Neft, Balt.*

Pacht, Johann Peter*

Riem, Niclas
Riet, Caspar
Riet, Lenhart
Rieth, Georg*
Rieth, John Leonard*
Rieth, Peter*
Ruell, Nicklas

Sab, Joseph*
Schadt, Antonis*
Schaeffer, Johannes Claus*
Schaffer, Friedrich
Schaffer, Niklas
Schitz, Conrad*
Schuchert, Johann Henrich
Stub, Marden

Walborn, Adam
Walborn, Andrew*
Wasserschmidt, Stephan

Zerbe, Lorentz*

THE LINDEMUTH LIST (II)

Anspach, Balthaser
Anspach, Leonhart
Batdorff, Martin
Blum, Ludwig
Boyer, Hans
Braun, Philip
Brossman, Francis
Cushwa, Isaiah
Deck, Nickolaus
Diffebach, Adam
Diffebach, Conrad
Ernst, Michael
Essel, Reinhold
Etchberger, Jacob
Fischer, Lawrence
Fischer, Sebastian
Fohrer, Johann
Goldman, Conrad
Heckedorn, Martin
Holston, Leonhard
Kapp, Jacob
Kayser, Christopher
Kinzer, Nicholas
Kitzmuller, Jonas
Lauks, Abraham
Lauer, Christian
Lebo, Peter
Lederman, Jacob

Lesch, Adam
Lesch, George
Long, Conrad
Minnich, Matthias
Reiss, Michael
Rieth, Caspar
Rieth, George
Rieth, John Leonhard
Rieth, Michael
Rieth, Nicholas
Schaeffer, Jacob
Schaeffer, Peter
Schell, Peter
Schmidt, Michael
Schuetz, Adam
Seigner, Hans George
Shump Christopher
Stupp, Adam
Unruh, George
Walborn, Christina
Walborn, Herman
Weiser, Christopher
Weiser, Conrad
Weiser, Michael
Weyant, Nicholas
Wenrich, Franz
Winter, Frederick
Zeh, George
Zeller, Johann
Zerbe, Peter

H. THE PETITION LIST OF PALATINES IN NORTH CAROLINA

THIS LIST is taken from a petition to the North Carolina authorities by the Palatines remaining at New Bern, against their dispossession by Cullen Pollock, son of Col. Pollock to whom Graffenried had assigned the lands as security for a debt. The petition was dated September 28, 1749 and is printed in the *N. C. Col. Rec.*, IV, 956. Although they referred to themselves as Palatines, a number of the petitioners were in all probability of Swiss origin, for a group of people deported from Berne, Switzerland were included in the original settlers of the town. The small number of families left from the original 650 Palatines is to be attributed to hardships of the voyage and first year of settlement, including an Indian massacre in 1711 and desertions from the colony to which Graffenried referred as early as 1711. *N. C. Col. Rec.*, I, 944.

Baver, Abraham
Baver, Christian
Busit, Abraham

Eibach, Jacob
Ender, Peter
Eslar, Christian

Feneyer, Philip

Ganter, Christian
Gesibel, Michael
Granade, John
Grest, Henry
Grum, Herman

Hubbach, Christian
Huber, Jacob

Kehler, Simon
Kinsey, John (appears twice)
Kiser, Michael

Lots, Peter

Market, Frederick
Miller, Jacob
Miller, Jno. Lekgan

Moor, Adam
Moor, Dennis
Morris, Henry

Omend, Phillip

Pillman, Peter
Pugar, Joseph

Reasonover, Mathias
Renege, George
Reyet, Peter
Rimer, John
Rimer, Nicholas
Risheed, Casper

Sheets, Jacob (from another petition of
    March 29, 1743)
Shelfer, Michael
Simons, Daniel
Sneidor, George

Tetchey, Daniel

Walker, Christian
Wallis, Andrew
Woolf, John Bernard Shone

L. PALATINE FAMILIES IN LIMERICK COUNTY IRELAND, JULY, 1934

THESE FAMILIES were listed from the memory of Mr. Julius Sheppard of Ballingarrane, a remarkable keen-witted descendant of Palatine ancestry. Palatines also lived in Bally-organ and Kilfinnane but their names were not mentioned. They are probably included in the "other Palatine Families" listed below, taken from William Crook, *The Palatines in Ireland*, (London, 1866), 251. Some of these names appear to be French or English in origin. They may be attributed to mixed marriage or perhaps a change of name by Palatine descendants.

Adare
Barkman, Fred and son, Erick
Bobanizer, John ⎫ sons of Moses
Bobanizer, James ⎭
Fitzell family

Hiffle family
Legeur, Fred
Legeur, James
Miller, Samuel and sons Richard and
    Fred

Miller, Richard and son Berty
Piper family (migrated to England in
    1916)
Ruckle (Ruttle), Daniel and son
    William
Sparling, Joseph
Shier, Pembroke
Shier, Jethro, Sr.
Shier, Jethro, Jr.
Shier, Jack
Tesky, Mrs. George

Askeaton
Cross, Mrs. Alice (formerly a Shier)
Ruttle, Thomas
Ruttle, William

Between Askeaton and Foynes
Shier, Ernest (bachelor)
Shier, Frederick (bachelor)

Between Askeaton and Ballingarrane
Ruttle, Edward
Ruttle, William (bachelor)

Ballisteen
Shier, Henry

Ballingarrane (Ballingrane)
Baker, Harry (bachelor)
Baker, John
Baker, Robert
Doupe, Edward (bachelor)
Doupe (Daub), John (brother and sister
    in Toronto, Canada)
Gilliard, Henry
Latchford, Richard (wife, a Ruttle)
Lowee, Mrs. William (brother and
    sister came to America fifty years
    ago)
Mick, William (bachelor)
Ruttle, Michael Heck
Ruttle, William
Sheppard, Julius (bachelor)
Sheppard, Uriah
Shier, George
Shier, John
Shier, Julius
Switzer, Nathaniel
Teskey, Augustus

Court Matrix (Court Matress)
Bowen, John
Delmege, Robert (Bertie)
Shier, Samuel
Shier, William
Switzer, Christopher
Switzer, Nathaniel (bachelor)
Switzer, John (bachelor)
Teskey, Albert
Teskey, Joseph

Killiheen
Bovenizer, Albert
Green, Edward (wife, a Switzer)
Modler, Edward
Teskey, Jack
Teskey, William

Pallaskenry (Pallas)
Hervaner, David } sons of Richard
Hervaner, Jack }
Lynch, Jack (mother, a Switzer)
Rennison, Thomas (daughter married
    Jack Lynch)
Switzer, Jack
Switzer, Peter

Rathskeal
Hudson, William (married a Sparling)
Sparling, James
Shier, Bertie
Stark, Samuel
Teskey, William

Other Palatine Families
Barabier
Bathomer
Benner
Bethel or Bother
Bowman
Cole
Roach
Corneil
Cronsberry
Embury
Gizzle
Glazier
Grunze
Guier
Heck
Hoffman
Lawrence
Ledwich
Long
Neizer
Rhinehead
Rodenbucher
Rose
Stack
St. John
St. Ledger
Strangle
Sleeper
Shoemaker
Smeltzer
Shoultace
Shanewise
Tattler
Urshelbough
Williams
Young

INDEX

Adams, sheriff from Albany, mistreated by Palatines, 202, 203.

Addison, Joseph, 82.

Admiralty, Dutch, assistance of, requested, 57, 61.

Adventure, Palatine desire for, 11.

Advertising, by Dayrolle, to stop emigration, 59; importance of Pa., in connection with later German immigration, 216, 217, 218; of English colonies in America, 12 ff., 216 ff.; use of circulars as, 62.

Albany, Palatines stop over in, 192.

Albrecht, J. Justin, 108.

Anabaptists, Swiss, 99, 103.

"Androboros," manuscript drama by Governor Hunter, footnote on 171, 200.

Anglican Church, aids Palatines, 69; Palatines in Ireland conform to, 89; pretended to be endangered by Palatine immigration, 181 ff.

Antigua, settlement of Palatines in, proposed, 35.

Apprentices, Palatine, 78, 149.

Archdale, John, correspondence of, 18, 26.

Arbuthnot, Dr. John, physician to Queen Anne, 182, 184.

Army, British, Palatines enlist in, 78.

Arnoldi, Dr. John, appointed Physician-General to Palatines, 163.

Ashhurst, Sir Henry, 116.

Bagge, Andrew, commissary for Palatines, complains of Cast, 166; referred to, 163, 164, 165, 166, 168.

Bahama Islands, 77.

Balance of trade, of England, with the Baltic countries, 113.

Baltic trade, conditions of, 112, 113.

Bank of England, 68.

Baptists, among Palatines, 8.

Baptists, United, of Amsterdam, 52.

Barbadoes, 77.

Barkley, Reverend, 45.

Bayard, Colonel Nicholas, the elder, referred to, 138, 150, 151, 154, 200.

Bayard, Nicholas, the younger, advances funds to the Palatines, 44; attacked by Palatines, 201; offers land-titles to Palatines, 200.

Beaufort, Duke of, one of the Carolina proprietors, 108.

Begging, by the Palatines in London, 70.

Bellomont, Governor of N. Y., see Coote, Richard.

Bendysh, Henry, secretary to the Commissioners for Collecting and Settling of the Palatines, arranges transportation of Palatines to N. Y., 143, 144.

Benson, Thomas, surgeon to the Palatines, 147.

Bern Land Company, 103; finances of, 104; members of, refuse to carry out agreement, 109; also see, Michel, François Louis.

Bern, Switzerland, 31, 99, 103.

Bishop of London, lacks minister for Palatines, 142.

Bishop of Oxford, proposes method for securing charity, 69.

Blackheath, Palatines on, 67, 72, 77, 80; visited, 8, 150.

Blankistore, Colonel, 109.

Bloome, Richard, pamphlet of, entitled *English America*, 18.

Board of Ordnance, see Ordnance.

Board of Trade, approves plan for N. Y. settlement, 130; approves proposals for colony of Swiss Protestants, 30; considers development of a staple commodity for the northern colonies, 122; considers Kocherthal's petition of 1708, 34 ff.; considers needs of Palatines in London, 73; informed of decision to send Palatines to N. Y., 128; lacks quorum, attendance required, 79; ordered to consider plans for settlement of Palatines in England, 72, 74; ordered to consult Attorney-General as to Palatine contract, 131; pushes bill for establishment of independent support for N. Y. government, 185; questions Sackett's tar-making methods, 176; recommends colonial naval stores as means of stopping colonial manufacturing, 121 ff.; reports on Swedish monopoly, 121; represents possibilities for colonial naval stores, 119; represents that Palatines be settled in Antigua, 35; in N. Y., 35, 127; in Jamaica, 35,

threats necessary to secure labor of, 174; unskilled labor of, 177; vital statistics of, 162, 198; winter in Albany and Schenectady, 192, 193; also see Hunter, Colonel Robert.

New York, dispersal of Palatines in, from Hudson River settlements, to Pa., 189; to Tulpehocken district, 205 ff., names of, Appendix G, 300 ff.; to New Jersey, settle in Hackensack, 230, names of, Appendix F, 291; to various parts of New York, to Livingston's lands, 189; to Mohawk Valley, 204, 205, 207 ff.; see Mohawk Valley; to New York City, 189, names of, Appendix F, 291; to Rhinebeck, 189; to Schoharie, 190, 193; see Schoharie Valley, Palatines in.

Newburgh, Palatines at, 40, 41 ff., 215, 216.

Newcastle, Duke of, 69.

Newfoundland fishery, 75.

Nichols, land grant of, criticized, 156.

Nicholson, Colonel Francis, 42, 156, footnote on 171.

Norris, Sir John, 128.

North Carolina, Graffenried purchases lands in, 100, 101; terms of, 100, 101; interest of Graffenried in Palatines as settlers in, 100 ff.; Michel purchases land in, 100; preparations for Palatine settlement in, 101, 102; proposals of Lords Proprietors of, for settlement in, 62, 98, terms offered, 62, 63, 99; subsidy to promoters of Palatine settlements in, 100, 101.

North Carolina, Palatines in, arrive, 102; ask aid of N. C. council, 110; condition of, 102, 104, 110; consider moving to Virginia or Maryland, 108; deserted by Graffenried, 109; Graffenried's agreement with, 105, 107; Indian massacre of, 107; lose their lands, 109, 110; moved to frontier, 110; petition Privy Council Committee, 110; settle New Bern, 105; settlement of, involved in local politics, 104, 105; also see Graffenried; Carolina; and Palatine settlements, proposed.

Northern War, the, 114.

Northey, Attorney-General, criticizes N.Y. naturalization act, 214; suggests, as alternative, confirmation of N. Y. land-titles, 215.

Nova Scotia, proposal for conquest of, 124, 125; proposal to settle Scots in, 124.

Nutten Island (now Governor's Island, N. Y.), 148, footnote on 217.

Oath of allegiance, required by general naturalization acts, 28, 215.

Ordnance, Board of, complains of loss of Palatine supplies without reimbursement by Parliament, 142; estimates cost of Palatine supplies, 142; issues tents for Palatines, 67.

Order-in-council, authorizing government aid in settling of Palatines, 35.

Origin of plan for government project to manufacture naval stores, 124 ff., 133.

Ormond, Duke of, see Butler, James.

Packet boat, used to transport Palatines, 57.

Palatine, as term, use of, footnote on 1.

Palatine Bridge, town of, 205.

Palatine court, Hudson River settlements, dissension in, 165; established, 164, 174.

Palatine emigration, anticipated, 50; at Rotterdam, 50, 51, 53 ff.; attempts to halt, 53, 58 ff.; causes of, Chapter I, summarized, 31; experiences of, 33, 47; forbidden by the Elector Palatine, 53; large number of children among, 57; names of, see Appendices A, 243 ff., B, 244 ff., C, 248 ff., D, 274 ff.; need of, great, 52, 56, 57, 63; preparations of, 47; size of, 1, 7, 32, 38, 65, 66; source of, 1, 2.

Palatine fever, 147.

Palatine immigration, to England, approved by Queen Anne, 52; arranged by Dayrolle, 53 ff.; attempts to halt, 56, 58 ff.; authorized by Marlborough, 54; authorized by Secretary of State Boyle, 55; condemned by House of Commons, 183; expected, 56, 72; expenditures by British government for, 183; forbidden by British authorities, 68; investigated by Parliament, 182, 183; landing of, not to be prevented, but no aid to be given, 63; names of, Appendices B, 244 ff., C, 248 ff., D, 274 ff.; not planned for, by British authorities, 29, 80, 100; numbers of, 65, 66; papists in, returned, 63, 66, 78, 79, for list of names, see Appendix D, 274 ff.; precedents for, 29; sail at own expense, 62, 64, 66; also see Dayrolle; England, Palatines in; and Palatine settlements, proposals for.